AF607967

PERCEPTION AND ITS DEVELOPMENT IN MERLEAU-PONTY'S PHENOMENOLOGY

Perception and Its Development in Merleau-Ponty's Phenomenology

EDITED BY KIRSTEN JACOBSON
AND JOHN RUSSON

UNIVERSITY OF TORONTO PRESS
Toronto Buffalo London

Toronto Buffalo London
www.utppublishing.com

ISBN 978-1-4875-0128-0

Library and Archives Canada Cataloguing in Publication

Perception and its development in Merleau-Ponty's Phenomenology / edited by Kirsten Jacobson and John Russon.

Includes bibliographical references and index.
ISBN 978-1-4875-0128-0 (cloth)

1. Merleau-Ponty, Maurice, 1908–1961. Phénoménologie de la perception. 2. Phenomenology. 3. Perception (Philosophy). I. Jacobson, Kirsten, 1973–, author, editor II. Russon, John, 1960–, author, editor

B2430.M376P4753 2017 142′.7 C2017-900114-0

This book has been published with the help of a grant from the Federation for the Humanities and Social Sciences, through the Awards to Scholarly Publications Program, using funds provided by the Social Sciences and Humanities Research Council of Canada.

University of Toronto Press acknowledges the financial assistance to its publishing program of the Canada Council for the Arts and the Ontario Arts Council, an agency of the Government of Ontario.

Funded by the Government of Canada
Financé par le gouvernement du Canada

Dedicated to Edward S. Casey,
for his kindness, friendship, and inspiration

Contents

Acknowledgments

This volume is a bit unlike other edited collections of essays. Generally, edited collections are a bit of a "grab bag," with a rather disparate set of works, each of which is self-contained and not intrinsically related either to the other essays or to the volume as a whole. The authors of the essays in this volume, however, are, by and large, participants in a small philosophical community that has consistently met and worked cooperatively for many years, and their essays consequently bear the mark of ongoing collaboration. As editors, we want first to acknowledge the substantial contribution offered by these writers through years of collective study, and we would like to express our appreciation for the deep commitment all of these writers have to *doing* phenomenology, rather than simply writing scholarly reports about it. Furthermore, all of the contributors to this volume made an effort to be responsive to the others' contributions, and we would like to thank them for the effort they put into making this such a coherent volume. We would also like to thank those contributors for their patience through the rather long process of bringing this volume into being; we hope that the quality of the completed work will be sufficient reward. We are also grateful to a number of colleagues in the profession who have been especially generous and helpful over the years, in matters both philosophical and professional. Specifically, we would like to thank Drew Leder, Len Lawlor, Tony Steinbock, Graeme Nicholson, and especially Ed Casey for years of support.

A Note on Citations

The essays in this volume are original phenomenological analyses, and not commentaries. Nonetheless, their central purpose is to illuminate, defend, and expand on the insights developed in Merleau-Ponty's *Phenomenology of Perception*. Because this work is a central point of orientation for these essays, references to this work will generally be incorporated directly into the text.

In both the text and the footnotes, references to this work will be to *PP* and will cite first the page number for the French text of Maurice Merleau-Ponty, *Phénomenologie de la Perception*, published by Gallimard in 2005, followed by the page number in the recent translation of this text by Donald A. Landes, published by Routledge in 2012.

Similarly, all references to Merleau-Ponty's posthumously published, incomplete work *Le Visible et l'Invisible* will be to *VI*, and will cite first the page number for the French text published by Gallimard in 1964, then the page number in the translation of this work as *The Visible and the Invisible* by Alphonso Lingis, published by Northwestern University Press in 1968.

PERCEPTION AND ITS DEVELOPMENT IN MERLEAU-PONTY'S PHENOMENOLOGY

Introduction: Perception and Its Development

KIRSTEN JACOBSON AND JOHN RUSSON

We call an individual "perceptive" who can detect the implicit significance of an event. We typically use this expression to mark someone out as uncommonly or unexpectedly astute, someone who, for example, notices something about one's dress or one's behaviour that others typically overlook, or, someone who, for example, detects the purpose behind the arrangement of items on a desk. To perceive is to recognize what is really there, whether the familiar things of the natural world – the deer grazing among the trees by the brook – or the secret depths of another's soul, as when we say, "I perceive in you a frustrated yearning to be heard." Perceiving can range from the simple behaviour of mere noticing to the highly refined behaviour of detection exemplified by Arthur Conan Doyle's character, Sherlock Holmes. Although these specific practices differ from one another, they all underscore the essential notion: perception means apprehending the truth of a situation, apprehending what is there.

Let us reflect briefly on the terms of this definition of perception. To call perception an "apprehension" is to emphasize the immediacy and passivity that characterizes the experience. Perception is fundamentally an encounter rather than a fabrication: in perception, one has the character of the other impressed upon one, rather than constructing something of one's own. Perception is something one allows for and undergoes, rather than something one makes. Perception is not an imposition of oneself, but a making way for the other.

The imposition of oneself, however, can be a matter of omission as much as a matter of commission: interjecting my prejudices can indeed obscure my apprehension of what is there, but equally, my ignorance can limit my ability to apprehend. One's apprehension may be superficial and misrepresentative because one is insufficiently responsive to what is happening, as when your infant daughter is in fact unable to perceive your adult anxiety concerning your own death, or when someone unacquainted with the forms of natural life does not recognize the difference between a floating log and a crocodile. The inexperienced person is indeed impressed by the sensible presentation of the father's expression or of the crocodile's bodily presence, but that person *fails to perceive* what is there, what it is that is appearing. Apprehension of what is really there, then, is a matter of apprehending the situation *truly*: *wahrnehmen* – "*truly*-taking" – as it is expressed in German.

Perception is the apprehension of the truth *of* a situation, and it is because perception is the apprehension of the *true* that this term "of" naturally comes up in the definition of perception: although perception is a matter of passive immediacy, it is not for that reason simply an apprehension of "the" immediate; instead, perception must apprehend the situation *in its true nature*, in its "essence," in its "depth" rather than in its "superficiality." To apprehend what is there *as if* it had no depth of its own, *as if* it were merely immediate, is precisely to misapprehend it. We might notice the immediate "thatness" of a phenomenon, but perception must be responsive to its "what," to the identity and nature *of* that "that," to see it *as* something. In perception, one must be responsive to *its* nature.

"Perception," the apprehension of the truth of a situation, thus names a rich behaviour, a behaviour that can take varied forms on varied occasions, and inasmuch as it must apprehend truly, it is a behaviour that is inherently responsive to norms – that is, to the norm given by the nature of its object. One of the most striking features of Maurice Merleau-Ponty's *Phenomenology of Perception* – perceptible already in its mere table of contents – is that his study of perception begins with sensation and ends with freedom. Merleau-Ponty's study makes clear that under the name "perception" are ranged all the forms of our apprehension of the real, from the most basic, minimal phenomena of bare sensitivity to our engagement with the deepest matters of existence. What it takes to perceive cannot be determined without determining the very nature of the real, the very nature of *that*, the true nature of which it is perception's mandate to apprehend. As reality itself runs the range from immediate sensible physicality through animal life to the very depths of the soul and the mind, so will perception itself take different forms in its engagement with reality. This breadth of scope is intimately related to another aspect of perception, one that is captured in Merleau-Ponty's notion of "the primacy of perception."[1]

Perception is not just one of the many things we do, it is not just an optional activity in which we might engage. Perception, rather, is *our native element*: we exist *as* practitioners of perception. It is our nature to be wrapped up in situations that call forth from us the question of their truth; it is our nature to be engaged in the endeavour to apprehend the truth of our situation. Typically, we think of ourselves as parts of the world – as "things" existing in the world of nature – and we think of perception as one of our capacities. We must note, however, that our very sense *that there is a world* is itself a phenomenon *of perception*. We are not organisms first and perceivers second; we *are* perceivers, that is, we exist *as* the fact – the *act* – of being aware, being responsive, and our very sense of ourselves as "a thing in the world" is itself a development of our perception.[2]

Identifying ourselves as "the act of perceiving," however, must not be confused with identifying ourselves as a representing mind. Descartes, in his famous argument that "I think therefore I am," similarly identified us with the act of experience, but he construed this "I" as the detached, self-contained mind from which the world is always inherently alien.[3] We must recognize, on the contrary, that we are *being-in-the-world*, that perception is not a power that travels outward from some "inner" space towards an alien reality, but that, instead, perception is situated, living engagement with the real.[4] We only ever occur *as* the experience *of things*, the experience *of a world*: "the perceiving mind," as Merleau-Ponty says, "is an incarnate mind."[5] For this reason, perception may equally be said to be "ours" and "its," that is, perception is as much called into being by things, such that our own identity is summoned up by the unique demands of responsiveness to the determinate situation, as it is a power we direct towards reality, allowing things to come to light.[6] The range of the phenomena of perception – from minimal sensation to maximal freedom – corresponds to the dimensions of our contact with the real, our being in the world: it is not an independent power hovering indifferently over things, but is enacted from the very determinacies of our situated existence.

Furthermore, this perception, inasmuch as it is not the act of a separate mind but is enacted in and as our bodily engagement with the world, is itself not a detached, tranquil contemplation; rather, it is a practice, a bodily doing. It is *through* walking that we perceive the spatial environment, *by* moving our eyes and head – and, indeed, by simultaneously touching the things around us with our hands – that we see our surroundings.[7] Perception is not a detached spectacle in detached mental space: it is enacted *in* and *through* our practical engagement with the world.

And this perception that is our own nature, our own element, is itself dynamic: the growth of our being in the world is the growth of perception, that is, perception – our very practice of being ourselves – becomes deeper and keener as we mature. As is already intimated in the example of the child, above, as one grows, one's perception becomes attuned more to the deeper matters of psychology and politics than to the more superficial matters of the still-new spectacle of life that captivates the attention of the child; indeed, one's growth as a person just *is* this growth of perception. Perception – apprehending what is there – runs, as we have noted, the whole range from simple apprehension of the immediate sensory contact with the real (for colours and sounds and "feels" really are "there") to the tortured apprehension of the deep reality of freedom – to the complexities of one's own feelings and of our global, historical, human situation. This perceptual range is not, however, a static range of options given from birth; it is the path of perception's dynamic development, *the path of our growth.*

Our development of perceptual capacity is equally our growth as persons, as beings-in-the-world. Merleau-Ponty's central thesis that our perception is "incarnate" does not mean simply that we perceive only because we are being-in-the-world; it means as well that perception is itself a worldly practice, as much transformative of as responsive to the world. The world itself and our relationship to it must themselves develop in order to accommodate the demands of perception. Indeed, to develop the capacity to perceive the rich complexities of freedom is equally to *establish* rich relations of freedom: our capacity for perception is afforded by the real, and transformative developments in our perception of the real must equally be transformative developments within our relationship to the world.

This idea of development – within perception, and within being-in-the-world – entails that the world itself is not a static, given determinacy but is, instead, the *possibility* for determinate meaning. The clarity and determinateness of our own identity and the correlative identity of the world to which we belong are themselves accomplishments within perception, but accomplishments always subtended by a further opacity and indeterminacy. "We must recognize the indeterminate as a positive phenomenon," writes Merleau-Ponty at the very beginning of his study of perception, and this indeterminacy remains the essential background to all our developed experience of the world.[8] Precisely because the terms of the world are always rooted in such indeterminacy, precisely because the fixed terms into which our perception is resolved are always accomplishments of perception rather than its pregiven parameters, the contour of – indeed the *meaning* of – our world always remains essentially open to revision. This openness of the world is the metaphysical counterpart of our creativity, our freedom: to say we are free is to say that the world is open to us, that it accommodates our creativity.

It is because of this openness of the world to our freedom that Merleau-Ponty's study of perception, which begins with consideration of the passivity of sensory reception, itself develops into a consideration of our *expressivity*, our creative transformation of our terms for engaging with the world and with each other.[9] If perception is the apprehension of the truth of the world, then it is *in* our creativity, we might say, that we experience – that we perceive – the nature of the world most truly, in that we apprehend its essential openness. And this apprehension that is creative expression is not just a static acknowledgment of the openness constitutive of reality, but is itself the performative enactment of that recognition. It is a recognition, indeed, that can only be made in and as a performance.[10]

Such creative expression draws our attention to a further dimension of our perceptual life, our being-in-the-world: our engagement with the real is an intersubjective engagement, that is, we inhabit a world *with others*.[11] An expression is a gesture made for others, and its meaning – the very sense of "my" gesture – is determined by how it is taken up by them. Language is inherently public, and my participation in the domain of language is a tacit commitment to the perspectives of others, a tacit acknowledgment that I cannot be myself on my own but that in order to be myself I depend on the support of others. Discussing expression, Merleau-Ponty writes: "I confirm the other person, and the other person confirms me."[12] Our perceptual life, then, is not a private affair but a collaborative one, a participation in a community of witnesses to the real, to the "true and exact world" that is our shared domain.[13]

Perception, then, is indeed our apprehension of the truth of a situation, but this apprehension, this passivity, is quite different from what we typically imagine when we think of passive apprehension. Our traditional prejudices about perception imagine it to be the establishing of a representation in a private mind by the mechanical impression of a fully formed world on a passive body. But on the contrary, perception is in fact the *bodily, intersubjective performance of engagement*: it is collaboration with the real itself in the simultaneous enactment of both seer and seen.[14] It is Merleau-Ponty's project to challenge these traditional prejudices by engaging in the rigorous description of the phenomena of perception – a phenomenology of perception.[15]

Merleau-Ponty's works have been of revolutionary importance in our intellectual world. They have transformed research in philosophy – whether in phenomenological studies proper, or in cognitive science or in philosophy of art – and have massively influenced work in other disciplines ranging from psychology and sociology to politics and artistic practice. From his early published work in *The Structure of Behavior* (1942), through the *Phenomenology of Perception* (1945), to his late work in the unfinished *The Visible and the Invisible*, and in his lecture courses throughout his years at the Sorbonne (1949–52) and the Collège de France (1952–61), the principle of his work remains the same: Merleau-Ponty's philosophy demonstrates throughout a resolute stance of being open to allowing perception itself to show its own nature, and his philosophy is precisely the attempt to give expression to the perception of perception itself. The authors in this volume have endeavoured to defend and develop this same project though studies of Merleau-Ponty's philosophy that are themselves oriented less towards commentary on his texts than towards descriptions and analyses of the phenomena themselves. The studies in this volume, like Merleau-Ponty's own chapters in the *Phenomenology of Perception*, move progressively from consideration of the most basic structures of perceptual life to consideration of the deepest and richest aspects of our expressive interpersonal and political life.

The four chapters in Part I, "Passivity and Intersubjectivity," address the fundamental dimensions – the "first principles" – of our existence as perceivers, challenging the familiar view that perception is the act of a self-possessed, detached, and individual agent mind that passes over its object like a searchlight. On the contrary, as we have seen, perception is most fundamentally an experience of passivity; it is also an engagement, and it is enacted in collaboration with others.

In chapter 1, "Freedom and Passivity: Attention, Work and Language," John Russon introduces the essential intertwining of activity and passivity in our experience by studying what might seem the definitive experience of perceptual life, namely, the act of "paying attention." Paying attention, more specifically, seems paradigmatically a matter of agency, and Russon uses progressively more sophisticated examples of studying, staring, listening, working, and communicating to discern the precise character of this perceptual activity – our perceptual freedom – in the context of a fundamental passivity that defines our experience.[16] Through this analysis, he demonstrates that our agency in general takes the form of answering a question posed by the environment and that it has "freedom of movement" within the parameters of possibility the object opens up. Our responsiveness has the effect of completing the identity of the object by bringing out of it what it cannot bring out of itself. It is thus inherent to the very nature of things to be open to our freedom. This openness of the thing to oneself, however, is also its openness to others, so in engaging with the thing one is in fact engaging in dialogue with others, co-inhabiting their space, and our attending to things is thus a "joint" attention.

In chapter 2, "The Image and the Workspace: Merleau-Ponty and Levinas on Passivity and Rhythmic Subjectivity," Maria Talero carries forward Russon's analysis of the intertwining of activity and passivity to clarify the fundamental (re)definition of subjectivity implied in Merleau-Ponty's phenomenology. In particular, she argues for an "enactive" subjectivity, more primary than the agency we typically associate with our conception of the human being as a self-defined and self-possessed subject who simply "is who she is." Merleau-Ponty, she argues, reveals experience to be "an enactive, bodily engagement with the lived environment," an engagement in which the body and the world are intertwined and mutually conditioning. Experience, she writes, "is the *coupling* of two incomplete terms, 'lived body' and 'world,' neither of which is a complete identity in its own right: each of which only exists as the potentiality of the other." Talero demonstrates the essential passivity inherent in this conception of experience by drawing upon Levinas's description of the rhythmic taking up of an image, according to which the viewer is someone who must become passively absorbed into a certain sort of rhythmic play. Using examples of being in a workspace and of playing basketball, Talero demonstrates that we succeed in our engagement in activities precisely by allowing ourselves to be rhythmically *pulled into* possibilities for motion that we can never actively predict or manage, and that we must *give ourselves over to* the work arena in much the same way that we give ourselves over to sleep. Thus our experience as a whole must be fundamentally understood as a kind of passivity. Indeed, like Levinas, Merleau-Ponty demonstrates that in many respects our experience resembles much more the experience of the dreamer than it resembles that of a fully conscious, self-possessed agent.

Both Russon and Talero develop the idea that our being as perceivers – indeed, as agents – is something received, and something performatively co-constituted with our objective situation. As Russon has noted in chapter 1, it is other people who in many ways make up the most significant dimension of this objective situation, and the passive, constitutive coupling of our subjectivity with that of others is Kym Maclaren's focus in chapter 3, "The 'Entre-Deux' of Emotions: Emotions as Institutions." Continuing the analysis of passivity, Maclaren approaches this topic through the theme of emotion, the "passions" that have long been thought to compromise our self-possessed agency. Drawing upon the notion of "institution" from Merleau-Ponty's later works to flesh out the ideas operative in the *Phenomenology of Perception*, and continuing the emphasis on the "enactive" character of experience introduced by Talero, Maclaren argues that our emotional life is thus not exactly "our own" – that it is not something "constituted" by an autonomous subject; rather, it is the delicate fabric established as an "entre-deux" – a collaborative reality "between two" – that is effectively our habituation to a form of behavioural "conversation" with the solicitations of our environment. It is the instituted character of these forms of coupling that explains their "passivity" – the way, that is, that we are not simply free to elect to change an emotion for another we might prefer. This instituted character also indicates, however, that these engrained "takes" on reality are not simply deterministic, alien forces; instead, as forms of coupling in which we participate, they are open to change. Such change, however, will not simply be by self-willed "fiat," but will be a re-entry into the sedimented conversation that draws upon the very resources made available to us by that perceptual "entre-deux."

In chapter 4, "Perceiving through Another: Incorporation and the Child Perceiver," Susan Bredlau further studies the theme of the inherent sharedness of our experience with others, which Maclaren explored in the context of our emotional experience. In keeping with the enactive model of perception outlined by Talero, Bredlau argues that the line between the perceiver and the perceived cannot be crisply drawn. Whether we notice it or not, our experience as perceivers regularly relies on our "incorporation" of things that we would normally presume to be on the side of the perceived into our very existence *as* perceivers: our powers of perception are made possible, as Russon showed, by "objects" that one would often, in a reflective state, identify as "not me." The perceiving body is thus not simply the isolatable packets of skin, bone, and muscle that an anatomy book might identify, but is, rather, the *system of perceptual possibility*, which may include a walking stick, a pair of glasses, and, perhaps most importantly, *another person's* know-how. Bredlau couples Merleau-Ponty's analyses of the child's experience with contemporary empirical studies in child psychology to show that the child in fact depends on the experience of others for her "own" perceptual possibilities. From the start, the child's experience is thus a matter of *perceptual cooperation*.

These four chapters of Part I thus analyse in detail what is really involved in the fact that our experience is "personal"; each reveals crucial ways in which this personal character of our experience does not, in fact, justify our (common) interpretation of ourselves as metaphysically autonomous subjects. Alongside this fact that our experience is always individualized – and in that sense always "personal" – it is also true that we experience the world as an impersonal realm of being "in itself." As Merleau-Ponty writes: "I ought to say that *one* perceives in me, and not that I perceive. Every sensation bears within itself the germ of a dream or depersonalization."[17] The four chapters of Part II, "Generality and Objectivity," examine the emergence within perception of the sense of the world as an independent reality. This is ultimately the experience of objectivity – that is, the experience of an independently existing world that is a norm to which we must answer.

In chapter 5, "Neglecting Space: Making Sense of a Partial Loss of One's World through a Phenomenological Account of the Spatiality of Embodiment," Kirsten Jacobson investigates the experience of "spatial neglect," a condition that often affects stroke victims and is characterized by a failure to notice a portion (typically an entire hemisphere) of their surrounding world. To understand this condition, which we might think of as a sort of inability to pay attention, Jacobson introduces Merleau-Ponty's conception of the "spatial level." Merleau-Ponty argues that experience is not just an immediate matter of presently grappling with present experience, but is in fact a more structured affair in which the sense of our experience crystallizes around privileged forms of significance that are the normative, general parameters from which we take our balance. These generalized parameters establish for us the "level" in experience, according to which we establish a lived sense of equilibrium. It is by means of this level that the body and the world are mutually attuned, and our explicit dealings are premised on this implicit sense of being-in-the-world. Although the actual details of our situation change moment by moment, a consistent identity to the self/world relation endures, not as a physical fact but as an *experience*, as Descartes showed in his wax argument;[18] *contra* Descartes, however, Merleau-Ponty establishes that this unity is also not given by an innate idea of the self-conscious mind, but is in fact an equilibrium established in our bodily grasp of the world.[19] The perceiving self, in other words, is not just the self-conscious mind, but is the *intelligent body*, the body by whose capacities for engagement a world – a space for possible action – has been opened up. Thus, our capacity for spatial engagement is not something simply "given" physiologically, nor is it a psychological function of the self-conscious mind; rather, it is the accomplishment of the lived body's establishing of an intelligent, attuned equilibrium with the world that lies below the engagement of the "self at this moment" and the "world at this moment."[20] Our spatial experience is a dimension of the generality of the world's identity established implicitly in our bodily being-in-the-world, a level that is itself a reflection of a person's lived engagement with his or her surroundings, an engagement rooted both in the vital parameters of our organic relation to the natural environment and in the processes of habituation by which we have established our developed being-in-the-world. The disturbance of one's spatial involvement is thus a disturbance of one's existential situation, rather than simply a "mental" or a "physical" problem: it is a problem of the intelligent "lived" body of existential interaction that establishes the implicit level of our experience that underlies our explicit perceptual behaviour.

This theme of the intelligent body is essential to Don Beith's study of embodied learning in chapter 6, "Moving into Being: The Motor Basis of Perception, Balance, and Reading." Through three connected case studies, Beith examines the experience of coming to inhabit new "levels" of body/world coupling. First, by examining the dynamic way in which an octopus body is jointed, Beith highlights how an animate body's existence and function are not given in advance, but rather always develop in coordination with its existential tasks and the surrounding situation that it encounters. He then draws on this insight to consider the higher-order activity of developing new possibilities for movement (specifically, kicking) beyond the habits one has already established, arguing that the sort of embodiment we see in human beings is not only that cooperative form of engagement captured by the notions "being-in-the-world" and "flesh," but also *intelligent* in the sense that the development of a new habit involves the grasping of a new "whole." Beith concludes by using an analysis of handwriting to show that it is only through the development of postures and movements supportive of the making of ideas that we can and do think. Our intelligence arises from and through our embodied relationship with the world, and, equally, our embodiment reflects our intelligent relationship with and grasp of our situation.

In chapter 7, "On the Nature of Space: Getting from Motricity to Reflection and Back Again," Noah Moss Brender continues the investigation of spatial experience, and investigates in particular the foundations of our experience of "objective space." Most importantly, Moss Brender, echoing Beith's analysis of bodily learning, argues that "objective space" is not natural and immediate, but is rather the object of a developed form of experience. The notion of objectivity is typically correlated with the notion of the detached, reflective intellect (akin to the "searchlight" notion of attention criticized by Russon in chapter 1), and Moss Brender argues that as objective space is derivative of a more basic spatiality, so is reflection derivative of a more basic experience of meaning. Through a reconsideration of Köhler's observations of chimpanzees, Moss Brender shows that, as Jacobson indicated in chapter 5, the subject/object opposition of mind and space is itself rooted in a more basic motor engagement with the world, a being-in-the-world characterized by a spatiality and a meaningfulness that are expressed in movement rather than in thought. Objective spatiality is derivative of motor-space but is not reducible to it, however. The power to reflect does indeed draw its resources from unacknowledged sources in the opacity of our bodily being-in-the-world, but it also opens up for us the unique domain of objective meaning, the domain in which it is possible to take up a position outside the immediacy of one's own perspective and to recognize the autonomy of things and of others.

In chapter 8, "Merleau-Ponty and the Phenomenology of Natural Time," David Ciavatta continues the study of the theme of generality within experience, now with respect to time rather than space. With the notion of the "level," Jacobson introduced the experience of generality, of an objective or "third person" realm not variable moment by moment or answerable to my immediate will. Echoing Kant's concerns in the "Analogies of Experience," Ciavatta pursues this theme specifically with respect to the experience of time: How, he asks, from within the immanent temporality of our first-person experience, can we come to have an experience of an "objective time," a third-person time "in itself"?[21] Ciavatta looks in particular to the experience of natural cycles as the basis for our experience of temporal generality or indifference, in that it is not this moment or even this day that captures the character of the cycles of nature, but rather the season or even the year and, ultimately, the indefinite progression of these. Similarly, the habit body is marked by a certain generality rather than specificity in that, as Jacobson showed, the habit body does not respond to this particular moment or activity, but is rather the enacting of a field of developed, general significance. In living out of our habit body, we live in an overarching time that to some extent ignores the demands and engrossing characteristics of our present situation. We live in a time that is both now and bygone at once; it is a "general now." It is thus ultimately the habit body that allows for the emergence within experience of a sense of a time that is indifferent to experience, that is, it is due to the habit body that there arises for us an experience of time "in itself."

Our perceptual relation to the world is thus simultaneously one of immersion and one of detachment: we are both participants in it and observers of it, and this odd duplicity, this vacillation between life and reflection, between lived experience and objectivity, defines the parameters of *meaning* in our lives. The three chapters of Part III, "Meaning and Ambiguity," investigate the distinct character of meaning in our experience.

David Morris, in chapter 9, "Institution, Expression, and the Temporality of Meaning in Merleau-Ponty," continues the investigation of temporality begun by Ciavatta. Arguing that the notion of difference is fundamental to Merleau-Ponty's understanding of meaning, but that mere difference is never enough to constitute meaning, Morris shows that orientation is also essential to meaning and that orientation is an inherently temporal notion of directedness from a past to a future. Meaning is, in other words, always wrapped up in an activity of *directional* differences. Further uniting the theme of orientation with the theme of the "level," Morris argues that meaning itself is always oriented in terms of the project of establishing an experiential "balance." Balance itself is never something actual (even though it is very real); one is never *at* a fixed balance point, but rather is always oscillating in such a way that one is relatively stable, the balance itself being a sort of governing norm enacted only within the efforts to achieve it. The norm of balance, then, is never itself a given reality, but is rather a "non-given" meaning that invokes within the situation an imperative to realize it. The temporality of our experience is this ongoing process of negotiation between the actual and the virtual, a negotiation that never admits of final resolution into a simple fixed determinacy, but instead leaves determinacy as always a provisional accomplishment within an irresolvably ambiguous domain.

This theme of the negotiation between ambiguity and resolution is further developed by Ömer Aygün, in chapter 10, "Implications of Merleau-Ponty's Account of Binocularity." By tracing the development of Merleau-Ponty's use of the example of binocular vision, Aygün explores the character not only of human vision but also of meaning in general. Aygün argues that Merleau-Ponty uses the phenomenon of binocular vision to demonstrate that negativity, self-opposition, and questioning are central to human perception, and that it is these characteristics of our perception, which we might ultimately capture with the term "ambiguity," that define us as beings who can partake in a life not marked by pre-givens. Aygün expands on Merleau-Ponty's own use of the story of Odysseus's meeting with the Cyclops Polyphemus in *The Odyssey* to show how a counter-example of the human life of choice, creativity, and cunning exists in a being who is monolithic, not only in his ways of "understanding" and behaving in the world, but also, quite significantly, in his way of seeing the world. The Cyclops has one eye – an eye that does not allow or call for an intentional or existential act, but rather that simply gives over the world in one self-sufficient swoop of positivity. Aygün's analysis brings to life the far-reaching implications of what otherwise might seem a topically limited example: binocular vision tells us not simply about the organs and processes of eyesight, but about sight understood as a rich and integrated power of perception that ultimately cannot be separated from an entire style of living – in this case a style marked by aiming, by ambiguity, and, thus, by meaning.

Chapter 11, "Alterity and Expression in Merleau-Ponty: A Response to Levinas," continues the emphasis on the inherent ambiguity of experience. Challenging Levinas's criticisms of Merleau-Ponty's philosophy as being marked by the "coincidence of the knowing and the known," Scott Marratto describes Merleau-Ponty as presenting consciousness and knowledge as fundamentally marked by *unknowing* – that is, knowledge is understood to be always working in a realm of ambiguities "that it can never close up." This is the power of knowledge, not its failure, since it is because of this that we are open to the world rather than simply captivated by it. Drawing especially on Merleau-Ponty's analysis of expression, Marratto argues that Merleau-Ponty's use of the painter to help him describe the character of vision is a move that demonstrates an overturning of previous philosophical conceptions of vision and its importance in capturing human knowledge. Unlike historical accounts of vision, which tended to rely on a dualistic conception of seer and seen, Merleau-Ponty's account insists that vision is akin to pregnancy insofar as it is simultaneously an activity and a passivity (the mother both tends to herself and "her" pregnancy and is subject to the demands of the pregnancy), is simultaneously us and not us (the fetus is both the mother and not the mother). Like pregnancy, vision cannot, he argues, be reduced to either a passive receptivity or an active positing. Instead, vision is as much a summons by the "outside" world as it is a voyage "outward" by the "self." The painter partakes in this intertwined relationship in a way that may be more visible to us than in the case of the average person looking about the world on a given day; the painter's work pushes us to notice that our way of seeing is not settled in advance, but is, rather, an open happening of communication, an invitation without end, an invitation unceasingly given and with no possibility for resolution. Our artistic traditions thus have a specially powerful capacity to make manifest to us the ambiguity that Morris and Aygün have demonstrated to be the characteristic nature of perception.

Part IV, "Expression," specifically addresses Merleau-Ponty's analysis of artistic expression and its unique role in perception. Drawing both upon Merleau-Ponty's writings on artists and on the work of contemporary artists, the four essays of Part IV bring us to the experience of perception at the point at which perception is itself performatively involved in enacting the world it perceives.[22]

In chapter 12, "Aesthetic Ideas: Developing the Phenomenology of Merleau-Ponty with the Art of Matta-Clark," Matthew J. Goodwin uses the architectural artwork of Gordon Matta-Clark to introduce and develop the distinction between first-order speech and second-order speech that Merleau-Ponty uses to understand the phenomenon of expression. Merleau-Ponty distinguishes two different ways in which lines function in our experience: as prosaic, and as flexuous.[23] Prosaic lines are akin to second-order language and thought, that is, they travel down already established paths. Flexuous lines, like first-order thought and language, generate meaning in a specific and inaugural creative act and equally summon into being our own selves as participants in that generated meaning. Goodwin argues that architecture often functions prosaically, imposing itself upon its inhabitants and shaping them in ways that fail to honour them *as* inhabitants. Matta-Clark's art, Goodwin argues, works precisely to disrupt the calcifying tendencies of prefabricated environments and to stimulate their viewers to become involved once again in the activity of bringing their space to life, so to speak.

This theme of "bringing our space to life" is further elaborated in chapter 13, "Flesh as the Space of Mourning: Maurice Merleau-Ponty Meets Ana Mendieta," in which Stefan Kristensen demonstrates how the time- and space-based artworks of Ana Mendieta engage and enact the notion of "phenomenal space." Kristensen describes phenomenal space as the perceptual domain in which space and time are not two distinct features, but rather are overlapping, and in which things are not juxtaposed, but rather encroach upon one another. Mendieta's artistic practice, which she called "Earth Body Art," typically involved creating human female body forms in various types of natural materials and leaving them to erode as memorials to the human form whose significance is inherently open to destruction. Kristensen sees here the performance of a reality that can never be simply and fully present, a reality that itself makes manifest the very nature of the reality that is perception. Perception, as the site for the emergence of ever-new spatio-temporal meaning, is always open-ended, always defined by a "not yet" that itself is engaged in the creative act of responding to our own past. The stability of the perceived present is accomplished precisely at the intersection of the embrace of the undecidability of the future and the "mourning" of the past. This mourning of which Kristensen speaks, however, is not a matter of grief or nostalgic longing. Mourning, rather, is a process of remembering one's past in such a way that one is precisely letting go of that past in order to find a new grasp on one's present. It is in this experience that Kristensen maintains we can see the indiscernability of space and time. Meaning is always realized "there," in and as the spatial presence of world, but that spatiality is itself always inherently defined by the "no longer" and the "not yet," by a temporal orientation that can never be discharged in simple presence. Mendieta's work makes clear that these "logical" structures of meaning are also the existential structures of the meaningfulness of our lives: a person lives her life-world in terms of her past, and whether her past is acknowledged in an act of simultaneously letting it go will determine whether her life-world breathes or suffocates her.

In chapter 14, "Phenomenology and the Body Politic: Merleau-Ponty, Cézanne, and Democracy," Peter Costello uses Merleau-Ponty's analysis of the artist to show the relevance of Merleau-Ponty's analysis of perception and his conception of "flesh" for our political life. The artist, in making visible what might otherwise go unnoticed, serves as an exemplary phenomenologist and for this reason also as a leader with political significance. Revisiting the theme of childhood development that Bredlau considered in chapter 4, Costello emphasizes the importance for the child's development both of developing a capacity to incorporate form and also, eventually, of making a creative, self-motivated move away from this guiding form. Costello argues that this is the rhythm of all human learning and freedom, and furthermore, that this process does not occur without the inspiration of others. This process defines the ultimate role of the artist: the artist offers "inspiring form" in this regular rhythm of learning and growth. Indeed, artists such as Gordon Matta-Clark and Ana Mendieta invite us precisely to participate in and thereby enact the perception of new ways of being human.

The volume concludes with chapter 15, "Phenomenology as First-Order Perception: Speech, Vision, and Reflection in Merleau-Ponty," in which Laura McMahon uses Merleau-Ponty's distinction between first- and second-order expression as a way to understand the practice of philosophy itself. Whereas it is our "natural attitude" to see the world and the meaning of the world as already established, as having been given in advance by nature or as having already been figured out by the experts who surround us, we must take up a "first order" attitude to perception in general if we are to engage adequately with the world and its perpetually open meanings. Phenomenology, McMahon argues, is such an originary perceiving: it is the perception of perception that itself creatively transforms perception itself. Furthermore, she argues, this originary responsiveness needs to be alive in our very practice of reading philosophical texts, such that we allow them to be sites for the emergence of new thoughts and new meanings instead of treating them as settled repositories of fully determinate doctrines. This conclusion in fact expresses well the founding motivation for this volume.

Although these fifteen essays are each written with the hand of a different author, this book represents a collaborative project rather than an assemblage of discrete studies. Most of the contributors to this volume have worked closely together for a number of years in something like a workshop or an artist's community, and these essays are generally the result of sustained discussion and cooperative interaction. Furthermore, almost all of the chapters have been developed through public presentation (primarily at various meetings of the International Merleau-Ponty Circle, but also at the American Philosophical Association, the Society for Phenomenology and Existential Philosophy, and smaller conferences), and have taken shape though collective discussion both before and after their presentation. Although the authors of these chapters draw on materials from the entire range of Merleau-Ponty's published work, our hope in bringing this collection together is primarily to offer a collaborative study of perception that runs roughly parallel to the study in the *Phenomenology of Perception*, and can act as a companion to that text. Instead of offering a "commentary," however, this volume is an attempt to engage with the living thought of Merleau-Ponty and to engage with it in answering to the phenomenological imperative to return "to the things themselves." We intend this work to be of independent value to scholars and to be a suitable teaching text for use in courses on Merleau-Ponty, offering helpful explications of his text as well as updating his analyses through consideration of more contemporary materials and showing how his mode of philosophizing can be pursued independently. But even more, it has been our intention to offer original philosophical studies in the spirit of Merleau-Ponty. In short, we have tried to take up Merleau-Ponty's phenomenology as a practice rather than as an object: we have tried creatively and collectively to perform phenomenology, with a goal of passing on to others the inspiration we have ourselves taken from Merleau-Ponty's work.

NOTES

1 Merleau-Ponty, "The Primacy of Perception," 25: "By these words, 'the primacy of perception,' we mean that the experience of perception is our presence at the moment when things, truths, values are constituted for us; that perception is a nascent *logos*; that it teaches us, outside all dogmatism, the true conditions of objectivity itself; that it summons us to the tasks of knowledge and action. It is not a question of reducing human knowledge to sensation, but of assisting at the birth of this knowledge, to make it as sensible as the sensible, to recover the consciousness of rationality. This experience of rationality is lost when we take it for granted as self."

2 Cf. Merleau-Ponty's discussion of "the Experience Error," *PP* 27[5]; cf. 40–1[17–18], 47[24–5]. Cf. also Merleau-Ponty, "An Unpublished Text," 3: "We never cease living in the world of perception, but we go beyond it in critical thought – almost to the point of forgetting the contribution of perception to our idea of truth."

3 Descartes, *Meditations*, Second Meditation, 18–19.

4 *PP* 106–14[80–7]. The notion of being-in-the-world is from Heidegger, *Being and Time*, Division I, ch. 2, s. 12, 49–55.

5 Merleau-Ponty, "An Unpublished Text," 4: "The perceiving mind is an incarnate mind. I have tried, first of all, to re-establish the roots of the

mind in its body and in its world, going against doctrines which treat perception as a simple result of the action of external things on our body as well as against those which insist on the autonomy of consciousness."

6 Cf. Merleau-Ponty's notion of "flesh" (*chair*), in "Intertwining – The Chiasm."

7 On the bodily character of perception, see Russon, "Merleau-Ponty and the New Science of the Soul," esp. 130–3. Cf. *PP* 31[9]: "At the elementary level of sensibility, we catch sight of a collaboration among partial stimuli and between the sensorial and the motor system that, through a variable physiological constellation, keeps the sensation constant, and thus rules out any definition of the nervous process as the simple transmission of a given message." On the non-separation of touch and vision (and of the different senses generally), see *PP* pt 1, ch. 4, 143–77[115–43], and pt 2, ch. 1, 251–76[214–39]; see also the discussion in *VI* 172–88[130–43]. This topic is discussed in Talero, "Intersubjectivity and Intermodal Perception."

8 *PP* 28[7]. Merleau-Ponty also emphasizes that the "figure–background" relationship is essential to all perception: "When Gestalt theory tells us that a figure against a background is the most basic sensible given we can have, this is not a contingent characteristic of factual perception … Rather, this is the very definition of the perceptual phenomenon, or that without which a phenomenon cannot be called perception" (*PP* 26[4]; see also 36[13ff]).

9 See *PP* pt 1, ch. 6, "The Body as Expression and Speech."

10 See Russon, "The Spatiality of Self-Consciousness," esp. 224–7.

11 See Merleau-Ponty, "The Child's Relations with Others"; see also *PP* pt 1, ch. 5, "The Bodily in Its Sexual Being," and pt 2, ch. 4, "Other Selves and the Human World." On the intersubjective character of our being-in-the-world, see Jacobson, "The Interpersonal Expression," esp. 158–60. See also Leder, *The Absent Body*, 94.

12 *PP* 225[191]. See also Maclaren, "Emotional Disorder," esp. 144–5.

13 *PP* 79–80[53].

14 This is the central thesis of contemporary "enactive" accounts of perception. See Thompson, *Mind in Life*, esp. ch. 4.

15 "Traditional Prejudices and the Return to Phenomena" is the title of the introductory section (chs. 1–4) of *PP*.

16 Cf. *VI*, working note from November 1959, 274[221]: "Philosophy has never spoken – I do not say of *passivity*: we are not effects – but I would say of the passivity of our activity."

17 *PP* 260[223]; cf. *VI*, working note of 2 May 1959, 244[190]: "I do not perceive any more than I speak – Perception has me as has language – And as it is necessary that all the same *I* be there in order to speak, *I* must

be there in order to perceive – But in what sense? As *one*." See also the working note of 22 October 1959 (cited in *The Merleau-Ponty Reader*, 426): "Subjectivity is truly *no one*. It is truly the desert. What is constitutive of the subject is to be integrally with the things of the world, to have no positively assignable interior, to be *generality*. Subjectivity is this foam at the mouth of the world, that the world never dissipates."

18 Descartes, *Meditations*, Second Meditation, 21.

19 *PP* 106–9[80–2].

20 Merleau-Ponty refers to the "body at this moment" (*le corps actuel*) at *PP* 111[84], and the "world at this moment" (*le monde actuel*) at *PP* 136[108]. (This is the translation by Colin Smith; Landes translates these expressions respectively as "the actual body" and "the present world.")

21 See Kant, *Critique of Pure Reason*, A176–218/B218–65.

22 On the significance of Merleau-Ponty for understanding contemporary art and vice versa, see Kristensen, "Le Mouvement de la Création" and "Merleau-Ponty."

23 See Merleau-Ponty, "Eye and Mind," 182–3; *VI*, working note of September 1959, 261[207]. The distinction between first-order and second-order expression is the subject of "The Body as Expression and Speech," pt 1, ch. 6 of *PP*; see esp. *PP* 217n2[530n6] (note to 183).

PART I

Passivity and Intersubjectivity

1 Freedom and Passivity: Attention, Work, and Language

JOHN RUSSON

We often think of our freedom as a kind of independent power of choice and action that floats over the surface of things, rather as a searchlight might selectively pass over things. I want to take up Merleau-Ponty's analysis of the act of paying attention – in which he criticizes a comparable "searchlight" model of attention – as an exemplary case study of freedom, to show how our freedom is always embedded in its situation.[1] I will consider, basically, how, in attention, our "free power" is in crucial ways *given by* the determinacies it addresses: this will be the inherent "passivity" of our "active" nature. This initial discerning of the passive dimension of the act of attention seems to limit the independent authority of freedom. Through considering the phenomena of habituation and work, however, we will eventually see that, because this passivity is the passivity of a practice, the things that give us our abilities are themselves vulnerable to our freedom while being insufficient to command it: although our experience is indeed fundamentally characterized by passivity, that passivity falls short of normativity. In the domain of communication, however, we will discover that intersubjectivity is an essential dimension of passivity that can constitute an inherent normative answerability within our freedom: it is ultimately by freedom that freedom can be definitively limited, so it will be through our passivity with respect to others that a compelling normative dimension emerges.

I. The Phenomenon of Attention

Let me first give three examples of experiences of paying attention.[2]

(1) If I am trying to become a better volleyball player, my coach might show me a video and say "pay attention to what the player at the net

does here." I would then watch the video with an explicit orientation towards a particular individual, and would pointedly look at that player with the expectation of seeing something significant happen. (2) A second attitude is a detached staring that could happen when I am (aggressively or defensively) experiencing my disengagement from a situation, and I address the object – perhaps a person – confrontationally with my direct gaze. (3) A third attitude is paying attention to music, which will mean giving myself over to absorption in it, either by listening or dancing, allowing myself to be overtaken by the rhythm and the emotional flow of the music instead of just hearing it in the background. These attitudes of looking at, staring, listening, and dancing can all legitimately be called "paying attention," although they can be stances of engagement *or* of disengagement, of analysis *or* of absorption. Let us note some constitutive features of these modes of attending.

(i) Paying attention is a *practice*, and it is a skill that must be developed. Imagine children in an elementary school classroom. Although there certainly are matters in which children can be absorbed for long periods, there is good reason for saying they have "short attention spans." One of the main tasks of their growing up is precisely to become more adept at paying attention, by developing patience and concentration, both of which require substantial emotional and bodily education. I must learn to control my emotions – to be self-possessed – if I am to be patient and to endure a process that might otherwise be boring, frustrating, or in other ways irritating.[3] To concentrate, I must be able, for example, to sit still in a chair for many hours or to hold my body in some other single posture unflinchingly. Paying attention also requires education. I cannot attend to what you are saying if I have not learned your language, and although I try, I cannot really pay adequate attention to the music – I cannot truly listen to it – without having learned how to appreciate it. To be sure, the ability to pay attention is a nascent power in the child, but it is a power that has a path of development over which it emerges in ever-richer forms.

(ii) Acts of paying attention are always embedded in particular *contexts*, and their enactment makes a difference in those contexts. My looking at the volleyball video is (a) a gesture of compliance with my coach's instructions, (b) a commitment to furthering my project of developing as a player, and (c) a particular placement of my body within the room as well as a usage of electricity. My staring at my colleague across the room (a) makes him uncomfortable and leads him to stop whispering to the person beside him, (b) is an expression of my irritation, and

(c) is a posture of uncommon stillness. My listening to the music (a) is an endorsement of shared activity of my companions and of the others in the music hall, (b) accomplishes a stepping out of the pressures of my workday, and (c) is a practice of sitting still with my eyes closed. In all of these cases, "paying attention" is a bodily action within a distinct and determinate spatial setting, an intersubjective gesture, and an engagement with the determinacies of my specific object.

(iii) The practice of paying attention has its *form dictated by the nature of that object*. It is the character of the music that dictates what it takes to pay attention to it: by virtue of being music, it requires that I attend to it by listening and/or by dancing, that I attend to it in a temporal process that can be neither rushed nor slowed, and so on; by virtue of being this piece of music, it requires that I "get inside" the unique musical space it is defining and that I appreciate its own internal norms and structures. Again, it is the volleyball lesson that sets the terms for my attention. As a student, I do not yet know how to play better – that is precisely what I must learn – so the very video I am watching will be teaching me about paying attention even as I engage in that practice: it will teach me what I need to notice. Paying heed entails being led by the object, and this "being led" is itself educational: to have the parameters of attending dictated by the object is to have "paying attention" as an activity that one cannot accomplish on one's own – that is, one can aim at it, but independently of engagement with the object, what one is to do is not available to one.

Finally, (iv) In all our examples of attending, we are imagining activities in which not-attending would be possible: to look at, to stare, to listen, and to dance are all practices of committing oneself to heeding something in situations in which one could have acted differently. In this sense, then, attention always actualizes a possibility and makes a perceptual figure out of something that could otherwise have remained in the background. As Sartre says in *Being and Nothingness*,

> no one object, no group of objects is especially designed to be organized as specifically either ground or figure; all depends on the direction of my attention. When I enter this café to search for Pierre, there is formed a synthetic organization of all the objects in the café, on the ground of which Pierre is given as about to appear. This organization of the café as the ground is an original nihilation ... The original nihilation of all the [possible] figures which appear and are swallowed up in the total neutrality

> of a *ground* is the necessary condition for the appearance of the principle figure, which is here the person of Pierre.[4]

All such "nihilations," Sartre argues, "derive their origin from an act, an expectation, or a project of a human being," and, using the negation that is a question as an exemplary case of this, he says, "it is essential therefore that the questioner have the permanent possibility of dissociating himself from the causal series which constitutes being."[5] The negation that is constitutive of the experience of a figure on a ground is, in short, a phenomenon of *freedom*. Indeed, this is just what is implied in calling the practice of paying attention "an act." Let us now look at the conditions of this free act.

II. The Conditions of Attention

(1) We have seen that attention, as a practice, is a meaningful and transformative contribution to a situation. Acts of attending are bodily practices – they involve positioning the eyes in certain ways, holding the body in a chair in certain ways, and so on – and, most basically, the condition of paying attention is the body. I cannot look at something without the eyes of a living body, or listen to something without the ears of a living body. The freedom to stare requires a body with mobile eyes, and so on.[6]

The very embodiment that enables my staring, my looking at, or my paying attention in general also makes this a necessary dimension of meaning within my experience. In other words, I cannot fail to be the kind of being for whom paying attention is an issue. Paying attention is a free act, but I am not free to choose to operate within these parameters.[7] As Hans Jonas says of organic life: "Its 'can' is a 'must,' since its execution is identical with its being. It can, but it cannot cease to do what it can without ceasing to be. Thus the sovereignty of form with respect to matter is also its subjection to the need of it."[8] Because the freedom to pay attention is embodied, it is a power given by the determinateness of that body. For that reason, this power is as much something by which I am constrained – something I undergo – as it is something I freely enact.[9] The power to pay attention is a power *of* this body, and the power thus stands in relations of necessary dependence upon the determinateness of this body.

(2) In addition to the organic powers that enable my action, the conditions of my attending to some aspect of a situation are the very

determinacies of that situation itself. As we just discussed, the power to grasp is a power *of* my fingers, palm, wrist, and so on, and in analogous ways, the power to attend to a situation is a power *of* that situation itself. Just as my hand makes available to me the power to grasp, it is the determinacies of my situation that *afford* me the possibilities of directing my gaze. The powers to think, to attend, to look, *are rooted in the objects of* those attitudes.[10] Let us consider how this is so.

Things *draw our attention*.[11] It is the nature of our experience of things to find them to be *charged* with significance, and the charge is one that needs our compliance in order to be *discharged*. The experience of attention is inherently defined by responsiveness and is realized in interaction: *it is an emergent transformation of the perceptual situation as a whole, rather than the application of an independent and independently defined power to a fixed object.*

As I gaze at the calendar on my wall, I experience the pressure it holds condensed within it: it is the map of my upcoming work responsibilities, and I feel its presence in my perceptual field as an imperative – an imperative to attend to what it says – but one that I can put off a bit longer. The very way the calendar is held within my perceptual field is as a kind of pressure, a kind of beckoning. It is not a deterministic force, however – it is, rather, a seed of possible significance that requires my compliance to grow – and I have some freedom of movement with respect to it, with respect to whether I address it directly, hold it at bay, or let it wither and die. The calendar is an offer and a provocation, and the question is whether I will give myself over to it.

Just as things can invite my attention, they can also repel it or refuse it. For example, in trying to learn how to play a song, I may find that I very much desire to listen to the melody the saxophone plays during the bridge section. Nonetheless, every time I listen to the tune, I find myself taken up in the flow of the song, and by the time the bridge section comes around, I have lost track of my mission. Despite my effort to hold on to my focused concentration, I find myself taken up in – overwhelmed by – the flow of the music. My attention is thus not strictly under my self-control, but is under the sway of the object to which it has directed itself.

Both as invitations and as refusals, the objects of our attention show themselves to be complicit in the accomplishing of the activity of paying attention. Some of the richness of this structure is evident in the familiar phenomenon of not being able to "get into" a sentence one is reading, an experience that has a few interesting dimensions. Sometimes, when one is trying to read, one finds oneself going through the words without making any real sense of them. Typically, this is because one is preoccupied by some other thought. One goes back and tries again, and the experience of trying to get into the meaning is a bit like the experience of diving into a swimming pool. In order to pay attention, one actually tries to give up one's detached control of one's consciousness in order to let the sentence take over. There are at least three related aspects to this familiar experience that pertain to my theme here. The first is that paying attention entails giving up one's detached, self-controlled stance and giving oneself over to the object, and to the way it gives itself: to pay heed to the object is to put it in the position of leadership and thus to let go of one's own ability to control how one's attending proceeds. The second is that the experience that the words – one's object – must let one in: they can function as a repelling surface off which one's attending intention bounces. The third is what is revealed in the initial experience of distraction: another thought held my attention and would not release it, such that, while I intended to attend to the reading, my attention was drawn back repeatedly to the "preoccupying" thought.[12]

To pay attention, then, is to make oneself answerable to the demands of the object.[13] The demands of the object are themselves *meaningful*, which is to say they speak to a free being (on which, more below), and for that reason they are themselves ambiguous. The demands of the object are not deterministic causes (as Sartre noted above), but "affordances" in that they afford different possible interactions, or "motivations," in the language of Merleau-Ponty and Sartre.[14] Attending is not simply a "yes/no" matter, not simply a butting up against each other of aliens, but a meaningful interaction, more like a dialogue between partners. My attending to the thing is a constructive interaction that involves decision and self-expression. Attention, then, is not like a detached, panoptic "searchlight" that indifferently surveys a set of fixed, determinate objects.[15] Rather, as Merleau-Ponty says, "attention, then, does not exist as a general and formal activity. There is in each case a particular freedom to gain, and a particular mental space to keep in order."[16] Attending to the thing is engaging with a meaningful field of possible developments in a dialogue in which one's own ability to attend to the thing is itself *contingent on the forms of engagement afforded by the thing*.[17]

(3) We said above that the "demands of the object" are themselves meaningful. This is because the objects of my world are already mediated by the parameters of my projects (vital, emotional, personal, etc.).[18]

Things can be meaningful calls to be heeded only if they are integrated within the fabric of one's world. The thing and I must first belong together if there is to be between us any issue of interaction, any issue of responsiveness. The thing can thus stand out as calling for my attention only if that call itself rests on a shared basic fabric, a shared participation in the real.[19] To experience the thing as a meaningful call, I must first be at home with it.

Being at home in the world is, most basically, being with things in such a way that they "make room" for one – one has a place in them. Indeed, whatever we might do to develop this, any such development can itself happen only because the things of our world are already in principle open to us. There must, first, be for us a world, be a world for us. Our very nature, in other words, must be being-in-the-world, an already-co-definedness of self and world. We do not accomplish our original relation to the world, but find ourselves already engaged, already stretched outside of ourselves "there." Our being is a being-there and hence determinate – already shaped by space, mood and others, by determinateness, our attitude towards it, and a perspective of others upon us.[20] In this way, our nature is by necessity passive at its root – it is only on the basis of this already givenness, this already determinate-ness, that there can be for us any possibility: our "I can" rests essentially on this givenness.

Beyond this original, *given* being-at-home, we also *accomplish* a more developed being-at-home through habituation.[21] We saw above that our acts of paying attention are always contextualized, and it is the hominess of our habituated being-in-the-world that provides this context. The processes of habituation through which we establish this developed hominess are primarily processes of establishing highly developed relationships of comfortable engagement with things, precisely such that we do not have to "pay attention" to them. Through practice, I develop a new power to act in the world. This new power is itself a "becoming at home" in things that were formerly alien to me. By developing this habit, I move from a situation of self-conscious alienated engagement, in which I must pay explicit heed to the thing, to a stance of absorption, in which I need not attend to the alienation of that thing, for it is now accommodated to me. But in thus allowing me to be at home in it, the thing has also taken power over me. I give over my agency to it and can no longer control it: I now rely upon the automatic agency of my habits to do the work for me of establishing my comfortable relationship with the world, and by establishing this situation by which I do not need to take explicit responsibility for carrying out my actions, I equally give away this power. My power is now the power *of* that definite habit, which gives itself to me and can be withdrawn. Just as our organic embodiment has a determinateness that empowers us precisely by binding us to it as a necessity outside our control, so do our processes of habituation establish for us determinate modes of relating to the world that empower us precisely by falling out of our reach and becoming, for us, necessities. Our acts of paying attention rest on such habituations.

These habitualities that come to provide a passive dimension to attention reveal the developed character of our perception. There has already been an investment of freedom – agency and work – involved in establishing this perceptual passivity. Habit – the fundamental "material" of our being at home in the world – ambiguously functions as both sides of the agency–passivity pair: it is itself an enactment of agency, but it plays the role of passivity to further agency. On the one hand, habits, like all the other conditions of perception, reveal that freedom is always an enactment of the freedom of movement afforded by the determinacies of a situation; on the other hand, habits, in their developed character, reveal that freedom is a *transformative* power that is capable of redefining the significance of those very determinacies. While freedom is emergent from the determinacies of our situation, it is not defined by those determinacies. What I want to consider now is the way in which our free activity reveals that what we might call the "worldly" dimensions of our passivity are not sufficient on their own to set a norm for our freedom, and that it is distinctly the intersubjective dimension of our freedom that offers the possibility of norms.

III. Freedom as Such: Work and Communication

The first thing for us to notice overall in these discussions is that the free and the determined are not opposed. Indeed, freedom just is determinacy. Freedom is the power to act, the "I can," and that is always the power *of* a given determinacy, and therefore a passivity. The very freedom that characterizes anything is also the givenness by which it is constrained. Let us consider this issue now in relation to the distinctive sense of freedom that is freedom as such, as opposed to any specific power: the freedom to dwell in the possible, to live a determinacy beyond its determinacy, to come at the present from the future. It is this freedom that, as we saw above, allows us to alter creatively the figure/

ground structure of experience through the act of "paying attention." I want now to consider this "living beyond" as such, or for itself. We saw above that the freedom of attention is embedded in the world: it is the freedom "of" determinateness, and it grows through a deepening of its *engagement* with things that is simultaneously a growth and a loss of itself. We will now consider further this theme of *engagement* as such, by considering the engagement with things that is the freedom of work and the engagement with persons that is the freedom of communication.

(1) In work, I engage with my object in order to bring forth from it something it makes possible. Work can never *simply* be an imposition of a pre-established reality upon a thing, for the condition of the imposition is that the thing itself make room for that imposition within its own nature. A child in frustration can wail at the world because its desires are not being fulfilled. The simple fact of its desire, however, is insufficient to transform the world. Work is committing oneself to operate within the terms the object makes available to bring about a fulfilment of one's desire. Work is therefore a coordinated engagement: to work is to learn how to have the world fulfil one's desires.

Because the product of work takes its definition from my desire, the object upon which I work is insufficient on its own to account for the product. The work operates within the terms the thing makes available, but it also exceeds those terms. The work brings into being a possibility *for the thing* that the thing alone was insufficient to accomplish. Work shows that things are not fully determinate in themselves, but are inherently open, that is, the "what" of a thing is always rooted in a domain of possibility: the thing itself opens itself up to possibilities of redefinition that are only possible through the freedom we bring to bear upon those things.[22] In principle, the things of our world are open to our definitive freedom – if they were not so in principle, our freedom could never affect them and there would be no such thing as work, as artifice. *This horizon of redefinition that is the possibility hovering above the determinacy of each thing is the same openness that characterized the object-as-motive that the act of attention transformed into a perceptual figure.* Attention is thus a form of work, and work a developed form of attention.

As I work upon the world, I am changed as much as the world is changed. The desire that refuses to learn the terms of possibility afforded by things is impotent, and is forced by its stubbornness into an isolated alienation from the world. This impotent subject will not learn the terms of the world and hence is ineffective; equally, it faces a world that is a hard, sealed surface, an impenetrable realm of fixity. This is the world of things that are wholly self-defined and determinate in themselves. The subject becomes potent in the same move by which the thing is removed from the presumption of essentialism. In working, I establish my own potency in the same move by which I realize the potentiality within the thing.[23] Approaching the thing so as to bring out of it what it cannot bring out of itself is also the move in which I become a being capable of participating, a being capable of making a difference within the domain opened up by the things of the world.

Inasmuch as it is through engagement that I move from impotence to a determinate "I can," it is through thus working *with* the world that I become meaningfully free. I am free in principle inasmuch as I inhabit the domain of possibility, the domain essentially defined by the primacy of the future (which rejects the authority of the "presentness" of the actuality of the thing). I am actually free to the extent that I inhabit this futurity by realizing possibilities in the world, to the extent that I *realize* this freedom, embody it in the world. What this means is that my freedom is realized as the world allowing me to act. I am free to the extent that the determinateness of my world admits of my power to realize the possible within it. Like the act of attention, the activity of working is a reality accomplished as a kind of dialogue in which I enact the possibilities *of* this thing: *my* freedom is *its* freedom to be otherwise. Work and attention are not impositions of one reality upon another, but the enactment of a co-reality. Let us take this up from the side of the "I."

In this work through which my freedom is accomplished, my engagement with reality is a kind of identification: what I am cannot be separated from the things through which I embodied this potency. In working I thus make myself determinate – I give my developed, free identity an embodiment in my things comparable to the embodiment of natural capacity that is my organic body. It is by committing myself (rather than holding back in withdrawn impotence) that I establish myself as a power, as a reality, and the more definite I am, the more powerful I am. At the same time, precisely by embedding my power and identity in these things, I am giving myself away, giving myself over to the supportive power of those things. I gain power to act in the world precisely by losing the power to control those powers – I commit myself to them and thus become dependent upon them, answerable to them. To be free *through* them requires that they be *necessary* for me. I become "me" through them precisely by having them become other to me – they embody my "I can" only by themselves being a zone of "I cannot."

But now notice also what this means from the side of the world. Merleau-Ponty criticizes both empiricism and rationalism for operating with the prejudice that the world is determinate in itself.[24] In the domain of attention, this means that the "what" of our perceptual object cannot be defined separately from the significance it acquires through our way of taking it up. Analogously, if things are open in principle to freedom – as they demonstrate themselves to be through our successfully working with them – then we cannot appeal to essentialism to call our acts "impositions" or to argue that we are mishandling them. If things by nature make room for our freedom, then they, on their own, are metaphysically insufficient to provide a norm for judging the legitimacy of our free transformations of their reality. How, then, might norms emerge within this domain of determinate freedom?

Here I think the crucial point is one we saw above, namely, that it is given that our world is a world with others. My involvement with other persons – other beings of possibility – is not something optional; rather, it is an ever-present dimension of significance within my experience. What this means experientially is that the very way in which the things of my world are given to me is *as* open to the freedom of others, just as they are open to my freedom. Thus, while the determinacy of the thing is insufficient by itself to establish its nature, it is also not the case that my say-so is automatically decisive, for the domain in which I realize the possible within the thing is a zone of contestation, a zone of engagement with the equally compelling engagements of others with that thing.[25] Inhabiting the world of freedom is thus necessarily inhabiting a world defined by the demand for communication. Let us now turn to this last domain, to complete our story of freedom.

(2) To engage with a thing is to participate in the world, to reject the zone of impotent alienation and commit oneself to determinacy. But participating in the world is making oneself answerable to the perspectives of others. This means that at root, *the meaning of "things" in our world is always a call to communication,* a call to community. And this coordination of our freedom with that of others is not some second action that follows on a basic involvement; it is, rather, what we must always be accomplishing in any engagement with things. We saw above that our developed identities are co-identities, that is, they are identifications with the world such that we exist as the freedom *of* a situation. This discussion of our inherent "being-with" entails that the very fabric of this developed co-reality is itself communication: we are "made out of" a successfully accomplished communication with others that is realized

as the meaningful things of our (shared) world. We are thus "made out of" language, so to speak, and the imperative inherent in our free realization of the possibilities in things is the imperative to communicate: my action is true, what I accomplish is real, when it is afforded room by the freedom of others that is implicit in the determinacy of things.

So freedom is ultimately enacted in transformative gestures that realize themselves in the accomplishment of a new, shared perception. When such gestures follow along familiar paths, this is the second-order expression of which Merleau-Ponty speaks.[26] But inasmuch as we experience our freedom as such, we experience in the situation the call of the future, and answering to this call is a special sort of gesture. The future is not prescribed, that is, the possibility of the situation is not reducible to its given determinacy. What this situation is to be – the very norm by which its present will be defined – is undecidable in that present.[27] *Living* freedom as freedom, *the experience of* freedom as such, is the experience of inhabiting this undecidable urgency. To be free is fully realized on its own terms in inhabiting the demand emergent from one's situation that one be that situation's deliverance, that one accomplish its future. The actions that enact such freedom are a distinct sort of gesture, unlike the familiar gestures of an already accomplished communication through the world. When gestures carry the weight of breaking new ground for our own freedom, that is, for realizing as such our identity as beings of possibility, this is art – first-order expression – in the broad sense.[28] It is in these gestures that we express our freedom as such, and they are thus gestures the explicit nature of which is to appeal to the freedom of others for their own realization and definition.

These originary gestures that ultimately and most fully enact our freedom are thus by their nature questions, that is, they call upon others to establish their meaning and, indeed, their very legitimacy.[29] Such gestures express our intention to deliver the situation of the identity it cannot accomplish on its own: the goal is not to impose but to deliver, to accomplish what it needs. But inasmuch as our actions are always single in a context that is inherently shared, we necessarily always act in such a way as to risk this imposition, and it is only after the fact that we will find whether the future we realized in the thing is accepted by reality. Said otherwise, we must wait upon the confirmation of the world to find out if we were acting idiosyncratically or truthfully, that is, on behalf of our shared world. Freedom is this experience of the world as the urgent demand to identify with it, and to identify with it as a shared inter-human world, but this urgent demand is constitutive of the very nature of the real and for that reason is not a demand that can ever be fulfilled in the sense of "disposed of." It is the permanent core of meaning in our lives that we struggle with this issue.

Conclusion: Freedom, Passivity, and Normativity

Taking attention as an exemplary phenomenon of freedom, I have argued that our active nature is inseparable from constitutive dimensions of passivity. The "freedom of movement," so to speak, that we experience in our ability to pay heed is rooted in the giving powers of the body, of our objects, of others, of the world, and of the history of our habituation: our power is the power *of* these determinacies, and *whatever we can describe as our own ability can equally be described as their affordance*. But the very fact that these things give themselves to the realization of freedom means they are vulnerable to that freedom and cannot by themselves define it. It is our answerability to others that is the dimension of passivity that is the reason we find ourselves answerable to an unfulfillable demand to make our freedom the deliverance of the true significance of the world rather than just an exploitation of its availability.[30]

NOTES

1 Introduction, chapter 3, "Attention and Judgment," *PP* 50–6[28–34].

2 For a nuanced discussion of the rich complexity of the phenomenon of attention, see Casey, "Attending and Glancing," esp. 311–35. See also Vermersch, "Attention," 52–4; and Bredlau, "Learning to See."

3 On the idea that the experience of self-possession must be accomplished through learning, compare Dewey, *Experience and Education*, 64: "The ideal aim of education is creation of power of self-control"; see also his *Human Nature and Conduct*, pt I, s. II, "Habit and Will," 24–42; and his *Democracy and Education*, ch. 6, "Education as Conservative and Progressive," 69–80.

4 Sartre, *Being and Nothingness*, 41. Cf. *PP* 53[32].

5 Ibid., 59, 58.

6 Cf. *PP* 74–5[48–9].

7 Cf. Depraz, "Where Is the Phenomenology of Attention?," 14–15.

8 Jonas, *The Phenomenon of Life*, 83.

9 See *VI* 274–5[221], working note from November 1959: "The soul always thinks: this is in it a property of its state, it cannot not think because a

field has been opened into which *something* or the *absence* of something is always inscribed. This is not an *activity* of the soul, nor a production of thoughts in the plural, and I am not even the author of the hollow that forms within me by the passage from the present to the retention, it is not I who makes myself think any more than it is I who makes my heart beat."

10 See *VI* 247194], working note from 20 May 1959: "The things have us, and ... not we who have the things."

11 The theme of the alluring, affective attraction of would-be objects of attention is richly explored in Steinbock, "Affection and Attraction."

12 Cf. ibid., 31.

13 See ibid., 32.

14 "Affordance" is the language of James J. Gibson. See, for example, his *Ecological Approach to Visual Perception*, 36 and *passim*, and the discussion in Greeno, "Gibson's Affordances." For Merleau-Ponty's discussion of "motivation, see *PP* 75–7[49–51].

15 For a critique of the "searchlight" model of attention, see Arvidson, "Toward a Phenomenology of Attention."

16 *PP* 53[32]. See also the references to the "field" (*champs*) of freedom in *PP* 501[462], and in *VI* 150[112], 274–5[221].

17 Cf. Noah Moss Brender's discussion of the confusion of "mobility of perspective" with "freedom from perspective" in ch. 7 of this volume.

18 Cf. *PP* 32–3[9–10].

19 This is a theme Merleau-Ponty discusses substantially under the heading "the flesh"; see esp. "The Intertwining – the Chiasm," ch. 4 of *VI* 181[137]: "If [the body] touches [things] and sees them, this is only because, being of their family, itself visible and tangible, it uses its own being as a means to participate in theirs, because each of the two beings is an archetype for the other, because the body belongs to the order of the things as the world is universal flesh."

20 On our being already defined by mood and intersubjectivity, see Maclaren, "Emotional Disorder," esp. 142–6.

21 On the theme of the habitually developed character of the experience of home, see Jacobson, "A Developed Nature."

22 See *PP* 28[6–7].

23 This is the essential point of Hegel's analysis of work in his discussion of the relationship of "master and slave" in *Phenomenology of Spirit*, paras. 194–6.

24 *PP* 50[28].

25 This is the core of Husserl's argument in the fifth of his *Cartesian Meditations* – that intersubjectivity is the condition for objectivity; see

89–108, esp. s. 49. This entails, as we shall see, that inasmuch as attention involves an appeal to objectivity, it is always implicitly joint attention and thus always implicitly presupposes communication.

26 See *PP* 217n2[530n6 (note to 183)].

27 Cf. *PP* 218[184]: "In understanding others, the problem is always indeterminate because only the solution to the problem will make the givens retrospectively appear as convergent."

28 See *PP* 216–19[182–5].

29 See *PP* 225[191]: "I confirm the other person, and the other person confirms me."

30 I am grateful to Len Lawlor for the invitation to deliver this paper as a keynote address to the 2007 meeting of the Merleau-Ponty Circle.

2 The Image and the Workspace: Merleau-Ponty and Levinas on Passivity and Rhythmic Subjectivity

MARIA TALERO

Although it is common for us to think of ourselves as agents, our experience is most basically a matter of passivity. This idea is central to the later philosophy of Merleau-Ponty (who lectured on the topic in 1954–55), and the theme of passivity has had substantial development in figures such as Levinas, Blanchot, Derrida, and Nancy.[1] It is sometimes thought, however, that Merleau-Ponty's philosophy of the body-subject in the *Phenomenology of Perception* is incompatible with these insights on the grounds that the notion of a body-subject harbours the idea of the body as an experiential "command centre" that exercises a kind of mastery over its experiences, "having" or "possessing" them rather than being possessed by them – in other words, a body-ego is still to some extent a subject in the traditional metaphysical sense. I will argue on the contrary that the notion of passivity is essential to the philosophy of Merleau-Ponty, not only in his later work but also in the very way he conceives of embodiment in the *Phenomenology of Perception*. My goal is not to prove that Merleau-Ponty's overall position in this work is identical to that of the other thinkers of passivity mentioned above; instead I am simply going to illuminate what I see as the deep and perhaps unexpected affinity between Merleau-Ponty's understanding of embodiment and Levinas's treatment of the image in "Reality and Its Shadow."[2] My strategy will be to open up some of the features of the Levinasian image and show how closely they resonate with Merleau-Ponty's view of embodied experience in the *Phenomenology of Perception* when we understand bodily experience as the *happening* or the *enactment* of what I will call an "experiential workspace." In addition to addressing peripherally the relationship between Merleau-Ponty and Levinas (an issue taken up more directly by Scott Marratto in chapter 11, below), this analysis will reveal the definitive passivity that characterizes the experience of perception.

I. Levinas and the Image

In his 1948 essay "Reality and Its Shadow," Levinas proposes to reinvigorate what he describes as the "somewhat worn-out notion of passivity" by examining the distinctive phenomenological and ontological status of the image.[3] By image he means "that which is engendered through the non-coincidence of being with itself" (135). In other words, despite our incurable temptation to regard images as passages towards the real, as if they were secondary or "derivative" windows helpfully framing "original" panoramas, Levinas wants to say that the image is the way that all substantial identities "leak" out of themselves, failing to live up to their own ontological claims of self-coincidence, sloughing off or "shedding" resemblances all around (135). To capture this movement of non-self-coincidence that engenders the image, he uses the example of a person (135).

A person confronts us as a being who, it would seem, "is what he is," as Levinas puts it: a substantial identity or a concentration of being, gathered and held within a single locus. My friend, a colleague, the mailman: these beings seem to possess their reality the way a glass of water bears its contents. Yet, Levinas says, the claim to self-coincidence that is made by the person "does not make us forget" – it cannot hide or dissemble – the movement of dispersal, of non-self-coincidence that is engendered at every moment in and through that very personhood, through "the objects he holds and the way he holds them, his gestures, limbs, gaze, thought, skin" (135). A person, in fact, is "like a torn sack," unable to contain its contents: that is, the very dimensions that constitute their personhood do so through a kind of ontological movement of dehiscence, of falling-away from substantial identity (135). The gestures my friend makes that are so typical of her, her distinctive mannerisms, are manifestations that refuse to be strictly identified with a primary locus. "Her gestures are so unique," we say; and it's true, those gestures *are her*, they superbly announce her identity, but in so doing, they are like torch-bearers for a unity that is nowhere given. As gestures, they point beyond themselves to an identity that is never consolidated on the other side of that pointing. This is true also of the whole repertoire of manifestations that make her *this person*, and *none other*: even her very body, her skin and her limbs, Levinas seems to be suggesting, partake in this movement of withdrawing, allowing the person to appear *in and through the radical insufficiency* they exhibit as harbingers of what she is: for *she is not this skin, these limbs*; that is to say, they do not contain or exhibit her identity like buckets of water drawn from a well: there is no well, no *source* that is her person, to which all of these manifestations of her owe their being: she is not given in any one of these things, but neither is she present when all of them are taken together. The person announced through the gestures is never given, yet each of them announces her identity precisely through its non-coincidence with that unconsolidated, never-to-be-encountered identity, in the absence of which it would not even stand out as one of her gestures.

It is in this sense then that we can say, with Levinas, that the person is a "dual being" (135), in that it manifests itself as a spreading-apart of two non-consolidated, non-existent terminus points, the person and the manifestations of personhood. This spreading, this unclosable spacing between two terms that are not themselves given as *relata*, is the relationship he calls *resemblance* (135–7). What is sloughed off from the density of substantial identity through the movement of resemblance is the *image*: images are the incapacity of being to contain itself "in one" (137), or to be identical with itself, fully consolidated. Being *resembles itself*, we can say, and thus proliferates images of itself everywhere, manifestations that point to a non-existent origin, just as the person resembles herself in her characteristic mannerisms, her distinctive way of walking, the way her face looks, all of which insistently point to or call for the disclosure of her identity in a way that can never be satisfied.

It is this dynamic of the image that I think is present also in Merleau-Ponty, but before showing how, I need to bring out something else in Levinas's account, namely, the inherent *musicality of the image*. Levinas links the operation of images with the phenomenon of musical rhythm – in particular, with the way that that musical rhythm takes up or inscribes the listener within itself as a setting in which her agency as a subject is put out of play, rendered fundamentally *passive* and vulnerable.[4] As he puts it: "Rhythm represents a unique situation where we cannot speak of consent, assumption, initiative or freedom, because the subject is caught and carried away by it" (132). The experience of rhythm *happens*: according to Levinas, it would be a mistake to say that I consent to it, for in the experience itself *I no longer remain*: "in rhythm there is no longer a oneself, but rather a sort of passage from oneself to anonymity" (133). This dissolution of subjective agency that takes place within rhythm is the fundamental *modality* of the image, according to

Levinas. "An image is musical," he insists, and by this he seems to mean that in our encounters with images we are taken up into a mode of passive, pre-subjective, pre-agential participation (132). He describes this transport as follows: "The particular automatic character of a walk or a dance to music is a mode of being where nothing is unconscious, but where consciousness, paralyzed in its freedom, *plays*, totally absorbed in this *playing* [emphasis mine]" (133). Thus we can add that images are not only musical but also lived by us as a kind of *absorbing play* – that in their grip, as in the grip of a musical rhythm, we are cast out of the world of objects which we grasp and cognize as agents, and into a realm of spectacle, of dream-things, into which we are absorbed through a kind of dreaming passivity that is like the absorption we undergo in play (133).

The two hallmarks of Levinas's treatment of the image in "Reality and Its Shadow," then, are these: (1) images are engendered by resemblance, or the self-fissuring movement of being by which being generates emblems of itself that have no originals, or in other words, that cannot be traced back to a source, and (2) the image operates on us in the mode of passivity, in the musical sense that Levinas has developed, where participation *happens* to the participant instead of being something *done* by her and where this happening can be described as a kind of absorbing play. We now turn to Merleau-Ponty's philosophy of embodiment, where we will find these very same marks of passivity in his account of embodied experience.

II. Merleau-Ponty and the Experiential Workspace

Although Levinas wants to distance his own account in "Reality and Its Shadow" from phenomenology – primarily Sartre's work on imagination – his account of the image as inducting the viewer into the passivity of an absorbing play seems to me to be very close to one of most important themes in Merleau-Ponty's *Phenomenology of Perception* – that is, Merleau-Ponty's view of experience as an enactive, bodily engagement with the lived environment.[5] What this means can be summarized as follows: On Merleau-Ponty's account, the embodied experiencer is behaviourally "coupled" with the affordances of the environment such that the phenomenal "look" of things and one's bodily behaviour mutually condition and constrain each other.[6] Thus, I experience my environment as harbouring behavioural possibilities for action – for example, the way that stairs appear "climbable" and cultural objects familiar and usable – and conversely, the bodily activities in which I engage at a practical, pre-reflective level constrain the terms in which things can appear to me (*PP* 164[133], 407[366]). Body and world are thus hermeneutically wedded to each other: the very phenomenal appearance of things for me harbours experiential cues to become absorbed in familiar behavioural repertoires, and conversely, my behavioural repertoires selectively allow certain phenomena to appear as salient, leaving others in the background (*PP* 111[84], 135–6[108]). My goal in the remainder of this chapter will be to bring to the fore the closeness – which at first may not be apparent – between Merleau-Ponty's theory of embodied experience as behavioural coupling and Levinas's theory of the passivity engendered by the image.

As a first step, I want to point out a basic hermeneutic principle operative in Merleau-Ponty's account of embodied experience: that *any singular identity, element, or dimension of experience is always embedded in an overarching modality of bodily comportment* (*PP* 128–9[101–2]). In other words, every "what" of experience is always embedded in a "how," or a mode of bodily comportment. In other words, there are no comportment-independent experiential givens. But we need to think carefully about the true nature of this bodily comportment. For we misunderstand it if we treat it as the product of a subjective agency that has simply been transposed from a transcendental ego onto a body-ego. Although Merleau-Ponty invokes Husserl's notion of the "I can" to designate the capacity for interaction that is definitive of our bodily comportment, there is nonetheless something misleading about using this expression as a way of designating it. In fact, on Merleau-Ponty's understanding, bodily experience is fundamentally *enactive* rather than *active* in nature.[7] This means, first of all, that there is no self-identical state of affairs that "constitutes" it – in other words, there "is" no such "thing" as an experience per se. Instead, experience is continually and dynamically enacted: it *happens* or *comes about* through a kind of mutual gearing-in to each other of body and world, in other words, of *bodily potentialities-for-action* and *potentialities-for-being-taken-up-by action* of the things in the world (*PP* 129[102], 297[291]). Thus, neither the bodily experiencer nor the things experienced are actual, self-subsistent things: experience is the *coupling* of two incomplete terms, "lived body" and "world," neither of which is a complete identity in its own right and each of which only exists as the potentiality of the other (*PP* pt I, ch. 1).

To capture the affinity between the passivity of the Levinasian image and the passivity of Merleau-Ponty's notion of embodied experience, I want to introduce the notion of the *experiential workspace*, which is my term for this enactive coupling of bodily and environmental potentialities, neither of which exists as an actuality. This concept will allow us to re-enter Merleau-Ponty's account of bodily experience through a less potentially misleading route than the idea that bodily experience consists of a tacit "I can" or an implicitly lived sense of bodily capacity – for, although I do not think the basic idea behind the "I can" is mistaken, I think that a different vocabulary may help better capture what is really at stake.[8] I will flesh out this notion of what I am calling "the experiential workspace" with two examples: working, and playing basketball.

First of all, think of what it is like to be at work. To be absorbed in one's work is to have certain matters become salient, issues that need to be painstakingly explained to someone else if that person is going to take over my work for me. In Merleau-Ponty's terms, when one settles down to work, one "gears in" to the task at hand – for example, when I relocate myself at my desk in order to get back to my work of the day before (*PP* 180–3[146–8], 297–8[260–1]).[9] On my desk, the usual props are arrayed before me: computer, books, papers arranged in piles. As I gaze, these props begin to shift their roles. Like the members of an improvisational troupe who have just received fresh parameters for a new improvised sketch, these individual things on the surface of my desk now seem to break with a previous ordering that has up to this moment defined them and that my gearing-in is just beginning to disrupt. It is as if they are rejoining a second ordering that is emerging even as the other dissolves: the "cast" or "look" of the situation starts to change, losing that distinctive, mildly unsettling appearance of a workspace in which one's tasks remain untouched and giving way to a new "look": it is as if my workspace is "warming" or "opening" up to me as one by one the specific parameters of the unfinished work start to reappear. A paragraph, a heading, a diagram remind me of what the issues were, and instantly, along with those issues, the *experiential contours* of the work have begun to once again become visible – those phenomenal "handholds" by which one is able to renew one's grip on it, dimensions through which it presents itself as able to be taken up, modified, improved; or conversely, which now, once again, thanks to my gearing-in, appear as impasses or fruitless dead ends that should be abandoned.

Through this phenomenological description of gearing-in to one's work, we can start to more precisely identify the enactive (as opposed to "active") aspects of Merleau-Ponty's account of experience and to show how this enactive approach to experience harbours an implicit understanding of passivity within it, even if sometimes Merleau-Ponty's own vocabulary in the *Phenomenology of Perception* might disguise this. More specifically, my goal now is to pinpoint how it is that his account is compatible with Levinas's view of the transport-like passivity into which we are absorbed through the encounter with images. Basically it is because on Merleau-Ponty's account, *experience unfolds in a workspace*, which is not an object-laden setting utilized by an agential body-subject but rather an enacted arena, one that is opened up *for* the experiencer rather than *by* her, one into which she must enter in a way exactly analogous to the way that someone gives themselves over to a musical rhythm. The experiential workspace is something that happens *to* us rather than something deployed *by* us. It is an arena that, in Levinas's language, "impose(s) itself on us without our assuming [it]" (132), and it does so through the operation of a dynamic, quasi-musical passivity.

This can be readily recognized by anyone who works on something. Work is not to be confused with any set of physical activities to which we might carelessly apply this label. True work is precisely that arena which we must enter, as Merleau-Ponty puts it, "as the faithful in Dionysian mysteries invoke the god by imitating the scenes of his life" (*PP* 201[166]) – in other words, through a mode of engagement that is inherently a dissolution of agency or an experiential transport. This is precisely why we frequently experience our work as frustrating or uninviting: it is precisely because the experiential workspace is not something deployed through our own agency. Rather, we are limited to guiding ourselves to its edge and allowing ourselves to be taken up within it, like a person trying to fall asleep by imitating its basic rhythms (*PP* 201–2[166–7]).

Now think of a game of basketball. Think of the way a basketball court appears to a person who is playing. When I am engaged in the game, the court appears to me as filled with navigational pathways that motivate and guide my action. The movements of other players open up pathways of possibility or block them off: I navigate these pathways of potential action precisely by being engaged in the flow of play. It is not as a volitional subject, or even as a sublimated yet still-volitional "body-subject," that I play basketball. Rather, it is more accurate to say that playing *happens to me*, in and through my embeddedness in the experiential workspace of the game. Like the person who has sat down at her desk and reconnected with her writing projects, administrative tasks, and e-mail responsibilities once more, the players absorbed in a game of basketball are engaged within an arena that releases its own parameters – its own unfolding norms – which are lived by the players as the *experiential contours* of play. The true elements of play, then, are the experiential contours of the workspace – the dynamically enacted navigational pathways that open and close as the play unfolds or, in our earlier example of getting back to work, the phenomenal handholds that allow me to get a grip on the demands of my task once more (or conversely, appear as navigational impasses that make the terrain of my task seem problematic, boring, or frustrating).[10]

And, most importantly of all, these experiential contours are not open to my action upon them as a volitional subject engaging with objects. The often-attested experience, among both athletes and amateurs, of being absorbed in a game to the point that it is as if "the game plays me" rather than the other way around, is, we should recognize, analogous to the way that musical rhythms absorb our agency and submerge us in a kind of experiential anonymity, a musical transport where it could be said that the rhythm *plays us*.

Thus the navigational pathways or "contours" of the experiential workspace take us up into a mode that should not be regarded as the agential action of a body-subject within her world, any more than the experience of being taken up into a musical rhythm should be. These pathways draw us out of ourselves and insert us into an essentially dream-like arena where our volitional activity is blunted, where it can get no purchase, and where we enter into participation by letting ourselves be "played" by *its* parameters (*PP* 201–2[166–7], 207[172]). When we work, or when we play, we are much more like dreamers than we are anything like the volitional subjects of traditional metaphysics. When we work or when we play, we are in close contact with the fundamental passivity of all embodied experience.

In the *Phenomenology of Perception*, then, Merleau-Ponty has, like Levinas, given us the coordinates for a dimension of being that is inherently characterized by passivity. Embodied experience, understood as unfolding within an experiential workspace, exhibits the very same fissured character, that fundamental duality or self-distancing that Levinas says is inherent in being itself, and that is revealed by *manifestations that point backwards to identities that are never given*. The experiential workspace is precisely such an unlocatable identity, discernible only through its traces, which are the experiential contours we have been discussing. In other words, these dynamic, enactive features of the experiential workspace are in fact *images* in Levinas's sense.

For the dynamism of the *contours* of the workspace announce the unclosable spread between lived body and world, just as through the operation of the image the fissured character of Being announces itself. In the same way that the gestures of the person point beyond themselves to an unconsolidated personhood that can never be directly encountered, the navigational pathways that draw us along within the workspace point beyond themselves to an unlivable and ungraspable non-origin: there is no point at which we directly encounter the play itself, or the work itself, no point at which these things are given to us as the sources to which the contours or pathways correspond. In other words, the experiential workspace is only given as non-coincidence with its traces, just as the personhood of the person is only given as non-coincidence with her gestures.

But what this also means is that workspaces are *labile, irreducibly "iterable" or open phenomena*; that is, they are inherently vulnerable to being taken over by new orderings that recontextualize and usurp their elements. Because workspaces are enacted only in and through the activity by which we engage in them, when we "gear in" to an experiential workspace, we do so precisely by transgressing on its open, labile edge, an edge that is permanently vulnerable to reinscription into a new ordering.

This intrinsic vulnerability to recontextualization means that workspaces are inherently defined by the possibility of their own non-being, their own phenomenal collapse as discernible identities. The labile, hidden surface of the experiential workspace, the very threshold by which we are able to enter into it and be taken up into its absorbing mode of passivity, is ultimately the feature of Merleau-Ponty's understanding of embodied experience that distinguishes it the most from the notion of an agential subject as the locus of experience. For what it shows is that the possibility of *workspace collapse*, or the dissolution of a given workspace as it gives way to another one ushered in by a different mode of activity, is embedded in the heart of every workspace-in-progress as the very ground of its being. *The very flow of experience can be viewed as a movement through one workspace collapse after another*, which we are no more and no less in control of as volitional agents than the participant in a musical rhythm or the person inviting sleep to take her over. In other words and in conclusion, our path from Levinas's notion of the image to the core of Merleau-Ponty's account of embodiment as a bodily coupling to an experiential workspace is an invitation to recognize, at the very core of embodied experience, the ontological dynamism of passivity at work.

Conclusion: Rhythmic Subjectivity

We are accustomed to thinking of ourselves as self-possessed subjects: as agents who exist independently of the world and who freely deploy the power of an autonomously defined will upon that world.[11] When Merleau-Ponty defines our experience in terms of the "I can," however, it is not such an "active" subject he describes, but rather an "enactive" subject that comes into being only in and through its world-embedded practices. The freedom of this enactive self is not an independently defined power that is freely deployed, like a spotlight directed towards whatever alien object it seeks to illuminate; rather, it is the freedom of "catching" the rhythm of a situation and "dancing" along with it.[11] Our developed situations present us with so many motivated solicitations, and our freedom is the responsiveness in which we undergo their summoning and make ourselves the medium for their realization.

NOTES

1 Merleau-Ponty, *Institution and Passivity*.
2 For a focused comparative study of Levinas and Merleau-Ponty on the theme of passivity, see Bergo, "Radical Passivity."
3 Levinas, "Reality and Its Shadow," 132. Subsequent page references to this work will be included in the text.
4 This "musical" conception of subjectivity is richly explored in Russon, *Bearing Witness to Epiphany*, esp. 11–22, 113–20. The "rhythmic" dimension of subjectivity is also extensively analysed in Lampert, *Simultaneity and Delay*; see esp. 22–3, 26–9. Some related themes are raised in Wiskus, *The Rhythm of Thought*, especially in relation to the interpretation of Cézanne, Proust, and Debussy.
5 Maurice Merleau-Ponty, *PP* pt 1, chs. 1 and 3.
6 On the theme of coupling, see Morris, "Touching Intelligence" and "Ecstatic Body, Ecstatic Nature." Cf. Kirsten Jacobson: "While it is often acknowledged in phenomenology that it is the gaze of a subject that makes possible the coherence and meaningfulness of a thing … this recognition does not give a special privilege to the subject; the subject is herself articulated through her having of those things … She is a walking being by means of the ground; has hands that grasp insofar as there are cups and tools and movable items to exercise that power"; "The Gift of Memory," 30.

7 For what is involved in the "enactive" model of perception, see Thompson, *Mind in Life*; and Noë, *Action in Perception*.
8 For the "I can" as the core sense of what it is to be a "self," see *PP* 171[139], 111[84].
9 On the theme of the spatial "level," see Bredlau, "Monstrous Faces"; and Talero, "Perception, Normativity, and Selfhood."
10 On perceptual terrains, see Bredlau, "Learning to See."
11 See Russon, *Bearing Witness to Epiphany*, 14–16.

3 The "Entre-Deux" of Emotions: Emotions as Institutions

KYM MACLAREN

Introduction

In the *Phenomenology of Perception,* Merleau-Ponty claims that "passionate feelings and behaviors are … in fact institutions" (*PP* 230[195]). What he means by this is not explicitly spelled out in the *Phenomenology;* indeed, it is not until nine years later, in his lecture course of 1954 on *institution,* that Merleau-Ponty returns to this idea and reflect on it thematically.[1] Yet if one reads the *Phenomenology* with the lectures on institution in mind, it is clear that the claim therein is not an off-hand remark – that already in this work "institution" is an important operative concept (although often referred to by different names or not named at all),[2] and that Merleau-Ponty has something sophisticated to say about emotion, although he does not have the opportunity to work it out in detail in that particular text.[3]

My aim in this chapter is, drawing upon Merleau-Ponty's mid-career writings, including the lectures on institution, to bring out the full force of the *Phenomenology*'s claim that passionate feelings and behaviours – what I will call emotions – are institutions. My interest is not so much in scholarly questions of how Merleau-Ponty's own thinking developed over time as it is in the (I hope more philosophical) question of how – given the new resources for understanding, the new organs of perception, that Merleau-Ponty develops in us through his writing – we are to understand institution, and emotion as institution. It is worth noting that Merleau-Ponty speaks provisionally of institution as occurring within both personal (or intersubjective) and public history – although ultimately he argues that these cannot be fully separated.[4] For the purposes of this chapter, I will focus on the more personal side of institutions – that is to say, on transformational moments within our personal and intersubjective lives where a new configuration of meaning and a new form of agency is inaugurated – and on what Merleau-Ponty calls the "subterranean logic" of this development. As we will see, the development involved is "subterranean" insofar as these transformational moments come in some sense from beyond the subject and are not simply the result of the subject's own constitutive powers. The notion of institution is thus yet another way in which Merleau-Ponty seeks to criticize and offer an alternative to intellectualism, with its idea of a constituting subject.

I begin by introducing the notion of institution in the first section. I then turn to two forms of personal institution other than emotion – artistic expression (in the second section) and perception (in the third section) – in order to show how the logic of institution is already at work in some of Merleau-Ponty's earliest central themes, and in order to build up our resources for thinking about emotion as institution. In these two sections, I argue that expression and perception involve not the *constitution* of a meaning by a subject, but rather the *institution* of a form in the "*entre-deux*" of embodied being and environment – the institution of a form that simultaneously *transforms* that embodied being rather than being simply constituted by it. The fourth section turns more explicitly to emotion and considers the commonly held idea that an emotional subject is always constituting others and its situation in terms of its emotion. Here, too, I argue that the emotional situation comes to be "*entre-deux*" and is not, as a philosophy of consciousness would suppose, simply the result of the subject's own projection. In other words, we come to see how, as Merleau-Ponty claimed, *emotion is an institution*. Since an inherent feature of institutions, according to Merleau-Ponty, is their tendency towards their own overcoming, the fifth and final section explores emotional transformation and the institution of new emotions. Here, again, my emphasis is on how the development of one's emotional life is not primarily the result of an autonomous subject's reflections and constitutions; rather, it emerges out of contingency and the "subterranean logic" (*IP* 124[77]) or "spontaneous method" (*PP* 160[129]) worked out in the repetition or reiteration of old institutions. Emotional transformation, on this account, needs to be understood as coming largely from beyond the subject and as allowing her to *become herself*, rather than being the result of her own autonomous powers.

1. Institution

Throughout his work, and thus in both the *Phenomenology of Perception* and the lectures on institution, a key project for Merleau-Ponty is a criticism of a "philosophy of consciousness" with its idea of a "constituting subject."[5] The constituting subject is conceived as absolute, as constituting the meaning of its object on the basis of its own powers, so that its object is only ever a reflection of the powers and acts of that consciousness. In the place of such a constituting subject, Merleau-Ponty argues in both the institution lectures and the *Phenomenology of Perception* (and arguably in all of his texts) for a conception of the subject as implicated in, and helping bring to determinate expression, a world of others and beings whose meaningful being exceeds that subject, and whose coming to expression equally transforms the subject itself. Thus Merleau-Ponty speaks in the institution lectures of a subject who "invests itself, i.e., animates itself with another meaning, transforms itself ... i.e., succeeds in making a meaning *which is transcendent to him* [my emphasis] dwell in his *I think* and in his body, as a meaning dwells in the book and the cultural object" (*IP* 40[10]); and in the *Phenomenology of Perception* he says that "it is the definition of the human body to appropriate, in an indefinite series of discontinuous acts, meaningful cores that transcend and transfigure its natural powers ... A system of definite powers suddenly decenters here and there, breaks apart, and is reorganized under a law that is unknown to the subject or to the external observer, and which is revealed to them in this very moment" (*PP* 235[199–200]). In both texts we find an argument for the relative *passivity* of the embodied subject, which, by virtue of being caught up in, *dispossessed* by, or *exposed* to meaningful vectors in being that outstrip it, while also taking up or resuming ("*reprendre*") those transcendent meanings, helps realize new ways of making sense of the world and of being itself.

It is, however, in the institution lectures that Merleau-Ponty develops a language that, arguably, better emphasizes and clarifies the passivity of the subject and the ways in which the meaning it realizes also always exceeds it. There, he speaks of an (inseparably) "instituted and instituting subject" (*IP* 35[6]) and contrasts this with the "constituting subject" to be criticized (*IP* 35[6]).

In the *Phenomenology of Perception*, by contrast, Merleau-Ponty has not yet developed a systematic vocabulary for distinguishing institution and constitution: there, he uses language of "constituting" to speak not only of the intellectualist notion of the subject which he is criticizing, but also of the coming to be of (the institution of) a new perceptual object which he wishes to bring to light. For example, he will criticize intellectualism for its conception of consciousness as a "constituting consciousness" (*PP* 65[42]) – whereby he means a consciousness that constitutes the object by virtue of "possess[ing] its law or secret" (*PP* 64[41]), a subject "who possesses, as fully realized, all of the knowledge of which our actual knowledge is merely the first approach" (*PP* 65[42]). Yet he will also say that intellectualism, with its emphasis on the conditions of possibility for perceptual objects, fails to account for the "constitutive dimension" of perception and knowledge – by which he points towards *not* a constituting subject but rather the "living cluster of perception ... the operation that makes it *actual*, or by which it is constituted" or "the 'hidden art' that causes a sense to spring up from the 'depths of nature'" (*PP* 64[40]). There is, therefore, a distinction in the *Phenomenology* between two ways of conceiving the emergence of meaningful being for consciousness – between what retrospectively we can call constitution and institution – although there Merleau-Ponty speaks of both sides of that distinction in terms of constitution. We might say, then, that even though (or perhaps because) institution is a central concept argued for within the *Phenomenology*, it remains more of an *operative concept* in that text insofar as it is not yet christened with a univocal name, not yet made to be a thematic concept in terms of which others are measured.

With the benefit of the lectures on institution, however, we can gain insight into the idea of institution that is at work even in the *Phenomenology*. We will see how artistic expression and perception – both of which are key topics in the *Phenomenology* – are characterized by a logic of institution, and this will equip us to see how, as the *Phenomenology* claims, emotions are institutions. First, though, allow me to complete the outline of the basic concept of institution so that we might recognize it in these other phenomena.

Once again, then, what Merleau-Ponty calls the "constituting subject" is the subject as it is conceived by intellectualism: intellectualism presents us with a conception of a "universal" (e.g., *PP* 82[56]) subject constituting objects that are only "the exact reflection of the acts and powers of consciousness" (*IP* 123[76]). Such a conception is problematic insofar as it allows the constituted objects "nothing ... that is able to launch consciousness anew into other perspectives ... no exchange, no movement [between consciousness and object]" (*IP* 123[76], translation modified); it thereby "strips the development of experience of its contingency and the object of its perceptual style" (*PP* 64[41]). Against this notion, Merleau-Ponty argues for a different kind of "constitution" of the object – a constitution that he later calls "institution" in part because the sense or meaning achieved is not *given by* consciousness – it is "not the act of a *Sinngebung*"(*IP* 38[8]), but rather comes to be in the embodied *exchange between* a self-in-the-making and an object-in-the-making. Here, "the perceived object is animated by a secret life" (*PP* 63[40]) that is never totally comprehended or made sense of by the subject. Furthermore, the realization of the perceptual object is as much a development and transformation of the subject as it is the realization of a new framework of sense-making and a (never-sufficient, never-finished) revelation of that perceptual object in its distinctive style.

Whether in the institution lectures or in the *Phenomenology*, then, what Merleau-Ponty requires of us is that we understand the coming to be of the subject as inseparable from the coming to be of the object, or that we move from a focus on either consciousness as primary (as in intellectualism) or the objective world as primary to a focus on the "in-between" or "*entre-deux*" (e.g., *IP* 66[30], 123[76]) – to the phenomenal field, where not a subject but *events* "endow the experience with durable dimensions, in relation to which a whole series of other experiences will make sense, will form a thinkable sequel or a history" (*IP* 124[77]). This endowment of a meaningful dimension or level that provides a framework for further sense-making, and thus allows new perceptual objects to emerge within experience, is what Merleau-Ponty comes to call "institution" (*IP* 124[77]).

How do "events" do this work of instituting? In the lectures on institution, Merleau-Ponty brings out explicitly the "subterranean logic" (*IP* 124[77]) that defines the development of institution. The logic of institution is "subterranean" because it is not a logic foreseen by the subject involved, because it operates outside the knowledge and intentions of that subject. When institution occurs, when a new dimension of meaning that sets the terms for future developments is inaugurated, we can retrospectively see how the past anticipated this development, how this development responded to the past and answered a question posed by it.[6] Yet this perspective is accessible only from the standpoint of the new institution, only *retrospectively*.[7] That past did not, in fact, fully contain its own answer; the answer exceeds it, transforms the very terms with which it functioned, and thus could never have been predicted or foreseen from that past, even though it answers to that past.[8] In other words, it is only retrospectively that it is even clear what we were asking, what question was being posed: "In exchange for what we had imagined, life gives us something else, and something else that was secretly wanted, not fortuitous. Realization is not what was foreseen, but all the same, what was wanted" (*IP* 75[38], translation modified).

Such a realization or epiphany comes about, Merleau-Ponty tells us, through errors, failures. By means of a kind of blind groping on the part of the living subject, that subject is diverted by various impasses to different investigations, and once again, it is only retrospectively that these investigations reveal their common theme. Somehow – and this is the marvel of institution – all of these errors open up a space for a new realization. To put it another way, caught up in our old institutions, we respond to the problems that present themselves by repeating in various ways these old ways of making sense. Since any institution is always finite, "particularizing" (e.g., *IP* 46[14]), since any institution reveals being only by foreclosing other possible articulations of being, these repetitions will always be inadequate for grasping the fullness of being. Yet their very inadequacy is what opens up a space where something else, something new, something unknowingly awaited, can announce itself. And the event is that moment in which, in the openness that constitutes seeking without even really knowing what the question is, some contingent occurrence in being ushers in a new way of seeing, a new configuration of meaning, a new institution. Thus, any particular institution tends – with the help of contingent happenings – towards its own overcoming. Although an expression of the past, institution is inherently futural, *à-venir*.[9]

Let us turn now to more concrete analyses of forms of human experience in order to further elucidate this notion of institution, and in order to prepare for an understanding of emotion as institution.

2. The Logic of Institution in Artistic Expression

Institution, as we have seen, is the "establishment in an experience … of dimensions … in relation to which a whole series of other experiences will make sense and will make a *sequel*, a history" (*IP* 38[8–9]). Such is the genius of an artist: through her particular mode of expression, she realizes for herself and for us a new way of experiencing the world. *Instituted* within her work is a new frame of reference by virtue of which new meanings, new perceptual objects, appear, and in response to which further expressions will now unfold. She institutes a new order that then becomes the *matrix* for future elaborations.[10]

The new order that is instituted or inaugurated is not, however, *simply new*; for it also seems to reveal a truth that was there all along, that had been prepared in the past and was simply waiting, latent, to be brought into the light. For instance, the institution of the Renaissance sense of perspective in art seems, once we have experienced it, to be the solution to a problem that had long been germinating and asking for resolution: it seems to be the *telos* towards which other art was heading. Yet this necessity and this *telos* appear only *retrospectively*: pre-Renaissance painters did not have clearly in mind the problem of how to represent three-dimensional space seen from one perspective; that is to say, they did not know the *telos* and simply lack the means. The problems they struggled with were articulated in different terms, and their continuity with the Renaissance problem of perspective is manifest only once this Renaissance perspective is instituted.

How, then, did this new institution come to be? Through a "blind logic" (*IP* 78[41]), says Merleau-Ponty, through a labour that is concerned with tensions internal to past institutions, which finds in those tensions vague, still ambiguous, suggestions of solutions, and which discovers that those solutions, once put to work, *mean more than we knew*. "Something more slips in," as Merleau-Ponty says (*IP* 76[39]). Writing is like this: one sets out to work on a problem that is still amorphous and slippery; in locating the precise words required to better formulate that problem, one discovers also that the richness of those words brings to light dimensions and tensions previously unsuspected, which reconfigure the problem at hand. We move forward gropingly, then, finding guidance and direction by looking backwards at what we have said, rather than forward at a predetermined end, until finally a last word choice or a final brushstroke establishes an equilibrium and crystallizes a meaning that settles everything into its place. In Merleau-Ponty's words: "Like the weaver, the writer works on the wrong side of his material. He has to do only with language, and it is thus that he suddenly finds himself surrounded by meaning" (*ILVS*, 45).

Here, then, we can see how institution is different from the work of a constituting subject. In artistic expression we do not have a subject who intends a determinate meaning and then finds the words, brushstrokes, or gestures to communicate it. Nor do we have a subject who communicates only the meanings in which she already lives. We rather have a landscape or experience that presents itself as a muddled problem, and words, brushstrokes or gestures that – through a meaningfulness that transcends the intentions of the author – work to clarify and articulate the problem, which is the same thing as disclosing its answer.

On the one hand, then, we have an emergence of meaning– or better, of a *matrix* of meaning – that transcends the intentions and even the current powers of the artist. The artistic object realized is something more than she intended and thus not her product so much as the product of her engagement with this situation and these words or brushstrokes – a product of the "*entre-deux.*" On the other hand, this also means that the artist herself is transformed, that she comes into possession, by virtue of this instituting act, of powers that were heretofore not yet hers. Thus Merleau-Ponty speaks of "the action of the work on the author" (*IP* 41[11]): "To have written or painted this or that changes him. To the point that he would not be able to make it again precisely because he has made it ... This is because what is written has realized certain instruments, operational concepts ... a new norm, in relation to which other divergences are possible." The thoroughgoing nature of this transformation of the subject by the meaning that is instituted is perhaps even more evident if we turn to consider institution in perception.

3. The Logic of Institution in Perception

Much work on the logic of expression and institution in Merleau-Ponty has focused on artistic expressions. But expression is endemic not only to art, and indeed, art is not the fundamental form of expression. Rather, as Merleau-Ponty says, artistic endeavours are merely the amplification and further articulation of a phenomenon of expression that resides already in action and perception, in our very bodies (*ILVS*, 54–5).[11] Moving and looking, says Merleau-Ponty, "already enclose the secret of expressive action ... All perception, all action which presupposes it, and in short every human use of the body is already *primordial expression* ... [They are] the primary operation which ... inaugurates an order and founds an institution" (*ILVS*, 66–7). Actions and perceptions, on Merleau-Ponty's account, take up, elaborate, and *realize* meaning and order in the world.

The very same retrospective logic that we noted in expression is to be found in this realization of a new perception. Over and over again in the *Phenomenology*, Merleau-Ponty argues against the view that perception is established through the association of pre-given determinate sensations or profiles; instead, he shows that it is only when a new perception is realized that we can identify, retrospectively, that which a perceptual object is "composed" of, or that which prepared its perception. For instance, in the case of an infant's development of colour perception, he says: "The first perception of colors, properly so called, is ... a change in the structure of consciousness, the institution of a new dimension of experience ... Once the quality 'color' is acquired, and only thanks to it, the previous givens appear as preparations for this quality" (*PP* 54[32]).

Similarly, in an earlier passage: "The unity of the thing in perception is not constructed through association, but rather, being the condition of association, this unity precedes the cross-checkings that verify and determine it, this unity precedes itself" (*PP* 40[17]). The idea that there are determinately given sense-data or components that a subject synthesizes or constitutes into a coherent perception is, Merleau-Ponty tells us, a *retrospective illusion.*

How, then, is the genesis of perception to be understood? One possibility is to suppose that the perceptual object is, rather than the result of a unilateral constitutive synthesis or sense-giving on the part of the subject, the result of an interaction between a subject with certain powers, capacities, or material resources, on the one hand, and an object with certain affordances for possible meanings, on the other.[12] But such a conception of perception still supposes, I contend, a subject that is more autonomous, more pre-established, more constituting than that for which Merleau-Ponty is arguing.

Certainly the perceptual meaning realized in the world is always conditioned by our material resources. How we take up and elaborate the world, the meaning that we realize in it, will depend upon our anatomy and motor capacities. When, for instance, we touch our foot to water, we realize a liquidity therein, a specific manner of giving way. But the water strider (*gerris remigis),* with its very different anatomy, realizes a different property in water: an elastic resistance, a surface of support. So it is tempting to suppose that the determinately perceived object is a product of what the subject and the object each contribute. But let me propose that, if we are to understand the true sense in which perception "inaugurates an order and founds an institution," we need to consider the possibility that the subject is itself determined, even *produced,* by the meaning realized.

Take for instance the case that Merleau-Ponty relates of vision in a person with hemianopsia.[13] Hemianopsia involves a loss of vision in half of the eye. People with hemianopsia do not, however, experience half of a healthy person's visual field, as one might expect. Rather, they experience an impoverished version of regular sight. This is because the eye becomes *reorganized* in such a way as best to realize perceptions: the eye rotates so as to put the most functional part of the eye in the centre, and at that central place the eye develops a new pseudo-fovea capable even of seeing colours to which, originally, that area of the eye was blind. The actual materiality of the eye is altered. The perception that forms is not, then, simply a matter of using what bodily resources we already have to articulate perceptually ambiguities and tensions in that which is to be perceived; it is not just within the perceptual field that reorganization takes place; the articulation of an equilibrium or form within the perceptual field is simultaneously the articulation of a new body, a new set of material resources. In other words, the production of the form of perception is equally the production of the form of the perceiver, as its material condition.

The same structure is evident even in healthy perception, where the movements that reveal and actualize aspects of things are also guided by those same aspects, yet to be fully realized. One cannot experience the texture of something if one merely pokes it; it is necessary to move one's hand back and forth over the surface of the thing. The speed and pressure of one's movements are, moreover, crucial: one cannot experience the texture of a certain kind of tree bark if one moves one's hand too slowly, and the soft fuzz of a baby's head is missed if one presses one's hand too firmly against it. Yet when we first encounter these surfaces, we do not need to experiment with infinite possible gestures in order to hit by chance upon the one that reveals the most. Instead, it seems that our movements are themselves guided by the thing to be perceived. What is to be perceived presents itself to our body as a problem to be solved, and like any real problem, it is initially muddled and ill-defined but it also offers us a general direction and inclines us to pursue a resolution in these ways rather than those. The particular movements that eventually resolve the problem and settle a perceptual meaning within experience are thus not chosen or willed by us; rather, they are propelled by the tensions and vectors internal to the perceptual situation itself. Far from being merely the playing out of previously possessed powers, our revelatory actions or gestures are learned, taught to us by the object whose meaning outstrips our current powers and that we seek to perceive.[14]

On the one hand, then, we can say that our bodily movements are the material conditions of the realization of a perception: they resolve the tensions within this sensible world and allow a particular texture to disclose itself for the first time. On the other hand, however, since the exact movements required are not clearly foreseen, since they are realized in their precise form only in the moment that a solution is found and a determinate perception crystallizes, we can also say that these movements are determined by the perception realized. There is, in other words, a retrospective logic to the subjective as well as the objective side of the institution of a perception: the perception achieved retrospectively sets out these particular movements as its necessary conditions.[15] Indeed, we could say that the productive experience produces its producer.

This is in good part what it means when we say that perceptions are institutions, and not phenomena constituted by a constituting subject. Perceptions have their source not in an already established, self-directing subject, but in a developing situation; and the meaning instituted determines the subject as much as the subject determines it.

A final example from the interpersonal sphere might help both to elucidate this logic of institution and to lead us towards a discussion of emotional life. Infants, we know, are first and foremost oriented towards other people. It is only around the age of sixteen weeks, when they develop material resources for reaching and haptically exploring inanimate things, that their dominant mode of attention seems to shift to those inanimate things. There is evidence that prior to developing these material resources, the infant is *dispossessed* by inanimate things to be perceived: confronted with an inanimate thing, the infant seems to become hooked by that thing; her behaviour becomes jerky and disorganized, and her heart rate and breathing are affected to such an extent that infants with congenital heart disease will turn blue in the face until they are able to break their gaze away from the thing.[16] Even in healthy babies this disorganization seems to build up to a point where the infant must violently break from looking at the thing in order to seek relief.[17] On the account of perception presented above, we can surmise that this is because the infant does not yet have the material resources required to respond to the solicitations of the thing, and thus a stable perceptual sense cannot realize itself. Because the material resources she has are insufficient to resolve the problem posed by the thing to be perceived, she is held captive of an impossible problem until its irresolvable tensions motivate breaking with that perceptual situation altogether.[18]

On the other hand, with other people who are appropriately responsive (and it is essential that they be *appropriately* responsive),[19] an *organized form of behaviour is instituted between infant and adult*. A proto-conversation emerges in the form of exchanged gazes, smiles, and vocalizations.[20] This institution of an organized form of interpersonal behaviour is, interestingly, accompanied by an institution of greater organization in the infant's body: her bodily gestures cease to be jerky and become smooth forms of behaviour like a pedalling of legs, or an easy turning away and towards the person perceived;[21] and better physiological regulation is associated with the mutually responsive exchange.[22] These phenomena suggest that the institution of a stable form within the situation, between adult and infant – *"entre-deux"* – is simultaneously the realization of an equilibrium or form *within the infant's body*. Again, we find that there is not a fully integrated body-subject that then proceeds to make sense of the situation; rather, the institution of sense in the situation is simultaneously the institution of a new order, a new organization within the body-subject. The infant's successful, harmonious perception of, and interaction with, the other is equally a harmonious organizing of her own bodily responses.

In this last example of an equilibrium established *entre-deux*, there is reason to think that the institution of a perception, or way of making sense of the world, has an affective side to it: what presents itself as a problem for perception brings with it affective tension and bodily disorganization; when, on the other hand, sense is able to be made of what is encountered in the world, and a settled perception and correlative way of being institutes itself, that tension is overcome and a harmonious, affectively positive orientation is established. Let us then turn, in the next two sections, to a consideration of the affective dimension of experience, and of emotion as institution. In the first place, this will require us to understand emotion as realized in the *"entre-deux"* and not simply as a constituting projection of a self-sufficient subject. Beyond that, we will see how emotional institutions tend to repeat themselves or to give way to new institutions, and also how those repetitions are the very "subterranean" working out of the logic of institution. In these ways, I hope to draw out the full meaning of the *Phenomenology*'s claim that emotion is an institution.

4. Constitution and Institution in Emotional Relations

In the lectures on institution, Merleau-Ponty considers love in Proust's *Remembrance of Things Past*. Merleau-Ponty traces the narrator's struggles with failed love in relation to Albertine, showing how these failures ultimately result in a crystallization or *institution* of love – in a realization (by which is intended both "acknowledgment" and "making real") of a very real love between himself and Albertine.

Initially, the struggles undergone by the narrator seem to reveal love as impossible. He has fallen in love with Albertine only by taking her to be someone who stands in for something he lacks, and thus who is other to him, who eludes him. He seeks, then, to possess her. Yet as soon as he seems to have overcome her alterity, to know her as she really is (in her banality, he feels), and to feel that she is wholly within his realm, he feels bored with her, uninterested, no longer desirous of love. Thus ensues an alternation, a "binary rhythm" (*IP* 68[32], 75[38]), of pursuit and boredom.

In this context, love appears as simply subjective – as an egocentric seeking to answer to one's own needs, and as an imaginary projection upon the desired person of the image of the person sought. One loves merely one's own interior image of the other, rather than the other herself; indeed, it seems that one is moved to do so by one's own contingent circumstances and not by anything essential about that other in her singularity. Love, in other words, is not in this situation really love *of the other*. When, from within this way of being, two people take themselves to be in love, in fact they are each only in love with their own image of the other, and they go along with the other's false image of themselves in order to feel themselves confirmed by the other – because, put simply, they want to be loved. Thus love seems to be the "mirage of a common life, which is sewn together by this double illusion" (*IP* 63[28]). This is essentially the story of (the impossibility of) love as felt by a *constituting subject* – that is, a subject who projects his own image upon the other, who finds only what he has put there, and who thus never succeeds in getting beyond himself: "the other is empty negation ... making sense only for me, through closed signification" (*IP* 33[5]).

Merleau-Ponty acknowledges that there is a truth to this vision of love – that we do constitute an image of the other for ourselves and project it upon her – and that the narrator in Proust's book does in fact begin with this kind of egocentric (failure of) love. But Merleau-Ponty argues that this is really only half the story, as Proust himself recognizes, and that in fact love can be (indeed *is*, in the case of Proust's narrator) instituted, crystallized, realized precisely through these kinds of failures.[23] The more fundamental truth, beyond that of a constituting subject, is the instituting and instituted subject.

What Proust's narrator comes to realize, on Merleau-Ponty's account, is that through and beyond the binary rhythm in which he has (and Albertine also has) been caught up, Albertine and he have been shaping each other, transforming each other: there is "productivity of what I am doing in the other and of what [she] is doing in me, true communication through lateral practicing" (*IP* 35[6]). In our relations with each other, we not only take these others as objects for us, but also come to be implicated through their gestures, words, and way of life in a meaningful world whose meaning transcends us – in a shared "intersubjective or symbolic field, [the field] of cultural objects, which is our milieu, our hinge, our jointure" (*IP* 35/6).[24] Others' behaviours reveal for us, and implicate us in the *institution* of, realms of meaning that we have not mastered, that transcend our own current powers of making sense and draw us beyond ourselves.[25] There is a kind of "encroachment" or "transgression"[26] of their ways of taking up the world on ours, and of ours on theirs, with the result that we learn through each other new ways of being towards the world, and thus new ways of being ourselves. This amounts to a kind of "co-existence"[27] with the other, a common way of being towards the world, a being-with – and the more one is "involved" with a person, the more one invests one's life in her, the more this coexistence comes to itself be a kind of institution, the framework in terms of which the world makes sense and is animated with meaning. Thus, the reality of love is to be found in the fact – sometimes not realized until we face the possible or real loss of the beloved – that the meaning of one's world is intimately tied up in a specific other's existence, that to lose that person would be not only to lose a figure within one's world, but also to lose that world itself, to find oneself suddenly groundless and the world itself drained of key structures of meaning that nourished and animated it, defined it even.[28]

This is the realization, the love, that crystallizes for Proust's narrator on the occasion of Albertine's death. He had been caught up in an orientation – an institution, in fact, inherited from his previous experiences of love (*IP* 124[77]) – that took love to be "domination, inquisition and suspicion, jealousy" (*IP* 68[32]) and that aimed at the impossible goal of removing all doubt, moment to moment, about her love for him and his capacity to love her. But even as he was caught up in this way of making sense of things, and troubled by her apparently impossibly elusive alterity, he was also shaping Albertine and being shaped by her. Thus the crystallization of love comes with the realization that "it is he who has made Albertine into a liar and a fugitive, that, in this jealousy, he has joined up with and made Albertine herself, made therefore the irreality, the non-realization of their love, and that this is to love – a way of loving" (*IP* 40[10]). This constitutes a revolution in the narrator's lived conception of love. There is, to be sure, a kind of elusiveness of the other, a true alterity of self and other. But at the same time, inseparable from this, is

> the fact that this self has ... married the form of another presence, or even has given birth to it such that the form of the other presence showed itself ... The instituting subject invests itself, i.e., animates itself with another meaning, transforms itself by means of its love, i.e., succeeds in making a meaning which is transcendent to him dwell in his *I think* and in his body, as a meaning dwells in the book and the cultural object. (*IP* 40[10])

The narrator discovers his coexistence with Albertine. Coexistence and alterity are, as it turns out, not two opposed experiences at odds with each other; rather, they are two sides of one coin (*PP* 417ff[376ff]).

Possession, then, is a foolish aim – and not only because of its impossibility, but also because this other is already in oneself and oneself already in her. Similarly, the removal of all doubt is a misguided aim: love is not of the order of knowledge or indubitability (were it knowledge, it would no longer be love). At any moment reason can be found to doubt the other's love. But love exists not in the moment-to-moment, but rather as a "transphenomenal reality": it is revealed not in any isolated moments that figure on the ground of our life, but in this ground itself, in the way that another has come to "occupy the entire horizon of my life" (*IP* 70[34]).

Love, then, is not something achieved through the active gaining possession of the other; nor is it a matter of simply coming to recognize her, if that means constituting an image of her that acknowledges or fits with her singularity. Indeed, love is not something that we *do*. It is, rather, something that takes hold of us (*IP* 63[28]), and it does this precisely through our living with each other and being transformed by each other. Love is a kind of giving over, a generosity that invests itself in/with a meaning that transcends it, and through this realizes a new way of seeing the world. This new vision of the world is the institution of a new perceptual field, and the institution of a new way of being oneself (a new self), and it happens not through our own constituting activity but only, necessarily, *entre-deux*. For we cannot transcend ourselves except through an investment in a way of being that outstrips us.

The "failures of love" that Proust's narrator experienced, then, were in fact experiences of alterity and coexistence, but lived, enacted from within a framework that prevented them from being experienced in their paradoxical complementarity – in the ways in which they give us to ourselves and to each other by taking us beyond ourselves – and thus in the form of real love. Yet it was also precisely these failures that opened a space where the narrator could experience the reality of love. These failures were not, then, simply failures; they were preparations, premeditations, essays ("*essais*") of love. Says Proust's narrator: these and other earlier struggles with love were "no more than slight and timid essays that were paving the way, appeals that were unconsciously clamoring, for this vaster love: my love for Albertine."[29] Such "essays" were blind: like the artist who does not see in advance exactly what she is moved to express, the lover does not see in advance the more profound truth that, *retrospectively*, we can say he sought. Rather, there is a kind of blind groping; and through this groping – along with the contingencies that present themselves, and the regular repetitions of impasses that form the "binary rhythm" – a new dimension of meaning inserts itself, advents, is inaugurated or instituted:

> Love is not created by circumstances, or by decision; it consists in the way questions and answers are linked together – by means of an attraction, something more slips in, we discover not exactly what we were seeking, but something else that is of concern. The initial *Sinngebung* [is] confirmed, but in a different direction, and yet that is not without a relation with the initial donation of sense. (*IP* 76–7[39], translation modified)

Let us consider further this institution of sense via errors, this subterranean logic by which a new institution realizes itself. To do so, we turn to another example that interested Merleau-Ponty – again an example of jealousy overcome, but this time in a toddler rather than an adult. By focusing on early childhood, we might better see how realizations of new emotional attitudes, new dimensions of meaning, new ways of being oneself, are not the product of a constituting subject who possesses in advance all the meanings it will find. Such emotional transformations are rather products of the *entre-deux*; they are *institutions*.

5. Emotional Institutions and Their Dialectic

Anyone who has struggled with emotional upheaval knows how oppressive it can be to be entangled in those emotions, and how difficult it can be to liberate oneself from them and to come out the other side. Often we try to deal with this by seeking to change our own ways of making sense of the situation. But, although we and others might say "you ought to think of it this way, rather than that," and although sometimes we can recognize at an intellectual level the sense of such claims, our own efforts at thinking differently often seem not to reach deeply enough into our lives. Frustratingly, we find that we cannot simply be the masters of our own minds, that emotions will often take hold of us in ways that we cannot shake by simply, stoically, choosing a different attitude.

Much more often, emotional transformation seems to happen in unexpected ways, and by virtue of some contingent event that suddenly brings upon us, as if from beyond us, an epiphany. Suddenly, we experience a revolution not just in our thoughts but in our very being, at the existential level. This, we will see, is the enactment of a new institution, a new emotional attitude; and the dialectic at work in this overcoming of an old institution and inauguration of a new one is, as Merleau-Ponty says, not an ideal but a *concrete* dialectic (*IP* 55–6[21]): it affects our being, not merely our thoughts.

Merleau-Ponty offers us an example of just such an institution – although he does not use the term "institution" – in his essay "The Child's Relations with Others."[30] Let us elaborate that example in order to see how it is indeed institution that is at issue here, and in order to shed further light on the subterranean logic by which institutions undergo revolutions and give birth to new institutions. We will need to note especially the key role that contingency and repetition, even regression, play in advancing this concrete dialectic. Before drawing attention to the logic of its development, I will first describe the example.

Gricha is a toddler, with one older brother (Jean). When a new sister is born, Gricha is afflicted with jealousy. This jealousy manifests itself sometimes in the development of a stutter, temper tantrums, sleepiness, a regression in Gricha's ability to control his excretions, negativity towards his sister, and a return to more infantile behaviour. Sometimes, however, it also seems to manifest itself in constantly shadowing his older brother, trying to imitate what he does, and the development of new motor abilities.

Why this alternation? Consider the problem that Gricha faces: he has grown up within an institution of relationships that he has experienced as absolute: reality has always been organized in terms of his being *the* youngest and the one cared for by others, and his brother being *the oldest*. This logic of absolutes is the "latent or lived metaphysics"[31] that structures Gricha's perceptions of his situation; it is an institution in the sense that institution is "the wherewithal on which I count at each moment, which is seen nowhere and is assumed by everything that is visible for a human being"; it is "the effective frame [translation modified]" (*IP* 43[12]) or the laying down of a "symbolic matrix" in terms of which all events within one's life make sense. The birth of a new sister, however, upsets this institution, and a drama ensues that we might understand as Gricha's lived attempt to make sense of the situation in the only terms he knows, by enacting variations on this same familiar institution.

Initially, due to his sense that he is *the youngest*, Gricha finds himself in his new sister, identifies with her. This identification results in a regression that manifests itself not only in Gricha's behaviour but also in his physiological capacities.[32] This regression does not, however, resolve the problem that has arisen, for Gricha's social environment clearly expects more of him than it does of the baby, and Gricha is, of course, not able to become fully his little sister. Gricha is then moved to try to incorporate and get rid of his sister: he stomps around and describes himself as the big bad wolf who is going to eat her up. His nanny's response to this apparently opens up a new possibility for him. She tells him, "Your little sister knows that her brother is strong as a wolf, but he's not really mean. She's not frightened, she's proud" (Hn 789) and this dissipates Gricha's antagonism; he approaches his sister sympathetically and feeds her her bottle.

It seems, however, that Gricha is able to assume this caring position only through an identification with his older brother, Jean. For he now begins to imitate his older brother regularly. It would appear, then, that Gricha has made no revolutionary advance and that he is still living within the absolute logic of the initial institution: he has simply swung from assuming himself to be *the youngest* to becoming *the oldest*. But this, too, is untenable, because Gricha cannot do all that Jean can, and Jean gets angry with him for constantly trying to imitate him. Gricha regresses again, and this alternation between infantile regressions and taking on his brother's behaviours – this "binary rhythm" – continues.

It is, finally, on the contingent occasion of a visit from another boy that Gricha totally overcomes his jealousy, resolves the problem that has been posed by the birth of his sister, and institutes a new way of being in the world. The visitor, Serge, is a boy older than Jean. Jean, Gricha, and Serge spend the day playing happily. Serge befriends Gricha; Jean, who within this threesome has become the middle child and is no longer the absolute oldest, likewise cares for Gricha, showing no jealousy. In the context of Gricha's current drama, this, it seems, reconfigures his world. On the basis of Gricha's identification with Jean, Jean's behaviour reveals to Gricha the possibility of being not *the youngest* or *the oldest*, but a middle child who is the youngest in relation to one but the oldest in relation to another. The logic of absolutes is overcome by a logic of relativity, and a new and tenable place within the world opens up for Gricha. The proof of this is that on one and the same day, Gricha's jealous behaviours disappear, he begins consistently to care for his little sister, and he develops suddenly the use of new verb tenses – the simple past, the imperfect, the simple future, and the future with the verb to go. These verb tenses express new dimensions of temporality that have opened up for Gricha and that allow him to make lived sense of his relative relations: "I *have been* the youngest, but I *am* the youngest no longer, and I *will become* the biggest [in relation to my sister]."[33] In effect, Gricha has moved out of the past in which he was stuck as an absolute present (the past of being *the* youngest), and his situation is now configured in terms of past, present, and future. This overcoming of jealousy is, then, the crystallization of a new institution, a new configuration of the world, a new existential logic in terms of which Gricha's situation finally makes good sense and through which Gricha realizes a caring relation to his new sister.

What this example shows us is the inherent historicity of human existence, the ways in which there are advents or developments within the individual's life that make for a "*personal* history." But how, precisely, should we understand this history? What accounts for its unfolding? What is the relation of the newly instituted form of existence to what came before it? It is here that we must make more precise our understanding of institution, and of emotion as institution.

In the first place, let us notice that there seems to be a *telos* at work here, but that this *telos* is realized only *retrospectively*. That is to say, it is only retrospectively that we can say that Gricha's regressions (his infantile way of being) and his anticipations (his imitation of his older brother) were the project of establishing a caring relationship with his new sister and his family at large. Such caring was not univocally what was *sought* for or *aimed at* in Gricha's regressions and anticipations. Clearly, with the birth of his sister, Gricha felt a problem arise, and his behaviours were embodied ways of trying to resolve that problem and to reinstitute an equilibrium in his relations with others. But from the vantage point of these behaviours, if we can articulate any goal at all, the goal seems to have been one of identification, of becoming his little sister or his older brother. No, the *telos* of a caring that allows each person to be himself or herself appears only at the moment of the institution of this new caring way of being, and only then does it announce itself as what was secretly wanted all along. Recall Merleau-Ponty: "In exchange for what we had imagined, life gives us something else, and something else that was secretly wanted, not fortuitous. Realization is not what was foreseen, but all the same, what was wanted" (*IP* 75[38], translation modified).

Here again, we see the logic of "a productive experience that produces its producer": Gricha is realized, *retrospectively*, as a boy whose actions were so many attempts or "*essais*" at caring. In the very same set of articles that describe Gricha, we are also given a description of another boy, Robert, who suffers from sibling jealousy as well, but who gets substantially stuck in that jealousy. Where Gricha learned to care for his sister, Robert became increasingly violent towards his, trying to poke scissors in her eye, hitting her, calling her stupid, and so on. In his case, we cannot accurately say of him that he was a boy seeking to care.[34] He was thus far only a boy jealously defending his habitual place in the world. Only the overcoming of jealousy and the institution of care allows us to speak retrospectively of a boy who, in a nascent, ambiguous, and groping manner, really sought to realize a caring relation.

Robert's case allows us to see that the overcoming of jealousy is not a necessary dialectic; there is no destiny, no metaphysical *telos* that propels us through pre-given stages of affective relations to others. Some people will live their whole lives caught up in jealousy. The institution of genuine care in Gricha's life came about not due to some inner *telos* determining the course of his life, but due to contingency: it was first of all the contingency of the birth of his sister that problematized the institution in which Gricha currently lives, and it was the contingent visit from Serge that allowed for the crystallization of a new institution that both revealed and overcame the limits of that first institution. Here Merleau-Ponty agrees with Weber: "There must be a fortuitous reunion [of events], but from these conditions a system with its own logic engenders itself" (*IP* 44[13], my translation). And later, "the idea of institution is precisely the foundation of a personal history on the basis of contingency" (*IP* 73[36]).

It is essential to note, however, that simple contingency is insufficient and that repetition also plays its part. Merleau-Ponty, as we have seen, speaks of a "binary rhythm" that is the alternation between the binary terms of our current institution but that is also "*prénotion*" (*IP* 75[38]) or premonition of the institution still to come, the *à-venir*. Gricha, through regressions and anticipations, regularly repeated the institution of absolutes, and this repetition helped to clear a space for, and to orient Gricha towards, the new institution of care and a logic of relativity. Having lived within the absolutes of *the* youngest and *the* oldest, when his world became troubled by the birth of his sister, he was moved to repeat these absolutes, to become the youngest, and when that failed, to become the oldest. It was precisely through the *failures* of these reiterations that Gricha was opened up to other possibilities. In other words, we can surmise that it was only in the context of these failures that Serge's visit could disclose for Gricha a new way of being-in-the-world. Had Serge visited earlier, his visit would likely have had no effect. Thus, in Merleau-Ponty's terms, "[there is] growth by successive waves, or by means of detours" (*IP* 59[24]), and "[there is a] future by means of a deepening of the past" (*IP* 57[22]).

Regressions and anticipations incline us towards a new institution because as actions and expressions they always mean in excess of what we intend, and they therefore disclose beyond themselves that which we had not fully anticipated. Again, "something more slips in, [and] we discover not exactly what we were seeking, but something else that is of concern" (*IP* 76–7[39], translation modified). In Gricha's case, his attempts to become his youngest sister or his oldest brother were not successful, but they suggested to him his difference from them, his need to assume a place in relation to them instead of becoming them. And his play day with Serge and Jean was not simply the enjoyable exchange that it seemed on the surface; it was simultaneously a revelation of what Gricha had not yet realized: the possibility of relative relations, a way of being that grants to everyone their proper place.

Ultimately, we can understand Gricha's initial occupation of a world of absolutes as itself an institution that realized *a response* to the lived, existential *question* of who he was in relation to others. This world of absolutes was the establishment of a certain affective relation between Gricha and his family. Recall, however, that an answer to a question is always a "particularizing" answer – that is, an answer that, although it reveals a truth, is also marked by the circumstances in which the question has appeared and that therefore forecloses the revelation of some dimensions of reality. Thus, this institution of absolute relations, too, is particularizing. It realizes only a limited or finite truth. Indeed, it is true that Gricha was *the youngest*, and his brother *the oldest*; it is even true that there is a kind of absoluteness to each subject. But this truth has a blindness built into it and cannot account for all possible scenarios or for its own conditions. Thus, it too will give rise to a question, a reactivation of the problem of how one is related to others, and it will be overcome by a new institution that responds in a new way to that question: "Human institution always resumes a prior institution, which has posed a *question*, i.e., a question that was its anticipation – and which has failed. It reactivates this problem and human institution reunites its givens in [a] totality that is centered otherwise" (*IP* 58[22–3]).

Precisely because each institution is "particularizing," the liberation it brings with it is always relative (*IP* 61[26]) and calls for a further self-overcoming. The dialectic of institution is "never finished" (*IP* 61[25]).

Conclusion

Emotion, I have proposed, is largely a function of the particular form, structure, or logic that characterizes our affective relations with others. My being-in-the-world raises the fundamental question of how I, others, and the world are related; in answer to this question, a particular logic of interpersonal relations is realized or instituted *entre-deux*.[35] The coming to be and eventual overcoming of this institution is to be understood as a concrete dialectic – as a dialectic that takes place in my living relations to others, and not merely in my own cognitive processes, nor merely in the eye of an onlooker.[36] This, on my account, is what it means to say that emotion is institution: it arises out of a familiar way of making sense of the world that has been instituted *entre-deux*; it involves a dialectic interaction with the world that is driven by the fact that that particular institution cannot adequately make sense of the reality it encounters; and, through the regressions, repetitions, and contingent revelations involved in that dialectic *entre-deux*, it can lead to the overcoming of that former institution and the establishment of a new frame of reference, a new institution, which ultimately, retrospectively, reveals the answer to the question that had secretly propelled that dialectic.

This account of emotion proposes itself as a refutation of a philosophy of consciousness and the idea of a constituting subject. For the emotional institutions that are realized in our lives *constitute us* as much as or more than we constitute them; and the dialectic these institutions undergo is a process driven not by self-reflection and the subject's unilateral constitution of meaning, but by contingency, repetition, and the indeterminate but fundamental question that our being in the world with others both poses and secretly, implicitly, ambiguously strives to work out.

To conclude, I would like to return briefly to the example of Gricha and Robert, in order to propose (a) that there is a danger in understanding emotion according to a philosophy of consciousness, and (b) that on the contrary, understanding emotion as institution has productive effects. Robert, you may remember, was the child who became stuck in his jealousy. It is noteworthy that his parents seemed to take a very different approach to jealousy than did Gricha's caretakers. Gricha's caretakers, as far as we can tell from Dolto-Marette's (autobiographical) account, assumed a compassionate attitude towards Gricha, acknowledging that the birth of his new sister was a situation that had put his very reality, his familiar institutions, into question. They treated his behaviours as expressions of his finitude, as ways of seeking an answer in the context of a certain blindness, rather than supposing that these behaviours were the outcome of Gricha's selfish construal of the situation. Believing that they could not *give* Gricha an answer to his problem and that the *realization* of an answer would have to emerge *for him*, they tried to do what they could (while also resisting his inadequate forms of behaviour) to provide him with possible resources. His nanny, as I have mentioned, seems (based on the effects) to have, in a minor way, reconfigured his situation for him by telling him that, as a big brother, he *mattered* to his sister. Similarly, when Gricha was in the midst of one of his greatest regressions, and calling himself by his sister's name (Katinka), his mother tried to encourage him to think of himself as having his own place in the world: she said, "Where's my big boy? I can see Katinka, but where is Gricha?" After Gricha shouted exuberantly, "Here, me," she reached out to him and said to the phantom of his sister, "Katinka, go back to your cradle, get out of Gricha's bed; you are too small for this big bed" (Hnj 791). And Gricha's parents supplied him with occasions for realizing a new relation to his sister by giving him a doll of his own and by encouraging play with other children. In other words, Gricha's caretakers understood his emotional reaction as a function of already instituted relations with the world and sought to *facilitate* the institution of a new form of relation between him and his world.[37]

Robert's parents, on the other hand, were oriented towards Robert in a manner that fit with an assumption of subjects as constituting. They accused him of being selfish and nasty, as if his antipathy towards his sister were *simply* a result of his own construal of the situation, and as if he could simply choose to construe it otherwise. In doing so, Robert's parents apparently bought into and consolidated Robert's sense that he no longer had a valuable place in his world; his ensuing behaviours suggest that his parents' attitudes *crystallized* his own indeterminate sense of being someone who didn't matter, a bad boy. The result was further regression and more "bad boy" behaviour – and bad behaviour that we can see was in fact the result of the dynamic occurring *entre-deux*. Robert did eventually overcome his jealousy and come to care responsibly for his sister, but only after his parents were directed to take up his situation compassionately, to recognize their co-responsibility in his behaviour, and to offer him new possible resources. On Dolto-Marette's account, rephrased in Merleau-Ponty's words, these parents needed to recognize, as did Proust's narrator, that they were themselves in large part responsible for who Robert was becoming, that because of the coexistence and *entre-deux* that characterizes human involvements, they had "joined up with and made" (*IP* 40[10]) Robert himself. In order to open up the kind of space where Robert could experience the epiphany of overcoming his current emotional institution for a new one, they needed to stop pressing for a new way of construing the situation, and to allow him to discover, to have instituted through his experiences – in the *entre-deux* – a new living way of being in relation to others.

I would like to propose, then, that the most productive attitude we might have towards our own and others' emotional lives is one that recognizes emotions as institution and as coming to be *entre-deux*.

NOTES

1 *L'Institution, la Passivité*, translated into English as *Institution and Passivity*. Henceforth, this text will be referred to as *IP* with the French pagination given first and the English translation pagination second. In the institution lecture course, Merleau-Ponty elucidates the idea of a passionate feeling as an institution through a focus on love as it is lived by the narrator in Proust's *Remembrance of Things Past*. Compared to some other commentators, I read the *Phenomenology* as much more in continuity with Merleau-Ponty's mid-career and later works, so that those ensuing works are really a radicalization or intensification of ideas already at work in the earlier texts, rather than a turn away from a philosophical perspective, in those earlier texts, that is too mired in "a philosophy of consciousness." On this point, I believe I am in agreement with Bernhard Waldenfels (see, for instance, his assessment of the development of Merleau-Ponty's thought in "The Paradox of Expression"), and I disagree with Renaud Barbaras (as he summarizes his view, for instance, in "Perception and

Movement"). Concerning the concept of institution in particular, I am in agreement with the logic of institution as Robert Vallier lays it out in his article "Institution," but I disagree with Vallier as well as with Claude Lefort in his foreword to the lectures on institution (*IP* 5–28[ix–xxxi]) that Merleau-Ponty makes a "turn" in the 1950s from the logic of expression, which proved to be inadequate to his project, to the logic of institution. As Véronique Fóti's article "Expression in Merleau-Ponty's Aesthetics, Philosophy of Nature, and Ontology" argues, expression is not left behind but remains central to Merleau-Ponty's later thought, and in particular to his conception of institution.

2 I will give further support for this claim in the next section, but let me remark here that, in the *Phenomenology*, Merleau-Ponty's central accounts of learning, creative expression, the acquisition of habit, and the coming to be of colour perception, spatial perception, and geometrical insights can be understood as putting to work the same logic of institution that he elaborates in his later lectures. Among the many different names that we find denoting institution in the *Phenomenology*, we find the following: "establishment (*établissement*)" (e.g., *PP* 54[32], 160[128–9] (translated by Landes as "institution"), "foundation (*fondation*)" (e.g., *PP* 160[129]), "everlasting acquisition (*acquisition pour toujours*)" (e.g., *PP* 453[413], or "*Stiftung*." See, for instance, *PP* 159–160[128–9], where Merleau-Ponty explicitly notes that he is translating Husserl's "favourite word" *Stiftung*, and where, in language very similar to that of the institution lectures, he claims that "the senses, and one's own body overall, present the mystery of a whole that, without leaving behind its *haecceity* and its particularity, emits beyond itself significations capable of offering a framework for a whole series of thoughts and experiences" and speaks of "the initial institution or founding of knowledge and action … the first grasp of being or of value whose concrete richness will never be exhausted by knowledge and action, and whose spontaneous method they will everywhere renew."

3 For extended explications of Merleau-Ponty's implicit account of emotions, two very worthwhile books are Glen Mazis's *Emotion and Embodiment* and Sue Cataldi's *Emotion, Depth, and Flesh*. I take my account of emotion here to be very much aligned with each of these texts; my intent is to supplement their accounts with a focus on the institutional or institutive character of emotion, and correlatively on the ways in which emotion comes to be "*entre-deux*."

4 The examples or case studies of personal history that Merleau-Ponty focuses on in the lectures on institution are transformations involved in puberty, love, and artistic expression. He then uses knowledge and culture

as transitional phenomena, between personal and public, to introduce us to the question of public history – the question, that is, of whether and how we might speak of a universal history, of transformations in the spirit of an age. The distinction between personal and public is, however, in fact one that cannot maintain itself as a simple distinction, as Merleau-Ponty goes on to note (*IP* 47[15]), since our own personal institutions are always informed by cultural institutions of our time – for instance, institutions surrounding gender, race, work, family, science, and so on – and our cultural institutions always take shape in communication with personal institutions (see also *IP* 78[41]).

5 That the project of the institution lecture course is to criticize and go beyond the idea of a constituting subject is made clear in both the introduction to the course (*IP* 33–48[5–15]) and the summary provided of the course (*IP* 76–9[123–6]). That one of the key projects of the *Phenomenology* is a criticism of this conception of the subject is evident in Merleau-Ponty's repeated criticism, in virtually every chapter, of intellectualism.

6 "Human institution always resumes a prior institution, which has posed a *question*, i.e., a question that was its anticipation" (*IP* 58[22]).

7 Thus Merleau-Ponty completes the quotation in footnote 6 above by noting that the prior institution, which implicitly poses a question, also fails in answering to, or even foreseeing the answer to, that question: "Human institution always resumes a prior institution, which has posed a *question*, i.e., a question that was its anticipation – and which has failed" (*IP* 58[22]).

8 Merleau-Ponty elucidates this with the example of painting (*IP* 125[78]): "in the history of painting, the problems (the problem of perspective, for example) are rarely resolved directly. The investigation stops at an impasse, other investigations seem to create a diversion, but the new impulse allows the obstacle to be overcome from another direction. Thus, rather than a *problem*, there is an 'interrogation' of painting, which is enough to give a common meaning to all its endeavors and which is enough to turn them into a history, but this common meaning never allows us to anticipate the history by means of concepts."

9 *IP* 38[9]: "The instituted will change but this very change is called for by its *Stiftung*. Goethe: genius [is] posthumous productivity. All institution is in this sense genius."

10 See *IP* 45, 54[13, 19]; and Merleau-Ponty, "Indirect Language and the Voices of Silence" [hereafter *ILVS*], 77.

11 In "Merleau-Ponty: Perception into Art," Paul Crowther, quoting from Merleau-Ponty's *Prose of the World*, argues that the common theme of all

of Merleau-Ponty's texts on art and aesthetics is this: "It is the expressive operation begun in the least perception, which amplifies into painting and art" (83).

12 Some secondary literature on the *Phenomenology* understands Merleau-Ponty's account of perception in this way – but mistakenly, as I will argue in this section.

13 Merleau-Ponty, *The Structure of Behavior*, 40–3; idem, *La structure du comportement*, 40–4.

14 *PP* 259[222]: "Thus a sensible that is about to be sensed poses to my body a sort of confused problem. I must find the attitude that will provide it with the means to become determinate and to become blue; I must find the response to a poorly formulated question. And yet, I do this only in response to its solicitation ... The sensible gives back to me what I had lent to it, but I received it from the sensible in the first place."

15 Bernhard Waldenfels identifies this retrospective logic as characteristic of the phenomenality of phenomena. In his often cited article "The Paradox of Expression," he speaks of it in terms of an "*après coup* ... a delayed effect ... a reverse movement of truth, or ... retrofiguration." See esp. 96. Waldenfels also understands the event of expression as a "founding event" (93) and thus as an institution.

16 Brazelton, "Joint Regulation of Neonate–Parent Behavior," 14–15.

17 Ibid., 14; Brazelton, Koslowski, and Main, "The Origins of Reciprocity," 54.

18 For a detailed argument to this effect, see Maclaren, "Embodied Perceptions of Others."

19 Faced with unresponsive adults, infants will make general gestures towards trying to engage the other, and when these fail, they will show negative affect, disorganized, jerky behaviours, and ultimately withdrawal (Brazelton, "Joint Regulation"; Brazelton, Koslowski, and Main, "The Origins of Reciprocity"; Field, *The Amazing Infant*, ch. 5; Legerstee, Corter and Kienapple, "Hand, Arm, and Facial Actions"; see also Adamson and Frick, "The Still Face," for a recent review of these "still-face" studies). Faced with overwhelmingly stimulating adults, infant behaviour becomes less organized and infants turn away (Brazelton, "Joint Regulation," 20–1; Brazelton, Koslowski, and Main, "The Origins of Reciprocity," 59; see also Cohn and Tronick, "Specificity of Infants' Response").

20 Papoušek, "Communication in Early Infancy"; Trevarthen, "Communication and Cooperation in Early Infancy."

21 Brazelton, Koslowski, and Main, "The Origins of Reciprocity."

22 Moore and Calkin, "Infants' Vagal Regulation." Cf. Porges's "polyvagal theory" (e.g., in "The Polyvagal Theory"), which proposes that vagal

regulation is used to foster social engagement and disengagement, and thus that there is a biological basis for social behaviour. In response to Porges, I would propose that the relation between vagal regulation and social behaviour cannot coherently be understood as a biological basis *causing* an interpersonal set of behaviours; we must instead understand physiological regulation as motivated and enabled by recognitive social exchanges.

23 See especially the section beginning at *IP* 64[29], where Merleau-Ponty lays out the criticisms of feelings as merely subjective, acknowledges them as true, but claims that they do not exhaust the question, that they are only "half of what is true." He then goes on to argue that "even as egocentric as the point of departure of love is, it becomes something other than a monologue" (*IP* 72[35]).

24 For support for and elaborations of Merleau-Ponty's idea that we learn to see with and through other people, see Maclaren, "Embodied Perceptions of Others" and "Intercorporeality, Intersubjectivity."

25 Recall *PP* 235[199]: "It is the definition of the human body to appropriate, in an indefinite series of discontinuous acts, meaningful cores that transcend and transfigure its natural powers. This act of transcendence is initially found in the acquisition of a behavior, and then in the silent communication of the gesture: the body opens itself to a new behavior and renders that behavior intelligible to external observers through the same power. A system of definite powers suddenly decenters here and there, breaks apart, and is reorganized under a law that is unknown to the subject or the external observer, and which is revealed to them in this very moment."

26 See especially Merleau-Ponty's "The Child's Relations with Others," 154–5; *Les relations avec autrui chez l'enfant*, 79–81. See also *PP* 235[199]: "For the speaking subject and for those who listen to him, the phonetic gesture produces a certain structuring of experience, a certain modulation of existence, just as a behavior of my body invests –for me and for others – the objects that surround me with a certain signification"; and *PP* 225[190–1]: "Communication or the understanding of gestures is achieved through the reciprocity between my intentions and the other person's gestures, and between my gestures and the intentions which can be read in the other person's behavior. Everything happens as if the other person's intention inhabited my body, or as if my intentions inhabited his body. The gesture I witness sketches out the first signs of an intentional object. This object becomes present and is fully understood when the powers of my body adjust to it and fit over it. The gesture is in front of me like a question, it

indicates to me specific sensible points in the world and invites me to join it there. Communication is accomplished when my behavior finds in this pathway its own pathway. I confirm the other person and the other person confirms me."

27 See especially *PP* 406ff[364ff]. But the notion of coexistence can be found throughout Merleau-Ponty's work, from his earliest text *The Structure of Behavior* onwards. "The Child's Relations with Others" can be read as an extended meditation on forms of coexistence and on the emergence of a realization of the alterity that comes with that.

28 In both the institution lectures and the *Phenomenology*, Merleau-Ponty calls attention to the difference between relatively authentic and inauthentic or hysterical emotions of love. And in both, his argument seems to be that what differentiates them is the degree to which the beloved has really become the fabric of one's world, the horizon in terms of which everything makes sense (*IP* 64[29], *PP* 437ff[397ff]).

29 Proust, *Remembrance of Things Past*, 253–4. Cited in a footnote to the institution lectures (*IP* 135–6n57[92–3n38]).

30 Merleau-Ponty takes the example from articles by Dolto-Marette, "Hypothèse nouvelle" [hereafter Hn], and Rostand, "Grammaire et affectivité." For what follows, I have consulted those articles, in addition to Merleau-Ponty's "The Child's Relations with Others."

31 Merleau-Ponty, "Metaphysics and the Novel."

32 He loses his ability to control his own excretions, for instance. Although some parents might interpret this as a way of "acting out," Dolto-Marette argues that it is more bodily than this (Hn 796–7), and she points to Gricha's genuine distress at wetting his bed as proof that this was not his aim (Hn 788).

33 Merleau-Ponty, "The Child's Relations with Others," 108–11; see also Hn as well as Rostand, "Grammaire et affectivité."

34 Robert does eventually overcome his jealousy, but only when his family transforms their way of taking up his jealous behaviours. For a considerable amount of time, Robert is stuck in his jealousy, and rather than improving, becomes increasingly violent towards his sister. Some people may be stuck in jealousy for a lifetime.

35 Merleau-Ponty claims that the medium of institution is "libido: it's the becoming of [our] total relation with [the] world and others" (*IP* 61). He says this in the context of his discussion of puberty as institution. Perhaps he means to say that it is only in the dialectic of puberty that the medium is our affective relations with others. Or perhaps this is true of all personal institution.

36 Ralón de Walton, in "Symbolic Matrices and the Institution of Meaning," explores the kind of meaning involved in symbolic matrices and institution and emphasizes the operative character of a structure of meaning that is really present, and not merely read into the data by an observer, but that is also not the product of a reflective subject.

37 This approach could be understood as exemplary of Heidegger's "leaping ahead" in *Being and Time* or *Sein und Zeit*, §26.

4 Perceiving through Another: Incorporation and the Child Perceiver

SUSAN M. BREDLAU

In the *Phenomenology of Perception*, Merleau-Ponty writes:

> The blind man's cane has ceased to be an object for him, it is no longer perceived for itself; rather, the cane's furthest point is transformed into a sensitive zone, it increases the scope and radius of the act of touching and has become analogous to a gaze. (*PP* 177[144])

The boundaries between perceiver and perceived can be redrawn.[1] Thus, for the blind man, his cane does not remain on the side of the perceived but instead shifts to the side of the perceiver. With this shift, the cane ceases being experienced by the blind man and, instead, becomes part of him; what was once sensed becomes sensitive. I will refer to such transformations of the perceived into the perceptive as incorporations. With incorporation, the cane becomes something *through* which the blind man perceives rather than something that he perceives. In the following four sections, I will examine the implications of incorporation for our understanding of the perceiving subject. I begin, in Section I, by arguing that other people, and not just other things, can be incorporated. Beyond perceiving other people in the world, one can also perceive the world through other people. In Section II, I draw on Merleau-Ponty's discussion of nascent perception in *The Structure of Behavior* and infant imitation in "The Child's Relations to Others" to argue that Merleau-Ponty conceives of infants as able to perceive through others. I argue as well that the incorporation of other people is especially critical to the child perceiver, who, unlike an adult, rarely acts alone. In Section III, I discuss some empirical research that supports the conception of the infant perceiver as defined by incorporation. Finally, in Section IV,

I briefly discuss the phenomenon of parental "scaffolding" and offer a phenomenological description of the impact that such incorporation might have on the child perceiver.

I. Incorporation and Other People

If what is perceived can be incorporated, then the limits of the perceiver need not be marked by her skin. Incorporation yields a perceiver who extends beyond an individual, human body.[2] Yet while this perceiver has what I will call an expanded body, incorporation cannot be understood in terms of simple addition and subtraction. When the blind man, for example, incorporates the cane, he does not continue to perceive a world that, although it is slightly closer to him and no longer contains the cane, is largely the same as before. The expansion of the body through the incorporation of the cane no more shortens the objective distance between the blind person and the world than the contraction of the body through the loss of a limb lengthens the objective distance between the amputee and the world. As Merleau-Ponty's discussion of the phantom limb reveals, to lose a limb is to have the entire structure of one's world altered (*PP* 95–122[82–95]). Likewise, to incorporate the cane into one's body is to acquire a new kind of sensitivity that is different from, although certainly not unrelated to, the sensitivity one previously enjoyed. For the blind man, for example, a series of steps that when perceived without the cane were experienced as grave obstacles, could now, when perceived through the cane, be experienced as navigable. With incorporation, both perceiver and perceived take on new identities; to annex fresh instruments, Merleau-Ponty writes, is to change our existence (*PP* 177[144]).

Before continuing, I want to emphasize here that incorporation is not synonymous with simple physical contact; it is not the presence of the cane next to the blind person that ensures its incorporation but, rather, its involvement in a new comportment. The cane can only become sensitive insofar as it, and the body of which it is now a part, arrange themselves in specific ways. Grabbed in the middle rather than held at its end, the cane will, for the blind person, likely remain primarily as perceived. Moreover, the kind of sensitivity that the cane allows will also depend on the comportments in which it is involved. When the cane is held at its end but jabbed at the world rather than run gently over it, its incorporation will yield an embattled perceiver rather an advancing one. The perceiver is neither matter nor mind but a dynamically arranged body. Thus it is insofar as the cane introduces and sustains comportments that an individual body alone was incapable of achieving that perceiver and perceived are formed anew. I will very shortly have more to say about how the comportments of the expanded body created by incorporation are sustained.

I remembered Merleau-Ponty's discussion of the blind person's cane as I was thinking about a recent trip to London. My first days in London were spent with a friend who had already visited the city many times; my last day there, however, I spent on my own. I was quite startled, on this last day, at how easily I could become disoriented, even as I simply retraced the same paths I had travelled just a few days earlier. A city that had, very recently, graciously invited my advances now seemed intent on repelling them. Distances once easily traversable were now intimidatingly long as the streets, which had previously seemed like broad boulevards that whisked me directly to my next destination, now seemed like close alleys that only diverted me away from where I wanted to go.

As much as I might try, I was unable to perceive the city as I had before; the previously welcoming city remained now obstinately closed. Yet as I thought about my situation, I realized that if I could not now, on my own, experience the city as open, this was because I had not previously, on my own, experienced the city as open; I felt it as open only when I was with my friend. While I was now alone, I had not been before. Moreover, as I started to think about my past experiences, I began to identify more and more situations that I had not handled alone. My friend had bought the train tickets. She had chosen which buses and subways to take. She had decided which streets to cross and even when to cross them. If, while with her, I could board the train nonchalantly, peer intently at the people passing by, and cross the streets with easy assurance, it was because I was perceiving these situations not on my own but rather *through* my friend.

Thus in travelling with me in the city, my friend had not simply accompanied me, as one person next to another; she was not just one thing among the many things I perceived. Instead, my relation to my friend was rather like the relation between the blind man and his cane. Incorporation, in other words, need not be restricted to inanimate things; incorporation may not only render perceptive what was previously not, as in the case of the cane and the blind man, but also render what is perceptive for itself also perceptive for another, as in the case of my friend and me.

Before discussing several similarities between these two examples of incorporation, I want to acknowledge two important differences between them. First, the blind man's incorporation of the cane is primarily a tactile incorporation. The blind man touches things through the cane. My incorporation of my friend, however, was, primarily visual, although it may have been tactile or aural as well. Second, my friend, unlike the blind man's cane, was perceptive in her own right. I did not, therefore, direct my friend's movements in the same way that the blind man directs the cane's movements; indeed, I was much more directed by my friend than she was by me.

In my experience, my friend was not simply perceived, nor was she even simply perceived as perceptive. That is, I did not merely observe that she was perceptive yet continue perceiving the world as I would if I were alone. Instead, I perceived *through* her; incorporation created a perceiver who was no longer confined to my individual body but expanded into hers, and this allowed me to perceive the world differently than I did when alone. My comportments, and the experiences they allowed, were achievable only insofar as my body was scaffolded by my friend's body. In using the word "scaffold," I want to draw attention to the intricate system of support on which my body relied. By enabling me to sustain comportments I could not have sustained on my own, my friend granted me a sensitivity to situations of which I would have otherwise remained insensible.

Incorporation accomplishes new sensitivities; this accomplishment, however, deserves to be carefully considered. First, one might be tempted to understand incorporation as, so to speak, opening one's eyes to the world around one. Yet my friend did not simply open my eyes to the city surrounding me any more than the blind man's cane simply opened his eyes to the steps ahead of him. Incorporation does not give access to a previously hidden world; rather, it allows the world to take on new meanings. My friend allowed me to take on very particular new comportments, and what I perceived reflected our unique relationship.[3] Incorporation is also not a one-time intervention; my friend's involvement in my perception was not only sustaining but also sustained.

Second, one might be tempted to understand incorporation as allowing one, so to speak, to see the world through another's eyes. This temptation seems particularly strong when that which is incorporated is another person rather than another thing. Yet although I have described the perceivers created through incorporation of another person as perceiving through this person, I want to stress that this formulation does not imply that the perceiver perceives exactly the same situations as whoever is incorporated. While my friend's involvement certainly allowed me to undertake and sustain comportments I could not have sustained alone, this involvement did not necessarily make me capable of sustaining comportments identical to hers. Thus although I would expect that my incorporation of my friend occurred together with my friend's incorporation of me, my involvement with her was rather different from her involvement with me. So even if there was a certain reciprocity between us insofar as each altered the other's perception, there need not have been any further equivalence between us, because these alterations were not alike.

Since it was through my friend that I was able to perceive the city as I had, my experiences of the city as welcoming were inseparable from her. Once the scaffolding of my friend's body was removed, the perceiver I had been collapsed; left with only my individual body, I could no longer sustain the same comportments as before. Stripped of my previous sensitivity to the city, I was unable to experience it in the same way. Thus in my present experience of disorientation, I recognized that my past experiences had not, in a certain sense, been mine.

If I was surprised, when alone, not to have the same experience as I had had before, this was because I had previously ascribed to my individual body a sensibility that was not truly mine. While walking around the city on those previous days, I had thought of myself as separate from all those around me. My experiences, however, were those of a perceiver expanded by incorporation. Thus I claimed to sustain on my own experiences that were, in fact, only sustained through another. As Merleau-Ponty writes, I can find in the world "other behaviors ... that intertwine with my own" (*PP* 415[374]); two bodies, like the parts of one body, can form a single system (*PP* 410[370]).[4] In thinking of myself as utterly separate from my friend, therefore, I had actually failed to properly distinguish myself from her. By ascribing to my individual body comportments that required incorporation of another's body, I had taken as mine what was only, so to speak, on loan from another.

Discovering that some of what one took to be one's individual experiences are actually only possible through others is not, I think, all that unusual. The loss of a companion – whether this is the temporary loss of a prolonged absence or the permanent loss of death – is often accompanied by the realization that certain structures of perception were joint rather than individual; as Joan Didion writes, following the sudden death of her husband, her house was still "our (I could not yet think *my*) … house."[5] With this loss, one's existence may be coloured by an anxiety that one did not feel before. Through one's partner, the world was secure; without one's partner, it is now more fraught. Likewise, one can visit the places one visited before or eat the food one ate before, yet now find these places or this food drained of their savour.

II. Incorporation and the Child

To recognize the phenomenon of incorporation is to recognize that a perceiver is not necessarily confined to a single human body; a perceiver may expand into other people as well as other things. Having explored the role of incorporation in adult perception, I will now focus on what role incorporation may play in infant perception. Insofar as the use of tools is a skill children do not immediately possess, one might think that incorporation is not particularly relevant to the infant perceiver. Yet insofar as other people can be involved in incorporation, the relevance of incorporation for the infant perceiver deserves to be reconsidered. After all, infants are hardly ever left alone, and thus the incorporation of others would seem to be much more a possibility for them than for adults. In addition, infants, much more often than adults, are quite literally joined with other people as they are held, carried, or embraced by another.

When first born, Merleau-Ponty writes in *The Structure of Behavior*, infants direct themselves disproportionately towards other people rather than to other things. Moreover, he continues, infants do not encounter these other people in the same way that they encounter other things: "Nascent perception has the double character of being directed toward human intentions rather than toward objects of nature or the pure qualities ... and of grasping them as experienced realities rather than as true objects."[6] Merleau-Ponty's focus here is on an infant's perception of a smile. First of all, he argues, we ought to understand the infant as perceiving a smile and not a face or a "mosaic of sensations."[7] An infant does not first perceive colours and lines and then, as she grows older, perceive a face and then a smile; an infant immediately perceives a smile. Second, and perhaps more importantly, Merleau-Ponty suggests that to perceive a smile is to perceive an intention of another person: "The human signification is given before the alleged sensible signs. A face is a center of human expression, the transparent envelope of the attitudes and desires of others, the place of manifestations, the barely material support for a multitude of intentions."[8] As

Merleau-Ponty describes it, then, nascent perception is defined by a kind of incorporation. The infant does not relate to other people as perceived, as one object among other objects in the world; rather, the infant relates to others' bodies as perceptive, as experiencing the world and acting intentionally within it. She sees, for example, others as smiling, and this smiling reflects how the other touches and hears the world as well as how the other sees the world.

Merleau-Ponty's discussion of child development in "The Child's Relations with Others" echoes his discussion of nascent perception. For a young child, he writes, "there is initially a stage of pre-communication (Max Scheler), wherein the other's intentions somehow play *across* my body while my intentions play across his."[9] As a result, he asserts, a young child does not begin life as a completely discrete, unique self; instead, she begins life immersed in a community of other people: "There is not one individual over against another but rather an anonymous collectivity, an undifferentiated group life."[10]

In the discussion that follows, my focus will be far more on Merleau-Ponty's claim that others' intentions can "play across" an infant's body than on his claim that such play implies an "anonymous collectivity, an undifferentiated group life." Nonetheless, I want to acknowledge that his description of the earliest stage of infant life as lacking a clear distinction between self and other has come under criticism. Gallagher, for example, argues that Merleau-Ponty's assertion that infants do not, at birth, distinguish themselves from others is simply not supported by contemporary research; as he writes, "the newborn infant's ability to imitate others, and its ability to correct its movement, which implies a recognition of the difference between its own gesture and the other's gesture, indicates a rudimentary differentiation between self and non-self."[11]

As Welsh notes, Merleau-Ponty's description of early infant life reflected the dominant views during his time.[12] Piaget, for example, wrote that "in the early stages of his development ... [the child] does not even recognise any definite limits between his self and the external world."[13] Similarly, Freud wrote that "an infant at the breast does not as yet distinguish his ego from the external world as the source of the sensations flowing in upon him."[14] Welsh acknowledges that these views have, in the face of contemporary research, given way to the view that "we come to the world with a preliminary understanding of the difference between self and other."[15] Nonetheless, she believes that Merleau-Ponty's emphasis on a lack of distinction between self and other "is not just influenced by the state of knowledge of infants in the mid-twentieth century, but is a search to find language that acknowledges human communication and connectivity without a mental, intellectualist bias."[16] She argues that "the value that is retained in Merleau-Ponty's lectures, despite their ignorance about the progress of the psychological sciences, is the appreciation of child experience as not just precursor to adult experience, but possessing its own rhythm and styles of interaction."[17]

Maclaren provides further defence for Merleau-Ponty's conception of early infant life by arguing that he "is right to claim that infants initially experience a 'syncretic sociability' (an indistinction between self and other) and a indistinction between subject and object."[18] Syncretic sociability does not, she argues, imply a total indistinction: "It is rather a relative sense of indeterminacy or ambiguity, an absence of clear boundaries, between what will later be realized as self and other."[19] Moreover, those who reject the idea of syncretic sociability assume "a fundamental sense of self-possession and self-governance ... [that] is an achievement, rather than a given."[20]

Following Welsh and Maclaren, I suggest that Merleau-Ponty's descriptions of early infant life as "an anonymous collectivity, an undifferentiated group life" be understood, at least in part, as a claim about infants' openness to others as perceptive. As I have noted, we often overlook the indebtedness of our own adult perceptual experiences to our perceiving through others. It seems especially critical, therefore, that we not repeat this mistake when considering infant perception. In other words, we could read Merleau-Ponty's description of infant life as an "anonymous collectivity" as resonating with his description of perception as having an "anonymous" or "pre-personal" dimension (*PP* 112[86], 203[168], 303[265] and elsewhere). This dimension certainly reflects a person's existence as a member of the human species, but it might also reflect a person's existence as a child who begins life perceiving through others. Before there is a fully developed personal self, who thinks about the world and decides how to act in it, there is a "prepersonal" self who is already acting in the world both as a natural being with a human body and as a social being through the bodies of others.

In both "Consciousness and the Acquisition of Language" and "The Child's Relations with Others," Merleau-Ponty draws on Guillaume's distinction between two kinds of imitation to support his own claim that children immediately perceive others as perceptive. Guillaume, he writes, "says that we do not at first imitate others but rather the actions of others, and that we find others at the point of origin of these actions."[21] Thus "at nine months and twenty-one days," Merleau-Ponty reports, "Guillaume's child seized the pencil upside down and used it to hit the table, but after several tries he turned the pencil over so as to place the point on the paper. This was not a question of the child reproducing the gesticulation of his father, but rather a question of obtaining the same result as he (i.e., the position of the pencil in relation to the paper)."[22]

When considering the child perceiver in the example above, if one consigns the father to the side of the perceived, then any imitation of his actions would seem to necessarily be a reproduction of his gesticulations. Yet, if one thinks of the father as, instead, on the side of the perceiver, then one can distinguish between an imitation of others and imitation of others' actions. For the child, the father was not so much sensed as sensitive. The child first perceives the situation as he did, as a situation "for writing," because he is not exploring it on his own but instead through his father. The child's incorporation of his father allows him to perceive the pencil and paper in a way he had not yet perceived for himself. Thus as the child presently attempts to write, it is the comportments sustained by his father, and not the image of his father, that the child is attempting to produce on his own. In other words, the child's comportments are similar to those of the adult, not because the child perceived the adult but because the child perceived *through* the adult; much as I tried to make my present experience of London conform to my past experiences of London, the child, albeit much more successfully, tries to make his present experiences with the pencil conform to his past experiences with the pencil.

Guillaume's distinction, in other words, can be understood as a distinction between the other as perceived by an individual body and the other as incorporated into an expanded body. Insofar as the father's involvement with the child through incorporation takes place primarily at the level of vision, it may be more difficult to consider the relation between the father and his child as similar to the relation between the blind man and his cane. However, just as one may touch a cane and yet be sensitive not to the cane itself but rather to the ground over which it travels, so too may one see a person but be sensitive not to the person herself but rather to the situation in which she is engaged.

I stress again that even with the imitation of his father's actions, the child's present experience is certainly not identical to his father's experiences; as Merleau-Ponty notes, albeit for a slightly different reason, the child's gestures "bear only an approximate and imperfect resemblance" to those of the father.[23] But I also want to stress a point that so far has not been thematized: Guillaume's example does entail imitation – that is, through incorporation, the child becomes able to assume not only a new comportment but also a comportment quite similar to his father's. Furthermore, Guillaume's example does not seem especially rare; the comportments that adults sustain in children are probably quite often similar to the comportments an adult would sustain on her own. For a child, one could say, others begin as incorporated so that they will not always remain so. It is by first extending into an adult body that the child will come to have an adult body of her own; through incorporation, adults allow a child to grow into the perceiver they themselves already are.

Merleau-Ponty's discussions of "nascent perception" and imitation are, therefore, consistent with the conception of infant perceivers as expanded through incorporation. Just as, in the case of the blind person, the perceiver must be considered not as an individual person but as person *and* cane, so too, in the case of infants, the perceiver must be considered not as an individual infant but rather as an infant *and* an adult. For the infant, others do not simply begin on the side of the perceived and only then cross over to the side of the perceiver; for the child, others often begin on the side of the perceiver. Indeed, one might think of the infant perceiver as beginning life expanded into others and only gradually contracting into the infant alone; as Merleau-Ponty writes, the child has "the attitude of a me which is unaware of itself and lives as easily in others as it does in itself – but which, being unaware of others in their own separateness as well, in truth is no more conscious of them than of itself."[24]

III. Empirical Research

Empirical research on child development recognizes that infants do experience others as, like themselves, experiencing the world. Yet researchers have typically argued that infants' experience of others as subjects requires infants to first develop a "theory of mind," and this development is usually thought to happen well after birth.[25] Similarly, the phenomenon of "joint attention," in which an infant treats others' eye movements as an attentive gaze that directs her own, has typically been thought to begin only when infants are around nine months old.[26]

One might think, therefore, that the conception of the child perceiver as defined, from birth, by incorporation of others is simply not supported by empirical research on child development. Not all researchers, however, argue that infants must develop a "theory of mind" before they can experience other people as subjects. Trevarthen, for example, argues that infants have an innate awareness of other people as subjects; he claims that "a child is born with motives to find and use the motives of other persons in 'conversational' negotiation of purposes, emotions, experiences and meaning."[27] He distinguishes between "primary intersubjectivity," which is enacted in dyadic infant–caregiver interactions, and "secondary intersubjectivity," which is enacted in triadic infant–caregiver–object interactions, and he claims that while primary intersubjectivity exists from birth, secondary intersubjectivity only begins to exist around nine months.[28]

Likewise, Reddy argues that infants begin life experiencing others as attentive and intentional.[29] Reddy calls for a second-person approach towards research into our experience of other people as subjects.[30] In contrast to a first-person approach, which argues that we know others as minds "by extension" of our own experiences as minds, or a third-person approach, which argues that we know other minds "from the outside through observation, inference, and theory," a second-person approach "suggests that others are experienced as others, in direct emotional engagement, and that this fundamentally undermines the 'problem' in the 'problem of other minds.'"[31] A second-person approach, Reddy writes, has three core features. First, it rejects the idea that other minds are "opaque to perception" and instead "sees minds as transparent within (and within the limits of) active, emotionally engaged perception."[32] Second, it "pluralises the other," arguing that we can have many different kinds of relations with others and that relations with others in the second person, as opposed to the third person, "allow[] us to experience others within our emotional responses to them *as* particular others."[33] Third, it "sees this active emotional engagement between people as constituting – or creating – the minds that each comes to have and develop, not merely providing information about each to the other."[34]

Reddy applies the second-person approach to research on infant development, and she argues that infants engage from birth with other people as subjects and enter into dialogue with them: "From birth, they prefer to look at faces which engage them in direct mutual gaze, and they are capable of engaging in imitative exchanges with adults that reveal not just an ability to recognize similarity between self and other but a motivation to invite engagement."[35] Reddy's work, then, offers a conception of infant experience that is compatible with the idea of the infant perceiver as expanded through incorporation. The infant perceiver does not first encounter other people as objects and only later come to experience them as subjects. Rather, the infant perceiver begins life perceiving others as perceptive.

Yet beyond offering a conception of infant experience that is compatible with the idea that infants, from birth, perceive through others, Reddy offers insight into the precise character of their perception through others. Reddy stresses that infants first experience others' attention and intentions as directed at them. As Reddy notes, to experience another person's attention as directed at you is very different from experiencing another person's attention as directed at someone or something else: "Imagine when, on catching a baby's eyes, you lean over and say hello and she bursts into tears. Then imagine observing the baby reacting that way to someone else saying hello to her. It matters powerfully whether the 'other mind' that you observe is turned towards you in engagement with you or towards someone else."[36] Although this is a description of adult experience, Reddy argues that an infant's experience is also powerfully informed by her perception of others as perceptive. Reddy's work suggests, therefore, that even in an infant's face-to-face engagements with others, a kind of incorporation is possible. In face-to-face engagement, it is the infant's experience of herself, rather than of some object or situation beyond her, that is informed by incorporation of others; the infant perceives through others to experience herself as attended to by others or as engaged in a kind of conversation with others.[37]

Furthermore, Reddy and others suggest that Trevarthen's distinction between primary and secondary intersubjectivity is not as pronounced as previously thought; they argue that infants, well before they are nine months old, experience others' attention as directed towards things other than the infants themselves. Reddy and Rossmanith, for example, note that infants "actively participate in joint cultural practices involving objects, e.g. looking at a book together from 3 months on, 'helpfully' lifting their bottom in nappy changing routines at 3 months, or covering and recovering their face with a blanket in peek-a-boo at 4 months.[38] Rossmanith and colleagues report that when three- to four-month-old infants and their caregivers are engaged in book-sharing activities, "infants actively participate by showing 'active interest' and being responsive, amenable to their caregivers['] lead, letting their attention and actions be guided, and readily accepting the caregivers' invitations to engage with objects offered."[39]

This research suggests that the phenomena of secondary intersubjectivity and joint attention may actually begin much earlier in life than previously thought. Even very young infants may not only perceive themselves through others but also perceive other things through others. This is not to say that important changes do not occur in the way infants interact with others as they grow older. Rather than conceiving of these changes as reflecting a shift from an experience of other people as objects to an experience of other people as subjects, however, these changes can be conceived, Reddy argues, as reflecting a shift in the meaning of others' attention.[40]

IV. Scaffolding

If, then, incorporation is conceived of as constitutive of the child perceiver, how might a child's perception be informed by her incorporation of others? In the first section of this chapter, I described my perception as "scaffolded" by my friend's, and references to a "scaffolding" relation between infants and other people do appear in empirical research on child development. The metaphor was first introduced in a 1978 paper by Wood, Bruner, and Ross titled "The Role of Tutoring in Problem Solving." "Scaffolding," they wrote, "consists essentially of the adult 'controlling' those elements of the task that are initially beyond the learner's capacity, thus permitting him to concentrate upon and complete only those elements that are within his range of competence."[41] Much of the research on parental scaffolding of infant activity focuses on children three years and older,[42] although Rossmanith and colleagues, whose work I discussed in the previous section, describe parental scaffolding behaviours with infants as young as three months old.[43]

Yet while the prevalence of scaffolding behaviours has since been documented quite extensively, there has been little discussion of them from a phenomenological perspective. I want, therefore, to conclude by exploring how such "scaffolding" – as a form of incorporation – might inform infant perception. My discussion will focus on three ways in which the world perceived by the infant might reflect the infant's existence as a body expanded through incorporation of another person; I will refer to these three ways as the dimensions of placement, engagement, and handling. In each of these dimensions, an infant does not so much perceive another person as perceive through her. While I will discuss each dimension as fairly distinct from the others, both temporally and conceptually, I think that in the end, they must be considered as inseparable. Thus even though one dimension may, in a particular situation, be dominant, it is probable that no dimension is ever completely absent. In addition, a child's perception may reflect these dimensions of incorporation even when there is no literal contact between a child and an adult: children see – and do not merely touch – through others. Finally, while I do not want to assign a strict age range to the term "child perceiver," incorporation is probably most easily discerned in infants and very young children. Nonetheless, I will use the more general term "child perceiver" because I do think that my comments are applicable to a much broader range of ages. Indeed, upon examination, many people who are otherwise considered adults may appear, as perceivers, to be much more like children.

First, unlike an adult, an infant's ability to move herself is quite limited. Thus while an adult usually carries herself from location to location, a child is usually carried by another person. It follows that the variety and range of locations in which a child perceives are available to the child only insofar as her movements are supported by an adult. While I can walk across a room to its far side, climb some stairs to an upper floor, or take a bus to the park on my own, these locations are available to a child only by incorporation. A child perceiver often has access only to those situations that another person gives her access to. Thus the perceptual experiences that are possible for the child are determined not by her individual body alone but rather by an expanded body that puts her in some locations and not in others. This first dimension of incorporation, then, is one of placement; a child's perceptions, one could say, take place through an adult.[44]

Second, once the child is carried to a particular location, the adult's involvement through incorporation usually does not end. An adult usually grasps situations without assistance, whereas a child often grasps situations while being held by an adult. The variety and range of comportments by which a child perceives, therefore, are available to her only insofar as they are sustained by an adult. I on my own can stand, turn my head, and bend without toppling over, but comportments like these, and the subsequent perceptual possibilities they offer, are often available to a child only by incorporation. A child's perceptual experiences are acquired with an expanded body that allows her comportments that her individual body would be incapable of. This second dimension of incorporation is one of engagement. Sometimes engagement is sustained through an adult's quite literal grasping of the child.

Yet the adult's incorporation into the grasping child may also be more subtle. An adult may sustain a child's comportment, for example, by specially preparing a location for her and thereby ensuring that she will be able to assume those comportments that are possible for her. Thus not only can adults make a place impervious to a child, by removing certain possibilities from it, but they can also make a place susceptible to a child, by adding certain possibilities to it. Adults, for example, may get a crib whose sides are both high enough to prevent a child from falling out and low enough to allow the child to pull herself up and look over the edge. Likewise, adults will usually fill a crib not with heavy barbells but with soft toys that the child can lift and move.

Finally, once the child is engaged in a particular situation, the adult's involvement through incorporation often still continues. Thus while an adult usually handles situations on her own, a child often handles situations with an adult. The precise comportments adopted by the child, therefore, are often only discovered insofar as her exploration is supported by an adult. For example, I guide my own hand over a dog with an appropriate pressure and motion for petting it; for a child, this comportment is often first achieved when an adult begins by petting the dog herself and then, with her hand on top of the child's, guides the child's hand over the dog. Similarly, a child may at first be able to bring a cup or utensil to her mouth only when her hand is escorted by an adult's. Thus the perceptual experiences of the child are achieved with her body expanded into another body that adjusts her comportments in ways that her individual body would not. This third dimension of incorporation is one of handling. As with engagement, handling may sometimes be sustained through tactile contact between a child and an adult. However, an adult may also adjust a child's comportment with her facial expressions or by making changes to the situation handled by the child; an adult, for example, may frown as a child attempts to climb a shaky chair, or she may instead steady it for her.

In conclusion, given the example of the blind man with which this chapter started, one might have assumed that incorporation is limited to tactile perception. Throughout the chapter, however, I have purposefully referred to incorporation as a shift from the perceived to the perceptive rather than from touched to touching. As Reddy's second-person approach captures so well, both adult and infant experience can be deeply informed by visual perceptions of other people as well as by the aural and tactile perceptions of others. When one is engaged with another person – whether this engagement is a dyadic face-to-face interaction or a triadic interaction focused on some third object or person – the entire structure of one's experience can be transformed by incorporation.

NOTES

1 Cf. James J. Gibson: "When in use, a tool is a sort of extension of the hand, almost an attachment to it or a part of the user's own body, and thus is no longer a part of the environment of the user. But when not in use, the tool is simply a detached object of the environment, graspable and portable, to be sure, but nevertheless external to the observer. This *capacity to attach something to the body* suggests that the boundary between the animal and the environment is not fixed at the surface of the skin but can shift" (*The Ecological Approach*, 41, italics Gibson's).
2 Gallagher and Cole's distinction between body schema and body image is also helpful for conceptualizing bodies whose limits are not marked out by the skin ("Body Image and Body Schema").
3 Cf. Plato: "Education isn't what some people declare it to be, namely, putting knowledge into souls that lack it, like putting sight into blind eyes ... Education takes for granted that sight is there but that it isn't turned the right way or looking where it ought to look, and it tries to redirect it appropriately" (*The Republic*, 190).
4 See also Merleau-Ponty's remarks about "intercorporeal being" in his discussion of "reversibility" in *VI*, 185–8/143–5.
5 Joan Didion, *The Year of Magical Thinking*, pg. 5, italics hers.
6 Merleau-Ponty, *Structure of Behavior*, 166.
7 Merleau-Ponty, *Structure of Behavior*, 166.
8 Merleau-Ponty, *The Structure of Behavior*, 143[167].
9 Merleau-Ponty, "The Child's Relations with Others," 119.
10 Ibid. 119.
11 Gallagher, *How the Body Shapes the Mind*, 83.
12 Welsh, *The Child as Natural Phenomenologist*, 42.
13 Piaget, *The Child's Conception of the World*, 169.
14 Freud, *Civilization and Its Discontents*, 13.
15 Welsh, *The Child as Natural Phenomenologist*, 72.
16 Ibid., 102.
17 Ibid., 105.
18 Maclaren, "Embodied Perceptions," 65
19 Ibid., 65.

20 Ibid., 65. See also Russon, "The Virtues of Agency" and "Between Two Intimacies"; and Simms, "Milk and Flesh."
21 Merleau-Ponty, "The Child's Relations with Others," 117.
22 Merleau-Ponty, *Consciousness and the Acquisition of Language*, 32–3[34].
23 Merleau-Ponty, *Consciousness and the Acquisition of Language*, 33[34].
24 Merleau-Ponty, "The Child's Relations with Others," 119.
25 See, for example, Gallagher, "The Practice of Mind," 83–108; and Stawarska, "Mutual Gaze and Social Cognition," 17–30.
26 See Reddy, *How Infants Know Minds*, 91.
27 Trevarthen, "The Concept and Foundations," 16.
28 Ibid., 17–18.
29 Reddy, *How Infants Know Minds*, 90–119, 150–82.
30 As I have argued elsewhere, it may be helpful to shift the focus away from other people as having minds and towards other people as perceptive; see Bredlau, "Husserl's Pairing Relation."
31 Reddy, *How Infants Know Minds*, 26. Meltzoff and Moore, for example, have demonstrated that infants less than seventy-two hours old can imitate adult facial expressions such as tongue protrusion and mouth openings ("Newborn Infants Imitate Adult Facial Gestures," 702–9). Since these infants have had no opportunity to observe their own facial expressions, their ability to imitate an adult's facial expressions demonstrates that they do not relate to adults simply as perceived. For additional discussion of Merleau-Ponty's claims about infant perception in light of studies on neonate imitation, see Gallagher and Meltzoff, "The Earliest Sense of Self and Others," 211–33.
32 Reddy, *How Infants Know Minds*, 26.
33 Ibid., 27, italics Reddy's.
34 Ibid., 27.
35 Ibid., 23.
36 Ibid., 27.
37 For further discussion of how a child's sense of herself is shaped by those around her, see Maclaren, "Embodied Perceptions," 63–93; and Russon, *Human Experience*, 51–74.
38 Rossmanith and Reddy, "Structure and Openness."
39 Rossmanith, Costall, and Reichelt, "Jointly Structuring Triadic Spaces," 9–10.
40 Reddy, *How Infants Know Minds*, 234.
41 Wood, Bruner, and Ross, "The Role of Tutoring," 90.
42 For a brief overview of some of this research, see Carr and Pike, "Maternal Scaffolding Behavior," 543–4.

43 Rossmanith, Costall, and Reichelt, "Jointly Structuring Triadic Spaces," 5, 9, 18.

44 I have selected the term "place" to evoke Edward S. Casey's rich discussion of place in *Getting Back into Place.*

PART II

Generality and Objectivity

5 Neglecting Space: Making Sense of a Partial Loss of One's World through a Phenomenological Account of the Spatiality of Embodiment

KIRSTEN JACOBSON

Merleau-Ponty criticizes both empirical and rationalist metaphysics for failing to explain or even to notice the way in which perception is forever involved in *discovering* and *creating* the meaning of objects and the world as a whole.[1] In his chapter "Space" in *Phenomenology of Perception*, he specifically argues that, contrary to the tenets of many rationalist and empiricist accounts, we are not in possession of our body as an object in a preset field. Our body is not something we experience as a conglomeration of fixed points that we know either by means of a "physical" map of neural data – as an empiricist would hold – or by means of a unifying map provided by consciousness – as a rationalist would claim.[2] Equally, our sense of orientation is not given to us as a pre-established feature of an existence bound either by the physical forces of gravity or by a perceptual form provided by one's consciousness – as the empiricist and the rationalist hold, respectively. Rather, our sense of orientation and even our basic sense of space are open to change and must be developed *in relationship with* our milieu.

This chapter begins by explicating Merleau-Ponty's insights into the role the body plays in shaping our sense of orientation and in shaping our basic experience of space. I then use Merleau-Ponty's notion of "spatial level" to provide a novel phenomenological interpretation of *spatial neglect* – a spatially revealing phenomenon that, I argue, common empiricist and rationalist approaches fail to explain adequately. I conclude that our ability to be oriented in different ways and even to neglect certain "objective" spaces altogether is only interpretable on the basis of a conception of spatiality that acknowledges the body's existential involvement in the production of space itself.

I. The Body and Space

Merleau-Ponty supports his criticisms of empiricist and rationalist analyses of spatial experience in part through his study of an experiment in which a person's "spatial level" is shown to shift from a "normal" level to one that is offset from this normal position. In this experiment, a man is situated such that he can see his surroundings only by means of mirrors that reflect his surroundings at a 45-degree angle with respect to his typical world axis. The man is then asked to perform basic tasks while looking at objects and their setting through this altered perspective. Initially, the man finds himself disoriented in this setting, and he cannot easily perform tasks that are otherwise quite familiar to him. Yet in spite of this initial experience of being out of sync or "oblique" with respect to his surroundings,

> after several minutes, and provided that he does not reinforce the initial anchorage by glancing away from the mirror ... the reflected room conjures up a subject capable of living in it. This virtual body displaces the real body, so much so that the subject no longer feels himself to be in the world he is actually in, and that, rather than his genuine legs and arms, he feels the legs and arms required for walking and acting in the reflected room – he inhabits the spectacle. (*PP* 297–8[260–1])

Merleau-Ponty argues that this man's new spatial level cannot be understood as a consequence of his learning a new set of correlations between his body's movements and the tilted scene – as the empiricist might contend – since this sort of correlative action would require a calculation for each new task and could not account for the experience he has of being ready and able to spring into any new action in any sector of the scene. Related experiments also rule out any rationalist explanation that assigns his shift to the powers of an overarching consciousness. For instance, Merleau-Ponty refers to an experiment in which subjects, who are able to make a shift in level like the one we have just described, are unable to experience a corresponding shift in the auditory levels of their surroundings.[3] Yet if the spatial level were a result of a power of an overarching consciousness, there would be no reason that the auditory shift should be difficult to establish.

Merleau-Ponty argues instead that the man's new spatial level is not connected to his body "such as it in fact exists, as a thing in objective space"; rather, it is connected to his body as a "system of possible actions, a virtual body whose phenomenal 'place' is defined by its task and by its situation" (*PP* 297[260]). In other words, his spatial level is *called for* by the situation with which he is confronted but is also brought about *in conjunction with* his abilities to find a way of moving and acting successfully in the given situation. The timing of the man's spatial shift when looking into the tilted mirror confirms this. The spectacle in the mirror becomes his own – *his* spatial level – at the same time that his sense of his body and its abilities aligns with the objects it encounters in a way that allows him to successfully carry out his tasks.[4] This possession may be of a wholly different orientation than that which he has in his daily life; nevertheless, he feels completely at home in this new level of embodiment.

Although the body has no pre-set or pre-given orientation that guarantees our spatial experience, it has been of central importance in collaborating to establish this level. As Merleau-Ponty writes: "But even if the body, considered as a mosaic of given sensations, does not trace out any direction, the body as an agent, on the contrary, plays an essential role in establishing a level" (*PP* 297[260]). The body should be understood as a *capacity for* shifting possibilities, for accepting shifting orientations. As Merleau-Ponty observes: "The possession of a body *brings with it the power of changing levels* and of 'understanding' space, just as the possession of a voice brings with it the power of changing pitches" (*PP* 299[262], my emphasis). Thus, the shift in spatial level following the experimental environmental shift of 45 degrees must be recognized as belonging to a cooperative or reciprocal relationship between the man's surrounding environmental situation and his own "personal" situation of embodiment. Neither works independently of the other; a spatial "home" is found when they are able to coordinate with each other and move forward together, and this can be said to owe neither solely to the "activity" of the man nor entirely to the "passivity" of the man under the pressure of environmental demands.

Since the body is intrinsically tied up in the development of our spatial levels, the body and its specificities not only allow us to achieve certain levels but can also serve to block the development of certain imaginable and even common spatial levels. Using only our own natural abilities, we cannot, for example, take up free-flowing movement in the sky as a bird can; nor can we make agile movements through treetops like a monkey or glide across the surface of water as a water spider does. In other cases, it is not a matter of "natural" human limitations or needs that keep us from certain spatial levels, but rather of a lack of developed habits. The rock climber, for instance, can scale steep cliffs owing to the years of practice she has put into learning how to move about in the levels of these settings; most people could not even set foot or hand on her familiar terrain. There are also some levels that are typically available to human beings and that require no extraordinary means of habituation, but that may not exist for others owing to fundamental differences connected to their bodies. Examining one example of such a difference – the phenomenon of spatial neglect – will allow us to see still further into the role the body plays in our spatiality and, at the same time, to see the inadequacies of common rationalist and empiricist accounts for explaining spatial experience.

II. Neglecting the Phenomenon of Spatial Neglect

After suffering a stroke, some people not only become paralysed on one side of the body but also "neglect" the world on the side of their paralysis – indeed, sometimes they do not even recognize that they are paralysed on that side.[5] These individuals generally fail to respond to questions about the "paralysed" side of the world, fail to report obvious events or features of that side, fail to acknowledge unaccomplished tasks on that side, and so forth. If such a person is rotated 180 degrees, however, she will come to acknowledge the previously neglected side, but will simultaneously fail to acknowledge the side of the world she had recognized prior to rotation.

Notwithstanding these "failures," these subjects are not *blind* to this paralysed side – a fact that proves problematic for any empirical or physiological explanation of this phenomenon. For instance, spatial neglect sufferers tend to notice vigorous or large motions on this side such as a quickly moving person or a flashing light. Even more strikingly, they demonstrate in certain cases that they can and do notice or respond to details that they fail to acknowledge explicitly. For instance, one study describes an experiment in which patients suffering from spatial neglect pertaining to their left side were shown two nearly identical drawings of houses. In one of the drawings, however, flames appeared in the left-hand windows of the house. Although the subjects reported the drawings to be identical, they also reported that if forced to choose between these "identical" houses, they would prefer to live in the house that – although they themselves did not explicitly mention this feature – did not have the flames coming out of its left side.[6] In another example, a spatial neglect patient would not eat the food on the left side of her plate; yet, "knowing" that she was missing something, she would, after finishing with the right side, move herself around the plate until she found more food, and continue doing so until no amount of turning would produce more food.[7] In both of these situations, there is a definite spatial omission: the subjects do not explicitly acknowledge that they are experiencing something on the "missing" side. Yet in both situations, as well as those in which vigorous movements are detected, they do show some type of recognition that they have noticed something on their "neglected" side. These examples demonstrate that these persons at some level have the ability to see their "neglected" side, even if they generally do not acknowledge this. Thus they cannot be described as *blind* to that side. These observations indicate that physiological and empirical accounts are inadequate on their own as explanations of this spatial phenomenon, for such accounts assume some sort of anatomical fault as the cause of the sensory deficiency, yet the phenomena of spatial neglect does not reflect the consistency or predictability associated purely with a damaged organ. Let us consider this problem more specifically in terms of one prominent physiological approach to explaining spatial neglect.[8]

A popular neurological explanation of spatial neglect focuses solely on patients with left-hemisphere spatial neglect and identifies the damage as existing in the right brain lobe and its accompanying neural circuitry.[9] Neurologists have associated the right lobe with "global" aspects of sensory perception; by contrast, the left lobe is considered to have a smaller "spotlight" and to be responsible for the perception of things happening *entirely* on the right side of the person's external world.[10] Thus, neurologists assert that when the right lobe is damaged, a person loses a "global" sense and has only the right-side-of-the-world "spotlight" provided by the left lobe. As a result, the patient does not notice the left half of the world.

There are significant problems with this explanation, however. To begin, this sort of account fails to explain how, as we have seen, such patients *are* able to notice things on the left side when the situation demands it. Moreover, this account cannot explain how many spatial neglect sufferers recover a "full" spatial view even though their paralysis and related brain damage persists.[11] Perhaps most significantly, such an account fails to offer an explanation for those persons suffering from *right*-hemisphere neglect. According to this account, people suffering damage to the left lobe should retain their ability to see the whole world, given that the global vision provided by the right lobe should compensate for the loss of the "spotlight" ability provided by the left lobe; yet a significant number of left-lobe stroke victims experience spatial neglect in the right hemisphere. Thus, this empirically based account, and its positing of a physical structure that should "perform" with consistency and predictability (or, at least, with shifts in behaviour for which the theory itself can readily account), does not have the flexibility needed to explain adequately the spatial neglect phenomenon.

It is also relevant to note here that it has been common in the literature on spatial neglect to emphasize or even to single out patients with left-hemisphere neglect.[12] Yet large numbers of people have right-hemisphere neglect that accompanies the paralysis of their right side and damage in their left-brain lobe. One study suggests that the existence of right-hemisphere neglect patients has been overlooked or at least underemphasized.[13] The authors reviewed a series of spatial neglect studies among stroke sufferers and noted that in these studies, 43 per cent of persons with right-brain damage were identified as showing signs of left-hemisphere spatial neglect, but also noted that a full *21 per cent* of patients with left-brain damage showed right-hemisphere spatial neglect. Already the sizeable occurrence of spatial neglect in left-brain stroke victims calls for a different account than the one given by the right-lobe damage theory. These numbers become even more striking when one considers that the same study found that reports of spatial neglect in left-brain-damaged stroke victims *were less likely to be reported* or were being *measured by inappropriate testing strategies*, given the other types of problems that arise in left-brain stroke victims. These points could suggest that studies into spatial neglect arising in conjunction with left-lobe damage may not be considered closely or carefully enough – perhaps because they cannot easily be accounted for by the prevailing neurological theory, which emphasizes the role of the right lobe.

A purely psychological or rationalist account also fails to capture the full nature of spatial neglect. A psychological account typically identifies this problem as arising out of an emotional need to repress the recognition of the horrible loss the person has suffered through the paralysis. Merleau-Ponty would argue that such an interpretation rightly addresses the significance of the problem in the person's life but that it does not properly identify the cause of the disability. Notably, it does not attend to the role of the body in shaping this disturbed perceptual experience.[14] Instead, it assigns the denial to a psyche that represses those representations of the world that are associated with the paralysed side of the body. Thus, the psychological account takes up a position similar to the rationalist one insofar as it conceives of the psyche as an overarching and unifying power that gives its form to all perceptual experience. As such, it cannot explain the perceptual *exceptions* experienced by these subjects. For instance, certain types of physical stimuli or apparatuses can trigger these patients to make open admissions regarding their "missing" side. Thus a mirror placed on the patient's "good" side can allow the patient to see and respond to objects on his or her "missing" side, and to do so with awareness and even pleasure.[15] Stimulating nystagmus or the use of prisms can also lead to voluntary recognition of the previously absent side.[16] If the psyche and its need for denial are responsible for and capable of securing the subject's spatial neglect, the stimuli in these experiments should not be able to break through to the subject. Thus, the psychological account joins the physiological account in falling short of explaining the complexity of this phenomenon.

III. The Spatial Level of Spatial Neglect

Returning to our analysis of spatial levels, we can, however, provide a *successful* account of spatial neglect.[17] Let us take as a starting point Merleau-Ponty's assessment of similar cases: "The motor disorders in cerebellar injury cases and those of psychic blindness can only be coordinated if the background of movement and vision is defined not by a stock of sensible qualities, but by *a certain manner of articulating or of structuring the surroundings* " (*PP* 145[117], my emphasis). Thus, rather than thinking of the paralysed person's spatial neglect as merely a sign of neurological damage or of an intellectual repression of such damage, we should understand this neglect as the general structure that this person is able to bring to his world. These patients have suffered a sudden widespread loss of capacities primarily based on one side of the body. Moreover, the reach of their condition does not apply just to one or two select activities; it has systemically affected their whole life. In other words, they are not facing an isolated impossible activity or even a set of them, but rather an entire *sphere* of brand new impossibilities.

Since, as we saw earlier, our spatial level arises as our body and its abilities align with the objects we encounter in a way that allows for our projects to be successfully carried out, it is no surprise that a person who has suddenly lost the use of an entire side of his body may experience a corresponding contraction in his spatial experience, in his experience of his world.[18] Merleau-Ponty's description of the experience of the phantom limb is helpful here:

> At the same moment that my usual world gives rise to habitual intentions in me, I can no longer actually unite with it if I have lost a limb. Manipulable objects, precisely insofar as they appear as manipulable, appeal to a hand that I no longer have.
>
> *Regions of silence* are thus marked out in the totality of my body. (*PP* 110[84], my emphasis)[19]

Thus the spatial neglect experienced by stroke victims can be understood as *tied up with* their inability to take up a particular range of actions; correspondingly, the spatial level they do experience reflects the world that the patients *can* inhabit. This claim is further supported by research showing that spatial neglect patients are often able to locate objects on their neglected side when they are asked to locate a thing *to use* for a specific purpose (instead of being asked to locate an object identified by its name) and when they are also able to take up this use in some meaningful way. For example, a person with spatial neglect may not explicitly notice "a cup" on her neglected side, but she may be successful when directed to find and use "something that can be used for drinking" on that side; this person's "neglected" side is, thus, "activated by *affordances* of objects."[20]

We begin to see the significance of this discrepancy in abilities when we consider Merleau-Ponty's discussion in *Phenomenology of Perception* of the patient Schneider, who is able to grasp an area of his body where a mosquito is biting him but who is unable to point to the same part of his body on mere command.[21] Merleau-Ponty argues that this shows an inability on Schneider's part to navigate in objective space; instead, he is wholly caught up in situational space – the space of habitual activity. Merleau-Ponty's argument suggests that Schneider's inability rests in a certain form of captivation: owing to his injuries, he has lost the ability to free himself from already established meanings; he cannot develop or even easily consider new forms of meaning. As such, he remains largely captivated within those motions and those spatial levels already set up by him in his past, and he struggles significantly when asked to depart from these to take on a form of behaviour that would diverge from an established grounding. Schneider's relative comfort with concrete movements and ineptness with abstract movements help Merleau-Ponty identify a crucial distinction between abstract and concrete movement: "The background to concrete movement is the given world, the background to abstract movement is, on the contrary, constructed ... [Concrete movement] takes place within being or within the actual, [abstract movement] within the possible or within non-being; the first adheres to a given background, the second itself sets up its own background" (*PP* 141–2[113–14]).

Schneider's inability to perform abstract movements points to the primordial character of spatial experience *as lived*; but it also underscores the significance for "normal" spatial experience of an ability to be able to step back and cease being captivated by already established ways of *living* space. Schneider's spatial experience has become frozen in its habitual ways, and thus he no longer possesses the element of openness that was essential for the development of those very habits by which he is now captivated.

Studies have shown that patients with spatial neglect tend to experience space much like Schneider. For instance, a patient with spatial neglect is able to bisect a line fairly accurately when allowed to grasp a pole at the mid-point, but, when asked merely to point at a mid-point of that same pole, demonstrates an imbalance that favours the side on which spatial neglect is not present.[22] As in the case of Schneider, the spatial neglect patient shows signs of being able to navigate space successfully when the spatial task is wrapped up in activity, but not when asked to step back (so to speak) and reflect on an abstracted spatial system. A person suffering from spatial neglect, like Schneider, is also stuck within a rigid habit body. Before considering the specifics of her situation, let us consider more closely the nature of habit and the habit body.[23]

As we have already begun to see in our discussion of the *established* character of habitual actions, a description of the habit body as "rigid" to a great extent successfully captures the habit body's very character: the habit body is the institution of a particular way of being that provides a stability from which a person confidently goes forth. But it is important to recognize that this stability has been *developed* and is, therefore, constitutively open to further development. Habit is *initially* inaugurated in situations in which a person's body is lived as a *body at this moment* – namely, in those situations when the body does not yet possess an already established means of responding to the given situation. In such situations, the body is actively called upon to respond in a specific, present way; the body must react here and now in order to *find* a way to navigate *this* situation. Over time, and through continued efforts at this particularized and particularizing behaviour, the body develops a habit for dealing with like situations. Future encounters with like situations are experienced as a general call to the body to respond in already established ways.[24] In this way, the situation and the body itself lose the character of particularity and presentness and instead are experienced according to generality and the past. The body recognizes a situation of this "general sort" and responds in a corresponding "general way."

For instance, a person must first learn the path to the location of a new job, and when doing so must pay explicit attention to the specific street names and required turns. This attentive action may need to be repeated multiple times if the pathway is sufficiently complicated, but eventually the path becomes integrated into the person's experience such that she no longer needs to attend actively to the required streets and turns. Instead, she finds herself able to direct her attention elsewhere – to a song on the radio, a problem she is working on solving, a conversation with a friend in the car, or the like – and while doing so finds herself arriving at her destination barely having noticed her effort to do so. She has been living out of her habit body – a body that typically does not announce its efforts insofar as these efforts have become woven into the body in much the same way as our breathing happens under the surface of our conscious activity. This "inattentive" and generalized relationship to our body can be so strong that we can be led by our bodies through actions that explicitly counter what we had set out to do. For instance, once having established her pathway to her job, a person may inadvertently find herself arriving at her workplace when she had intended to head to a nearby store; while she was immersed in thinking about something else, her body led her along the path to which it had become habituated. In this example, we see how a person's body lives significantly out of the past. While the present to a certain extent is responsible for calling up certain ways of behaving in a person, this very present is often experienced in terms of past experiences that serve to generalize the very way the present is encountered by the person. In a significant way, then, it is not the present that is encountered, but rather the past that is here and now being re-encountered. It takes a certain commitment to activity on behalf of a person to be able to respond with particularity to this moment – that is, to live from her body-in-this-moment. It is in such moments that a person can work to develop new possibilities for taking up and living out a situation.

The spatial neglect sufferer's habit body has ceased in significant ways to remain open to this possibility of new development. Her body is holding on tightly to one way of having and navigating a world even though it is no longer capable of having such a world; as a result, her perception of that world closes her off from noticing those arenas where the "I-cannot" looms. Similarly, the person with the phantom limb lives out of a no longer actualizable world, but her repressive attachment to the past world is experienced in such a way that she cannot see her limb's absence and the ways in which this absence fails to allow her to connect fully to that past world she retains. The sufferer of spatial neglect represses that portion of her world that would push her to address the need to develop a new world relation, a new habit body. A spatial level, like a limb, is a development and a capacity of ours. The sufferer of spatial neglect, like the phantom limb sufferer, lives out of her past capacity and in doing so overlooks her arena of present incapacity – not as a mere psychological blind spot, but rather insofar as the past, not *this* present, is what is being lived – and that past cannot be maintained if the present demands of the situation are to be incorporated into it.

Thus, like Schneider, the spatial neglect patient lives within those givens that were developed prior to her bodily injury and cannot "set up" a new, spontaneous background for a spatial engagement that abstracts from what is already given in her experience. The spatial neglect patient *can* grasp successfully at the middle of the pole, because this is an activity she has performed countless times prior to this moment in comparable situations – such as picking up a stick, carrying a ladder, grasping a door handle, etc.; this action is a generalized activity that builds upon her past habits of manipulating her surrounding world. In such situations, she finds herself in a recognizable world. Merleau-Ponty makes a parallel claim about the world of the person with a phantom limb:

> The body is the vehicle of being in the world and, for a living being, having a body means being united with a definite milieu, merging with certain projects, and being perpetually engaged therein. In the evidentness of this complete world in which manipulable objects still figure, in the impulse of movement that goes toward it and where the project of writing or of playing the piano still figures, the patient finds the certainty of his [bodily] integrity. (*PP* 110[84])

In the case of the sufferer of spatial neglect maintaining this wholeness does not involve preserving a missing limb and its capacities, but rather overlooking that region of the world where a whole sphere of incapacity presently looms. The spatial neglect patient encounters trouble, then, when asked to take herself out of her already established habits of spatial engagement, because such a demand asks her to live *creatively* in the here and now, to develop a spatial relationship that has not already been established, even while her body, in its state of partial paralysis, is hindered in doing so. Thus to enter fully into the realm of the present is to ask her to consider her body and its spatial possibilities not in terms of what has already been established, but in terms of what could be done now. Since with such a question she is confronted with what she can no longer do, she will, as far as she can, avoid facing this question. She is asked in this scenario to respond on the basis of her body at this moment, but it is *this* body out of which she is not yet living; she continues to live through the habit body of her past.[25] To maintain this unmaintainable stance, she lives in a contracted world that corresponds to that arena in which she can continue to carry out her life through the established general ways of her past.

In significant ways, this explanation resembles (and Merleau-Ponty acknowledges this) that of the psychologist whom Merleau-Ponty criticizes. Spatial neglect *is* a form of denial regarding the inaccessible side of the world. But this is not simply a "psychological" denial; it is wrapped up as well with what the person *can do*.[26] The important shift here is to recognize that consciousness is a matter not of having certain volitional attitudes, such as "I think," "I affirm," "I deny," and so forth, but rather of being able to partake in certain activities, such as "I watch," "I desire," "I move," and so on. As Merleau-Ponty writes: "Consciousness is originarily not an 'I think that,' but rather an 'I can'" (*PP* 171[139]). Thus the stroke victim's denial is not one relegated to an isolatable thought or emotion about a certain isolatable fact of her existence. Rather, the subject is suffering from a systemic lived inability to propel herself forward from the one side of her body, and her consciousness reflects this inability. Merleau-Ponty supports this assessment when he writes that

> the life of consciousness – epistemic life, the life of desire, or perceptual life – is underpinned by an "intentional arc" *that projects around us* our past, our future, *our human milieu, our physical situation,* our ideological situation, and our moral situation, or rather, *that ensures that we are situated* within all of these relationships. This intentional arc creates the unity of the senses, the unity of the senses with intelligence, and the unity of sensitivity and motricity. And this is what "goes limp" in the disorder. (*PP* 169[137], my emphasis)

Thus, the person's loss of the ability to do things on one side of her body is conjoined with an inability to find herself in the situation belonging to that side. She cannot act or reach out to this side of the world, for *there* is a world of "I cannot."[27] Insofar as she, as being-in-the-world, cannot summon up or experience her agential self there, she does not find this part of the "objective" world. Instead, she lives within a spatial level – a world – that matches her current existential possibilities.

This spatial level effectively seals off that part of the "present" world that cannot be accessed by the subject; her world is thereby preserved according to the abilities of her past. She lives in that world that is delimited by the "I can" that is able to express itself without challenge – that is, within the realm marked out by her "I cannot." The realm she no longer "sees" is, then, that arena where she would fundamentally encounter her current self not in terms of an "I can" but of an "I cannot." Merleau-Ponty's analysis of the phantom limb again helps delineate this phenomenon. Substituting "contracted world" for "imaginary arm" in his recognition of the repressive character of the lived experience of the phantom limb patient, we can extend his point to spatial neglect and recognize this experience also as an existential clinging to a former way of being:

> The phantom limb [or contracted spatial world] is thus, like a repressed experience, a previous present that cannot commit to becoming past. The memories called back before the amputee's mind induce a phantom limb [or contracted spatial world] not in the manner in which one image calls forth another in associationism, but because every memory reopens lost time and invites us to again take up the situation that it evokes. (*PP* 114[88])

The spatial neglect sufferer lives out her body and her present through her past – something that all of us do insofar as we live in and through our habits, but also something that, as long as her "illness" persists, she, like the person with a phantom limb, does to the exclusion of present demands that ask her to work on developing new habits, that ask her, in other words, to respond from her body at this moment.

Spatial neglect does not, of course, accompany all injuries or bodily limitations and is not experienced by many paralysis victims. The fact that there is a *range* of spatial possibilities supports the claim that spatial levels are tied up with our overall ability to open onto our world by means of our bodies. So for an "able-bodied" person, an impossible activity may be a source of frustration, but it does not – as it does for the stroke victim – signal a sudden change in what one is able to do, nor is it usually connected to an entire sphere of impossibilities. Still, as we have seen with the rock climber, people are not equally open to all spatial levels. Thus, an objectively identical place can have entirely different meanings for different people depending on their possibilities for acting in that place. Insofar as the non–rock climber would claim that there is no path to ascend the cliff wall, she may be viewed as neglecting this spatial realm or, at least, as not being open to it. But this neglect does not generally pose or point to a problem for this person, since it is not a lack that permeates the person's daily experience of moving about or her basic life concerns and interests; it is limited to this particular instance – and to an optional form of entertainment at that. Perhaps as importantly, neglecting the paths up a steep cliff is not noted by others as a "problem" – that is, as an inability to see something that people for the most part are required to see in order to function "normally" in a shared interpersonal world. Again, for most people, the cliff as a pathway is an optional, personal sort of sight. Put another way, the non-climber's "spatial neglect" is not wrapped up with a fundamental existential change or lack in her bodily means of opening onto a world. Thus, for an "able-bodied" person, an inability to attain a certain spatial level does not lead to the type of spatial contractions experienced by the stroke victim. Even in persons who do suffer from spatial neglect, this neglect often diminishes or even disappears even though their paralysis remains. Once again, for this to occur, these "disabled" persons must have been able to find a new way of *creating* and *discovering* the spatial level of a "full" world – whatever that may mean for each particular person, and they must do so from within the bodily abilities they possess.

Conclusion

It is the *establishment* of a spatial level that provides us with our stability, with our orientation, and this establishment is one of co-creativity – that is, the mutually interpenetrating relationship of our body and our milieu. Merleau-Ponty supports this conclusion when he writes that "we do not stand up straight because of the skeletal mechanism nor even through the nervous system's regulation of muscular tonus, but because *we are engaged in a world*. If this engagement is absent, the body collapses and again becomes an object" (*PP* 303[541–2], my emphasis).

In these moments of collapse, we also catch sight of the *contingency* of our experiences of an "upright" world, as well as of ourselves as oriented beings who have a *developed* spatial setting.[28]

Thus, our surroundings (e.g., the forces of gravity and buoyancy) place certain demands on our bodies, but this does not determine in advance how we will establish our spatial level in light of those demands. Moreover, if the body is to be capable of taking on new spatial levels – as it, in fact, is – it must be *creatively open* to the demands of the new situation.[29] Spatial variations and even *spatial neglect* are possible because the body does not *guarantee* that we will or *insist* that we have to do things in a *given* way. Rather, it is *through our bodies* that we can find *varying* ways to take up the demands of our situations. As we have seen, it is *as* a person's body *finds* a way to become coordinated with the demands of his situation that a spatial level unfolds before him. In other words, "he is his body and his body is the power for a certain world" (*PP* 136[109]). The space that arises therein is a space of bodily based potentialities, not that of a pre-given, "impersonal" Euclidean framework. Our ability to achieve a sense of space as "objective" finds its very basis in a lived experience of space in which the body at this moment and its *struggles* to grapple with the particular demands of a situation are paramount. Indeed, as we have also seen, our creative attempts to establish our spatial level can be more or less attuned to or capable of responding to the demands of certain aspects of our lives, and thus can be more or less effective with respect to certain contingencies we face. It is at moments when this particularizing character of our body fails us – such as in the case of sufferers of spatial neglect – that we can especially see the necessarily *creative* element that is essential to our ability to develop our own spatial levels *and* also a "healthy" – that is, sustainable and intersubjectively sharable – notion of generalized space.

It is equally at this point that we can find certain implications for therapeutic work for spatial neglect (and similar disorders).[30] In identifying spatial neglect as a "disorder," we are asserting that there is something inadequate about a human stance that presumes that its private way of seeing the world is *the* truth of reality. While the person with spatial neglect indeed demonstrates her own co-creative engagement between her body and her surrounding situation, we recognize the stance of someone with spatial neglect as one that meets with resistance and likely some form of failure, because the subject is forcing her own terms onto the givens of the situation in such a way as to obscure the particular demands of those givens. By contrast, mental and physical health – and, by extension, successful human living – requires an ability to be vulnerable and creatively receptive to the demands of the world in its givenness. In other words, it requires that a person be able to act as a subject that respects the character of subjectivity *as a realization of objectivity*. The world must be able to show itself through us. This does not amount to reducing the subject to a projector of an alien reality; rather, it acknowledges that the very nature of subjectivity is *to be* insofar as it is engaged with what *is* beyond itself. In any case, the problem here seems to arise from an inability to see the situation as it stands on its own terms.

Yet as our analysis of spatial neglect demonstrates, this reflection is not guaranteed. As subjects, we are essentially characterized by our freedom. No immediate one-to-one correspondence between subjectivity and the world could exist, for this would be a situation lacking any reflection; it would be a situation of necessity, of natural law. Thus, central to subjectivity is the possibility for misinterpretation of the world and its demands. And here it is important to note that the world does not have one and only one interpretation. The givens it offers will, according to the situation in which they are taken up, have different, equally "valid" interpretations. That said, it is not *any* interpretation that gears adequately onto the givens of reality. Mental health is characterized by a subject's ability to reflect adequately the reality of his or her situation, and the sufferer of spatial neglect demonstrates multiple ways in which her reflection falls short of a full engagement with this reality.

Therapy for the person with spatial neglect would, then, entail helping bring the subject into a new way of being that more adequately opens her onto the present demands being made upon her by the givens of the world.[31] As in any area of growth, this involves opening a person to a situation of vulnerability, a situation in which the way of being for which a person is aiming is not yet securely hers. It is because of this vulnerability that guidance is needed, in part because it is in moments of vulnerability that a person is most likely to revert to ways of seeing or acting that are most engrained in her – that is, that she is likely to retreat to her private stances on the world. The therapist can offer the spatial neglect sufferer a stability and a guidance that is not yet hers and that will allow her to maintain a stance of vulnerability to the world that she is not yet seeing because of her tendency to reflect only what she has already established for herself.[32]

Therapy is, then, a coming to reflect the world in its diversity, as that diversity can be reflected in you. Therapy is, in other words, nothing other than making a home in reality. This making of a home in reality is grounded in ongoing cooperation between living in vulnerability and living in security. It is living in such a way that our habit body is able to retain its character as a reliable home while also being open to the alien and the demand the alien places upon us for creating ourselves anew.

NOTES

1 Merleau-Ponty discusses these issues throughout his chapter "The Spatiality of One's Own Body and Motoricity" in *PP*. For the most relevant criticisms of empiricism and rationalism by Merleau-Ponty, see *PP* 36–9[13–17] and 50–6[28–34]. Note that while certain empirical and rationalist accounts may avoid some of the problems Merleau-Ponty identifies, the basic orientation of these schools of thought is rooted in ontologies that Merleau-Ponty argues will lead them to *miss* the very phenomena they are trying to explain.

2 For Merleau-Ponty's full criticism of the rationalist's and empiricist's accounts of orientation, see *PP* 290–303[253–65].

3 For this aspect of the experiment under discussion, see Merleau-Ponty, *PP* 296–8[259–61].

4 John Russon supports a similar conclusion in "Embodiment and Responsibility": "The world is what it is for us only because we commune with it bodily, and its meaningfulness is a significance in which we are already implicated. This is true from our primitive spatial inhabiting of the world, in which the orientation of things derives from our motor projects, all the way to the extremely sophisticated determinacies which are our social and intellectual existence" (294).

5 For clear discussions of this phenomenon (albeit with analyses of the phenomenon that Merleau-Ponty would largely dismiss), see Halligan and Marshall, "Neglect of Awareness"; Marotta, McKeeff, and Behrmann, "Hemispatial Neglect"; and Ramachandran and Blakeslee, *Phantoms in the Brain*, ch. 6.

6 See ibid., 117–18.

7 See ibid., 118.

8 While I will criticize here a neurological accounting of the phenomenon of spatial neglect, I also want to acknowledge that there is contemporary research in cognitive science that quite excellently utilizes and analyses

neurological data to offer phenomenologically adequate accounts of various "normal" and "abnormal" experiences. Prime examples of contemporary research include Gallagher, *How the Body Shapes the Mind;* Johnson and Lakoff, *Philosophy in the Flesh;* and Thompson, *Mind in Life.* Merleau-Ponty was himself inspired by the research conducted by Gestalt psychologists such as Köhler (e.g., see *Dynamics in Psychology*) and Goldstein (e.g., see *The Organism*).

9 For a full account of this position, see Halligan and Marshall, "Neglect of Awareness." See also Ramachandran and Blakeslee, *Phantoms in the Brain,* 44–6, 50–1, 115–17.

10 See ibid., 117.

11 See ibid., 119.

12 Ramachandran and Blakeslee, for example, in *Phantoms in the Brain,* claim that "neglect occurs primarily after injury to the right parietal lobe and not to the left" (117).

13 See Bowen, McKenna, and Tallis, "Reasons for Variability."

14 See Merleau-Ponty, *PP* 103–5[78–80], 142–3[114–15].

15 See Ramachandran and Blakeslee, *Phantoms in the Brain,* 124.

16 See respectively ibid., 144–7; and Parton and Husain, "Spatial Neglect," 118.

17 I make a related argument about the contraction of one's space as it relates to one's embodied existential situation in an article titled "The Interpersonal Expression of Human Spatiality." In it, I argue that the experience of the anorectic is one in which her bodily contraction and retractive gestures of not eating or participating in other common and significant human exchanges (around food of course, but also significantly around issues of communication) reflect a tangible spatial contraction in her world, a contraction rooted in an ailing interpersonal situation (usually that of the family) in which her voice is not heard and does not count. Supporting the idea (albeit certainly not intentionally) that the anorectic's world is contracted, the sister of one anorectic comments: "It is like her world is tunneled from here to there [points from her body to the floor] down to where the number points on the scale" (Charmaz, "Loss of Self, 176). Ultimately, I would argue that despite the difference in origin of the disorders, the anorectic's experience of embodiment has similar features of limitation to those of the person who has suffered a stroke, and that she also experiences a corresponding spatial contraction. For a relevant analysis of the experience of "losing one's self" in people with chronic illness and the corresponding constriction of one's world, see Charmaz, "Loss of Self."

18 Kvinge, Gjengedal, and Kirkevold support this conclusion in their analysis of the changed "life-world" of persons who have suffered a stroke ("Gaining Access to the Life-World," see esp. 64). Note that the discussion of the lived body presented in this paper (and by Merleau-Ponty) allows for the possibility that a person suffering a stroke may *not* develop spatial neglect; the way in which a person is able to take up his or her body is not dictated by his or her past even though it is very significantly supported by that past.

19 Russon, in "Embodiment and Responsibility," supports Merleau-Ponty's assessment when he writes that the body is "the parameters for possible bodily involvement which define the matrix of possible dimensions of perceptual experience" (294).

20 Behrmann, Ebert, and Black, "Hemispatial Neglect and Visual Search," 261 (my emphasis).

21 See Merleau-Ponty, *PP* 132–43[105–15] for a discussion of this example and of the distinction between pointing (*Zeigen*) and grasping (*Greifen*). For Kurt Goldstein's original discussions of this differentiation, see his essay "Über Zeigen und Greifen" and the also relevant "Abstract and Concrete Behavior" in *Kurt Goldstein: Selected Papers / Ausgewählte Schriften*.

22 See Robertson, Nico, and Hood, "Believing What You Feel." See also Goodale, Millner, Jacobson, et al., "A Neurological Dissociation." For significant research on the ability of action-based searches to "activate" previously neglected areas, see also Humphreys and Riddoch, "Detecting Action" and "Knowing What You Need"; see also Riddoch, Humphreys, Edwards, et al., "Seeing the Action." Also see McIntosh, McClements, and Dijkerman, "Preserved Obstacle Avoidance," for a related study in which neglect patients are unable to equally divide a line between two objects, but are able to *reach* "correctly" for something midway between the same two objects. See also Michel, Pisella, Halligan, et al., "Simulating Unilateral Neglect," for a study of induced spatial neglect in "normal" subjects that concludes that sensorimotor activity is crucial in establishing one's spatial range, and that spatial neglect cannot be understood merely as the effect of damage to the cortical brain areas.

23 The following discussion of habit and the habit body is informed significantly by Merleau-Ponty's analysis in *PP*, esp. 108–18[82–91] and 176–82[143–8].

24 For a related discussion of generality by Merleau-Ponty, see *PP* 197–8[162–3] and 259–60[223–4].

25 Although I have here been arguing that this behaviour marks an avoidance of abstraction, there is a certain way in which we could describe

this behaviour as a form of abstraction insofar as the patient is, in acting so, avoiding or repressing the particular demands of this situation and thus, as Merleau-Ponty argues, making a "passage from first person existence to a sort of scholastic view of this existence, which is sustained by a previous experience, or rather by the memory of having had this experience, and then by the memory of having had this memory, and so on, to the point that in the end it only retains its essential form" (*PP* 111[85]). The abstraction here is, however, one of having developed in the past a form of generalized experience and action, not one of a creative grappling with a present or future possibility. On the theme of living from a past, as this is played out in Merleau-Ponty's analysis of the phantom limb, see Russon, "The Impossibilities of the I."

26 John Hull, who went blind in his forties, uses Merleau-Ponty's discussion of the phantom limb to explain his own experience of the interrelationship of the psychic and the physiological, and the opening (or closing) of the world that arises when something impairs this "duo": "The problem for the disabled person is that the ordinary, habitual body, which relates us to the world, is no longer the same as the actual body. This knowledge is unacceptable, because one would be exiled from one's world ... The disabled person *cannot expect to adjust to the memory of the accident* or illness which caused the disablement, as other sad losses in life. *The moment of disablement is not one painful memory amongst others, but represents a change in the world itself, which is negotiated and understood through the whole body* ... What the disabled person remembers is not so much the accident as the world before the accident, and that past becomes blurred with the present ... One lives on a former experience ... So deeply imprinted into us are the stereotypes of our bodily action in the world, that we never really escape from them" (Hull, *On Sight and Insight*, 176). The phantom limb (or, in Hull's case, the bodily experiences of continuing to be and act in a world of sight) is an expression of an embodied conviction that one lives in a world that has been one's own – a world to which one belongs – and that cannot simply be dismissed or forgotten either "physically" or "psychically."

27 On the relation of the "I can" and the "I cannot," see Russon, *Bearing Witness to Epiphany*, 50–8; and "Spatiality and Self-Consciousness," esp. 223.

28 The sight of this contingency brings with it a sense of "vertigo" similar to that which Sartre discusses in *Being and Nothingness*, 50–2 and 65–81. On this theme, Merleau-Ponty writes: "The lability of levels gives not merely the intellectual experience of disorder, but also the living experience

of vertigo and nausea, which is the consciousness of, and the horror caused by, our contingency. The positing of a level is the forgetting of this contingency, and space is established upon our facticity" (*PP* 303[265]).

29 In "Lived Body and Environment," Shaun Gallagher offers a clear discussion of the symbiotic relationship, so to speak, between body posture and environment (see esp. 163–5). See also Leder, *The Absent Body*, 34–5.

30 I wish to thank Drew Leder and his commentary on a shorter version of this essay at the 2009 Eastern Division Meeting of the APA for helping me to consider further the therapeutic implications implied in my analysis of spatial neglect. The following section of the chapter owes in part to Leder's insights on this issue. I have also published work on the nature of agoraphobia (and to a lesser extent on hypochondria and anorexia), and on alternative therapeutic models for understanding these disorders. In this work, I began to develop my insights into how therapy and psychological health should be understood and pursued in light of the recognition that our experience of the world is dialogic rather than determinate. On this theme, see also my articles "The Interpersonal Expression of Human Spatiality" and "Agoraphobia and Hypochondria as Disorders of Dwelling."

31 There is an interesting parallel to make here between the therapy I am suggesting for someone suffering from spatial neglect and a possible extension of Merleau-Ponty's discussion of the empiricist as someone suffering from a certain "sort of mental blindness" insofar as he is a person whose system of thought may be able to build up "approximate equivalents" of the original structures of perception, but who is fundamentally operating in a realm of "subordinate truth" – i.e., within a realm of truth that "distorts experience" by failing to respond to its lived demands (*PP* 48–9[26–7]). Merleau-Ponty's phenomenological project could, then, be seen as a certain form of rehabilitative therapy for the empiricist (as well as for the psychologist) – a therapy that could allow these thinkers to return to what Merleau-Ponty calls "the *homeland* of our thoughts" (*PP* 48[26]). My argument in this chapter would suggest that the lack of being-at-home is the problem faced by both the sufferer of spatial neglect and the empiricist insofar as their ways of being-in-the-world have ceased being the supportive ground that allows them to be creatively responsive to the demands made upon them by their world. A fitting form of therapy for them would, then, be an invitation to return to a *participatory* form of paying attention to the world – an invitation to phenomenology, in other words – that may allow them to make a *living* home for themselves.

For a related discussion of the *developed* character of home, see my essay "A Developed Nature."

32 The practical details of such a therapy are beyond the scope of this chapter, but there are promising developments that support my proposal occurring in the intersecting work of phenomenologists and neuropsychologists. See, for example, Klinke, Zahavi, Hjaltason, et al., "Getting the Left Right"; and Klinke, Thorsteinsson, and Jónsdóttir, "Advancing Phenomenological Research."

6 Moving into Being: The Motor Basis of Perception, Balance, and Reading

DON BEITH

We tend to explain the movement of our bodies mechanically. When we do so, we assume that the body moves in a pre-existent space, by virtue of cause-and-effect relationships between its anatomical parts. On this view, the body moves according to its position in uniform space. Also, we tend to explain *learning* mechanically. This is true both in situations of explicitly learning to move and in other "cognitive" situations that do not manifestly involve movement. On such a view, learning involves understanding associations between already formed terms. For example, a child learns first to recognize objects, such as letters and sounds, then to recognize associations between these objects, as in reading letter/sound correspondences. This view of learning as cognitive association posits our capacity to learn as an independently relevant domain, one that is distinct from our capacity to move. These respective views of moving and learning, while separating the two domains, share the premise that each is a mechanical function in an already established world. I challenge these assumptions, employing insights from Maurice Merleau-Ponty's *Phenomenology of Perception,* first by demonstrating that moving and learning are *not* mechanical functions in an already established space, then by asserting that moving and learning are in fact concerted activities of establishing space that develop mutually.

I begin, in Section I, with Merleau-Ponty's conception of "motor intentionality," the idea that the body does not move according to the positions of an abstract space; rather, the body's movement is oriented by a sensitive awareness of its living situation. To demonstrate this point, I turn to a recent empirical study of joint formation in octopuses. The formation of the octopus joint is not ordered by measurable positions or anatomical components; rather, it is shaped by the vital projects of the octopus, such as grasping. The joints formed by the octopus do not reflect the imposition of limits on movement, but instead are vitally responsive developments that generate and increase possibilities of movement.

In Section II, I pursue this point about the self-developing character of movement, which is at the core of Merleau-Ponty's conception of habit. I use the example of learning a spinning kick in Taekwondo to demonstrate how the moving body concomitantly accumulates abilities of movement and sensitivities to spatial orientation. Learning to spin-kick involves developing increasingly sophisticated levels of the kinaesthetic sense of balance. Balance is not a cognitive capacity to locate the body in space, but a power of spatial orientation that the body develops by feeling itself in movement. The example of the spin-kick will demonstrate that perceptual and motor learning are inseparable and that they develop together successively in habit formation.

In Section III, I take a manifestly perceptual habit, reading – one seemingly defined by cognitive associations – and demonstrate that it is in fact accomplished as a development of bodily movement. I first draw on studies that demonstrate that reading development hinges on a pre-literate background of motor habits, such as posture and balance. Second, I argue that kinaesthetic memories developed by drawing and handwriting – learning to perceive words as expressive enactments of the body – are connected to good habits of reading. Taking up studies of dyslexia, I demonstrate that diminished motor habits, such as posture, balance, and handwriting, are linked with impaired reading habits. I contend that the habits we have to learn in order to read are embedded in a nexus of background motor habits, particularly habits of relating to words as means of bodily expression.

I. The Space of Movement: The Dynamic Formation of the Body

To have a body is not to look on it from the outside, as if it were just another thing in the world. When I move my body, I do not effect this movement as if my body were a piece on a chessboard. Nor am I contained by my body, or subject to it as to so many mechanical impulses and reflexes. I am my body, but this body is not a thing in an already determined space. I experience my coming to be as body, and my coming to be as body is equally the coming to be of space. In the *Phenomenology of Perception*, Merleau-Ponty describes this as a spatiality of "situation," opposed to a spatiality of "position" (*PP* 127[100]). My hand, for example, is not given to me as a thing defined by a set of measured distances and joint angles. My hand lies at no distance from me as an immediate potential for action, a vehicle with which I can move into space through vitally oriented movements, such as grasping. Grasping takes things and integrates them into my body: handrail, cane, pen, telephone, steering wheel, and more all become conduits of the handy action of my body. I have my body in the specific ways it comes to have space – grasping, walking, working, writing, speaking, driving, and so on. In each of these cases of moving, the moving configuration of my body and its orientation to and of the space around it are inseparable: "The spatiality of the body is the deployment of its being as a body, and the manner in which it is actualized as a body. By seeking to analyze it, we thus did nothing but anticipate what we have to say concerning bodily synthesis in general" (*PP* 185[150]).

The body is a potentiality that is realized in its moving spatial relations. It does not pre-exist these relations as an anatomical thing. The body does not move as a thing does, as a solid entity propelled by some external force through a change in locations. The body is *self-moving*. As mover and moved at once, the body is a mediated and dynamic identity. Aristotle, in his *Movement of Animals*, demonstrates that an animal can locomote not because its body is a solid "one," but because it is a "one that is a two," because it internally self-differentiates through its joints.[1] This internal differentiation allows a part of the animal to push while another part of the animal is pushed. Here motion and rest, as well as activity and passivity, depend on each other. Indeed, motion and rest, passivity and activity, cannot be conceived of as already constituted identities that then require each other. Rather, these roles are assigned relationally in the changing context of which parts are pushing and being pushed. The term that encompasses this relation of complimentary roles, one that therefore precedes the binary distinctions of moving/resting and active/passive, is the joint.

The moving body is not a fixed form of identity. The "parts" of the animal body and their roles are not given fixedly, but are cast and recast by ongoing movement. When I walk, my knees oscillate between extension and flexion as my lower legs reverse roles as ground-pushing platform and striding step. "In the case of joints," Aristotle writes, "the centres become now one potentially and divided actually, and now one actually and divided potentially"[2]: in the functional joint, the parts play relative, changing roles such that they are in themselves only potentially passive or active. When I injure myself, a part of the joint becomes fixedly passive, at which point the joint ceases to move because roles within it are fixedly divided. In the functioning joint, and in the moving body as a whole, the moving and resting, active and passive parts are not separable roles or even discrete "parts," such that Merleau-Ponty describes the parts of the body as "enveloping" each other (*PP* 185[150]). The body is organized as a self-moving institution, both in and as movement: it is the self-enactment of the very difference through which it is realized.

It can be difficult to perceive the body as the potentiality to deploy space, rather than as a part a part of already determined space. When we look at human joints, for example, we see fixed points of articulation. Articulated joints are sediments of evolution that derive from a more basic self-articulating movement. Unlike the human, the octopus does not start out with articulated joints. In their study of grasping movement, Germán Sumbre, Graziano Fiorito, Tamar Flash, and Binyamin Hochner discovered that the octopus forms its joints on the move, by generating self-opposed, self-differentiating movements along its arms:

> When retrieving food to its mouth, the octopus actually shapes its arm into a quasi-articulated structure by forming three bends that act like skeletal joints ... The octopus manages to transform its extremely flexible arm into a structure that acts like a jointed appendage ... The arm generates two waves of muscle contraction that propagate towards each other, setting the second, or medial, joint at their collision point. This is a remarkably simple mechanism for adjusting the length of the arm segments according to where the object is grasped along the arm. The arm also forms a proximal joint near where the arm meets the body, and a distal joint near the suckers that have grasped the food.[3]

As with the human limb, there is a self-opposition between two interdependent but opposed muscular contractions. What is remarkable here, however, is that this self-opposition is not enabled by an anatomical joint, but rather institutes the joint itself as "these two waves stiffen the quasi-articulated structure, and the pattern of muscle activation responsible for the medial-joint formation and is generated or initiated around their collision point."[4] The self-moving body, through self-opposed motion, articulates a joint, and this joint in turn allows more particularized self-opposed movements within the arm segments it generates, allowing for the formation of proximal and distal joints as well as the activity of grasping.

The body exists as actualization of potential: not the mathematical potentiality of a fixed anatomy but the expanding organic potentiality of a living body. As Merleau-Ponty explains: "The mechanics of the skeleton cannot, even at the level of science, account for the privileged movements and positions of my body" (*PP* 187ff[151ff]). The octopus limb counters the skeletal "bad faith" of our everyday interpretation of bodily movement because here there is no skeletal anatomy. In the octopus, joints come to be in movement and appear more immediately as a dynamic "structure" or *Gestalt*, the term Merleau-Ponty uses to characterize the living body as a "being in which the expression is indistinguishable from the thing expressed."[5] The octopus arm, unlike our own, has a "virtually infinite" range of motion. Here we see the openness of the body – its existence as potentiality – in the seemingly infinite range of possible articulations of the octopus arm. At the same time, in watching the joints materialize in the arm we see that the arm does not exist in an infinite Cartesian space of "positions," but in a vital, living space of situations. The possibilities of the octopus arm are located in a lived "spatiality of situation," where movement is immediately meaningful in the terms of grasping, eating, and so on.

In the case of locomotion, we saw that the internal dividedness, the *intensive dynamics* of the leg joints amounted to an *extensive difference*, the expression of a meaning: walking. In the octopus we see that this holistic bodily self-enactment is an expressive response to the vital demands of the environment. Motor articulation does not occur across static, preformed positions but develops through sensitive engagement with a vital situation.[6] Yet in their study, Sumbre and colleagues nonetheless employ an interpretive schema that presupposes a Cartesian spatiality of position. They assume that the octopus either orients itself according to internal joint angles or by the relative coordinates of the limb and the grasped object:

> A still unresolved issue is whether movements are represented in the central nervous system by external coordinates (location in three dimensional space, x, y, z) or intrinsic coordinates (joint angle, muscle force). The premise is that the octopus relates to its own body and spatial environment cognitively, via its motor cortex. This poses a severe problem in the octopus because, abstractly conceived, the joint possesses virtually infinite "degrees of freedom."[7]

In this analysis, the joint is posited as a formation that happens to reduce the "degrees of freedom" in the octopus arm, simplifying space into terms that the "motor control" system can "master."[8] On this view, the joint is only accidental: it happens to represent a manageable subset of spatial coordinates that can achieve the grasping of an object. Yet the description of the joint articulation as "object-dependent" belies another explanation that does not separate "intrinsic" and "extrinsic" space by situating the body and the object as isolated spatial coordinates in indifferent space.

The motor coordination of the body is first a matter of perceptual orientation, and conversely perceptions are revealed as motile dispositions and potentialities of the body. This relation is not mediated by abstract spatial position; rather, it appears as an already achieved, immediate correlation between body and world. The octopus arm, in this view, is ordered not to physical coordinates but to a *graspable* thing within reach. Merleau-Ponty writes of how this functional, vital value institutes a holistic bodily coordination: "In the very first attempts at grasping, children do not look at their hand, but at the object. The different segments of the body are only known through their functional value and their coordination is not learned" (*PP* 185[150]). It is within the terms of practical movement that bodily coordinates unfold. Grasping involves a double-movement of reaching and contracting or pulling, but where these two movements meet and are orchestrated hinges on the dynamic terms of the practical relationship with the grasped thing. The point of muscular collision in the octopus arm determines the position of the medial joint, but this point fluctuates and self-adjusts according to how the object is grasped.[9] The octopus does not merely happen upon a "kinematic constraint" in the abstract control of a geometrical orientation.[10] The joint angles fall out of the practical task – they are intrinsic to the self-opposed movement of grasping.

Merleau-Ponty's "spatiality of situation" explains how the "kinematic constraint" of the joint is no accident of "evolutionary convergence" but a mechanism that unfolds within the intrinsic demands of animal movement.[11] That joints are dynamic formations entails that movement precedes anatomy; therefore, as Scott L. Hooper writes, in an analysis of octopus joint studies, "muscles predate the evolution of hard body parts."[12] Hooper suggests that the joint as a motor control mechanism is not a "late, derived and specialized natural mechanism"; rather, "flexibly creating different 'skeletons' of stiffened muscles against which other muscles can act may be the mother of all motor control."[13] It is tempting to look at the octopus and to imagine the freedom we could enjoy if we had freely articulating limbs. This amounts to seeing our own articulated joints as mere physical limitations, which again implies prioritizing geometric over lived space. But in fact, grasping joints in the human and the octopus are formed out of a common vital demand. Indeed, our own sedimented joint structures enable us a more general freedom than that of the octopus. Human joint structures are internalized articulations rather than tasks we must attend to in each movement. That we do not have to form an arm in every movement allows us to move the threshold of our motion into more complexly self-opposed movements in our wrists, knuckles and fingers. Our general capacity to grasp in sophisticated ways is built upon the foundational readiness of our skeletal joints. Passivity is intrinsic to our most developed activities, which rely on past activities, which are not left behind but remain integrated – in this case skeletally – within present activity as its scaffold.

II. Formative Movements: The Systematic Articulation of Bodily Habits

In acting against itself and forming limits within itself, the body expands its possibilities of movement. The self-opposition of the body is the opening up of a space of possible motion, which provides a scaffold for more precise and particularized self-limiting movements, which are themselves more sophisticated relations with the environment. After the octopus forms the medial joint, it can send opposed muscular contractions along each limb segment and form further joints. This means that possibilities of action or "degrees of freedom" in the moving body are not abstractly present in advance, to be selected among; rather, the body generates more generally meaningful possibilities of movement by increasingly particularizing itself.

This cumulative intensification of the body's possibilities to concomitantly move and perceive is Merleau-Ponty's conception of habit. In habit, movements that begin as contingent and optional are integrated by the body such that the body's subsequent movement is ordered to them, rendering them necessary and automatic. Movements that are initially difficult and that demand explicit attention become familiarly ready and inconspicuously fluid potencies of the body. Habits are not volitional activities, for situations themselves immediately prompt and impel our habitual actions. When I am driving the car and an animal runs into the road, I immediately step on the brake pedal, yell for my passengers to hold on, and look through the rear-view mirror. These actions are not optional, and these things – brake pedal, word, mirror – are not indifferent pieces of the world: they may have been this when I first learned to use them, but they become far more – the immediate portals of my bodily action and perception.[14]

Habits are not spontaneous acts; rather, they depend on and continue a past. This past is not merely passed over, elapsed; instead, what was a particular, peculiar past remains active in the present as the general form of what it means to live in the present. Our passive dependence on the past is not a matter of strict determination: the past action in its particularity does not mandate the same habitual response every time, although neurotic habits can tend to this. Rather, the development of specificity into generality in habit means that unprecedented situations can appear as meaningful, such as when I hear configurations of words I have not yet encountered. In our earlier analysis, the joint showed us that space is not originally uniform; in an analogous way, habits disclose to us that all times are not strictly commensurate, that some *formative* moments have pivotal, privileged impact. As we develop, the present is increasingly structured by these habitual accumulations of past significance, such as these words that I cannot but hear as English. This structuring of the present by the past means that the more we develop, the less there can appear a neutral present as such – the "truth" of the present is embedded in its past. Yet these "past" habits, as they enable the significance of the present, are not thematically or explicitly present to us – we perceive and act *through* them, so these habits are never immediate objects of our study or manipulation.[15] Understanding this structure of habit yields ontological insights about time and meaning and also exposes teachers' and learners' basic terms of practice.

As a teacher of the Korean martial art Taekwondo, I generally find I can recognize when students are ready for new, challenging stages of learning. When I discern that a novice has a good sense of balance and pivoting, as well as proficiency with some of the more complex kicks, I have them begin practicing a spinning kick (*duirochagi*) by integrating the more basic moves with which they are already comfortable. The challenge is for the student to divide each leg into a separate function. In the ground leg, one by one, the toes, foot, ankle, leg, hip, torso, arms, and head must rapidly spin around into a resting position, each in turn snapping into place as the "ground" for the subsequently pivotal part. The issues of coordination that are raised by the need to balance their weight over their feet while spinning are further complicated by the fact that they must learn to kick with precision by timing the phases of the kick to the different moments of shifting balance, having both spin and balance culminate in a resting position at the final instant of the kick. Each one of the spin-kick's movements involves a finely developed habit. Body parts move to serve as platforms for the others, and *pari passu* one habit must serve as a ground for subsequent, more sophisticated habits. First one learns to kick laterally (turning kick), then to flex the knee joint while kicking laterally (hooking kick), then to spin, then to kick while spinning (and, indeed, much earlier than all of this, one had to learn to walk, stand, and understand instructions). These preliminary movements must all become background habits – they are not thematized in the spin-kick itself. When I, the expert, spin-kick, I do not thematize spin plus kick: I simply spin-kick. And this is why the movement is so hard to teach to an uninitiated beginner: the student must learn to *perform the movement as a whole.* It is the movement as a whole that determines the roles and functions of the parts in their intertwined activity and passivity.

This "whole" movement of the body is not simply self-oriented – it is oriented by the world, but here body and world are related dynamically and developmentally. Through increasingly self-opposed movements are achieved richer engagements with the world. Merleau-Ponty says of habit that "the body, then, has understood and the habit has been acquired when the body allows itself to be penetrated by a new signification, when it has assimilated a new meaningful core" (*PP* 182[148]). This is precisely what happens when I learn to do the spinning kick: I integrate two significances into a new one. The new significance is not *ex nihilo,* but neither yet is it a simple combination of existent habits: it is a transformation of them. As Merleau-Ponty movingly writes, "in this sense ... our body is comparable to the work of art. It is a knot of living significations and not the law of a certain number of covariant terms" (*PP* 188[153]). In forming new habits the body surpasses old habits but retains them as ground. The habitual stages of our formative past are pivotal in everything that follows.

III. From Movement to Perception: Learning to Read by Learning to Write

So far we have seen that motor habits are oriented to and ordered by relations with the *perceived world.* Motor habits such as the spin-kick involve a finely attuned sense of balance, whereas grasping and limb articulation require a coordination with the grasped object. Conversely, all perceptual habits are *motor oriented and realized.* This central thesis of the

Phenomenology of Perception is twofold: motility is not mere mechanism but is sensitive to the world, *and* perception is not merely receptive or disincarnated but always involves *moving* in the world. This coordination of motility and perception is the ongoing cumulative enactment of habit: "The analysis of motor habit as an extension of existence continues, then, into an analysis of perceptual habit as an acquisition of a world. Reciprocally, every perceptual habit is still a motor habit, and here again the grasping of a signification is accomplished by the body" (*PP* 189[154]).

In this section I study the correlate thesis to the idea that bodily movement is sensitively oriented: that perception is embedded in the development of motor capacities. Perception and movement are the mutually instituting dimensions of habit. To demonstrate this, I turn to a seemingly autonomous perceptual function, reading, and link its development to the acquisition of motor habits, particularly the habits of *making* written words in drawing and handwriting.

According to Merleau-Ponty, movement is "neither [mere] motility nor [pure] thought." Rather, "between movement as a third person process and thought as a representation of movement, an anticipation or a grasp of the result assured by the body itself as a motor power, a 'motor project,' or a 'motor intentionality'... movement is, indissolubly, movement and consciousness of movement" (*PP* 141[113]).

Moving and perceiving are not distinctly active and passive, doing and receiving, but are integrated, mutually enabling aspects of the body. Esther Thelen and Linda Smith note that in infancy, the distinction is far less established:

> If the infant accidentally moves [a rattle], and sees and hears the consequences, the infant will become captured by the activity – moving and shaking, looking and listening – and incrementally through this repeated action gaining intentional control over the shaking of the rattle. Piaget thought that this ... accidental action that leads to an interesting and arousing outcome and thus more activity and the re-experience of the outcome – [is] foundational to development itself. Circular reactions are perception-action loops that create opportunities for learning. In the case of the rattle, the repeated activity teaches how to control one's body, which actions bring held objects into view, and how sights, sounds and actions correspond.[16]

The child does not pre-possess a full awareness of its body. Moving is the discovery of body and world, but this discovery involves creativity, and the infant movement is the mutual *expression* of body and world. The perceived contours of things are shown through the body's new capacities for moving, and vice versa. Merleau-Ponty says of speech that "the word, far from being the simple sign of objects and significations, inhabits things and bears significations" (*PP* 217[183]). Original developments of movement and initial perceptions of the world are what Merleau-Ponty terms first-order expressions and not already established realities, or conventional, second-order expressions.

Of all of our perceptual capacities, reading is the one that seems most manifestly concerned with an established reality – namely, the text. On such a view of reading as passive, reading does not compose a text but instead involves first memorizing sounds, written symbols, and concepts, which are already established entities. Second, on this account, is the stage of learning the associations between these entities, associations that are themselves also predetermined. It is common that research into reading development is premised on the relationship between read-symbols and the ability to correlate them with already acquired auditory phonemes, spoken or heard.[17] This view of reading as passive – one that is held by many literacy researchers – opposes reading to the *activities* of speaking and writing. Like the motor theory that claims that the body must know determinate positions in space in order to position its limbs, these theories take visual and auditory symbols to be already possessed units, whose meaning is available and ready to be correlated with other already established meanings.

What this understanding of reading as passive overlooks is that *forming* written signs is crucial to the symbolic identification of those written signs with sounds and meanings. Many researchers in the fields of education, learning disability, and child psychology lament the lack of studies seeking to understand the developmental relation between handwriting and reading.[18] There are, however, "constructivist" investigations that begin with the premise that "readers construct or create [meanings] through a variety of active processes [i.e., construction, elaboration, prediction, etc.]."[19] If true of learning to read, this confirms Merleau-Ponty's criticism that "the link from the word to its living sense is not an external link of association" and supports his argument that meaning "inhabits the word" and that the subject does not receive, but so too *inhabits* the word and enters into the sphere of words by creating them (*PP* 234–5[199]). I contend that reading is a perceptual capacity rooted in our earliest childhood habits of moving, specifically in our habits of *establishing space* in posture and in drawing or *forming shapes*.

Learning to read involves taking motor habits that children already have and developing them towards perceptual habits. In her *Stages of Reading Development*, Jeanne Chall delineates a pre-literate stage and identifies kinaesthetic associations – including making sounds, name-scribbling, and even holding books – that will later play a central role in developing reading habits.[20] Yet many studies of learning to read English presuppose that these pre-literate sources of reading are strictly perceptual, encompassing the ability to aurally discern phonemes. This approach elides an examination of the child's pre-literate capacity to recognize and capacity to make pre-alphabetic marks. Countering this assumption, Li-Hai Tan, Theodore Spinks, Guinevere Eden, Charles Perfetti, and Wai Ting Siok, in a study of pre-literate development, show that in Chinese –a "logographic" language in which there are no systematic phoneme-to-grapheme correlations – the role of the *written* figure is critical. The pivotal skill in learning to read in Chinese is neither phonemic nor orthographic, since the words do not correlate to sounds or comprise a system of alphabetic spellings. Learning to make and distinguish increasingly precise written marks is the fulcrum of literate development:

> We sought to elucidate how writing mediates reading development ... The ability to draw simple objects does not involve orthographic processes and thus should not be related to reading ability ... Writing of Chinese characters requires a high-order organization of strokes and components that constitute the internal structure of the character. This motor activity may result in pairing of hand movement patterns and language stimuli and may help form long-term motor memory of Chinese characters ... On this motoric mechanism, writing [characters, as well as] ... other sorts of activities involving precise, coordinated movements such as picture drawing should be also correlated with reading performance. Furthermore, because pictures of objects possess higher visual complexities than do many Chinese characters, picture drawing, in general, demands finer motor activity than writing.[21]

Through early experiences of feeling herself originating written shapes, irrespective of spelling knowledge, the child founds habitual associations that will later be pivotal for developed habits of reading. Kinaesthetic awareness during habit formation is described by Betty Sheffield as the "earliest, strongest, and most reliable memory channel."[22] This research in Chinese literacy formation sheds light on this neglected aspect of English literacy.

Learning to make shapes and sounds is the bedrock habit of literacy. Describing the first phase of English literacy as preceding the recognition of visual word-symbols, Chall explains how a child develops the prerequisite habits kinaesthetically. At first, via semi-phonetic associations, the child discovers written words as a capacity to make sounds, to break these sounds into parts.[23] This method of alphabetic instruction is extensively employed in Waldorf schools' "Living Alphabet" method, which makes alliterative connections between letters and sounds or letters that sound or look like objects (e.g., B is drawn on a page with a pictured bee, while the teacher says "bee"/"B"). Other methods use "inventive spelling" whereby a child is encouraged to develop complete phonetic associations between sounds and letters by spelling phonetically. The experience of initiating the *formation* of letters is paramount here. Marilyn Jager Adams notes that "the act of writing newly learned words results in a significant strengthening of their perceptual integrity in recognition. This is surely a factor underlying the documented advantages of programs that emphasize writing and spelling activities."[24] Research suggests that forming words out of pre-formed letters (i.e., typing) involves less motor-neural activity than forming the words by writing.[25] Further studies have found that adults learning a foreign alphabet by handwriting (i.e., rather than typing) achieve consistently higher retention scores.[26] Still other studies have demonstrated a negative result, correlating difficulty in learning to read with dysfunctional or substandard writing.[27]

In short, the background to perceptual abilities is a kinaesthetic one: "Hand kinaesthetic elements seem to be the essential link between the visual cue and the various associations which give [a] word meaning. In other words it seems to be necessary for the child to develop a certain kinaesthetic background before he can apperceive the visual sensations for which the printed words form the stimulus."[28] It is by feeling words as eliciting movement, encountering them as things the child can *do* with her body, that the child can take them up into her body and enter into a figurative comportment through them, such as the moment Merleau-Ponty describes when a "contraction of the throat, the sibilant emission of air between the tongue and teeth, a certain manner of playing with our body suddenly allows itself to be invested with a *figurative sense* and signifies this externally. This is no more and no less miraculous than the emergence of love from desire, or that of the gesture from the uncoordinated movements at the start of life" (*PP* 235[200]). By forming these kinesthetic habits in early childhood, we are "conveyed out of ourselves" into the reality of the words among which our body can move. The basic motor habits of handwriting must become sufficiently reliable that they remain "past" and function in the background of more *figurative* habitual syntheses.[29]

To further demonstrate the link between writing and reading, and *a fortiori* moving and perceiving, I demonstrate how an impediment to a motor habit can be an impediment to a perceptual habit, and vice versa, and in complex ways. The body is a constellation of developed/developing motor-perceptual habits. Merleau-Ponty writes, for example, that there is no such thing as a "purely motor" disturbance "that does not, to some extent, affect the sense of language" (*PP* 236[201]). Once they develop a relation to linguistic expression, motor habits are strongly imbued with expressive significance. People can be impaired in their ability to speak creatively and purposefully by generating their own words, demonstrates Merleau-Ponty, while still being able to habitually respond to questions and to read provided texts while "putting expression into it." Thus even if the capacity to express new meanings is impaired, the words still bear a trace of the style that learned to first give them expression: the "speech or words carry a primary layer of signification that adheres to them and that gives the thought as a style, as an affective value ... rather than as a conceptual statement" (*PP* 222[188]). The point is that *how* we learn to express ourselves in our basic *style* of speech and writing is one of the most engrained, irreversible habits. The motor style with which we make speech is our vehicle into more developed, expressive linguistic experience; it brings meaning to life as "an organism of words, it installs this new signification in the writer or the reader like a new sense organ, and it opens a new field or a new dimension to our experience" (*PP* 222–3[188]). It follows that early, basic motor habits of expressive style are the basis of more developed linguistic capacities, such as expression and reading, such that an impediment in one of these firmly rooted motor habits can be a tenacious obstacle to language development.

Some educators and psychologists have noted that dyslexia is not a mere cognitive impairment, but often involves an idiosyncratic complex of motor habits and gestural capacities. These researchers have connected dyslexics to a range of different motor difficulties, such as troubled manual dexterity, or balance and coordination. Notably, Michael Wolff has researched coordination issues in dyslexia, Mary Haslum has studied issues of balance and hand drawing in dyslexics,

Samuel Orton has pioneered a multisensory approach to reading education, and educators have employed the Waldorf method of holistic learning.[30] Orton's research in the 1930s called for dyslexia to be viewed as inseparable "from accompanying conditions, [declaring] that poor handwriting, left-handedness, inverted letters, and stuttering ... all went together in severe cases."[31] For focused perceptual habits to operate, a host of motor habits must be reliably in place. Not unlike the fixed point of the joint that is necessary as a fulcrum, these motor habits are a platform for more developed activities. Indeed, posture itself is a precondition for more developed habits such as writing, reading, and learning. When writing, one needs to sit or stand and stabilize most of the body in order to concentrate on the autonomy of the wrist and fingers. This motor ability to sit and focus equally undergirds the perceptual ability to hold fast and listen to what someone else is saying. To be taught, students must learn to occupy and express themselves in educational settings, such as classrooms. Some researchers have zeroed in on a lack of postural control as an impediment in the attention and general motor skills of dyslexics.[32]

Reading and writing also depend on habits of motor fluidity. An inconsistent, arhythmic writing speed has been linked to difficulties in attention and focused ability to read. Writing fluently requires simpler habits such as a sufficiently firm yet relaxed pencil grip and pressure on the page, as well as the aforementioned balance and stability. Furthermore, the ability to write smoothly without pauses or backtracking contributes to reading from left-to-right and moving with the direction (or *sens*) of the text.[33] Indeed, left-handed writers subjected to right-hand–oriented writing conventions and lessons often experience difficulty moving with the grain of this *sens*. Even more, ambidextrous students often perceive certain letters (such as d, b, q, and p) as indistinguishably reversible.[34] For such an ambidextrous child, learning to spell by rote memory alone, rather than by consistently assigned writing tasks involving directional coordination, "is apt to be very short lived."[35] In light of these studies, I contend that students benefit in reading development when they are trained to do more than recognize a word as a pure formula, an ordering of letters – they need to learn to make these words, to integrate what they might immediately perceive as reversible letters as *belonging* to the directed context of their body's capacity to move, in this case to write. Cursive writing could be a facilitator in teaching the contextual directedness of reading, by fostering both a sense of letter orientation and a steady writing speed. Writing and reading, like walking and so many other habits, are skills that need to function autonomously without moment-to-moment attention. In cursive, as opposed to printing, the formation of each letter is not a discrete motor task but belongs to the movement as a whole. Writing a word as a whole, as a *Gestalt*, on my hypothesis, is of a piece with seeing it as a whole: with *reading* it.

The habits that enable this autonomy of writing are not necessarily habits of writing. Roderick Nicolson, a dyslexia researcher, supports a dyslexic "automation hypothesis" where dyslexics originally have difficulty with habits such as balancing, which preoccupy conscious attention.[36] When a child has to focus on balancing and cannot facilely associate words, word association can disrupt or block the formation of reading habits.[37] For early printing to figure as a task, so that it too can become background for more advanced writing, other habitual skills must first "handily" abide in the background.

The study of habit reveals the import of formative educational habits, and of the practical habits of fine motor control cultivated by such activities as drawing. Learning to draw and hand-write at an early age has been broadly linked to strong early reading development, and "virtually all children who lag in reading skill in K-1 are dysfluent printers."[38] This supports Betty Sheffield's thesis that dyslexic students often "need to use writing in order to learn how to read."[39] Any melioration of dyslexia needs to be contextualized by the particular habits of each student: perhaps the student has a poor sense of balance, posture, and attention but a strong capacity to draw, or perhaps the student has a fine sense of balance but has difficulty orienting letters. While writing is a keystone of reading, writing itself pivots on more basic skills.

These studies demonstrate that what is important is that children not be merely subjected to formal training in habits and repetitive drills that reverse errors or develop motor/word associations. A motor impediment can involve an existential crisis, a felt lack of self-expression, a need to discover oneself in grasping and apprehending the world, in finding oneself confirmed there rather than being made to move there. It is crucial, then, to expose children to drawing and handwriting as a space of confirmation, as a space where they can express themselves and encounter writing and reading conventions as something they *do*, and to be attentive to their specific habits when they cannot read or write.

Conclusion

I have argued that Merleau-Ponty's philosophy offers resources to challenge our habitual way of understanding the body as a mechanical thing in a physical world. Also, I have demonstrated that learning is not a merely mechanical associative practice and that learning has bodily as well as cognitive dimensions. Learning is bodily accomplished, yet at the same time the body is always accomplished by learning to move. In consulting studies of octopus joint formation, we discovered that from its earliest stages the body itself is accomplished by orienting its movements towards vital purposes, such as grasping food. It is by developing habits of this body that senses by moving, and whose moving is always sensibly oriented, that we can attain developed perceptual abilities. We saw – for example, in learning to perform a spin-kick – that sophisticated motor habits depend not only on a background of more basic motor habits but also on a similar progressively developed background of perceptual habits, such as balance. Developed perceptual activities, even those most putatively independent of bodily movement, remain bodily activities. Reading, we saw, was nested in bodily habits such as posture, habit, and left-to-right motor orientation. Moreover, motor habits related to the creative expression of words, such as drawing and handwriting, are strongly correlated with the perceptual capacity of reading. Impediments in these motor habits, as I demonstrated by consulting studies of dyslexia, are often at the root of impediments of perceptual habits. Just like the body that expressively establishes space, perceptual learning depends on habituated capacities of movement and expression. In this chapter I developed the insight that the body learns to move by learning to orient itself to the world, as in the octopus and the spin-kick, into the correlate thesis that even our most presumably cognitive orientations to the world, like reading, are bodily realized.

NOTES

1 Aristotle, *The Movement of* Animals, ch. 1.
2 Ibid., ch. 2.
3 Sumbre et al., "Octopuses Arm Movements," 767–72.
4 Ibid., 770.
5 For Merleau-Ponty's definition of dynamic *structure* or *form*, see his *The Structure of Behavior*, 49[47], 101[91], 147–8[137].

6 Merleau-Ponty describes the system by which movements self-orient around practical norms: "The workbench, the scissors, and the pieces of leather are presented to the subject as poles of action; they define, through their combined value, a particular situation that remains open, that calls for a certain mode of resolution, a certain labor. The body is but one element in the system of subject and his world, and the task obtains the necessary movements from him through a sort of distant attraction" (*PP* 136[108–9]).
7 Sumbre et al., "Octopuses," 770. See also Hooper, "Motor Control," 283–5.
8 Sumbre et al., "Octopuses," 771.
9 Ibid., 767.
10 Ibid., 767.
11 Ibid., 771.
12 Hooper, "Motor Control," 284.
13 Ibid., 284.
14 "To habituate oneself to a hat, an automobile, or a cane is to take up residence in them, or, inversely, to make them participate within the voluminosity of one's own body. Habit expresses the power we have of dilating our being in the world, or of altering our existence through incorporating new instruments" (*PP* 179[145]).
15 For a further phenomenological account of habit, see Russon, *Human Experience*, esp. chs. 2, 3, 5.
16 Thelen and Smith, *A Dynamic Systems Approach*, 167.
17 On this predominant view, the primary indicator of reading proficiency is a child's "battery" of phonemic distinctions. See Noble and McCandliss, "Reading Development," 370–8.
18 Several authors who propose a relation between handwriting and reading express disappointment that there have not been more studies of this relation. See Adams, *Beginning to Read*; and Nicolson and Fawcett, "Dyslexia"; Sheffield, "Handwriting"; and Vernon and Ferreiro, "Writing Development."
19 Shanahan, "Nature of the Reading-Writing Relation," 466–77.
20 Chall, *Stages of Reading Development*, 13.
21 Tan, Spinks, Eden, et al., "Reading Depends on Writing," 8781–5.
22 Sheffield, "Handwriting," 22. Thelen and Smith also cite a study by Reeke and Edelman of a computer program that learned by forming "self-organizing" categories by tracing out letter shapes. Thelen and Smith, *A Dynamic Systems Approach*, 167.
23 Chall, *Stages of Reading Development*, 13.
24 Adams, *Beginning to Read*, 131.

25 See Mangen, "The Haptics of Writing."
26 Longchamp, Boucard, Gilhodes, et al., "Learning Through Hand- or Typewriting Influences," 802–15.
27 Rose, "The Writing–Reading Connection." Rose cites empirical studies, by teachers he interviewed, of early writers and correlates writing fluently, at a high speed, with reading well.
28 Henry, "Structured, Sequential," 3–26.
29 "Consciousness trails behind itself the completed syntheses, they remain available, they could be reactivated, and as such they are taken up and transcended in the total act of numeration. What is called pure number or authentic number is only a promotion or an extension through repetition of the constitutive movement of every perception" (*PP* 168[136]).
30 These relationships are widely documented. See Wolff, Michel, Ovrut, et al., "Rate and Timing," 349–59; and Haslum, "Predictors of Dyslexia?," 622–30; Nicolson and Fawcett, "Dyslexia"; and Ramus, Pidgeon, and Frith, "The Relationship," 712–22.
31 Henry, "Multisensory Teaching," 8, citing a letter from Orton.
32 Ramus, Pidgeon, and Frith, "The Relationship," 719.
33 Thomson and Gilchrist, *Dyslexia*, 45. Here the authors explicitly connect impediments in writing speed and direction to dyslexia. This study is also extremely useful for understanding the motor "ergonomics" of dyslexia and other perceptual linguistic impairments.
34 Sheffield, "Handwriting," 33, citing Eglington, "Handedness and Dyslexia," 1611–16.
35 Henry, "Structured, Sequential," 8.
36 The automation hypothesis is further explored by Ramus, Pidgeon, and Frith, "The Relationship," 713.
37 See Nicolson and Fawcett, "Dyslexia."
38 Sheffield, "Handwriting," 31, citing Martlew, "Handwriting and Spelling," 275–90.
39 Sheffield, "Handwriting," 22.

7 On the Nature of Space: Getting from Motricity to Reflection and Back Again

NOAH MOSS BRENDER

> Bodily space can only truly become a fragment of objective space if, within its singularity as bodily space, it contains the dialectical ferment that will transform it into universal space.
>
> *PP* 131[104]

In our everyday dealings with the world, we tend to think of the world as a collection of more or less independent things. These things are spread out in space, occupying definite positions at various distances from one another. My body is one of these objects, and I navigate the world by moving through this space and dealing with the various things I find within it. To make this navigation easier, I can construct a map that represents the relative positions of things in the world. If I want to be even more systematic, I can place these things within a system of coordinates that captures the distances from any one thing in the world to any other. This familiar experience of space as measurable and calculable, as something that can be represented and reckoned with, is what drives most traditional philosophical accounts of space.

If, like the empiricist, we make this objective space the object of our investigations, we discover a closed system of exact relations that encompasses all of being. The parts of this system, like the parts of a machine, are external and indifferent to one another – *partes extra partes*, as Merleau-Ponty often puts it.[1] Everything is spatially related to everything else, but these spatial relations are entirely extrinsic to the things they relate. My body must have its place within this world-machine, and be subject to the same mechanistic laws as every other piece of extension.

If, on the other hand, we follow the idealist in turning our attention to the *knower* who is presupposed by this description of space, we find that we have implicitly taken up a position outside of the system we were describing. From this Archimedean vantage point, we can see the whole of being spread out before us and comprehend it all at once. Indeed, it turns out to be precisely this comprehension that holds space together: since the parts of space are perfectly indifferent to one another, they require a consciousness to synthesize them into a whole, in the same way that a craftsman puts together the parts of a machine. My body is still one of these parts, but I discover that I have taken leave of it, that I am something quite different: a constituting consciousness, for whom my body is just another constituted object.[2]

It turns out that the seemingly innocuous description of space with which we began generates an untenable Cartesian dualism of body and mind, or the unsatisfactory alternatives of empiricism and idealism. Either I am part of space, and must myself be subsumed under the mechanistic laws I use to describe it; or space is nothing but the thought of space, and so it is part of me, a structure or content of my consciousness. Merleau-Ponty offers us a way out of this dilemma by calling into question the traditional assumption – underlying both empiricism and idealism – that objective space is identical with being itself.

Although objective space appears to us as something natural and immediate, it is in fact a product of reflection. It is a space rendered transparent and ideal, purified of opacity and ambiguity, of anything that cannot be made explicit and univocal. Everything personal has been removed from this space, leaving a universal framework that stands above and encompasses every particular point of view. In the *Phenomenology of Perception*, Merleau-Ponty calls our attention to a different experience of space, equally familiar but largely ignored by traditional philosophical accounts. This is the experience of space as we live it through our bodies: the experience of my body's "knowing" where things are and how to move with respect to them, without my being able to articulate this knowledge explicitly or to say how I have come by it. This is the space of what Merleau-Ponty calls "motricity [*motricité*]," a space of movement and action rather than contemplation and knowledge. It is organized around my own body, and it orients my movements and perceptions. Things have meaning in this space, not in terms of their objective positions, but in terms of my bodily "I can" (*PP* 171[139]). Merleau-Ponty gives this spatial, bodily meaning the name "motor significance [*signification motrice*]" (*PP* 178[144], translation modified). In contrast with the meaning produced by reflection, motor significance is characterized by ambiguity, generality, and opacity. The motor significance of my world is not explicit or transparent to me, but forms the invisible background of my familiar movements.

The great importance of Merleau-Ponty's rediscovery of lived space lies in its revelation of a kind of meaning that is not symbolic or discursive, a bodily sense expressed in movement rather than represented in thought. This motor significance is of a different order than the meanings produced by reflection. Indeed, the two look so different that reflection typically refuses to recognize the former as meanings at all. Merleau-Ponty argues, however, that the bodily meanings that reflection disavows are in fact its root and source. Thus the space of reflection, which has traditionally been identified with being itself, is actually derivative of lived space:

> [F]rom the moment I want to thematize bodily space or to work out its sense, I find in it nothing but intelligible space. But at the same time, this intelligible space is not extricated from oriented space, it is in fact nothing but the making explicit of it, and, detached from this source, it has absolutely no sense. Homogeneous space can only express the sense of oriented space because it received this sense from oriented space. (*PP* 131[104])

This chapter will examine the relation between these two spaces in order to describe precisely how objective space is constituted and how it expresses the sense of lived space. Our investigation of the nature of space will equally be an investigation of the nature of reflection. The power of reflection – in which we seem to take up a universal standpoint outside of our own bodies and survey being as a whole – is what drives traditional claims that we are disembodied minds or transcendental egos. In order to refute these claims, this chapter will attempt to show that reflection is a *bodily* capacity, a power given to bodies with *logos* – the distinctive capacity for *symbolic* conduct. By placing reflection in its bodily context and returning it to its roots in pre-reflective meaning, we will also arrive at a new understanding of space as a natural meaning – a sense without thought – that is not fixed but evolving, a way of making sense that our bodies have inherited from the living bodies that came before us.

This chapter's argument will be drawn principally from a dense and under-studied passage in Merleau-Ponty's first book, *The Structure of*

Behavior.[3] We will follow the *Structure*'s strategy of illuminating human experience via the study of animal behaviour – in this case, that of the chimpanzee. The purpose of this is twofold. First, the contrast with the chimp's experience of space will reveal and problematize structures of human spatiality that we ordinarily take for granted. Second, it will allow us to show how our experience of space as uniform and universal is a development of the animal's sense of space as oriented around its own body.

I. Multiplicity of Perspective and the World of Things

Our discussion of chimpanzee behaviour will draw on two experiments by the *Gestalt* psychologist Wolfgang Köhler, which Merleau-Ponty describes in *The Structure of Behavior*.[4] In the first of these, Köhler noticed that a chimp who had learned to use boxes as instruments would not use a given box in this capacity as long as another chimp was sitting on it (*SB* 127[116]).[5] It might sit or lean on the box, but it seemed incapable of perceiving the box as an instrument until the other chimp stopped using it as a seat.[6] According to Merleau-Ponty, this shows that the chimpanzee experiences the box-as-seat and the box-as-instrument as two entirely different objects (*SB* 127[116–17]). It cannot see the box as a seat that can be used as a tool, or a tool that was once a seat. In other words, the chimp does not experience the box as a single *thing* that can appear in different ways and be used for different purposes. Rather, the box appears only as part of an integral situation. When this situation changes, the box is transformed along with it, leaving no trace of its earlier meaning. The chimpanzee cannot switch back and forth at will between perceiving the box as a seat and as an instrument; it is not free to adopt different points of view at its own discretion. The situation as a whole has an immediate value – it is given as already configured in a certain way, and this will only change when the situation itself changes, for example, when the other chimp stops sitting on the box.

In other words, the chimpanzee experiences its situation as a *Gestalt*: a whole in which each part affects and is affected by every other part. Furthermore, this *Gestalt* situation is not an object of knowledge for the chimp. The chimp does not experience its situation as a spectacle that could be divided into parts. Rather, the chimp lives its situation as an immediate call to action, an imperative or compulsion that cannot be denied. It is not a matter of first discerning the meaning of the situation and then formulating an appropriate response. Rather, the meaning of the situation *just is* the demand for action. Significance for the chimp is *motor* significance: it is not represented in consciousness, but enacted in the world through movement. The chimp's behaviour and its situation thus form a larger *Gestalt*: it is impossible to separate the one from the other, the meaning of the animal's situation from the movements by which it takes up that situation. Crucially, these movements *express* the meaning of the situation, but the chimp does not *know* this meaning; it does not make the meaning explicit or thematic for itself. According to Merleau-Ponty, this is the basic form that meaning takes – not just for chimpanzees but for all living bodies, including our own.

Given this account of what it is to have a meaningful situation, the chimpanzee's behaviour towards the box should not surprise us. What calls for explanation is not the chimpanzee's behaviour but our own: How is it that we are able to isolate objects from the total situation in which we encounter them, and see them as the same *thing* in different contexts? This is a variant of Descartes's famous question, in the Second Meditation, of how we recognize the wax as the self-same substance through changes in the sensory profiles it presents to us.[7] For Descartes, the answer is that we, as thinking beings, are not compelled by the evidence of bodily sensation. However, if this compulsion is the very structure of meaning, as Merleau-Ponty claims, then we must seek a different answer. It cannot be that we simply transcend or abandon the *Gestalt* structure of perception. Rather, the thing-structure must somehow arise as an elaboration or complication of the *Gestalt*-structure.[8] Merleau-Ponty's suggestion is that this occurs through a certain "multiplicity of perspective" that we possess and that chimps lack (*SB* 133[122]). Like the chimpanzee, we experience our situation as a *Gestalt*, an organized and oriented whole. But unlike the chimp, we are able to reorganize or reorient this whole, to "*Gestalt*-shift" more or less at will between different possible configurations of the situation. This allows us to achieve a certain distance, a certain remove, from any particular perspective. The chimpanzee experiences its situation as an immediate and irresistible call to action; by contrast, human beings are able, at least some of the time, to resist these demands. In resisting the call of the situation – which is to say, the motor significance it has for us – we become able to thematize this significance to some extent. The animal *lives in* the meaning of its immediate situation without *perceiving* this meaning as such. But we, thanks to our multiplicity of perspective, can see the situation's *immediate* significance as only one among many and consider this significance in its own right. To be able to choose between multiple perspectives is to become (at least implicitly) aware of perspective as such.

This first experiment has led us to pose the problem of how we perceive objects as *things*, but it does not give us the resources we need to fully resolve this problem. In order to deepen the account we have begun, we must turn to a second experiment of Köhler's, this one focused on the chimpanzee's perception of spatial relations.

II. Mobility of Perspective and Homogeneous Space

In this experiment, Köhler placed a piece of fruit behind a grill, out of reach of the chimpanzee, but gave the chimp a stick, which it learned to use to pull the fruit to within reach. Köhler then repeated the experiment, this time placing a three-sided frame around the fruit, with its open side facing away from the chimp. In this new situation, the chimp still tried to pull the fruit towards itself, even though the presence of the frame now made this impossible. Only rarely and with great difficulty would a chimp discover that it could first push the fruit away from itself towards the open side, making a detour around the frame so as to eventually pull the fruit into reach (*SB* 127[117]).[9]

This is liable to strike us as a bizarre failure on the part of the chimpanzee. After all, the chimp would be perfectly capable of making this detour with its own body, if it were a matter of moving around the frame to get to the banana (*SB* 127[117]).[10] But to move the *banana* along this same path is somehow beyond the chimp's capacities. To us these appear to be equivalent tasks, presenting equivalent spatial relations: the path from A to B is plainly identical to the path from B to A. Yet it is clear that they are not equivalent for the chimpanzee. This is not simply a failure of perception or intelligence on the part of the animal. Rather, it reveals that space has a different meaning for the chimp than it does for us. The chimp can solve spatial problems that require moving itself towards a goal, but not the reverse; the organism is mobile and the goal fixed, and these roles cannot be exchanged (*SB* 127[117]). This shows that the animal's own body occupies a privileged position in its experience of space. Space for the chimpanzee is not a homogeneous field of extension, *partes extra partes*. Its points are not all equivalent and interchangeable. On the contrary, it has a centre-point – namely, the chimp's own body – and all of space is organized around this point. This *organization* of space, its intrinsic *orientation* around a central point, is what gives it its meaning, its *sens*.[11] Chimp-space is a *Gestalt*, a structure whose parts are not external or indifferent to one another. A change in one part of this structure affects every other part: when the centre shifts, all of space is reconfigured.

The chimp does not, therefore, experience itself as an object moving through a fixed landscape; rather, it is the landscape that shifts around the animal in response to the animal's movements. The oriented, organized space of the chimpanzee calls for a different understanding of movement than the one we are used to. Movement for the chimp is not the exchange of one position for another within an indifferent space. Rather, it is a *transformation* of space, a reconfiguration of the chimp's *Gestalt* situation. In moving, the chimp does not simply navigate a space whose meaning is already settled; rather, it actively makes sense out of a spatial situation whose meaning is ambiguous, problematic, and yet to be determined.[12] Thus, when the chimpanzee executes a complex route towards a goal, it is not tracing a geometrical path through a static field of pre-established positions; it is responding on the fly to the shifting demands of a landscape whose meaning keeps changing in response to the chimp's own movements.

To move the fruit around obstacles while remaining stationary oneself is an entirely different task: here the landscape as a whole must remain fixed while an *object* is moved around within it. Of course, the chimpanzee can move objects around with respect to its own body, just as it can move one part of its body with respect to another. The chimp has no experience, however, of moving its hand *away* from its mouth in order to bring whatever it is holding *towards* its mouth; thus the space of the chimp's own body is of no help in this task. The problem is one of spatial relations between one object and another, which is why it presents such difficulties to the animal. Chimp-space is organized radially, its lines of force all emanating from the organism's own body; objects do not have independent spatial relations with one another, but only relations to this origin.

Once again, we must come to see that it is not the animal's experience that calls for explanation, but our own. The chimp's inability to see the path from A to B as identical to that from B to A is not evidence of a bizarre spatial blindness. Rather, it demonstrates that the equivalence of these two paths is a feature not of space itself but of a distinctly human sense of space. The animal's perception is not a deficient version of our own, but an older one, of which ours is a development. Thus we must try to understand how our experience of space as uniform could develop out of the animal's sense of space as oriented around its own body. Returning to Köhler's experiment, we must try to see how the resources of oriented space could be mobilized in order to make the detour with the object possible. As we have seen, the problem is that the chimpanzee's body is mobile in a way that the objects in its world are not. If the chimp and the banana could exchange positions, the animal would easily escape the enclosure and reach the banana. To succeed in this experiment, then, the organism must somehow effect this very reversal without actually moving its own body. It must imaginatively put itself in the place of the banana and see its own body as the goal. To manoeuvre an object around obstacles as easily as I manoeuvre my own body, I must imagine myself in the place of the object and move *it* as *I* would move if I were in its place.

The fact that we can make detours with objects, while chimps cannot, suggests that we possess a *mobility of perspective* that chimpanzees lack (*SB* 128[118]). This mobility goes beyond the *multiplicity* of perspective that we saw above in the example of the box-as-seat and box-as-instrument. Mobility of perpective is the capacity, not just to vary one's own perspective on the object, but to leave the perspective of one's own body and take up the *object*'s point of view. The privilege of one's own body can be overcome only by ceding this privilege to some object and transferring it to a point outside of oneself. We can perceive space as uniform, *not* because it has no centre, but because for us this centre is *mobile*. What we have is not a view from nowhere, but a mobile vantage point, the capacity to take up a *virtual* point of view without actually moving our body to that location. Thus, if the path from A to B seems to us equivalent to the path from B to A, it is not because space has for us no *sens*, no intrinsic orientation, but because we are able to *reverse* that orientation by projecting ourselves virtually to another location. Similarly, if we (unlike the chimpanzee) can understand spatial relations between objects, it is not because these relations do not originate in our bodies but because we can shift this origin virtually to objects outside of ourselves. Merleau-Ponty makes the same point in the *Phenomenology of Perception*: when I say that the book is on the table, I am implicitly putting myself in the place of the book or the table and applying categories drawn from my body's relation to objects (*PP* 131[103]).

This insight into our mobility of perspective allows us to deepen our account of how we perceive objects as *things*. The only *thing* in the animal's world – the only identity that can maintain itself through changing contexts and relations – is the animal's own body (*SB* 128[118]). In order to transform an object into a *thing*, then, I must transfer to it the thing-liness of my own body. I do this by taking up the object's perspective on the world so that it becomes a virtual body, a vantage point that remains the same while the world changes around it. From this virtual perspective outside of myself, my actual body can cease to be the centre of my universe and appear instead as just another object. This point anticipates and perhaps sheds some light on Merleau-Ponty's claim in "Eye and Mind" that things look back at us: to perceive an object as a *thing*, an independent and persistent entity whose meaning is greater than its meaning for me, is to take it as a quasi-organism with its own point of view on the world.[13] We should note that the capacity to perceive *things* is not simply a power, but also a form of passivity. To have this ability is to give objects power over me, the power to pull me out of myself. No sooner do I focus on the object than I find myself there with it, seeing things from its perspective. I can escape the object's gravitational pull only by moving – by shifting my attention to a different object or engaging in some motor activity that pulls me back to myself and relocates me in my own body.

III. Mobility of Perspective as Symbolic Conduct

We have now seen how our experience of the world as made up of *things* and our experience of space as uniform extension are both made possible by our mobility of perspective – that is, by our capacity to elaborate a space of virtual relations out of our body's actual, *sens*-ed situation. It remains for us to show how this mobility of perspective is a form of *symbolic* conduct.

Consider again what is required of the chimp who is asked to make a detour with the banana. We have said that the solution here is to put oneself in the place of the fruit and move it as one would move one's own body. To do this, one must imagine oneself following this route without actually performing the movement. Merleau-Ponty points out that this is analogous to the task of giving directions (*SB* 127[117]): to explain a complex itinerary to someone else, I must imagine myself actually following the path in question and then translate these virtual movements into spoken instructions. Similarly, the chimp would have to translate its own virtual movements into the non-verbal "instructions" it gives to the banana. Indeed, the difficulty we find in explaining a complex itinerary to someone, as opposed to simply following it ourselves, is precisely analogous to the chimp's difficulty in performing the detour with the banana. Merleau-Ponty observes that we are often unable to formulate directions at all without resorting to a "motor mimic," some set of gestures that helps us imaginatively orient ourselves along the path we are describing (*SB* 127[117]); for example, as I imagine myself turning left, I might actually rotate my body ninety degrees to the left in order to help me visualize what comes next.[14] This difficulty, and our ways of compensating for it, reveal that an immediate experience of the body's actual, oriented space is still operating beneath the mobile perspective of virtual space. We cannot sustain a virtual perspective for long without resorting to actual movements that re-establish its roots in the oriented space of our body: "By the gestures which we sketch we make the principal directions of the virtual field in which our description is unfolding correspond momentarily with the strong structures – right and left, high and low – of our own body" (*SB* 128[117]).

The task of performing a detour with an object is actually more complex than that of giving directions, because the chimp cannot direct the banana from the banana's own point of view – the perspective the chimp would occupy were it performing the movement itself – but must do so from its own position behind the grill. Thus it is a matter of not only composing a virtual movement but also imagining what this movement would look like *from a perspective outside of the movement itself*. This is less like giving directions and more like reading a map or plan (*SB* 128[117]). Consider the various elements involved in plotting a route on a map. First, I must imagine myself traversing a space without actually doing so. Furthermore, I must imagine what this movement would look like from a bird's-eye view – a perspective I have never occupied in my actual movements. Finally, I must *represent* the spectacle of this movement *graphically* – "transcribing a kinetic melody into a visual diagram … establishing relations of reciprocal correspondence and mutual expression between them" (*SB* 128[118]). This is precisely what is required of the chimpanzee in Köhler's experiment: first, one would have to imagine oneself traversing the path from the banana to the grill; furthermore, one would have to imagine what this traversal would look like to an observer positioned behind the grill; and finally, one would have to move the banana along this very path, "trac[ing] by our very gesture the *symbol* of the movement which we would have to make if we were in its place" (*SB* 128[118], my emphasis).

To take up the perspective of an object outside of me, then, is to perform a kind of translation, to re-present a familiar series of movements in a different way. It is to set up a correspondence between the space of my actual body and the virtual space of an imaginary body, and to do so in such a way that they *express the same sense* despite being differently located and oriented. The power we have been calling "mobility of perspective" thus turns out to be a *symbolic* capacity: rather than simply moving, and thus enacting a sense, we take up the already enacted sense of our own familiar movements and *express* it in a gesture, in words, or in a diagram. Merleau-Ponty calls this a "structure or an intention of the second power" or a "relation between relations" (*SB* 128[118]) – what the Greeks called *logos*.[15] It is a movement that responds, not to my immediate situation, but to the meaning of my own familiar movements – to the sense that I myself have enacted in building up habitual ways of moving through a given situation.

In symbolic conduct, the immanent signification of things becomes thematic for us – not as an object of knowledge but as a stimulus, a demand for meaningful action that *expresses* the sense it is responding to.[16] The animal enacts a meaningful world through its behaviour, but it does so without *knowing* the meanings it enacts, without making them thematic. It sings a melody it cannot hear. Human *logos* is an awakening to the song that is all around us. It is the power to perceive meanings as such, rather than simply living in them. This does not mean that we cease *enacting* meanings in favour of *knowing* them. Rather, we enact meanings of a second order: the meaningful world that our bodies respond to includes the meanings that we and others are enacting. It is this capacity to perceive meanings as such that allows us to inquire into the meaning that space has for the chimpanzee, to express in words the sense that the chimp can only express in movement.

The rise of symbolic conduct opens up, for the first time, the question of truth and objectivity.[17] In symbolic conduct, I can ask what things mean in themselves rather than simply acting out their meaning for me. I can take up a position outside of my own immediate situation and see my own actions from an outside perspective. I can give up my privileged place at the centre of my world and see my own body as one object among many. The power of *logos* is the power of reflection. With reflection, however, comes the possibility of error. The chimpanzee is never mistaken about the meaning of its own actions – but that is because it never asks after this meaning. The human being, the being with *logos*, is the being for whom the meaning of its own conduct is an issue. Thus, we are also the beings who can be wrong about ourselves, who can misunderstand the sense of our own conduct.

IV. Pre-reflective Meaning and the Nature of Space

We now see what Merleau-Ponty means when he says, in the *Phenomenology of Perception*, that intelligible, homogeneous space expresses the sense of oriented space (*PP* 131[104]). I can experience space as homogeneous, and my body as just another object, because I am constantly taking up virtual perspectives outside of my own body. To take up such a virtual perspective is to translate the sense of my body's oriented space and the motor significance of my habitual movements into a virtual space and virtual movements that express the same sense.

With practice, these translations become so easy that we no longer notice we are making them. We are thus liable to mistake our *mobility* of perspective for a *freedom from* perspective: our virtual standpoint moves from place to place so quickly and effortlessly that we seem to be everywhere at once, to be taking in being as a whole in the same way that we survey a map from above. This is how we form the idea of space as a system of uniform positions existing simultaneously, spread out before our gaze, each point external to and independent of every other. Our capacity to take up virtual perspectives also makes it possible for us to perceive objects as *things* that maintain their own identities through changes of context and relation. This is how we form the idea of the world as a collection of independent parts, like a great machine – *partes extra partes*.

If we take this pure exteriority to be the structure of being itself, we will be trapped in the traditional antinomies of reflection. There is no room in the machine for reflection, and no meaning in the machine except for that which reflection gives it; reflection must therefore posit itself as outside of being, at the origin of the world. Yet we are bodies; we are born; we do not make the world. Reflection is right to identify itself as the origin of objective space. Its mistake is to identify this constituted space with being itself. Empiricism, no less than idealism, makes being into an idea, for in each case reflection take its own criteria of intelligibility – transparency, givenness, presence – to be the measure of being. Whether they make space into a thing outside of me or a structure of my consciousness, philosophies of reflection are alike in demanding that space be something fully given and fully present. There can be motion *in* space, but not *of* space: in order to be thinkable, space must be fixed, determinate, and singular. We have been speaking of a reflection that takes its roots for granted and that recognizes only the meanings it has made. However, Merleau-Ponty shows that a more radical reflection is possible, one that discovers as its own origin a world of meanings that are prior to thought – meanings that are not ideas and that do not need me to constitute them. It is in this world that we will find the true meaning of space.

In the *Phenomenology of Perception*, Merleau-Ponty shows that space is not only organized around my body but also oriented by my history. That is, the spatial organization of my present situation – the *spatial level* that establishes the basic directions of up and down – cannot be explained by the contents of the situation itself, but only by the spatial norms and habits my body has developed in the past (*PP* 291–9[254–62]). Space thus has an irreducibly *temporal* dimension to it: its meaning is not fixed, but constantly evolving as my body learns to move in new ways by encountering new spatial situations.

This might appear to make space into something completely personal. And indeed, there is something personal about space, as Merleau-Ponty is concerned to show. My body, my way of moving, my way of relating spatially to things and other people in the world, all express a personal style that is unique to me, formed by my particular history and life. But space also has an *impersonal* dimension, a dimension of *generality*. This is because the history of space does not begin with my birth. As Merleau-Ponty writes in the *Phenomenology of Perception*, "each of our experiences in sequence, *back to and including the first*, passes forward an already acquired spatiality" (*PP* 302[264], emphasis added). We are born into space: that is, our very first movements, and the very first situations we encounter, already have a spatial significance. But as we have just noted, spatial significance is always oriented by a past, always taking up a sense that is already in motion. The meaning space has for me must therefore be oriented by a past that is not my own: "My history must be the sequel to a pre-history whose acquired results it uses; my personal existence must be the taking up of a pre-personal tradition" (*PP* 302[265]). We are born with bodies that already incline towards certain determinate ways of moving and making sense, inherited from the living bodies that came before us. I am thus connected, through my body, to a past that is not my personal past. This is not the past of any one particular life, but a *general* past – an evolutionary history that blends together countless lives, stretching back to the origin of life on this planet. Our bodies are not geared in advance to any *particular* situation, but they do reflect an "ancient pact established between *X* and the world in general" – an adaptation to the *kinds* of spaces that shaped the bodies of our ancestors (*PP* 302[265]). "At the core of the subject, space and perception in general mark the fact of his birth, the perpetual contribution of his corporeality, and a communication with the world more ancient than thought. And this is why they saturate consciousness and are opaque to reflection" (*PP* 302[265]). The general spatiality that I have inherited is not transparent to me, for it is a motor significance, not an idea. It is sedimented in the complex, personal habits and norms that my body has developed over the course of my life, the invisible background that orients my movements and perceptions.

Space is a *tradition* – or as Merleau-Ponty will later say, an *institution*.[18] It is a way of making sense that I participate in without possessing, a meaning that makes sense without me. I do not have to constitute space, but neither am I passively inserted into it like a part into a machine. Space is both a movement in which I am swept up and an inheritance that I carry forward, taking it up in my own way. Space is *natural*, but not in the sense this word has come to have of something universal and already determined. "Nature," Merleau-Ponty writes in the summary of his 1956–57 lecture course on the subject, "is what has a meaning, without this meaning being posited by thought: it is the autoproduction of a meaning."[19] Space is a natural meaning in this sense, a self-moving, self-producing significance, and my body participates in this autoproduction.

The rediscovery of a meaning prior to reflection is also the rediscovery of nature: a nature that we do not constitute, that does not depend on us for its meaning. The reflection that takes itself to be the source of all meaning unwittingly substitutes a dead, ideal nature for the concrete, living one. But radical reflection finds that nature is already generating its own meanings before thought arrives on the scene. Nature is intrinsically meaningful: it is self-moving and self-showing. It does not passively submit to our sense-making, but actively participates in it. To think about nature, then, is to take up a tradition of significance; it is to express or give voice to a sense we did not make, to a meaning that is already under way. It is in this spirit that we must think about space. We can reflect on space – name it, measure it, question it – only because, as living bodies, we are already participant in it, and it in us.

In this chapter, we have tried to understand how our reflective sense of space as universal could have developed out of something like the chimpanzee's pre-reflective space of motricity. Thus, we have been thinking all along about the evolution or institution of space in nature, about the growth of new ways of making sense out of older ones. The power of reflection is a way of moving and making sense that developed naturally over time. This inherited, bodily power of *logos* allows us to take space up as something universal, measurable, and univocal. However, this universal space is not the space of nature, but merely an idealized expression of it. There is no truly universal space. There is only a *general* space that each of us inherits, inhabits, and makes our own; a self-propagating tradition of meaning that is prior to thought.

NOTES

1 Merleau-Ponty takes this formula from René Descartes, who used it in a 1649 letter to Henry More: "I call extended only what is imaginable as having parts outside of parts [*ita illud solum quod est imaginabile, ut habens partes extra partes … dico esse extensum*]" (*The Philosophical Writings*, vol. 3, 362). (I have modified the English translation, which renders "partes extra partes" as "parts within parts.") Merleau-Ponty cites this passage in his lectures on *The Incarnate Subject* (50). I am indebted to Donald Landes for locating this citation.

2 See *PP* 64[41]: "We began from a world in itself that acted upon our eyes in order to make itself seen by us; we have arrived now at a consciousness or a thought about the world, but the very nature of this world is unchanged. It is still defined by the absolute exteriority of its parts and is merely doubled across its extension by a thought that sustains it. We pass from an absolute objectivity to an absolute subjectivity, but this second idea is worth only as much as the first, and only finds support in contrast to the first, which is to say, through it."

3 Merleau-Ponty's *The Structure of Behavior* (hereafter *SB*) will be cited in-text, with page numbers first from the French and then from the Fisher translation.

4 Köhler was the director of an anthropoid research station in the Canary Islands when the First World War broke out, stranding him there for several years. It was during this time that he performed his pioneering research on chimpanzee problem solving, published in 1917 as *The Mentality of Apes*. His results are widely cited by psychologists, but few have attempted to reproduce them exactly. This may be due in part to the unusual circumstances in which Köhler conducted his research: he lived with and observed the chimpanzees over a number of years, giving them names and becoming very familiar with their individual personalities and habits. Schiller repeated several of the chimpanzee experiments that Köhler had performed, but not the two we will examine here. He reports

behaviours in the chimpanzees similar to those found by Köhler, although he argues for a behaviourist, mechanistic interpretation of them (Schiller, "Innate Constituents").

5 One might think that the one chimp was simply waiting for the other to get off the box before using it; according to Köhler, however, other experiments showed that had this been the case, the first chimp would have pleaded and pulled at the second to persuade it to move, or simply tried to move the box with the other chimp still sitting on it (*The Mentality of Apes*, 178–9). Merleau-Ponty first describes this experiment at *SB* 124[114].

6 Psychologists call this phenomenon "functional fixedness" and report a similar phenomenon in humans: subjects are quicker to use a tool if it is not already being used for some other purpose (Duncker, "On Problem Solving"). This is consistent with the analysis presented below, namely, that the structures of chimpanzee perception form the basis of the more complex structures of human perception and can still be seen at work within the latter.

7 Descartes, *Philosophical Writings*, vol. 2, 20–2.

8 The phenomenon of "functional fixedness" in humans supports Merleau-Ponty's claim that the Gestalt-structure underlies human perception of objects as *things*: if we *only* saw objects as *things* independent of their context, it would be hard to explain why we take longer to notice a tool when it is being used for some other purpose. (See note 6.)

9 See Köhler, *The Mentality of Apes*, 226–34. Merleau-Ponty describes a variation on this experiment at *SB* 108[98]. Anderson cites this experiment by Köhler and notes that human problem solvers are often similarly "reluctant to pursue paths that temporarily take them in the direction of states less similar to the goal" ("Problem Solving and Learning," 37). Brainerd repeated this experiment with a three-year-old human subject, whose performance was similar to that of Köhler's chimpanzees; older children, however, solved the problem easily ("The Mentality of a Child"). This is consistent with the claims I make below that the human perception of space develops out of a spatiality similar to that of the chimpanzee. It further suggests that these more complex structures of perception are learned, and take time to develop in humans.

10 Köhler makes this same point in *The Mentality of Apes*, 228–9.

11 Merleau-Ponty plays on the double-meaning of the French word *sens*, which means both *meaning* and *direction*. See, for example, *PP* 301[263–4].

12 In other words, the chimp's movement is *expressive*, in Merleau-Ponty's sense: it does not give voice to a ready-made meaning, but generates a

new significance by engaging with its situation. See the chapter in *PP* on "The Body as Expression, and Speech." For more on the logic of expression and the living body, see Maclaren, "Life Is Inherently Expressive"; and Morris, "What Is Living."

13 Merleau-Ponty, "Eye and Mind," 358–9.

14 Merleau-Ponty notes that such "motor mimics" were also used by Gelb and Goldstein's patient "Schneider," to compensate for the cognitive deficits caused by his brain injury (*SB* 127[117]). See also *PP* 132–43[105–15].

15 In mathematics, a relation between relations is a *proportion*. The ancient Greek mathematicians who established the theory of proportions chose for this concept the term "logos."

16 As Merleau-Ponty writes, "genuine *aptitudes* demand that the 'stimulus' become efficacious through its internal properties of structure, by its immanent signification; and they demand that the response symbolize along with the stimulus … Here behavior no longer only *has* a signification, it *is* itself signification" (*SB* 133[122], translation modified).

17 Merleau-Ponty writes: "With symbolic forms, a conduct appears, which expresses the stimulus for itself, which is open to truth and to the proper value of things, which tends to the adequation of the signifying and signified, of the intention and that which it intends" (*SB* 133[122]).

18 Merleau-Ponty develops this concept in his 1954–55 lecture course, "Institution in Personal and Public History."

19 Merleau-Ponty, "The Concept of Nature," 3.

8 Merleau-Ponty and the Phenomenology of Natural Time

DAVID CIAVATTA

The account of time that Merleau-Ponty develops in the *Phenomenology of Perception* aims to describe time as it is lived by us in our concrete, embodied experience. From this phenomenological perspective, time presents itself, in its most original form, for instance in our experience of living in anticipation of, and of thereby bringing to bear in the here and now, what has not yet occurred; or it presents itself in our lived experience of the weight that the past, although no longer present to perception, still has on us as setting the tone of our present situation. On Merleau-Ponty's account, such basic experiences of time's perpetually "ecstatic" character – whereby the temporal dimensions exist, not as merely external to or as merely following one another, but as intimately informing one another throughout – cannot ultimately be explained in terms of some sort of passive registering of a purportedly objective time that exists in external things. On the contrary, these experiences reveal that we have time at issue for us in our very being as living subjects – that as experiencing beings, we are essentially constituted in terms of the *ecstasis* of the temporal dimensions.

Indeed, for Merleau-Ponty, as for Heidegger, there is not only an intimate link, but ultimately an identity, between time and subjectivity, in the sense that it is precisely in and through the existential dynamics of our lived experience as finite subjects engaged with the world that the world itself takes on a temporal meaning in the first place.[1] Thus Merleau-Ponty comes to argue that "there is no such thing as natural time if we understand this to mean a time of objects without subjectivity" (*PP* 517[479]). For him, the basic features of our more familiar, objectively-oriented conceptions of time – for instance, the notion that time flows at a constant, uniform rate, and that this flow admits of being divided up into determinate, quantifiable moments or points of full presence ("nows"), such that time comes to take the form of an ideal formal register in which all events have their clear and determinate place in relation to one another – are, while not without their place in our everyday engagements with the world, nevertheless derivative, abstract forms of the more fundamental way in which the dimensions of time are first brought to life, and first come to inform one another, in and through the unfolding of lived experience.[2]

Besides contrasting the lived and ecstatic "time of subjectivity" with the objective conception of time – with the "time of objects without subjectivity" – Merleau-Ponty regularly contrasts it specifically with the time distinctive of the ongoing, repetitive cycles of nature (for instance, the articulation of time into day and night or into the broader cycle of the seasons, or the time of our own organism's various metabolic cycles). It is not altogether clear, however, whether natural time in this more specific sense – the temporality specific to cyclicality and repetition – shares the same fate in his account as objective time generally; that is, it is not clear whether it too is taken to be a merely derivative, abstract form of the more original, ecstatic time of lived experience. Of course, we tend to think of natural cycles, and particularly such large-scale cycles as that of the earth around the sun, as being essentially indifferent to our experience, and in this sense as "without subjectivity." And it is precisely such indifference – the fact that this day is passing into night, in the same way and at the same rate as it did yesterday, regardless of the fact that, experientially, today is radically distinct from yesterday, at least in the sense that it is thoroughly informed by yesterday's events as its past horizon – that would seem to lend credence to the objective conception of time generally. It would seem, then, that if Merleau-Ponty is out to show the derivative character of objective time generally, the time of the natural cycle in particular will also be shown to be derivative. And, as I will discuss in the first section of this chapter, Merleau-Ponty does indeed give us reason to think of cyclical time as being in certain respects a kind of deficient, derivative modality of the ecstatic time of subjectivity.

Merleau-Ponty also argues, however, that the time of cyclicality has its own original contribution to make to our lived experience of time, and at various points in the *Phenomenology of Perception* we find him concerned to show that structures of cyclicality, particularly insofar as they are characteristic of the body's own internal processes and of the body's various modes of engagement with the natural world, play an irreducible role in shaping the very character of experience itself. That is, the phenomenology of lived time reveals that there is a kind of temporal cyclicality *internal to lived experience itself*, and, in this respect, we can say that the lived time of subjectivity is not simply to be contrasted with natural time, but that it encompasses, within itself, certain dimensions of cyclical temporality.

From this point of view, it is not solely a question of how we experience natural cycles, where those cycles are still posited as one among many external *objects* of experience; rather, it is a question of grasping how such cyclical patterns inform the temporal character of experiencing itself. I will be suggesting that certain cycles, such as the day/night cycle, and the body's cycle of breathing, have a form akin to the bodily or species *a priori* that Merleau-Ponty uncovers – that is, they constitute the general horizons that contextualize and thus inform *all* of our experience in advance of our having this or that particular experience.[3] This general horizon, although internal to experience, is best described as something we see "through" or "in terms of," rather than being a discrete, circumscribed *object of* experience in its own right – much as we perceive the world "in terms of" our lived bodies, instead of having our bodies as express objects before us.[4]

Merleau-Ponty characterizes this natural dimension of our own temporal experience as having the form of a "generalized time" (*PP* 517[479]), by which he means to capture those general, recurring features of our own lived experience that are always on the horizon of the more immediate, more circumscribed, passing temporal events that occupy us from moment to moment. This generalized time is not simply *external* to experience – rather, for Merleau-Ponty, it is an irreducible, qualitatively distinct way in which experience itself articulates time for itself; in its generality, however, this time is nevertheless *relatively indifferent* to the way in which our more immediate, moment-to-moment experiences unfold. Indeed, we can say that it is relatively indifferent to the ecstatic character of what Merleau-Ponty identifies as the perceptual "field of presence" that constitutes the core of our experience of time; for, whereas in perception we are constitutively alive to the historical individuality and immediacy of the present, uniquely informed as it is by its unique horizon of immediate past and impending future, in our reckoning with generalized time we ourselves display a kind of indifference to the individuality of this immediate field of presence, treating it rather as one among many phases of a constantly present, recurring cycle. Thus, for Merleau-Ponty there are certain crucial ways in which experience, in its temporal generality, *is constitutively indifferent to itself.*

By uncovering a dimension of temporal generality and indifference operative *within* lived experience, Merleau-Ponty thus offers us a conception of experience – and of subjectivity itself – that diverges markedly from traditional conceptions. In contrast to the rationalist or intellectualist ideal of experience as constitutively and thoroughly self-transparent, we find here an experience that is, in certain of its dimensions, indifferent to, or, we might say, unaffected by, itself. And in contrast to the empiricist model of experience as thoroughly atomized into discrete, self-contained temporal moments or episodes (a model that Kant, too, adopted), we are here confronted with a dimension of experience that is itself general – with a kind of experiencing that is not thoroughly individuated into the fits and starts of discrete, passing instances, but that itself displays the sort of constancy characteristic of natural cycles.

Thus, while Merleau-Ponty sometimes speaks as though cyclical time is simply derivative upon the lived temporality of subjectivity – likening cyclical time to a constantly frustrated subjective commitment, or identifying it as a "natural outline of a subjectivity" (*PP* 517[479]) – there is also an important sense in which Merleau-Ponty's conception of subjectivity, along with his corresponding conception of its commitment-based character, are clearly informed by structures that are, in the end, derived from the cyclicality of natural time. Or perhaps it is better to say, as Merleau-Ponty does, that it is precisely in the arena of temporality that the fundamental ambiguity of the nature/subjectivity distinction comes to the fore.[5]

In what follows I offer an analysis of certain aspects of Merleau-Ponty's account of experience, with a view towards revealing how the generality and repetitiveness distinctive of natural time comes to structure the temporality of lived experience itself. We can, I suggest, look to such appearances of natural temporality within experience as providing a kind of indirect phenomenology of natural time; and, at once, we can find in them one of the main springs of Merleau-Ponty's challenge to traditional conceptions of subjectivity.[6] I begin, however, with an analysis of Merleau-Ponty's attempt to link cyclical time with the objective account of time whose seeming dominance he ultimately seeks to dismantle.

I. The Cyclicality and Indifference of Nature

It seems that a process that exists in the peculiar way of happening again and again, and that continues in this way indefinitely – as natural cycles do – can only be *experienced* as such on the basis of a temporal succession of relatively distinct moments or episodes that, despite their successive and distinct character, nevertheless merge with one another in the sense that a current episode presents itself as essentially the same as *previous* episodes and episodes *to come.* To have this experience of return – of coming back, once again, to where we started – requires, at the very least, a holding on to the past within the present, such that the present in a way collapses into this past. And experiencing this return as a cycle that is *ongoing* – that has a kind of iterative impetus of its own – requires the anticipation that the future will likewise present again what *has already been present.* In this way, we can start to see how our lived experience of the overlapping, mutually determining character of the temporal dimensions might be a condition for the possibility of experiencing temporal cyclicality.

This sort of transcendental argument is clearly at work in Merleau-Ponty's approach to cyclical time. The core of Merleau-Ponty's argument for viewing the cyclical time of nature as conditioned by, and thus derivative upon, lived time, with its constitutive structures of anticipation and retention, seems to be that we could not gain experiential access to repetitive natural cycles *as* cycles except insofar as we actually distinguish, within the cycle, between definite moments of departure and arrival (*PP* 486[447]). It is only insofar as we as finite subjects are situated experientially *within* a cycle's concrete movement in the here and now, and thereby treat one of its particular, finite stages as an actual *starting point* from which to project an *arrival* at some particular future stage in its movement – for instance, as we experience today's late afternoon sun *as a foreshadowing* of the darkness that will soon enfold us, thereby enabling the sun's setting to occur as an *anticipated point of arrival* – that we can gain access to the temporal differentiation occurring within the cycle. And it is based on the experience of coming back to where we started, the lived experience of the *dissolution* of this temporal differentiation – the experience, for instance, of the night (formerly a distinct arrival point in relation to a waning daylight that specifically anticipated it) gradually "departing" or transitioning into *yet another* day, complete with *its* own late afternoon sunlight – that we gain access to its cyclical character as such.

For Merleau-Ponty the time of departures and arrivals, of beginnings and endings, can be construed as the *time of the event*, or as *historical time,* in that history is precisely the forum in which such inaugurations and resolutions, and the temporal differentiation they imply, matter as such. It is in historical time that the present gets its individuated character *qua* this unique present, in virtue of its being located within an unfolding drama – or, we can say, in virtue of its backward reference towards some past starting point that kicked off a new duration, and a forward reference towards some temporal end. It is with the time of history and of narrative – the time of subjectivity proper – that the ecstatic character of temporality is most clearly revealed. On this basis, then, we can say that for Merleau-Ponty, it is only insofar as the self-iterating cycle of nature is, as it were, "historicized" into an unfolding narrative, into an individuated duration that exists only in reference to its own (past) *beginning* and (future) *end*, that we can access it *as* an ongoing cycle in the first place. Historical time is thus prior to, or more original than, the cyclicality of natural time, and Merleau-Ponty goes as far as to call the latter a merely "secondary attribute" that can only be understood as an *inauthentic* or *negative* mode of this more narrative-like structure of time (*PP* 486[447]).

This is what Merleau-Ponty means when he likens natural time to a "disappointment and a repeated failure," describing it as only "the outline and the abstract form of a commitment" (*PP* 517[479]). The time of subjectivity is characterized by the essentially ecstatic, narrative structure of a commitment, as for instance when the subject, in the present moment, commits itself in such a way that it kicks off a new drama within whose future unfolding the present decision is kept alive as this drama's inaugural context – in such a way that this present is *not simply undone* by what happens next. If on a given morning I decide to spend the day travelling to another city, I thereby reach out from the present moment of the decision towards the future goal, committing the rest of my day in such a way that *its* present, when it comes, will constantly refer back to my morning's resolution and the future it projected; it is on this condition, for instance, that I come to experience the boredom that comes with some delay I encounter during my travels, for I experience this present circumstance not just as a fresh "now" in its own right, but in terms of its being a frustrating delaying of my anticipated future. My capacity to make such ordinary commitments is thus grounded in the more basic capacity of experience to implicate the temporal dimensions with one another.[7] In the case of the continuous natural cycle, however, the present "is never present for good, since it is already past when it appears, and the future has there but the appearance of a goal towards which we are moving, since it soon arrives in the present and since we then turn toward another future" (*PP* 517[479], translation modified). Just as no one episode of breathing settles our respiratory needs "for good" – for every act of exhaling, while it seems to *end* a particular cycle of breathing, just as immediately calls for *yet another* act of inhaling, one that is wholly new in that it bears no significant, *internal* temporal reference to the one that immediately preceded it – so natural time in general "continuously gnaws away at itself and undoes what it has just done" (*PP* 517[479]).[8] Thus with natural time the relationship of ecstatic temporal implication is unravelled, and we are left with moments of time that are essentially external and indifferent to one another.[9] Each cycle presents itself more or less as a self-sufficient present that as such does not "develop" out of prior instantiations of the cycle, or anticipate future instantiations.

Merleau-Ponty implies that it is in part this "externalizing" tendency of natural time that motivates the objectivist conception of time as a uniform series of quantifiable "nows" that are essentially external to one another. In moving from our lived experience of what it is like to have night on our horizon as our busy day reaches its final hours, to a conception of day and night, in general, as perpetual reiterations of the earth's ongoing rotation around the sun, we are moving away from lived time in its rich multidimensionality, towards a conception of time that is premised on the claim to stand *beyond* time, beyond my perceptual immersion in *this* singular field of presence with its imbricated horizons of past and future. From the point of view of the objective movement of the earth's rotation, my experience of *this* day slipping away from me is a matter of indifference, and the multidimensionality of time's lived flow is flattened, so to speak, into a "conceived time" according to which past, present, and future are *equally present* to the (essentially atemporal) conceiving mind as a series of uniform, measurable "nows," each external to the other.[10] In arguing for the derivative, inauthentic character of natural time, Merleau-Ponty seems to be targeting precisely this attempt to idealize time, this transformation of it into uniform, intelligible units.

It is crucial to note, however, that Merleau-Ponty does not thereby rule out the possibility of developing a phenomenology of natural time that is free of such problematic, unphenomenological idealization. Although he perhaps does not pursue such a phenomenology head-on in the *Phenomenology of Perception*, we will find hints of it at work in Merleau-Ponty's account of the manner in which structures of cyclicality and repetition inform experience itself. Before getting there, though, it would be helpful to distinguish between two dimensions of our experience of the natural cycle. First, there is the question of what it is like to experience a single cycle – for instance, a day–night–day cycle, or an inhale–exhale–inhale cycle, or a hunger–satisfaction–hunger cycle. This is the dimension we have already focused on: by putting ourselves *within* a finite stage of the single cycle, and by witnessing how our essential historicality as subjects both differentiates singular moments from one another and envelops them within one another such that they exist as one another's determinate past and future horizons, we cannot help experiencing the cycle, with its fresh new (i.e., non-enveloped) presents, as inherently frustrating, as mere adumbrations of a temporality that they themselves ultimately fail to display. Second, however, there is also the question of how we come to access the *constancy of the cycle itself* – that is, of how we come to experience not just this or that rotation within a *particular* cycle, but the cycling itself as something general and constant, something that *keeps on repeating* and is, as such, of an *indefinite duration*. I will suggest that it is with respect to this second dimension that we find Merleau-Ponty pointing to something in cyclical time that is not *simply* conditional on historical time; moreover, it is with respect to this second dimension that we will eventually come to see how features of natural time inform the structure of experience itself.

If it is the case that we only ever experience the cycle from the point of view of one of the particular, finite stages in which the cycle is instantiated here and now, it would seem that the experience of the cycling movement as something that is itself constant – as something that continues to cycle through again and again, indefinitely – must be arrived at through some sort of Humean induction, based on the assumption that the future will resemble the past; that is, based on our experience of a multiplicity of instances of particular day/night/day transitions, we come to project that this cycling is not merely a matter of contingent, isolated instances, but the expression of a unified, constantly present, general reality or law that explains *all* instances and that warrants our expectation of instances to come. And, just as Hume sought to show that such an inductive move can never be adequately justified, we might expect that if, on Merleau-Ponty's account, our *only* access to the recurring, general character of a cycle is by way of our various, individual experiences of being immersed in particular instantiations of that cycle, then the idea that there is a cyclical time, understood as an enduring, objective feature of reality itself, must likewise be regarded as an unfounded, unphenomenological, and merely derivative induction.

I will be arguing, however, that Merleau-Ponty does not in fact think that our experience of the constancy, or indefinitely repeating character, of such cycles comes by way of an induction from isolated instances to something more general. On the contrary, we will see that there is for Merleau-Ponty a much more direct, *lived* relation to the constancy and generality of the cycle's ongoing character; in other words, there is a lived, phenomenal character peculiar to this generality as such, one that is not reducible to the phenomenality (of departure and arrival, and their frustrations) that is specific to this generality's individual experiential instantiations. The irreducibility of the phenomenality of the general will enable us to see how cyclical time and its constitutive generality inform the character of lived experience itself.

II. Temporal Experience, Indifference, and the Phenomenality of the General

As Merleau-Ponty notes, we are inclined to conceive of the cycles of nature as themselves atemporal – or as a "quasi-eternity," as Merleau-Ponty puts it (*PP* 486[447])[11] – precisely insofar as the cyclical processes themselves, as distinct from their moment-to-moment instantiations, are in a certain sense *ever-present*. From the point of view of the ongoing character of the circular movement itself, there are not really any beginnings or endings, which would imply the movement's *not* being present – whether in the form of an absence prior to the movement's beginning, or an absence after it ends. For at each point of the cycle's movement, what is really most at issue is the *constant flow*, the *continuous reiteration* of the *selfsame process* through the different moments. As I have suggested, no single breath I take presents itself as the "culminating" breath, as the climactic and long-anticipated "breath to end all breaths." Rather, each single breath presents itself merely as one among many moments in a continuous process – the stability of breathing, in general – a process that, from the point of view of this or that breath, continues indefinitely, perhaps even endlessly. Of course, my breathing is coextensive with my life, so it began and will end with that life. But from the point of view of breathing itself, even my dying breath is not significantly different from any other breath I have taken. As an essentially constant process that as such recedes into the background of my lived experience – such that no one breath becomes especially conspicuous to me – my breathing does not itself seem to bear the trace of its own beginning and impending end, and thus has no historicality or narrativity to it; it *exists precisely as something of indefinite duration*. Although there is a sort of narrativity that comes with the qualitative differentiations *within* each cycle (e.g., in the way my current inhale is "released" into the exhale it has anticipated), these differences are essentially subsumed and to a large extent dissolved within a larger, essentially unchanging, constantly present identity (the enduring, continuous flow of the respiratory system insofar as it maintains its regular rhythm).

So we can say that from the point of view of this ongoing flow as a whole, the concrete moments of the process do not matter *in their individuality* as circumscribed episodes, each differentiating itself from its past and future in the unique historical series; all that matters is the essentially *generic* way in which each contributes to the maintenance of the whole.[12] Each is, as it were, obliterated and "undone" in its individuality and historicality as soon as it comes to exist, and presents itself merely as one among many substitutable "ephemera" of a more general process that is itself *constantly* present.

This erosion of the singular, historical present can equally be understood as the persistence of an enduring, overarching, *general present*. As in our example, the exigencies of respiration are, so to speak, *ever-present*, in that they constitute a *general, continuous "now"* that is, in the end, coextensive with the "now" of my whole life. Indeed, Merleau-Ponty at one point speaks as though the rhythm of our breathing puts us in touch with a process that exceeds the boundaries of even our own individual lives – thus his reference to the "immense lung" that each of us participates in, particularly when we are asleep and thus are not as actively engaged in the personal, temporally individuated projects peculiar to our conscious life.[13] It is nature's privileging of the general over the individual, of the constantly present over that which exists as temporally situated within this or that singular present, that leads Merleau-Ponty to speak of natural – in distinction to historical – time as a "generalized time" (see *PP* 517[479]).[14]

Although we as individual subjects are in principle alive to the individuality of our own experiences,[15] and as such are caught up in the temporal individuality and historical distinctness of each passing episode of our experience, we do not exist purely as individuals in all aspects of our being. As Merleau-Ponty argues, we as subjects are *also* inescapably *general*, and this "zone of generalized existence" (*PP* 514[476]) forms an inherent part of our experiential relationship to ourselves, particularly insofar as we are embodied agents living in a natural world.[16] This means that, while we might be experientially occupied with the immediate content of our current, idiosyncratic perceptual episode – with what is singularly happening to us right now, in this instant – we are *at once* experientially alive to the more general experiential context in and through which *all* of our particular, episodic experiences take shape.

For instance, I am constitutively alive to the general ways in which the world presents itself according to those general, constantly available intentional projects that I share with "all psycho-physical subjects who have a similar organization to my own" (*PP* 503[465]). As Merleau-Ponty notes, regardless of the idiosyncratic, historically distinct project we are involved in at the moment, we always experience the mountain in front of us *as large*, and the molehill *as small*, precisely because we all have similarly organized bodies that, being possessed of similar types and rates of motion, cannot fail to project a general horizon of motility in terms of which molehills appear as capable being traversed in one quick stride, while mountains present a much more formidable, arduous, and time-consuming challenge (see *PP* 503[464]). Thus Merleau-Ponty draws attention to an impersonal, general rhythm of experience that lies beneath each of our individuated, unique, and more personal experiences:

> Insofar as I have "sense organs," a "body," and "psychical functions" comparable to those of others, each moment of my experience ceases to be an integrated or rigorously unique totality ... Insofar as I inhabit a "physical world," where consistent "stimuli" and typical situations are discovered – and not merely the historical world in which situations are never comparable – my life is made up of rhythms that do not have their *reason* in what I have chosen to be, but rather have their *condition* in the banal milieu that surrounds me. (*PP* 112–13[86])

This general, natural setting, with its recurring rhythms, is akin to a medium *through* which we see, rather than something that itself strikes us as an express object of our experience.[17] Merleau-Ponty notes that, due to its generality and medium-character, we can abstract from the specific objects of our most immediate perceptual situation even while maintaining the general form of this overall context. Thus, for instance, in my imagination I can fantasize about what it would be like to experience the Alps as molehills, but even within this imaginary field my experience is still informed by my body's general system of relative spatial equivalencies, so that even if I can take the Alps in one stride, I can still appreciate that the distance from the Alps to the Himalayas, or to the moon, is more formidable and time-consuming (not to mention the invariant character of those basic articulations such as "up" and "down" or "right" and "left").[18] This general system of spatial equivalences enacted through the body thus functions as a sort of bodily *a priori* in the sense that *all* of my particular spatial experiences, and even my acts of imagination, are *always already* conditioned by, and oriented in terms of, these equivalencies. It is this, our body's inescapable, spontaneous commitment to our general "terrestrial situation" (*PP* 503[464]), that remains constantly operative, regardless of what is peculiar to my individual, historically specific experience. Although it is not as thoroughly discussed as the body's system of spatial articulation, we can presume that there is for Merleau-Ponty a comparable general system of *temporal* articulation at work in our experience, a system that is likewise rooted in our natural, "terrestrial situation" and that likewise involves a basic orientation towards certain general features of the temporal field (as, for instance, day and night, or the recurring systole and diastole rhythm of the circulatory system) that underlie all of our specific temporal experiences.[19]

Before pursuing this suggestion further, we should note that the dimension of generality that structures our particular experiences in advance is, although general in character, not some sort of ideal or universal category that resides in our intellect and that as such *derives from*, or is to be *applied to*, our particular, concrete experiences. We often think of perceptual experience, along with whatever specific objects are intended in perception, as being in all aspects fully individuated and concrete, such that anything general must be regarded as an abstraction that takes on meaning only by way of some sort of indirect reference to the concrete, perceptual world. Thus any talk of how we "experience the world in general," or of the "general form" the phenomenal world takes, would seem to involve some abstraction from our *actual* experiences, which are one and all singular. Merleau-Ponty proposes, however, that the sort of bodily generality he takes to be basic to experience *has its own way of appearing in and for experience* – that is, that there is a *phenomenality* peculiar to this layer of generality. Thus, what is general in experience is not simply inferred by the intellect (for instance, in an inductive move), or the product of an intellectual reflection on experience's ideal conditions (as in the case of the Kantian categories), but something that an attentive description of experience reveals to be an actual, lived feature of what and how we experience.[20]

The notion of the phenomenality of the general comes to the fore most prominently in Merleau-Ponty's discussion of style, and in particular in his discussion of the manner in which individual agents reveal themselves to have a certain character or general style of comportment that underlies a wide range of their particular gestures and actions.[21] But it also constitutes an essential feature of Merleau-Ponty's more basic account of our embodied perception. Thus he refers to the "global presence" that our perceptual situations have for us (*PP* 108[81]), or to the "evidentness of [the] complete world" that our body affords us (*PP* 111[84]). He also draws attention in various places to the fact that we are alive to the "atmospheric" (i.e., inherently non-individuated, indefinite, horizonal) character of our situation (see, for example, *PP* 207[172], 440[400], 506[467]), and he correlates this palpable generality to the fact that our own body's responses to the world immediately exist for us not as particular, occasion-by-occasion responses, but are "sketched out once and for all in their generality" (*PP* 117[89]). As we approach an understanding of generalized time, then, we must likewise concern ourselves first of all with its phenomenal character, with its peculiar way of *being given* in and for lived experience.

III. Indifference and the Phenomenality of the General Now

We can begin by noticing the distinctive phenomenal character of the longer temporal durations in which we find ourselves situated. For instance, Merleau-Ponty draws attention to the fact that, while we might be inclined to think of our experience of the present as an experience of "this [individuated] instant" – for, according to our objective conception of time, time is constantly flowing at a uniform rate, so the present must be such as to disappear *instantaneously*, as soon as it arrives – we must recognize that the *experiential now* also trails off into the more general terrain of "today, this year or even my entire life" (*PP* 483[444]). That is, part of what is constitutive of our perceptual "field of presence" is that we are experientially alive to being in the midst of more general and more gradually unfolding durations, and that we can look to our experience of the *continuity* of these longer durations as a mode of access to the phenomenal givenness of general time.

In the context of his account of the phenomenological genesis of the objective conception of time, Merleau-Ponty draws attention to the fact that our experience of the continuity of time always takes place by way of a differentiation of a continuous duration from the more discontinuous, passing character of our particular, episodic experiences (see *PP* 481–3[442–4]).

In effect, our lived experience of continuous durations takes the form of a certain *indifference to experience in its more episodic character*, and we shall see that it is precisely the phenomenal character of this indifference – an indifference to experience, but that is itself apparent *in* and *to* experience – that affords us access to time's generality more broadly.

To elucidate this point, Merleau-Ponty unpacks our experience of time's continuity by way of an analogy with the fact that, in experiencing our own movements through space, we are alive, not only to the way the more immediate, proximate, and individuated features of our environment change as we move through it, but also to the way in which the less determinate, more distant, and more general features on the horizon stay *the same*, despite our movements. As Merleau-Ponty writes, when we are looking at a landscape through the window of a train, "we do not really believe that the landscape moves; the attendant at the railway crossing whizzes by, but the hill in the distance hardly moves" (*PP* 182[443]). Thus, although particular objects in the immediate environment whiz by – and thus appear as relative to, or as expressions of, the movement we identify ourselves with as embodied subjects (i.e., the train's movement, experienced as an extension of *our* bodily movement[22]) – the distant landscape appears precisely in its fixity and in its relative indifference to this movement. Merleau-Ponty seems to be suggesting that it is precisely in experiencing the difference between that which moves "with us" and that which is indifferent to our movement, that we come to posit an "object out there" in space (the unchanging landscape) that is taken to be *independent* of our experience.

Merleau-Ponty likens this spatial experience of indifference to the way in which the longer events or durations in which we are immersed (for instance, the current week or month) appear to us likewise as "fixed points" when compared to the shorter, more immediate, and more clearly defined episodes of experience (for instance, this morning, this hour, or this minute), whose passing has a more palpable dimension in our experience: "even if the start of my journey has already moved off, the start of my week remains a fixed point; an objective time is sketched out upon the horizon and must therefore be taking shape in my immediate past" (*PP* 482[443]).[23] Because I experience my week as being, so to speak, *as present to me* this afternoon as it was at the opening of my day (and as it will be tomorrow morning), because it appears as a more enduring, continuous "now" that does not simply pass away with – or, that is relatively indifferent to – the various episodic experiences in which I am embroiled in a moment-to-moment manner, we can say that it is through an experience of indifference that my experience itself gives rise to a time that runs its course relatively independently of such moment-to-moment to experience, a time that passes in a manner that is relatively indifferent to the way in which our most immediate and engrossing experiences – each with its horizon of recent past and impending future – enact the *ecstasis* of time's dimensions. Merleau-Ponty suggests that it is precisely this lived experience of indifference that forms the phenomenological basis of our conception of an objective time.

Of course, just as the hill in the distance, although it may have presented itself as the fixed point in my landscape for several kilometres of travel, eventually disappears from my view altogether, so too do the longer spans of time that form the more distant horizons of our current situation pass away like minutes and hours do. Thus these reference points in the more distant temporal horizon, although they are *relatively* indifferent to the changes I experience in my most immediate, moment-to-moment bodily experience, are not *absolutely* indifferent to, or independent of, this more ephemeral experience; they pass away too, and this more gradual passing is itself something to which our experience is alive. Presumably our experience of the passing of the more general durations also occurs by way of a reference to relatively "fixed" durations that are more general still – just as, in the spatial case, where the specific distant horizons gradually change as we move, but the fact that there is always some distant horizon, in general, is "fixed." But this dependence does not imply that these longer, more gradual durations are experientially *reducible to* the more ephemeral and distinct episodes, as though they amounted to a mere *aggregate* of these more circumscribed moments of presence. Rather, there is clearly a phenomenological difference between these "strata" of experience, a difference that lived experience is *constantly* alive to and *constantly* involved in negotiating. Indeed, it would seem that negotiating these temporal differences is a constitutive feature of our way of taking up time at all.[24]

Of course, we cannot simply say that these strata are *simultaneous* with one another – for indeed, precisely what is in question is the distinction between distinct experiences of presence, in terms of which relations of simultaneity can be determined in the first place. Indeed, we should not even call them *distinct experiences* of presence, for this would suggest that they are somehow on a par with one another, each having its own clear and fully present "object," when in fact the experience of the more general duration is really a way of experiencing the *disintegration* or *indistinction* of our more circumscribed, moment-by-moment temporality: it is our way of being alive to the fact that the temporal distinctions we are otherwise concerned to be making at the level of our moment-to-moment, historical experiences *are also being unmade*. There is, as it were, a kind of *forgetting* of the distinctness of this distinct present moment – a disintegration of this otherwise unique moment of presence into a more indeterminate, amorphous, general field of presence – *already at work* in the very perception, the very "making-present," of it.[25] Just as distant landscapes have a certain look to them – they actually appear to us *as far away*, and in seeing them we are alive to the fact that we are only getting general contours, we *see* that *there is much more to see* in them than is currently visible[26] – so too do longer time spans have their own distinctive manner of presenting themselves in experience, their own phenomenality. But this phenomenality is, as it were, a negative phenomenality, the givenness to experience of a kind of indistinction, or an indifference to differences that are given at another level of experience; it is, as it were, the visibility of a kind of invisibility.

It seems that our *experience* of such general durations, and thus of an indifference to our own more distinct, moment-by-moment experiences, must *itself* be stretched out over time, and rather than taking the form of a simple accumulation or synthesis of individual instances of experience, has rather the form of a single, continuous, drawn-out experience. For while it might be true that I have insight, at this *current* moment of time, into what it means to experience my most immediate situation as happening "this year" – for instance, insofar as I locate what is happening at the moment within "the summer during which my first child was born," thereby experiencing its temporal specificity as continuous with a more gradual and general duration that envelopes the preceding winter and spring, in which I lived in anticipation of the birth[27] – it is also clear that I could not have this experiential insight at the moment were it not for the fact that I myself have actually lived through the unfolding of this longer duration. Experience itself takes time, and the experience of the *phenomenal sense* of longer durations (as compared, for instance, to an intellectual construction of such durations, by way of a calendar) must itself be a "living through" or "living out" of those longer durations. In arguing for the continuity of experience over time, and thus indirectly for the phenomenality of the general now, Merleau-Ponty (focusing in particular on the now that is my life) goes so far as to call my first perception an "ever-present event" that I am still in the midst of, arguing that "I am not a series of psychical acts, nor for that matter a central I who gathers them together in a synthetic unity, but rather a single experience that is inseparable from itself, a single 'cohesion of life,' a single temporality" (*PP* 469[430]).[28] It is this living cohesion, this single experience that is, from the point of view of my lived experience, of indefinite duration, that alone allows the notion of "'my life,' my 'total being'" to be, not "contestable constructions," but "phenomena that are presented to reflection as evident" (*PP* 439[399]).[29]

IV. The General Now of the Species and of the World

Having articulated the basic character of the general now as grounded in an experience of indifference, we must note that in all of the examples we have considered thus far of the "general now" – *this* week, *this* summer, or the now of *this* (i.e., *my own*) life as a whole – our experience is still to some extent grounded in the historical singularity (the "thisness") of such nows, for we cannot fail to be alive to what makes the more general period at issue temporally individuated when compared to other such general periods. This individuation is in each case grounded in a certain inaugural event (the beginning of my week, the birth of my child, my own birth), an event that kicks off a historically new and unique duration that underlies and unifies the significance of the particular events within that duration. Thus, even in our experience of time's more general durations we are still drawing upon the distinctive character of historical time. This raises the question of whether there are *any* general durations operative in our lived experience that are *purely* ahistorical, and that as such are indifferent to *any and all* historical instantiation – the question of whether there are in lived experience any pure repetitions that carry on indefinitely, without any internal reference to their own beginning or end.[30] Such pure repetition, apparently ungrounded in any historically specific inaugural event, is, we recall, the feature that most characterizes *natural* cycles. So what we are asking is whether there are strata of our lived experience – perhaps those strata that are farthest removed from the most immediate, most individuated now of my current perception – that in effect comprise an experiential merging with natural cyclicality.

It would seem that any singular now (even if it is of a more general duration, when compared to the more immediate nows that are enveloped into it) must exist for us, to some extent, as *one among many nows* in a natural rhythm that is of indefinite duration. For instance, it seems that our experience of this summer, in its temporal thisness, hinges on our capacity to experience the "summerness" of this summer, which amounts to the capacity to locate this historically individuated "moment" in an indefinitely recurring cycle of seasons that is at bottom indifferent to any of its particular, historical instantiations. Indeed, on Merleau-Ponty's argument even the experience of "this, my [singular] life" is premised on a first-order apperception that originally reveals me to myself as "*a* consciousness (or as a man or an embodied subject)," and ultimately as a terrestrial being thrown into the natural world (*PP* 515[478]) – a world that is, in the end, characterized by recurring, cyclical rhythms that exceed the boundaries not only of my own individual life but even of the life of my species. Thus Merleau-Ponty implies that, even in my original experiential relation to myself, I cannot fail to locate myself within a time that is indifferent to *all* of the inaugural events, *all* of the departure points – including that of my own birth – that ground the historical narratives through which I typically make sense of the world.

In the end, Merleau-Ponty works towards the idea that the natural world as a whole is *itself* historical, that it too, in its totality, is "temporally individuated" in the sense that there is ultimately only one singular unfolding time that encompasses all times. Thus he argues that there is phenomenological justification for the common personification of time as a "single, concrete being, fully present in each of its manifestations just as a man is fully present in each of his spoken words" (*PP* 484[445]), for just as the individual has a determinate style, there is in fact a "temporal style of the world, and time remains the same because the past is a previous future and a recent present, the present is an impending past and a recent future, and finally, the future is a present and even a past to come" (*PP* 484[445]). In the terms I have been developing, we can say that the world itself has its own duration, that the world's time "remains the same" insofar as it is, despite the temporal ecstasies of its various manifestations, an indefinitely drawn-out "now" – a now that is "ever-present" within each of the particular "nows" of my episodic experience. Thus, at the level of this more fundamental analysis, there are in the final analysis no pure, *eternal* repetitions in the concrete natural world, for all repetitions – even the large-scale movements of the solar system – are ultimately rooted in contingent, finite, inaugural events located in the historical series, a series that is ultimately continuous with, and forms the ultimate horizon of, the singular "now" of even our most ephemeral and singularized perceptual experience.[31]

Nevertheless, we as finite, terrestrial subjects, constantly engaged with the natural world for the whole extent of our lives, must necessarily reckon with the fact that we are living in and through certain temporal trajectories opened up by founding inaugural events *to which we can have no experiential access*. From our point of view, such events as the beginning of the world or the beginning of our species (or, indeed, even the event of our own birth[32]) comprise, as it were, an original past – a past that was *never present*[33] – in the sense that *all* of our experiences can only exist *after*, and *in the wake of*, these events, within the general duration (the duration of the world itself, or of "now" of our species) they have kicked off. Such events are, thus, the concrete conditions of all of our experience; they are, as it were, time's historical *a priori*. But they are also properly understood as time's *natural a priori*. For insofar as their starting points are, from the point of view of our experience, always deferred into a general, non-individuated past, and insofar as their endpoints in the future (if they do in fact end) are likewise deferred indefinitely, our experience – as the specifically *human* experience of *this singular* world – is tantamount to an indefinite, ongoing repetition of what these events inaugurated. These inaugural events, having been generalized in such a way as to lose contact with their original historical definiteness as singular events, become the *ever-present, ever-repeated context* of *all* our experience, in that *everything* we experience is *already* located within their indefinite durations, within these most general and most unhistorical of "nows."

Thus, regarding the question of whether there are pure, non-historical repetitions operative within lived experience, it seems that for Merleau-Ponty, we must offer a qualified response: while time is, through its whole extent, historical in the sense of being both individuating and individuated, there is nevertheless a kind of pure repetition operative in and as the generality of experience itself, insofar as experience is constitutively unable to make direct contact with the singular founding events that inaugurated the most general, indefinite durations that comprise the all-encompassing temporal strata of our experiential engagement with the world. Insofar as these events are merged into a past that can never be recovered by lived experience – into what Merleau-Ponty, in referring specifically to the repetitive organic processes we all inherit *qua* human beings, calls the "past of all pasts" (*PP* 114[87]) – they are for us tantamount to the given, *a priori*, and *ever-present* conditions of all our experiences. Precisely insofar as subjectivity, as being-in-the-world, carries within it *a priori* – that is, prior to any particular, individuated experiences – the most general form that the phenomenal world takes (and, more specifically, the general form the world takes for "psycho-physical subjects who have a similar organization to my own" (*PP* 503[465]), our embodied experience can *itself* be understood as a kind of pure repetition that thereby embodies a kind of indifference with respect to the individuated moments of its own concrete unfolding. It is thus that nature, insofar as it is characterized by ongoing cyclical repetition, finds its place *within* experience itself. The phenomenology of temporal experience leads to a conception of natural temporality precisely as that which is recalcitrant to the structure of *historical inauguration* or *institution*.[34]

V. The "General Now" of the Body and the Temporality of Repression

The notion that an individual subject can be out of touch with the individuated historical events that inaugurated the general atmosphere that permeates all of this individual's experiences forms the core of Merleau-Ponty's account of the logic of *repression*, which in his view is one of the basic and pervading psychological mechanisms structuring our existence.[35] As I will discuss in this concluding section, Merleau-Ponty focuses on the fact that in repression a traumatic event in the course of a person's life ends up losing its individual character and comes to inform the general contours of all of that person's experience, such that everything new that appears to the person unwittingly appears already in terms of – or, we can say, as part of a repetition of – that original event. Thus what was a singular, relatively isolated "now" becomes, in effect, a general now – the now of *all* experience – and the otherwise individuated, historical event of the past becomes *ever-present* in such a way as to lose touch with its own historicality. What is of particular interest for our purposes is that, for Merleau-Ponty, the logic of repression forms the basic temporal model for conceiving of the way in which all of our experience is inherently informed in advance by the repetitive processes we have inherited from our species. The ongoing, repetitive rhythms of our various organic processes exist for us, within experience, precisely as the general, ever-present context – the general now – of *all* we see and touch; they are, as I have already suggested, our bodily *a priori*. But in the case of these "natural" *a priori* – as distinct from the case of those psychological repressions that are formed in the course of our lives, and that are thus mediated specifically by our personal projects – what has been generalized are certain inaugural events (for instance, the "prehistorical" events in the evolution of our species) of which we can have no personal experience or memory. Thus the mechanism of repression will help shed further light on how it is that experience is internally informed by a natural temporality, one that is structured in terms of cycles that have lost touch with all historical temporality and that thus tend towards pure repetition.

Merleau-Ponty's initial discussion of repression is sparked by an attempt to uncover the specifically temporal conditions of the phenomenon of the phantom limb (see *PP* 108–18[80–91]). For him, this phenomenon challenges both our strictly physiological and our strictly psychological accounts of human existence. While this phenomenon has psychological dimensions – insofar as the continued sensations are of a limb that is not "actually there," and moreover manifest a certain attitude of refusal on the part of the patient, an attempt to keep a hold on the body that is now lost – patients are not straightforwardly conscious of their project of refusal and seem in many respects to be genuinely unconscious of their actual loss. And while the phenomenon also has clear physiological correlates – as is shown, for instance, by the fact that when certain of the patient's afferent nerves are severed, the phantom limb disappears (*PP* 116[88]) – Merleau-Ponty shows that the physiological account alone (insofar as it reduces the body to a system of objectively present, causally connected forces) cannot fully account for the virtual, past-ridden, ghostly character of the phantom limb.

Merleau-Ponty's own "existential" account of the phenomenon hinges on demonstrating that the phantom limb has an essentially "ambiguous presence" for the patient – that it is, for the patient, both there and not there, or, put in other terms, the patient is both conscious of the loss of his limb and, at the same time, not conscious of it. And rather than resorting to the positing of some sort of hidden unconscious domain in the psyche – thereby reinscribing the body/mind dualism within the psyche itself, in the form of a dualism between actually present, effective drives, and a consciousness that is wholly unaware of them – Merleau-Ponty appeals rather to the generality of experiential time to account for the nature of this inherently ambiguous experience. His argument is essentially that the limb is, for the patient, *present in general*, but *not specifically present in this particular moment*, so his account hinges ultimately on demonstrating the ambiguity of the temporal present itself, the ambiguity of a present that is irreducibly both singular and general, both an immediate, momentary now and a general, persisting now that exists across, and that is relatively indifferent to, momentary nows.[36] Just as, in our previous examples, we saw that, experientially, the now can be both the singular moment of perception, but also the now of this day, this year, or this life as a whole, here we see that it is precisely the play of these two strata – and, in particular, in the indifference of the former to the latter – that is at issue.

In the case of the phantom limb, our experiential attunement to the generality of the now takes the form of what Merleau-Ponty terms the "habit body," which in this context is to be understood as a critique of the physiological body: whereas the physiological body, traditionally conceived, is constituted in terms of objective forces that must be fully present in some physical form in order to be effectual, the habit body is never wholly present in this or that instant of time, but is essentially spread across time. It is not just that the habit body contains, at the moment, in its full physical presence, the actual, still-effective traces of past bodily events; rather, the habit body exists as *keeping open* and *reliving* its past, *qua* past, in the sense that it gives rise to a indefinite present that merges with this past.[37] Merleau-Ponty argues that the patient's impersonal habit-body *continues to inhabit* and thereby *continuously repeat* the general, impersonal "now" of the body for which the limb is still *present*, thereby giving rise to a perceptual field that, on the whole or in general, continues to motivate the activity of that limb. Although the limb is in fact *not present* in the body physiologically conceived, it *is* present – within an indefinite, general present, indifferent to moment-to-moment experience – in the habit-body, which continues to bring it to bear in the very way it continues to comport itself towards the world.

This general comportment continues to structure experience, even though the patient cannot fail to be alive to the fact that, with respect to this or that particular project his "body at this moment" might personally initiate in the singular "now" of his unique situation, he no longer has the use of this limb (see *PP* 111[84]). Thus Merleau-Ponty draws attention to the fact that even though patients experiencing a phantom limb continue to operate as though the limb were still there in practice, these same patients can, when focusing specific attention on the limb, describe certain peculiarities of the limb and of its motile capacities (*PP* 110[83]).[38] This specific awareness is, however, "repressed" when the patient feels called upon to engage in some action that the world solicits from him, for "like the normal [i.e., uninjured] subject, he has no need of a clear and articulated perception of his body in order to begin moving. It is enough that his body is 'available' as an indivisible power" (*PP*

110[83]). For, as I mentioned above, our own body's responses to the world immediately exist for us not as particular, occasion-by-occasion responses, but are "sketched out once and for all in their generality" (*PP* 117[89]).

Merleau-Ponty models the phenomenon of the phantom limb on the phenomenon of repression in order to draw attention to the way in which experience itself compulsively re-enacts or continues its general past in the present, to the point that experience becomes relatively indifferent to what is new and peculiar in the singular situations it faces in the episodic present. In the case of repression, experience remains imprisoned in the reiteration of the now of a traumatic past episode; Merleau-Ponty claims that this very specific now grows into a general now, such that it comes to "displace" any new nows and "relieves them of their value as authentic present moments" (*PP* 112[85]) – that is, it deprives them of their historical singularity, self-evidence, and autonomy, of their capacity to fully occupy or "fill up" an instant of consciousness (*PP* 114[87]) in their own right. As Merleau-Ponty writes, "new perceptions replace previous ones, and even new emotions replace those that came before, but this renewal only has to do with the content of our experience and not with its structure" (*PP* 112[85]). That is, in repression we become relatively indifferent to our new experiences, because we are compelled to experience the traumatic "now" of the past as though it were the general structure of all subsequent experiences; thus nothing new really happens to us, and "personal time [or we might also say narrative, historical time] is arrested" (*PP* 112[85]). Thus the "forgetting" that, I argued, is already on the horizon of every present experience – the forgetting that comes with submerging the present into a more distant, general, less articulate past – in this case dominates. The "new" present is, as it were, forgotten before it is even articulated.

The patient experiencing a phantom limb is likewise engaged in a kind of repression insofar as she continues to inhabit – or, we can also say, continues to be committed to – the general world that solicits the once-familiar activities of her limb, to the point that she becomes indifferent to or untouched by the signs in her *present* perceptual situations that would make evident to her that her limb is no longer present. As Merleau-Ponty writes, "in hysteria and repression, we can be ignorant of something while knowing it because our memories and our body, rather than being given to us through singular and determinate acts of consciousness, are enveloped by generality" (*PP* 200[165]). The patient who experiences a phantom limb "knows" her limb is not present, but she overlooks this insofar as she immerses herself in the generality of a present that reopens, and thus continues, the past in which it was still at her general disposal. As Merleau-Ponty writes,

> sensory messages or memories are only explicitly grasped or known by us [in the present] given a general adhesion to the zone of our body and of our life that they concern. This adhesion or refusal places the subject into a definite situation and delimits his immediately available mental field, just as the acquisition or the loss of a sensory organ offers or subtracts an object of the physical field from his direct grasp. (*PP* 200[165])

In the case of the phantom limb, there is similarly a kind of compulsive reiteration and displacement of the present, but here the reiteration is not of a particular "now" in the patient's past, but of a kind of general, impersonal "now" that was never itself present as a singular episode that "filled up" the patient's consciousness as such. For just as the acquisition of a new bodily organ itself opens up a whole field of presence, so too does having a functioning limb itself open up a whole field of presence in which manipulable objects figure. Although one might, in the course of one's life, have the occasion to consciously develop specific abilities with one's arms, one cannot recall having had to learn to have one's arms at one's disposal in general, and correspondingly, one cannot recall having had to learn that the world is generally open, say, to being reached at by one's arms.[39] That I experience the world thus as manipulable in general is not something I have ever been expressly conscious of as such in one of my particular perceptions, but it *is* something that has *always already* been in place as a general horizon of each of my particular engagements with the world. In this way, the body itself constitutes a "general now" that serves as the medium in and through which all of my particular, episodic experiences of self-directed arm use take place.

Insofar as we are bodies that participate in the pre-personal, reiterative time of natural life, then, there is always some dimension of us that is untouched by what we are experiencing in the singular here and now. As Merleau-Ponty notes, even when, upon the death of a loved one, I seem to be "wholly absorbed in" my sorrow, and am thus wholly defined by this historically singular moment of personal experience, "my gaze already wanders out before me, it quietly takes interest in some bright object, it resumes its autonomous existence" (*PP* 113–14[86]). While the "now" of such personal sorrow would seem to be an example of an "integrated or rigorously unique totality" of experience (*PP* 113[86]) – for even my body, insofar as it is overtaken with crying, for example, is "integrated" into this singular distress – my body nevertheless maintains a sliver of indifference with respect to this singular "now," for it is also operating in other, more general, relatively autonomous impersonal domains, thereby also giving rise to more general, impersonal domains of experience.[40] Sorrow or not, my eyes *do what they always do*, responding to *ever-present* imperatives of the visible world, so there is, in a certain sense, nothing singular about their activity – they are constantly caught up in adjusting themselves so as to discover the optimal focusing movements through which to make sense of what is before them, which is why they are particularly solicited by a bright object that is, at first, hard to fixate upon. I am thereby engaged in a constantly repeating bodily process that operates according to its own, relatively autonomous rhythms and temporality, and it is being caught up in the body's general "now" that gives me some distance from – or, we can also say, *represses* – the singular now of my personal distress. Thus in his discussion of repression, Merleau-Ponty likens the body's constitutive generality to a kind of repression, calling it "an anonymous and general existence" that plays the role of an "*innate complex*" (*PP* 113[86]). Our bodies, and what is "innate" in them, are themselves the compulsive reiteration, in the present, of an impersonal, irretrievable past – whether the past of our own earliest stages of bodily development, or even the "past of the species" (*le passé spécifique*), which our own body "secretly feeds … because this past remains its present" (*PP* 114[87], translation modified).

It is true, the impersonal rhythms we repeat in the lived present of our bodies, and the distinctive temporality of repetition these rhythms inscribe in us, are not just an impassive background against which all our specific, more personal projects take place. They are also constantly being "sublimated" into the individuated historical events and narratives that make up our lives; they are, as it were, constantly *becoming historical*. Consider, for instance, the way in which the otherwise generic repetition of the breathing cycle comes to be given a musicality of its own in the playing of certain jazz trumpeters who have adopted a "breathy" sound, or breath-length units of phrasing: we certainly "hear" the rhythm of breathing in their playing, but this rhythm has been *transformed* by, and thus becomes *meaningful within*, the narrative or historical structure of the melody or solo. Similarly, a person who develops an overly anxious way of being-in-the-world can also come to develop shorter, choppier breathing rhythms that in effect become personal expressions of this individual's overall way of being.[41] Merleau-Ponty would have us see, however, that our ability to experience these sublimated "institutions" of meaning depends to some extent on our appreciating the dialectical relationship they maintain with the non-instituted, generic "norms" they serve to transform. For how else would we be able to experience a certain pattern of breathing as "short and choppy," or how would we be able to hear the solo as a "sublimation" or "narrativization" of breath, if we were not in touch with the constancy, regularity, and essentially non-narrative character of breathing in general?[42] Moreover, Merleau-Ponty is also concerned to draw attention to the way in which the impersonal, repetitive currents of our bodily existence can, at times, reassert themselves as our dominant way of experiencing time. For instance, in certain illnesses our "bodily events become the events of the day" (*PP* 114[87]), in the sense that the main articulations of our day are determined, not by our personal capacity to initiate certain projects and see them through, but rather by the generic, repetitive cycles of our organism. Such cases would suggest that the generalized existence of our body continues to *exist, in its generality,* even while being sublimated into more personalized, individualized forms – that the natural time of the body never *quite* gives itself wholly over to the historical time of personal life, that there is always operative, within experience, a certain indifference to what we are experiencing, and thus a certain recalcitrance to historical time.

The time of nature, we have seen, is thus not merely derivative upon the historical time of subjectivity; rather, it is an irreducible dimension of our lived experience, revealing itself in the constitutive indifference that we ourselves have in regard to our own more circumscribed experiences. I have suggested that the way to approach an understanding of Merleau-Ponty's phenomenology of time is to see both of these temporal dimensions, the natural and the historical, as being operative at once, and it is precisely in the resulting ambiguity of the present – a present that is, at once, this unique, individuated now, as well as the general now of my life, my species, and even of the world – that we can approach an understanding of the fundamental, irresolvable ambiguity of an existence that is both nature and subjectivity.

NOTES

1 See Merleau-Ponty's claim that "[time] must be understood as a subject, and the subject must be understood as time" (*PP* 484[445]). For a helpful general discussion of the significance of this link between time and subjectivity, see Matthews, "Temporality, Subjectivity, and History."

2 For instance, Merleau-Ponty argues that we could not even conceive of events as thus laid out into fixed points in time, were we not already immersed in experiencing the way time maintains a dynamic unity in its passing by way of structures of anticipation and retention (*PP* 481–2[442–3]).

3 For Merleau-Ponty's reference to the *"a priori* of the species," see *PP* 107[80].

4 On the theme of the repetitive rhythms of natural cycles being that through which we experience our situations, see Russon, *Bearing Witness to Epiphany*, chs. 1 and 5.

5 See *PP* 114[87], where Merleau-Ponty speaks of the ambiguity of time itself – in particular, the ambiguity of our past as something that is both present and absent – as being at the core of our attempt to understand the ambiguity between the personal (subjective existence) and the impersonal domain of the body in its natural being.

6 I am also thus meaning to imply that there is at work in *PP* a conception of nature that anticipates some of the core ideas about nature's inherent *generality* that come to the fore in Merleau-Ponty's later course notes on nature. See Merleau-Ponty, *Nature*; especially relevant in this connection are Merleau-Ponty's discussion of Whitehead (113–22) and his various discussions of the philosophical implications of modern biology, and in particular of the ontological status of that which grounds the particular, observable phenomena of growth and generation (for instance, 178–90, 229–66). As a contrast, compare Renaud Barbaras's argument in "Merleau-Ponty and Nature" that the phenomenological project contained in the *PP* is incapable of questioning the sense of nature as such, and thus does not approach the conception of nature developed in Merleau-Ponty's later work. My approach thus shares more with Bernet's attempt to show that the main outlines of the later philosophy of nature have already been laid out in *PP*; see Rudolf Bernet, "The Subject in Nature," 56.

7 For a helpful elaboration of some of the complicated ways in which the temporal dimensions implicate one another – and, specifically, the way in which the past "becomes past" in virtue of the present that references it as past – see Glen A. Mazis, "Merleau-Ponty and the 'Backward Flow' of Time," 53–68.

8 In contrast to the experience of seeing a city in the distance grow larger on our horizon as we drive towards it – an experience in which there is an unbroken continuity of "transition syntheses" of the various *Abschattungen* of the city, but in which the continuity involves a *development* towards an anticipated, organic "completion," namely, the increasingly more articulate vision of the city (see *PP* 386[344–5]) – the experience of natural cycles promises some sort of development towards a completion, but in the end we find ourselves back exactly where we started; it is as though we were driving toward something, only to find that the completion of the journey coincided exactly with the place we started from.

9 Merleau-Ponty's description of the experience of time of a patient who is engaged in repressing a traumatic event is particularly helpful in illustrating this dissolution into natural time: "for the patient, nothing ever happens ... nothing comes to pass but always identical 'nows'; life flows back upon itself and history is dissolved into natural time" (*PP* 202–3[167]). I will return below to Merleau-Ponty's discussion of repression and its relevance for illuminating natural time.

10 For Merleau-Ponty's account of this idealized time, see *PP* 474–5[435–6].

11 Merleau-Ponty here speaks of the "feeling of eternity" that can be elicited, for instance, in the face of the continuity of the water flow in a fountain: rather than perceiving distinct spurts, repeated again and again, we feel as though there is essentially one arc-like continuity, whose uninterrupted flow bespeaks a kind of static identity that overrides what might otherwise appear as distinct temporal episodes (*PP* 486[447]). Merleau-Ponty reminds us, however, that insofar as we are alive to the constant *pressing* or *thrusting* of the water, our subjectivity in effect "comes to shatter the plenitude of being in itself" by introducing a structure of transcendence or a "reach[ing] out toward" (*PP* 483[444]), thereby sneaking in a non-cyclical (or historical) trajectory into the otherwise "complete" movement; this *ever-incomplete* trajectory is what the feeling of eternity "feeds on."

12 See Barbaras's insightful discussion of Merleau-Ponty's later challenge to the idea that nature, understood essentially as generality and totality, can be individuated into distinct temporal moments; Barbaras, "Merleau-Ponty and Nature," 32–6.

13 "Sleep arrives when a certain voluntary attitude suddenly receives from outside the very confirmation that it was expecting. *I* breathe slowly and deeply to call forth sleep, and suddenly, one might say, my mouth communicates with some immense external lung that calls my breath forth and forces it back. A certain respiratory rhythm, desired by me just a moment ago, becomes my very being (*PP* 256[219]).

14 For an excellent discussion of what is at stake in conceiving of nature as a generalized existence, see Barbaras, "Merleau-Ponty and Nature."

15 "Just as every experience – insofar as it has to do with impressions – is in the same way strictly my own, it seems that a unique and never doubled subject embraces them all (*PP* 515[477]).

16 For a helpful discussion of the significance of Merleau-Ponty's conception of our constitutive generality, see Lawlor, "The End of Phenomenology."

17 Compare Merleau-Ponty's claim that "[e]ach thing appears to us through a medium that it colors with its fundamental quality" (*PP* 514[476]).

18 See again *PP* 503[464]. See also Merleau-Ponty's discussion of the "body image," conceived as a "system of equivalences" and an "immediately given invariant" through which the world is given to us (*PP* 176[142).

19 In saying that we must "eat and breathe before perceiving or reaching a relational life" (*PP* 197[162]), Merleau-Ponty is not just making the obvious point that we must be alive in order to perceive and to engage in interpersonal experience, but is rather drawing attention to the fact that our impersonal, cyclical processes give rise to a *general field of possibilities*, within which our particular, more articulated perceptions and interactions can crystallize (on this point, see *PP* 199–200[164–5]). Compare here Alia Al-Saji's discussion of sensation as a process of rhythmic differentiation arising out of the less differentiated rhythms of the body; Al-Saji, "'A Past Which Has Never Been Present.'"

20 For an insightful discussion of the how the problem of grasping generalities is reframed in the context of phenomenology, see David Morris, "Bergsonian Intuition."

21 In his discussion of how agents develop practical characters, or styles of acting, that underlie their particular instances of action, Merleau-Ponty comes to argue that "Generality and probability are not fictions, they are phenomena" (*PP* 506[467]). For a further discussion of style as it pertains both to human character and to artworks, see Merleau-Ponty, "Indirect Language," 39–83, esp. 52–5.

22 As in Merleau-Ponty's example of how the car we are accustomed to driving comes to be incorporated into our body (*PP* 178–9[144]), here too we can think of the train and its movement as incorporated into, or as "dilations" of, our lived body.

23 Presumably, in referring to the week as a duration of time, Merleau-Ponty does not intend us to think of a 168-hour or 7-day period, starting on Sunday, as strictly defined by the specific calendar we have adopted, for this would be to presuppose the objective conception of time that he is claiming to derive here. Rather, what is at issue is the "lived week," as

defined most essentially by the longer-term projects we are involved in, projects that encompass and thereby act as a horizon for the various "sub-projects" that we undertake in a day-to-day way.

24 Compare Merleau-Ponty's remark that the "'shrivelling up' of the past whose extreme would be oblivion" is not an accident of memory, or a "degradation in the empirical existence of a consciousness of time that is in principle total; rather they express the initial ambiguity of memory: to retain is to hold onto, but at a distance" (*PP* 485[446]). That is, the fact that the past becomes less articulate to us ("shrivels up"), and thus becomes more and more a "past in general," as it gets further away, is an irreducible, constitutive feature of what it is to have a past, not merely an accidental result of our empirical memory's incapacity to hold on to all of the episodic articulations that composed it. Analogously, the longer durations in which we are involved – those that stretch out further into the past and future – are likewise *constitutively* general and vague, in a way that is simply not reducible to an aggregate of our episodic experience.

25 Compare here Alia Al-Saji's argument, in contrast, that in the *Phenomenology of Perception*, "forgetting is sidestepped as a phenomenon, but also as a structural dimension of time itself"; Alia Al-Saji, "The Temporality of Life," 182. However, see Al-Saji's "'A Past Which Has Never Been Present'" for the argument that Merleau-Ponty, in his account of sensation, does in the end operate with a sense of the essentiality of forgetfulness, or of a disruption of full presence.

26 Compare Merleau-Ponty's discussion of perceiving "size at a distance," for instance in "Indirect Language," 49. Merleau-Ponty argues here that the reason why we see the moon as large even though, if we measure all of the things in our field of vision according to the same one uniform standard, the "space" taken up by the moon is quite small, is because we see it *as distant*.

27 Compare Merleau-Ponty's observation that "we consider, for example, everything that has a meaningful relation with our present worries as belonging to our present; and thus we implicitly recognize that time and sense [which is essentially general in nature] are one" (*PP* 489[450]).

28 Merleau-Ponty notes that he is adopting the notion of the "cohesion of life" from Heidegger's *Being and Time*, and it is noteworthy that he returns to this notion again in the chapter on "Temporality," there in service of his argument that "I am myself time" (*PP* 483[445]).

29 In referring to *reflection* here, I take it that Merleau-Ponty means the sort of radical reflection characteristic of phenomenology, a reflection that gains access precisely to the unreflective, to what we are alive to in our lived

experience. For it is in our lived experience that this general "now" has its phenomenality and is thus precluded from being a mere "construction."

30 Compare Lawlor's discussion of Merleau-Ponty's conception of the original past in comparison to the Deleuzean notion of pure repetition; Leonard Lawlor, "The End of Phenomenology."

31 I take this to be an implication of Merleau-Ponty's argument that the "feeling of eternity" that is elicited by the natural cycle is ultimately grounded in the historical temporality of the *event* (see *PP* 485–6[446–7]), and of the argument, discussed above, that our access to cyclicality is conditioned by the historical time of arrival and departure.

32 See Merleau-Ponty's claim that "nothing was perceived in intra-uterine life, and this is why there is nothing to remember. There was nothing but the sketch of a natural self and of a natural time. This anonymous life is merely the limit of the temporal dispersion that always threatens the historical present" (*PP* 404[362]).

33 Merleau-Ponty's mention of the "original past, a past that has never been a present," comes at the end of the chapter on "Sense Experience" (*PP* 289[252]). The interpretation of the concept of an "original past" has been a matter of some controversy in the secondary literature on Merleau-Ponty. For a discussion of some aspects of this controversy, and for an interesting interpretation of this concept, see Al-Saji, "'A Past Which Has Never Been Present.'" My own reading, which situates this original past in the natural rhythms of the body, is consistent with Al-Saji's, although my interest is to show how this original past comes hand in hand with the essentially repetitive or cyclical character of experience as informed by bodily *a priori*, a character that is left largely in the background in her reading.

34 Compare here Renaud Barbaras's claim that, in the later work of Merleau-Ponty, nature is conceived precisely in terms of its difference from the instituted; Barbaras, "Merleau-Ponty and Nature."

35 See Talero's "Merleau-Ponty and the Bodily Subject" for an insightful account of the indispensable role that repression plays in all embodied experience.

36 Thus in this context Merleau-Ponty concludes that "the ambiguity of being-in-the-world is expressed by the ambiguity of our body, and this latter is understood through the ambiguity of time" (*PP* 114[87]).

37 For an incisive account of the habit body specifically as a form of memory, see Casey, "Habitual Body and Memory."

38 Merleau-Ponty here also draws attention to the fact that anosognosic patients develop behaviours that leave their paralysed limbs out of account, precisely so as not to have to face their deficiency head-on; this

avoidance behaviour is an indication of a repressed, vague awareness of the paralysis.

39 It appears that newborn humans do not yet have the ability to perceive their environments as cohering into a stable whole that contains definite, manipulable objects that they can reach out and touch. The flailing of limbs that is so typical of newborns suggests a lack of any determinate motor control of their limbs, and a lack of even any operative intentionality toward the project of specific reaching or grasping. Still, the current of their existence still runs through their limbs, and the spontaneous flailing presumably expresses the indeterminacy and non-articulacy of their experience, thus constituting the general, "non-instituted" background of all further developments of limb motility. It is worth noting, however, that the so-called rooting reflex, apparent from birth, implies that, at least through its mouth in relation to the breast, the infant can experience something like a "space to traverse" to get to the breast that is to be "grasped" by the mouth.

40 For a helpful discussion of Merleau-Ponty's use of the concept of "integration" in his account of the relation of the psychological and the physical, see Olkowski, "Merleau-Ponty's Freudianism."

41 I am grateful to Alia Al-Saji for introducing this example in the course of a discussion of a paper I presented to the Canadian Society of Continental Philosophy in 2008. Compare here Merleau-Ponty's remark that "even reflexes have a sense, and the style of each individual is still visible in them" (*PP* 114[87]).

42 Compare Merleau-Ponty's claim that one can detect a person's whole style of being from her gait, but only insofar as her body appears as a "very noticeable variation of the *norm* of walking, looking, touching and speaking that I possess in my self-awareness because I am incarnate"; Merleau-Ponty, "Indirect Language," 54, my emphasis.

PART III

Meaning and Ambiguity

9 Institution, Expression, and the Temporality of Meaning in Merleau-Ponty

DAVID MORRIS

We often conceptualize meaning as something that is "in the head" or that could be fully present and possessed by the subject. I might, for example, claim that "love" is something whose meaning I myself could already and fully grasp.[1] Indeed, our language limns this linkage between meaning and possessing things in speaking of grasping, mistaking, comprehending, or misapprehending meanings, the latter two terms having roots in Latin words for grasping, a connection at play in the French *comprendre*.[2]

From the start, Merleau-Ponty criticizes this conception of meaning. *The Structure of Behavior*[3] argues that meaning emerges in interwoven physical, living, and human structures; the *Phenomenology of Perception* shows how meaning arises in temporally open-ended fields and expressive movements;[4] and his later work shows how meaning arises in a being that is never fully present. In all these cases, meaning is *not* something a subject could possess, because it operates through something beyond the subject and is meaningful only in transcending us. An initial illustration is given by Merleau-Ponty's point that objects such as houses (or even ideal objects such as triangles) have meaning in open-endedly foreshadowing aspects that cannot now or ever be fully given.[5] The paradoxical condition of meaning is thus that it *not* be fully given or present, that it transcend comprehension. As Merleau-Ponty notes in his lectures on passivity, "we never have closed significations ... [we] have only open significations and situations whose sense is in genesis" (*IP* 179[134]).[6] But none of this implies that meaning transcends us as an idea completely present in another realm. Rather, meaning's transcending is internal to the very flow of grasping meaning: meaning's transcending is *temporal.*

Merleau-Ponty's philosophy weaves between two versions of this claim. Descriptively, he shows how temporality is the "medium" of meaning's open-ended flow. Ontologically, and more radically, he shows how temporality is the very being and operation of meaning: meaning is not so much *in* time as made "of" temporality – meaning *is* temporality.[7] Contra Descartes's argument that meaning is a present content found in a special place interior to the subject, meaning is temporally dispersed and is never fully present any place – a point anticipating many central insights of Derrida.[8]

This chapter aims to give insight into meaning as an inherently temporal phenomenon. It does so to shed light on Merleau-Ponty's later concept of institution, which names an event that generates meaning without, however, being an act of constitution anchored in an already given subject or concepts. Institution thus undoes any full presence behind meaning. It does so precisely by conceptualizing meaning in temporal terms, as in Merleau-Ponty's formula that institution designates "those events in an experience which endow the experience with durable dimensions, in relation to which a whole series of other experiences will make sense" (*IP* 124[77]). The chapter clarifies these issues by tracing the linkage between temporality and meaning across Merleau-Ponty's philosophy, to show how meaning eventuates in a peculiar gap between the present and past, in which the past is not present but is nonetheless operative as orienting or weighing down the present so as to enable meaning. The chapter's strategy is synthetic: it digs behind oft-cited terms and moments across Merleau-Ponty's philosophy so as to gradually lay bare the concepts and lines of argument that bind them together in relation to temporality and meaning. In Merleau-Ponty's philosophy there is no simple, linear development from the descriptive to the ontological claim about meaning's temporality: even though the latter is more emphatic in his later philosophy, it percolates behind the *Phenomenology*'s constant engagement with temporality, and we will see that *The Structure of Behavior* already anticipates it. Nonetheless, for clarity, this chapter generally moves from the descriptive to the ontological. To keep the argument clear and accessible, many of the references and supports in Merleau-Ponty's work, as well as qualifications and objections, will be submerged in notes, for the issue explored here is a tiny tip of an immense iceberg of issues that floats beneath Merleau-Ponty's philosophy.

I. Meaning as Mediated by the Non-Given

Let us begin by simply describing a few key features of the phenomenon of meaning. Meaning is most notably a phenomenon of difference. Love is not hate. This difference is crucial to love appearing as a meaningful phenomenon; someone indifferent to this difference does not engage in or encounter love as such. The connection between meaning and difference is obvious in efforts to define meaningful terms, so far as these cross-reference other meaningful terms by way of contrast or distinction. This is most explicit in definitions rendered in genus-difference form.

Mere difference, though, is not sufficient for meaning. Myriad non-denumerable and indeterminate differences can be detected everywhere in the world – for example, between the density or porosity of any two bits of rock, or the temperature of a rock's top and bottom surfaces. As scientists we conceptualize the rock as determined by particular differences that we pick out in this myriad. But the rock is indifferent to these differences as such: it just *is* this myriad difference, its operation does not hinge on picking out any particular difference as such. In contrast, temperature differences of the rock matter and make a difference as such in the lizard's behaviour of warming its blood by sun-basking on the rock's top *but not* bottom. (We can say this without claiming that the lizard is *aware* of this difference as we are, which is not to deny that it has some kind of awareness of this difference.) This "but not" is key to meaning: meaning entails not only difference (this *not being* that), but something in virtue of which this but not that difference is the way to go (this *but not* that is warmth, food, love). (A complication that does not impact the argument is here left aside.[9]) That is, in meaningful phenomena, differences do not operate on a merely immediate level but are mediated by and reference something else in virtue of which they are salient: the high temperature of the rock's top is not meaningful in itself but in relation to the lizard's differential behaviour as enacting and referencing norms for warm versus cool temperatures. In sum, meaning involves differences that make a difference, that operate or are marked as such – in virtue of something.

A crucial consequence is that although meaning bears upon differences, it is not reducible to given differences themselves.[10] Encryption vividly demonstrates this. In Poe's famous story *The Gold Bug*, all the differences that would matter for meaning are in fact right there in the encrypted cipher-text (which begins "53‡‡†305))6*;4826)"). Yet in themselves these differences are meaningless, since they could say anything and therefore make no determinate difference or sense. The text makes sense only in light of something else: a code. In virtue of the decrypting code, the text's differences make a difference as just so many characters, each of which figures as this but not that plain-text letter (which letters in turn make sense only in light of English and its orthography).[11] Conversely, an observer who sees the lizard's movements as driven by immediate causes and does not see them as diverging from paths *not* taken, in virtue of the lizard's movements enacting a "code of behaviour," cannot "decrypt" living meanings in this phenomenon.[12]

The point that the lizard's "code of behaviour" involves paths *not* taken emphasizes how meaning exceeds givenness and presence. To wit, the "but not" that is key to meaning relates immediate, given differences (the rock *being* this, not that, temperature) to other differences *not* immediately given – paths *not* taken. A spot of rock is its own temperature. But it is not, and does not refer to, the salient temperatures that it is not. And the latter, which are *not given,* are crucial to the "but not" character of meaning. The thermostat differentially reacts to differing temperatures, turning on the furnace when the temperature is below a certain value. But its reaction hinges on the present temperature. Its operation does not refer to, let alone determine or discriminate, temperatures at which it is *not* going on. In short, while the thermostat goes on at specific temperatures, it does not exhibit a *preference* for this *but not* that temperature; it detects differences, but not as differences that make a difference in light of some further "code." Evidence for this is that the thermostat indifferently goes on either when the outside temperature drops or when its set-point is raised. The two are equivalent because the thermostat's operation is driven by merely given differences.[13] In contrast, we feel sick when our "set-point" raises in fever, and the lizard's "operation," its "code of behaviour," is "driven" by differences over and above the given.[14]

II. The Paradoxical Doubling of Meaning – and Being

The key result of the above is that meaning is manifest in differences yet is irreducible to present differences given in themselves. Given differences thus make sense only in virtue of something further, for example, a "code of behaviour," that is not and cannot be given at the same time and in the same way – meaning exceeds reduction to presence. Indeed, meaning could not hide in plain sight, be encrypted, if it were reducible to immediate givens, which is what empiricism wants to do. And as Merleau-Ponty shows, empiricism also renders ambiguity and learning inexplicable. This is because learning, ambiguity, and encryption all require something over and above the given, such that the given can remain the same while its meaning differs (or is encrypted and decrypted). On the other hand, Merleau-Ponty shows that the "something more" that bestows differing meanings could not, as intellectualism claims, be rooted in an active constituting consciousness wholly above the given, because learning and ambiguity are mediated by and passive to givens.[15]

These seemingly basic points together define a profound paradox at the heart of Merleau-Ponty's philosophy – namely, that *the phenomenon of meaning entails that something more than the given be given within the given.*[16] (We can think here of Merleau-Ponty's argument that children learn to distinguish red and green by encountering things that do not yet give red and green, yet give something more than the colour distinctions already grasped by the child. In this way the givens themselves prompt an "overturning of the givens"; *PP* 50–3[28–31]).

Everything said below simply unpacks this paradox and its consequences, which are central to such Merleau-Pontian concepts as expression, institution, resumption (*reprise*),[17] and divergence (*écart*) – processes whereby the given internally divides, doubles, or overlaps itself with something more than what is (initially) given so that meaning can accrue within givenness itself. What Merleau-Ponty discovers is that such processes entail a paradoxical ontology in which being internally doubles itself: being is not a plenum of immediately given differences but is "hollow," such that a sort of internal excess operates in being, thus allowing the given to double with non-given "codes" that emerge from within being, rather than descending from ready-made ideas. This "doubling" is a basic feature of Merleau-Ponty's philosophy and is also at work in themes such as these: the fold; figure–ground; field; chiasm; ontological depth; his critique of ontological "diplopia"; the invisible *of* the visible; the point that phenomena are not the appearance of invisible essences; and, as we will see, level and structure.[18] Ultimately this doubling is to be understood in terms of a temporal overlapping of the present with the past and future. The ontological paradox is that being engenders something more than the given only because of a temporal non-givenness of being: being is something more than the given only by being less than fully given.

This crucially anticipates where we are going. But to understand the paradox and its consequences we need to back up and excavate the line of thought from meaning to temporality and ontology within Merleau-Ponty's philosophy. To do this let us first of all recast the previous section's result (that differences are meaningful only in light of something further than those differences themselves) in terms of Merleau-Ponty's constant attention to the fact that the French word for meaning, *sens*, also connotes direction.[19] In French, a one-way street has a *sens unique* that sets up a domain of orienting, directional differences in which one is to do this but not that, such that going the wrong way has the meaning of a traffic violation. Similarly, in its environment, the lizard's body sets up a domain of orienting differences in which the warm top of the rock is the right way to go at certain periods of the day. For Merleau-Ponty, *sens*, meaning, is never an immediately given, point-like content; rather, it is a moving vector that has determinate sense in figuring against an orienting domain of directional differences. Meaning thus has what I will call a "double structure," in which the given is doubled by something further that orients it – yet this doubling is generated within givenness itself.

In the *Phenomenology*, for example, Merleau-Ponty argues that the meaning of "up" and "down" is irreducible to given visual or intellectual contents and instead involves a spatial "level" (*niveau*) in virtue of which this but not that way is up. By "level" Merleau-Ponty means not some objectively inscribed standard for determining up and down, but something dynamic – namely, the ongoing, habitual manner in which situations typically call upon us to work with them: the person working at her desk, the mechanic lying beneath her car and working on its underside, the astronaut floating in front of variously aligned instruments, each has different sorts of levels requisite to her or his work. "Up" and "down" fall out of working with things via such levels.[20]

The level is not immediately given in or alongside other content, since it is the mediating term that makes sense of differential content. Indeed, the level is something more than what is immediately given because it emerges from the body's inhabiting a situation as soliciting habitual, virtual action – and habit precisely exceeds immediate givens. Yet this habitual level emerges *within* situations: in Merleau-Ponty's analysis of an experiment by Wertheimer, it is precisely the perceiver's bodily inhabitation of a situation visually tilted by mirrors that leads to the acquisition of a new level that sets things to rights (*contra* intellectualist appeals to a constituting consciousness that would not need and could not take the time to learn how to make sense of new situations) (*PP* 291–303[254–65]).

In short, the level is a habitual code of conduct in virtue of which things make sense. In showing how levels are crucial to perception, Merleau-Ponty shows how making sense of things – and there being *sens* at all – requires that our involvement with things, from within itself and not by way of transcendent ideas, double itself with a level that exceeds and thence orients the given.

The point of this section is that meaning requires mediating norms that are, however, dynamically inherent in the phenomena. Such norms do not have the fixity, conventionality, and so on, usually connoted by "norm" or "code." Merleau-Ponty's concept of level is well suited to designating such inherently dynamic norms, so I here expand his concept of level, beyond perception strictly, to designate norms of meaningful phenomena in general – a terminological expansion already at play in Merleau-Ponty.

III. The Genesis of Meaning and Levels by Internal Divergence

In the *Phenomenology*, the level and the double-structure of perception are first of all rooted in the body as doubled with habits. The study of bodily movement reveals that the body "comprises two distinct layers, that of the habitual body and that of the body at this moment" (*PP* 111[84]). This amounts to the discovery of "a new sense of the word 'sense [*sens*],'" a meaning that "is not the work of a universal constituting consciousness" (*PP* 182–3[148]), precisely because the doubling that enables perceptual *sens* is rooted not in ideas but in bodily habit. Given its rootedness in habit, meaning is obviously a temporal phenomenon: something further can double over and orient the given with something more than the given because habit overlays givens with a bodily past exceeding the present. Yet it is no mere matter of fact or accident that meaning and its double-structure are rooted in temporality and something like habit. To grasp this we need to dig further into the logic of meaning, first of all to understand how mediating norms (such as provided by habitual levels) are in fact intrinsic conditions pervasive to all of perception and how they must arise by way of a "divergence" within phenomena.

Consider Merleau-Ponty's analysis of colour constancy – for example, seeing paper as constantly white even as it is variously shaded or lit by the sun or by light bulbs with different spectra. He shows that constancy depends on taking changing givens (the paper variously lit) in two ways: as manifesting a level of illumination, and as manifesting a colour that is constant in virtue of the level of lighting.[21] The complication is that the terms of this double-structure of lighting and lit are obviously given by way of each other – they fold into each other. (Here I draw on the sense of *com-plicare* as folding together: "*com*" is the Latin suffix for "with," and "*plico*" means "to fold"; in French, a fold is a *pli*.)

There is a similar complication with seeing a house as solid and real. This is because we can never directly encounter the house-as-a-whole, with all sides present at once. We perceive its reality only in a moving flow of perception that continually turns up visible sides in light of and as leading to hidden sides – but this means seeing the given in light of a never directly visible house-as-a-whole. Again, this requires taking changing givens in two ways: as manifesting the house-as-a-whole (*qua* level never directly visible); and as sides of a house-as-a-whole. Again, these are given by way of each other, since it is only as sides-of-a-house that things manifest the house-as-a-whole ... in virtue of which they stand as sides.[22]

These two examples illustrate our previous result that meaning requires a level over and above given differences. But the examples, by emphasizing the ever-changing dynamics of things and light, also let us see how this requirement is no mere descriptive matter of fact, but a transcendental requirement intrinsic to meaningful experience. When we step out of experience and analyse it, all we find is an ever-changing flow of differences (Hume's problem); yet within experience what we find are stable "this but not that" structures crucial to meaning. This must mean that we never encounter a pure flow of differences, but something that is always already arrested and gathered together (synthesized) as a stable level against which, for example, what would be myriad minutely shifting indeterminate shades appear as white, but not grey or yellow. Merleau-Ponty's criticism of intellectualism (which bases this synthesis in a constituting consciousness beyond the fray of experience) tells us that this arresting must arise *within the flow of differences*. We can now see how our paradoxical point – that meaning entails that something more than the given be given *within the given* – is a transcendental condition of the possibility of meaningful experience.[23]

But we can also see how it leads to the complication noted in our two examples: if levels must inhere in the given, then the given must figure as double, must manifest itself in two ways, as varying content and as the dynamically invariant level for making sense of content. The wonder is that a flow of differences (changing shades) internally factors or divides against itself so as to manifest two interactants (the lit and the level of lighting) that mutually determine each other as relatively stable.

Yet this sort of internal division of a flow is not so unusual. Consider balancing.[24] It is only by always diverging from balance that you balance; you are never actually *at* a balance "point" (even a building glacially creaks around its balance). Balance, although very real, is never fully present. (The notion of a balance "point" is thus misleading, which is why it is here dropped in favour of balance as an always dynamic term.) You stay upright by muscles constantly twitching this way and that; your vertebrae are not like cylinders cemented in a column, but like shimmying saucers swaying in a stack as a waiter totters to stay their toppling. Each sway at once diverges from balance and engenders the balance from which it is a divergence, the one by way of the other. Balance as level of balancing thus gives a model of levels as inherently dynamic and non-given. (And it illustrates Merleau-Ponty's profound concept of *écart*, of something internally diverging from itself so as to engender its own sense.)

But this complication, that balance only is by way of divergence from balance, entails that balance is a *phenomenon of time*. Indeed, in a universe in which masses lacked momentum, inertia, and gravity, the phenomenon of balance would not be possible, because balance depends on masses carrying the momentum of the past along with them in a gravitational field that accelerates masses and thus weighs them with a future that threatens their toppling. Balance is a phenomenon of time *doubling and carrying the past over the present in light of a future.*

IV. The Paradox and Temporality of Expression

What we next need to understand is how the internal divergence of flowing differences (into levels and differences meaningful in light of levels) likewise depends on a temporality that weighs the present with a past that carries over the present in light of a future.

The phenomenon of balance may nicely illustrate how levels can internally arise in flows, yet our perceptual examples still seem miraculous: seeing a colour as determinately meaningful, which entails grasping lighting and lit by way of changing differences between them, differences that at once link them to and differentiate them from each other. This appears akin to spontaneously grasping, in non-sensical, encrypted cypher-characters, the code that decrypts their sense. How could you do this from within the flow of cypher-characters if you did not already have a sense of the code or of characters as meaningful letters? How could a flow entirely lacking sense internally accrue levels for grasping sense? In the case of balancing we can admit that balance emerges only in swaying away from it, yet still claim that finding balance entails an already given ability to balance. Similarly, we can admit that our sense of familiar perceptual objects or texts emerges only in interactive flows, yet still claim that finding their sense entails our already possessing abilities for grasping their meaning. Even if levels do emerge within flows, does this not depend on abilities or standards given in advance of such flows?

Problems such as these are behind Socrates's claim (in Plato's *Phaedo*) that learning the concept of equality would already entail being able to conceptualize objects (e.g., two sticks) as exemplars of equality (since encountering sticks as examples of equality *but not* twoness, stickness, lengthiness, or linearity would already require the sense that equality, but not something else, is the issue common to the examples). We can learn equality from examples because examples merely prompt recollection of an already possessed code. From Merleau-Ponty's perspective, this fails to truly pose or answer the following questions: How does genuinely new meaning arise? Why, if we already possess a code, are we incapable of deploying it until we engage in learning? And why is learning to deploy a code so determinately dependent on time, repetition, and details of learning situations?[25]

Here we will shift, in Merleau-Ponty, from the problem of perceptual meaning to the problem of meaning in language and expression. The two are linked, since for Merleau-Ponty resolving a perceptual situation's meaning is a matter of making its latent sense express (as for example, in resolving an ambiguous object), and the peculiar temporality of expression (discussed below) is akin to the peculiar temporality of perception that was broached above and that Merleau-Ponty detects in the child learning to distinguish red and green for the first time (*PP* 50–6[28–34]). In other words, for Merleau-Ponty, perceptual and linguistic meaning, seeing red and saying "red," are not disjoint phenomena: things perceived are in themselves already far more laden with a language-like, meaningful future than a reductionist empiricism might admit, and language is far more freighted with bodily and perceptual pasts than an inflationist intellectualism would allow.

So let us now turn to Merleau-Ponty's account, in the *Phenomenology*'s chapter on expression, of expression in the case of what he calls primary expression, where, for example, a child or poet is learning a new meaning for the first time (as opposed to secondary expression, where already available meanings or terms are redeployed). The aim is first to show, descriptively, how expression involves divergence and generation of a level – by way of a paradoxical temporality in which the past carries over into the present in light of a future, such that these mutually illuminate each other. We will then draw on the above to conceptualize the ontological underpinnings of expression, showing how the genesis of sense is structurally akin to finding a new balance point in a terrain that has shifted beneath us, or a terrain that our balancing movements have dug out and undermined in a new way.

The key point in Merleau-Ponty's description of primary expression is that in engendering a new word, or figuring out how to say something for the first time, I do not already possess, in advance of speaking, writing, or silent expression, that which I want to express, but only in non-linguistic form. If that were the case, then expression would amount to *translating* a non-linguistic idea into linguistic form, as if the meaning I wished to express could already be there in advance of the language I forge for expressing it. Against this view, Merleau-Ponty directs our attention to concrete details of the phenomenon – for example, the way in which I struggle to figure out the words for saying what I want to say, in which what I want to say does not become clear until I say it, in which what I want to say is changed by my saying or writing things, in which I learn from saying – as the painter learns from trying to paint and the painting changes as different strokes reconfigure the tensions and problems being addressed. Thus, if we could call expression a translation, it is, according to Merleau-Ponty, a peculiar form of translation that does not shift an already given original text into a different language but rather, as Bernhard Waldenfels emphasizes, *creates* the original that it translates only in the course of translating it.[26]

Note that this is akin to decrypting a text, in which process we discover in the cipher-text a not yet given code and a not yet decrypted plain-text by way of each other. In expression we likewise find a not yet given code and plain-text by way of one another. The difference is that in decryption the plain-text had been previously given to someone else, whereas in primary expression the plain-text had never been before. Expression is thus like decrypting a message that had never existed or was sent by no one. Perhaps this is why prophets grasping their world anew take what they are saying as voicing the divine.

On the other hand, while expression creates its original, we have to remember that this is not a creation from nothing. In struggling to say X, it is X, *this* but not that, that I am struggling to say. It is *this X* that I am trying to say, and the "this but not that" structure (the level) is crucial to my eventually saying it: it directs and orients the expressive process, which fails if I cannot articulate the sense of X as *not* being the sense of something else. The paradox is that the level that directs and orients expression is not yet given, but rather comes to be given in the very process it orients. In expression, the emerging figure (what I end up saying, on this one occasion) reciprocally shapes and clarifies its emerging ground (the new linguistic level in virtue of which I could say it in the first place – and on all occasions henceforth).

Here, once again, we have meaning by way of doubling and divergence, but the description lets us see clearly how the genesis of new meaning entails a peculiar and paradoxical temporality. For what we are discussing above – and what we feel in the gestural arc of expression – is an indeterminate past becoming ever more determinate in a present that manifests this determinacy only insofar as it figures against this past which is still at work in the present as futurally orienting its working direction. The original text, the past of expression, becomes determinate only in guiding the futurally unfolding work of expressive translation to the point where the present translation can look back and claim (in a reprise) the original as the original that it in fact translates. The level as past of expression becomes determinate only in light of that which it eventually balances, ballasts, and levels. Experientially this is manifest in a sort of "aha" moment, finding balance, in the realization: that's what I was trying to say all along, it was there with me all along, how could I not have figured it out right away? We are here tracing quite complex structures via coordinately complex claims – but note that the complexity here is kith and kin to the one traced in the case of the house and colour constancy. We get to the level of the house or lighting, that will clarify what we have been seeing all along (as sides-of-a-house, or unambiguous colours), only by moving forward through multiply flowing sides or shades to the "aha" balance where these at once stand (are reprised) as the level and what the level renders meaningful.

In short, the phenomenon of expression is not one in which something determinate, present and fully given, is re-presented in a new way (in external language versus internal ideas); it is, rather, a phenomenon in which the non-givenness of something, a vagueness, a problem, destabilizes and thence opens the way for a balance that resolves vagueness into something determinate. Note that this non-givenness is not entirely void or indeterminate – such a void would be mere presence with a minus sign in front of it. We are here encountering something far more ontologically radical or ambiguous. And the key consequence for us is that meaning does not arise from an already given starting point, from presence – yet this non-presence is already doubled with enough directedness that it can diverge into a new level and meaning.

V. The Doubling of Temporality and the Weight of the Past

What we next need to understand is how a non-presence in being can already be doubled with directedness, a *sens* in the making, a pregnancy, as Merleau-Ponty oft puts it – which is not, however, a pregnancy in the sense of something already given, waiting to be born, as if birth is a matter of opening the door to someone already waiting to walk in (see *IP* 37[8]). How can there be this excess?

The whole of Merleau-Ponty's thought on institution, I think, grapples with the thought that this excess is not just *manifest* in the temporality of expression – this excess *is* temporality: being is pregnant with *sens*, doubled and overlaid with direction, because the past carries over the present into the future. (The latter formula here acquires a conceptual meaning; it conceptualizes the past as carrying over, doubling, into the present, by open-endedly carrying the present over into a future yet-to-be.) The present is at least twofold: the present now happening; and a past still operative in the present that is distinct yet complicit in the present. In other words, the sort of doubling that is manifest in the present body doubled with habit is manifest in a deeper way, in an ontological doubling of temporality itself. As Merleau-Ponty puts it, "to be conscious is to realize a certain divergence, a certain variation in an already instituted existential field, which is always behind us and whose weight, like that of a flywheel [*volant*], intervenes up into the actions by which we transform it" (*IP* 267[206]). We can be oriented and meaningfully conscious because the weight of past movements and institutions intervenes in present action, in the same way that past momentum stored in the present movement of a flywheel regulates the present system – and our present actions can reciprocally modify this operative past. Again, he writes that childhood dramas are "neither cause nor effect" of current dramas and their meaning; the childhood past "is a *flywheel*, a grain of sand on which the oyster makes its pearl with time" (*IP* 242[185]).[27] Meaning is not just *manifest* in the paradoxical temporality of expression but is made with, engendered from, temporality paradoxically doubling over itself.

To understand what is at work in and behind this claim, let us rework our previous point about expression in light of our analysis of divergence and balance. As a phenomenon of divergence, meaning is a phenomenon of resolution, of resolving meanings and levels by way of their complicity in one another. We could think here of visually resolving something blurry or out of focus (which is much like resolving constant colour in changing light). How do you do this? Do you need to have an already given norm of focus, either in general (what it means for something to be in focus) or in particular (how to get this particular thing in focus)? The answer is "no." To get this particular thing in focus, I don't already need to know how to focus on it, all I need to do is something rather like balance: I shift focus back and forth and let that shifting set up the variations against which this but not that counts as in focus; it is in diverging from focus that I converge on the level of focus. The blurred thing, in our movement with it, engenders, by divergence, the level of its resolution.[28] But what provides the criterion for things in general being in focus, for this but not that being sharp? Without this criterion my relation to blurred things would never settle to a level. Here we can appeal, by way of example, to levels engendered in species handling things. Once again we would not have to appeal to levels specified in advance; we would need only attend to the ways in which creatures, in their remote engagements with the environment, evolve various senses and focusing abilities that let them get different kinds of grips on things. We can take "focus" to be whatever enables and stabilizes this characteristic grip, a kind of balance that settles these engagements. I have no idea what counts as the equivalent of focus for insectile species with compound eyes or for echolocating bats, but I can think there is something in their relation to the environment that has diverged and settled, in evolution, into a level of handling things in light of things handled. Just as balance emerges in wobbling calling a halt to itself, it is possibilities internal to moving interaction itself, not criteria fixed in advance, that engender levels by divergence. And all that is required for this level and thence meaning to arise is that in nature, materiality, being, *the past carry over and operate in the present of the system in such a way that the system is not fully present but lags behind and ahead of itself, such that this lag can intrude in the present, like a flywheel, and accumulate, by divergence, a level that directs or steers the present in doubling over it.*[29] (In the passages from *IP* cited above, Merleau-Ponty's term *volant* has the sense of both flywheel and steering wheel.) Ultimately, this temporal carry-over is not just the condition of meaning but the very "stuff" of it, for if we try to cash out this carry-over in terms of mere materials, and so on, we will land in a presence that betrays the dynamics and ambiguity of meaning and that undermines our ability to account for the genesis of sense.

In other words, the difference that makes a difference to meaning is ultimately the difference between the past and the present. This is paradoxical, because if this difference is to register, if it is to be determinate, the past cannot *go away* but rather must operate as different from the present and as directed towards a still ongoing future. (Note that this requires a curious gap between the past and the present that disjoins them without, however, dividing them such that the past is not present at all.[30]) The genesis of meaning hinges on being being non-given via its temporality, where this temporality is structured such that the past carries over into the not-yet-given present, such that this doubling of the present with the past introduces an excess into present events, such that the past can thence as it were enable a "clog" or "jam" in the present, a stand[31] that institutes a divergence between a flow and its level.

This discussion helps us grasp Merleau-Ponty's formula for institution as referring to "those events in an experience which endow the experience with durable dimensions, in relation to which a whole series of other experiences will make sense" (*IP* 124[77]). Experience is a flow of events. But that flow is not merely a series of given occurrences. It has more in it than that, because it has less in it than that. The present and temporality itself are never fully given. This emptiness structures temporality such that there is "room" for the past of this present to intervene, flywheel-like, in the present, and to be modified in turn by the ongoing present. This enables a divergence, a bilaminar flow, in which the layers of the flow can jam one another and produce something new, an event that is not like other events, not alongside them, but transformative of the whole series: a new level – more precisely, an institution – that changes the sense of given events *from within*.

The logic here is tricky, so let us unpack the issue via an example that Merleau-Ponty gives in the institution lectures. The example is of the way in which what he calls pre-maturation (an organism's developing ways of behaving prior to puberty) sets up behaviours that, once the organism does reach puberty, can be seen to be still operative, flywheel-like, in the organism – yet transformed by puberty so that they figure in new ways. The transformation to puberty depends on the pre-maturational past, like a habit, continually overlaying present behaviours in such a way as to *at once* (1) build up ongoing behaviours; and (2) in finally accomplishing that build-up, drive it into a jam, a difference or inappropriateness, that is manifest in being at odds with – diverging from – the present. We could think here of pre-sexual play that at once builds up our ways of engaging and touching others but becomes and is felt as different (or inappropriate) only when these behaviours and the body eventually accomplish actual sexual conduct: the playful kiss or hug all of a sudden stands out as sexual, as all of a sudden divergent or different from the present (or therefore inappropriate) precisely when it finally operates as sexual, when the flywheel has enough momentum. This is the phenomenon of a sudden "Did I really do that?" that calls a halt to our forward momentum, thus marking it as divergent into a new issue in the present. The interesting point here is that it is only by the past, gradual operation of the not-yet-sexual, finally eventuating as sexuality in the present, that the present behaviour can stand out as sexual *but not* just playful. The fabric of the "but not" structure is temporality. If the behaviour merely happened in the present, it would be sexual for us observers looking on at it – but for the one engaged in the behaviour it would not operate as meaningfully sexual, as this *but not* that. We observers can see that the child is already behaving sexually, but it is only when the child experiences present behaviour diverging from her past behavioural build-up *precisely in accomplishing it* that she or he experiences the wonder of sexuality as a meaningfully different phenomenon. In other words, it is only in the child experiencing the present as *reprising* the past that she experiences the present as sexual *but not* pre-sexual; and the experience of reprise entails that the present at once be experienced as built-up in continuity with the past yet discontinuous from it *precisely as accomplishing what was building up.* (Notice that the structure here is akin to Merleau-Ponty's account of the child learning to see colours: prior to distinguishing red and green, the child does not fail to see red and green for what they are, she experiences very different colours; prior to the event that institutes sexuality, the child does not experience sexuality versus non-sexuality or pre-sexuality, she has an entirely different spectrum of experience. Also, the logic of discontinuity by continuity echoes passages from *Structure* discussed below.) It is only by lagging ahead and behind, by stumbling, that we stumble into meaning. Meaning is not constituted by the clear light of reason, but instituted by twilit stumbling.

In the initial description of expression above, we are just seeing this process of institution working at a macro-level.[32] Institution names the finer, slower workings of expression and shows us how expression's resolution of vagueness into sense is not just manifest in time but ontologically depends on the non-givenness of being and being's non-given past carrying over into the present. Living, feeling, expressive, thinking beings just make this carry-over ever more explicitly operative in the present. The operation of the machine's flywheel *is* the momentum it carries with it, its behaviour approximates to an identity of past and present (which is why physics, in describing flywheels and so on, can take time as unreal[33]). In contrast, in our behaviour we and other animals ever more operate in the divergence of past and present and ever more manifest an explicit marking and remarking of our past. Memory is ontologically key here.[34]

VI. Reprise: The Temporality of *Structure* and the Structure of Temporality

In this chapter it is not possible to fully unpack the complex intersection, which has just been broached, of meaning and temporality with nature, life, and memory. But we can get a sense of some underlying conceptual issues by turning back from institution to Merleau-Ponty's first book, *The Structure of Behavior*. This will also let us see how *Structure* anticipates – and enriches – the thought of institution.

To connect with *Structure*, let us note that the philosophical issue underlying the above discussion has to do with conditions and what they condition. Levels are conditions of meaning. The paradox we have been digging out via divergence, doubling, and so on, is that the conditions of meaning are in fact conditioned by the meaningful differences they condition. For example, the new linguistic level eventually expressed is conditioned by the coming to utterance it enables. In other words, the conditions of meaningful experience themselves appear: they are not given in advance of the phenomena, but appear *within* the phenomena.[35] That conditions of meaning and experience appear is a key commitment of and methodological constraint on Merleau-Ponty's analysis of meaning and being: do not appeal to things that do not appear; hence, discard intellectualist appeals to *a priori* conditions that, as such, would never appear; in any case, appeal to purely *a priori* conditions creates difficulties explaining the factual dynamics of appearances (e.g., learning, ambiguity).

That is, Merleau-Ponty's philosophy undoes divisions between the *a priori* and *a posteriori*. Meaning, expression, and institution all operate with an *a priori*, for meaning entails a level through which alone things mean this but not that; but these phenomena engender their own *a priori* *from within* the *a posteriori*. This engendering is what happens when we express something new, and it is also what Merleau-Ponty argues happens, in a manner quite analogous to expression, in perception – for example, in the case of touch, where the moving hand, in its situation, puts together the spatial *a priori* that makes sense of what is touched (*PP* 266–7[229–30]).

This indistinction between the *a priori* and the *a posteriori*, and the point that meaning entails systems producing their own conditions, is crucial to *Structure* and its central concept: structure. He defines structure as "the joining of an idea and an existence which are indiscernible, the contingent arrangement by which materials begin to have meaning in our presence, intelligibility in the nascent state" (*SB* 223[206–7]). Here, as in the *Phenomenology*'s opening remark that phenomenology "puts essences back into existence" (7[lxx]), the crucial point is that meaning – which intellectualism would put in a special place that is *a priori* insulated from experience – is in fact joined with the flow of existence.

What is interesting is the way that Merleau-Ponty's grappling with structure as this indiscernibility of *a priori* and *a posteriori*, idea and existence, already anticipates the temporality of institution. Briefly, in *Structure*, Merleau-Ponty appeals to structures to make sense of the relation between soul/mind and body within nature. His conclusion is that soul and body are relative terms, such that

> the body in general is an ensemble of paths already traced, of powers already constituted; the body is the acquired dialectical soil upon which a higher "formation" is accomplished, and the soul is the meaning which is then established. The relations of the soul and the body can indeed be compared to those of concept and word, but on the condition of perceiving, beneath the separated products, the constituting operation which joins them and of rediscovering ... the living *word* which is its unique actualization, in which the meaning is formulated for the first time and thus founds itself as meaning and becomes available for later operations. (*SB* 227[210])

The relation between soul and body is comparable to the relation between concepts and words in primary expression. Merleau-Ponty here writes about this in terms of a constituting operation that bestows sense, but his text suggests that sense arises through a process closer to institution. When he details consciousness's relation to the conditions from which it arises, he writes that for "adult consciousness," "the historical becoming which prepared it was not *before* it, it is only *for* it; the time during which it progressed is no longer the time *of* its constitution, but a time which it constitutes; and the series of events is subordinated to its eternity" (*SB* 222[206]). But Merleau-Ponty argues that this already constituted view of (adult) consciousness, which reduces the past to the present and thus refuses passivity to originating temporality (by claiming to constitute temporality), is wrong-headed. A "reversal of perspective" is required in which we see that "for life, as for the mind, there is no past which is absolutely past; 'the moments which the mind seems to have behind it are also borne in its present depths.' Higher behavior retains the subordinated dialectics in the present depths of its existence, from that of the physical system and its topographical conditions to that of the organism and its milieu" (*SB* 224[207]).[36]

That is, Merleau-Ponty is already starting to criticize the claim that meaning arises as present in the act or time of constitution and is beginning to see that the genesis of meaning requires the non-presence of a flywheel operation of the past in the present. Moreover, elsewhere in his analysis of physical, vital, and human structures and their interrelation, he writes that "already, in the physical world, the passage from conditions to consequences is discontinuous" (*SB* 144[134]). Thus, with form [structure], a principle of discontinuity is introduced, and the conditions for a development by leaps or crises, for an event or for a history, are given (*SB* 148[137]):

> In our image of the physical world, we are obliged to introduce partial totalities ... [which are] precisely what we understood above by form[37] ... To treat the physical world as if it were an intersecting linear causal series in which each keeps its individuality, as if it were a world in which there is no duration, is an illegitimate extrapolation; science must be linked to a history of the universe in which the development is discontinuous. (*SB* 149–50[139])

All of this means that he is already seeing that this "flywheel" operation requires a time that is not a continuous, already given dimension, but a domain of being that itself eventuates, that is "total because it is partial" (*IP* 36[7]), that leaves room for disruptive events – which yet enable meaning to take hold (by reprise). But these points from *Structure* also tell us that the self-eventuating, discontinuous temporality of institution is not simply an artefact of or internal to subjectivity or even the body subject: it is operative on the deepest ontological levels. It is not just in the human order that we find structures that accomplish themselves by building up into and instituting temporal discontinuities that leap back to the past via an operative memory. This is crucial to the physical order too, where structure is accomplished via past momentum carrying over into the present so as to enact a new behavioural regime, as in a system now arriving at an ongoing balance, or a soap bubble snapping into a shimmying sphere – although operative memory and past are not explicitly marked in such systems.

That *Structure* anticipates the logic of institution becomes quite clear when we note that Merleau-Ponty's 1952 synopsis of *Structure* summarizes the results traced above as follows: "The perceiving organism seems to show us a Cartesian mixture of the soul with the body. Higher-order behaviours give a new meaning to the life of the organism, but the mind here disposes of only a limited freedom; it needs simpler activities in order *to stabilize itself in durable institutions* and to realize itself truly as mind" (Merleau-Ponty *Parcours deux*). This language of durable institutions echoes and anticipates the above-cited formula for institution that appears in the 1954–55 institution lecture course.[38] This should tell us that already in *Structure* Merleau-Ponty is beginning to see that the relation between meaning and its roots, between mind and body, is one of institution, in which flows of events generate something new by carrying the past over the present towards the future so as to catch something new in the present.

Put otherwise, the condition of the genesis of sense appears as temporality itself.[39] That is, the analysis of temporality as the condition of institution ultimately pertains to the ontological structure of temporality itself and *not just the structure of our experience of temporality*. This is suggested by the way *Structure* anticipates the concept of institution, in terms of discontinuities and transformative events in the universe itself. And it also flagged in a note on time in *The Visible and the Invisible* that seems to reprise some of the above points from *Structure*. This note remarks the paradox that time must constitute itself, yet not be all present, but points out that the paradox dissolves when we realize that "time is not an absolute series of events, a tempo – not even the tempo of the consciousness – it is an institution" (*VI* 238[184]). Time itself institutes itself, is itself institution – and this institution-structure of time, we can see from the above, ontologically enables all other instituting events.[40] The institution of institution in Merleau-Ponty is a long time eventuating.[41]

NOTES

1 Love is a key example in Merleau-Ponty's continual grappling with meaning and its temporality. See the "Cogito" and "Temporality" chapters of *PP* and the resumption of this example in the institution lectures. Proust is Merleau-Ponty's touchstone, and the consequence is a temporal opacity of love.

2 *PP* plays on the connection between *comprendre*, to understand, and *prendre*, to grasp, but does not reduce comprehension of meaning to a model of fully grasping physical things. Quite the opposite: *PP* shows how meaningfully grasping physical things is a temporally open-ended act and then shows how other sorts of meaning are also open-ended.

3 Merleau-Ponty, *La Structure du Comportement* (*The Structure of Behavior*), hereafter cited as *SB*, with the French pagination followed by the English.

4 See, for example, the comment in "The Phenomenal Field" chapter of *PP* that phenomenological reflection is not intellectualist but must be regarded as "a creative operation which itself participates in the facticity" of the experience on which it reflects (*PP* 88[62]). This means that the phenomenal field is creative of new meaning. On the significance of this point, see Lawlor, "The End of Phenomenology." On the connections between the field, sense genesis, and temporality, see Merleau-Ponty's later and profound remark that "time is the very model of institution: passivity–activity, it continues, because it has been instituted, it fuses, it cannot stop being, it is total because it is partial, it is a field"; *L'Institution, la Passivité*, 36 (*Institution and Passivity*, 7). (Hereafter, this text will be referred to as *IP*, with the page number in the French edition followed by the page number in the English translation.) The non-givenness of temporality is key to fields and institution.

5 This point is a running theme of *PP* (on ideal objects, see the "Cogito" chapter); see also "The Primacy of Perception" in Merleau-Ponty's *The Primacy of Perception*. Merleau-Ponty is developing Husserl's increasingly radical insights into the horizonal and incomplete structure of experience; see especially Edmund Husserl, *Analyses*, part 2, "Self-Giving in Perception."

6 See *IP* for his lecture notes on the closely intertwined themes of institution and passivity. Vallier, "Institution," gives helpful background. Also see Renaud Barbaras, "Merleau-Ponty and Nature."

7 The complex weave between the descriptive and ontological claims couples with Merleau-Ponty's criticism of his earlier philosophy in its relation to Husserl, an issue signalled in the sentence just after the one quoted from *IP*: "consciousness [is neither] a flux of absolutely individual *Erlebnisse,* nor a place of eternal significations." That is, absolutely individual, already given *Erlebnisse* are as much of a problem as "eternal significations," even though the series of these would exceed us in temporal flows. What is needed is a radical ontology in which the sense of *Erlebnisse* is never presently given.

8 See, for example, "Différance" and "Signature Event Context" in Derrida's *Margins of Philosophy* and the discussion of dangerous supplement in *Of Grammatology*. This Derridean resonance should not be surprising given that both are captivated by Husserl's "The Origin of Geometry": see Derrida, *Edmund Husserl's Origin of Geometry* and *The Problem of Genesis;* and Merleau-Ponty, *Husserl at the Limits*. Lawlor's introductory essay in the latter helpfully traces some of these connections; also see Lawlor, *Thinking Through French Philosophy*.

9 The complication is that the "not" in the "this *but not* that" structure is not exclusive or binary: it leaves room for ambiguity and polyvalence, for example, it overlaps between love and hate, or multiple contrastive terms (this is love, but not hate, yet also not passionate ardour), and so on. But this still requires the operation of a "but not" mediated by a level, which is the important issue here.

10 This is not to deny that meaning arises from differences, just that meaning is not *reducible* to *given* differences. The claim here is that meaning arises from differences that, in virtue of temporality, could never have been fully given. So a reduction to already guaranteed differences given in themselves is impossible; the latter are *artefacts*, results, of meaningful embodiment and language, not primary phenomena. Genesis of difference goes all the way down. This is anticipated by the point, in *PP* (289[252]), that perception depends on a "past which has never been a present." Compare Merleau-Ponty's thought (discussed in Barbaras, "Merleau-Ponty and Nature"), that even the elemental differences of sulfur are temporally generated through lateral relations between spread-out bits of the cosmos.

11 In formalized information theory, the issue here is that information is measured against a space of possible signals not given in the signals themselves. For example, in the ASCII computer code, "5" carries

information in virtue of *not being* one of the other 255 characters possible in that code. Encryption turns a plain-text, with a non-random, differential distribution of signals, into a cipher-text in which the signal distribution approximates an indifferent randomness, as if there is no code against which these differences matter. The better the encryption, the more its output approaches pure noise and may not even be recognized as a signal. In Poe's story, the non-random frequency distribution of characters is key to cracking the code. As in the position developed here, information theory conceptualizes information as differences that make a difference in virtue of something further. But the something further is an already fixed space of possible differences. From Merleau-Ponty's point of view, this amounts to an intellectualism that is good for analysing communication of already given meanings, but not for analysing the genesis of meaning. See Atlan and Cohen, "Immune Information," for a resonant argument that information theory is inadequate to account for the immune's system ability to identify previously unencountered substances as pathogens. Interestingly, they argue that immunological meaning arises in the temporality of dynamic processes.

12 On meaning as arising in living behaviour, compare *SB*; Heidegger, *The Fundamental Concepts of Metaphysics* (which inspired my lizard example) and the discussion thereof in Buchanan, *Onto-Ethologies*; Varela, "Organism"; and Thompson, *Mind in Life*.

13 Put otherwise, specifying the set-point at once determines the difference that the thermostat detects and the would-be "code of behaviour" by which it operates, and the thermostat is indifferent to what its set-point is. So there is no "code of behaviour" over and above differences presently detected and no reference in its operation to temperatures at which it is not going on. But there is a complication here. If it immediately switched on when the temperature dropped below the set-point, a thermostat (especially one in a small room attached to a powerful heater) can plunge into hysteresis, wildly clicking on and off. So thermostats are designed, for example, to switch on only after the temperature remains below the set point for a period of time. The thermostat thus effectively uses the environment as a memory-store of past temperature. To this extent the thermostat references something not now given. But the thermostat is indifferent to what this non-given is to be. A human who regulates to the wrong temperature is sick, whereas the thermostat indifferently regulates to whatever it is set to. Nonetheless, in the thermostat's temporal interaction with the environment we find the germ of the sort of temporality of meaningful systems and balance discussed below.

On similar lines, someone might claim that unlike a thermostat, an accelerometer (for example) detects changes in velocity (in rates of change of position) by reference to something not given, that is, by comparison to past positions, so its operation cannot be reduced to present differences. This mistakes the issue. However it measures acceleration, the accelerometer indifferently outputs acceleration at this moment, while the fighter pilot blacks out at so many Gs of acceleration, because this but not that acceleration is liveable and thus meaningful for her. Moreover, we can build accelerometers that work by measuring present deflections of accelerating masses, because physical systems are operatively related to their past by inertia, and so on.

The issue with the thermostat and accelerometer is *how* a system is related to its past: in non-meaningful systems, the past and future vanish in the present even while determining it, whereas meaning depends on the past and future standing out as different from the present. This echoes Merleau-Ponty's argument that memory is not reducible to present traces, since this would not explain how those traces have a pastness different from the present.

14 These claims invite the objection that over its long course, evolution produces differences that make a difference (e.g., the lizard "code of behaviour") from mere differences (of molecules moving). The response from Merleau-Pontian phenomenology (and from some evolutionary scientists and philosophers of biology) is to argue that evolutionary science often and typically (although subtly) turns the environment into a selective cause that acts so as to "drive" evolution. Here this amounts to packing the standard by which differences make a difference into the environment. This begs the question of how selectivity actually arises. The argument is that selectivity depends on the organism's reciprocal coupling with its environment such that it participates in producing the environment that "selects" it. Rooting this in evolution would require a kind of nascent activity and divergence in matter, nature and being (see below), and it is because of this that Merleau-Ponty's studies of meaning and institution are coupled with studies of embryology and nature (in *IP* and *La nature*). On the organism as active, see, for example, Fox Keller, *Making Sense of Life*; Lewontin, *Biology as Ideology*; Varela, "Organism"; Thompson, *Mind in Life*; and Russon, "Embodiment and Responsibility."

15 See the introductory chapters of *PP*. On these issues, see, for example, Mallin, *Merleau-Ponty's Philosophy*; Rojcewicz, "Depth Perception in Merleau-Ponty"; Madison, *The Phenomenology of Merleau-Ponty*; Hass, *Merleau-Ponty's Philosophy*; and Talero, "Perception, Normativity." In

temporal terms, empiricism's reduction of meaning to sensory givens does not see that meaning entails a futural excess that is yet to be determined and the intellectualist inflation of meaning to ideas does not see that meaning entails a past not constituted by consciousness. Empiricism is too passivist, intellectualism too activist (see the lectures on passivity).

16 This paradox is precisely at stake in what Barbaras helpfully calls phenomenality, in which the phenomena are not the appearance of an essence behind the scenes, yet the appearance of the phenomena exceeds what is presently given. See Barbaras, "The Movement of the Living"; *Le Désir et la Distance*; and *The Being of the Phenomenon*. That is, phenomena have an internal, ontological depth.

17 *Reprendre* becomes ever prominent in *PP*'s interweaving of *prendre* and *comprendre* and in the institution lectures. In both, it names a movement that comes back to a present's past so as to generate something new. See below on this logic.

18 Briefly: The theme of the hollow goes back to *SB* and persists through to the later work. The image indicates a latitude within being for more to eventuate; the fold conceives this latitude in terms of being doubling over itself. The field is "total because it is partial" (*IP* 36[7]), that is, it is generative because hollow, and institution "is itself and beyond itself" (*IP* 43[12]), that is, it has a "double aspect." As indicated in note 16, for Merleau-Ponty phenomena are not manifestations of invisible essences behind the scenes; rather, being is a phenomenality in which appearance is the appearance of appearance, of something further than is immediately given, where this something further is however, within the given, which is why the invisible is, crucially, *of* the visible, in it. (See Merleau-Ponty, *VI* 247[300–1].) Being thus has internal depths and is double: the invisible is the lining, *doublure* (*VI* 195[149]), of the visible. Doubleness is a pervasive theme in *VI*, which, however, criticizes an "ontological diplopia" (cf. *VI* 220n[166n]) that overlays objects with a *separable* layer of meaning (as in Cartesian dualism). But doubleness goes back to the body as doubled with habits (see below). In terms of this chapter, chiasm is simply the doubling of being arising through the interrelation of complicity and divergence.

19 See the point, discussed below, that the study of movement amounts to a discovery of "a new sense of the word 'sense'" (*PP* 182–3[148]) and the passage from "Temporality" in *PP* discussed in note 32.

20 On the level, see Kockelmans, "Merleau-Ponty on Space Perception"; Mallin, *Merleau-Ponty's Philosophy*, and Bredlau, "Learning to See." On the dynamics of this level in spatial perception, see Morris, "Optical Idealism." For the broader importance of the level to Merleau-Ponty's

account of perception, see Talero, "Perception, Normativity"; and Kelly, "Seeing Things in Merleau-Ponty." For another argument that perception is based on living norms, see Thompson, *Mind in Life*.

21 On levels and lighting, see Kelly, "Seeing Things in Merleau-Ponty"; and Mallin, *Merleau-Ponty's Philosophy*.

22 On this issue, see note 6; see also Jay Lampert, *Synthesis and Backward Reference*, for a masterful study that shows how Husserlian synthesis requires a "backward reference" with a temporally complex structure. This chapter shows how backward reference is "ontologized" in doubling, divergence, institution, and so on.

23 This point goes back to Hegel's deduction of universals from singulars in *Phenomenology of Spirit*. Although this cannot be detailed here, Hegel is in fact background to Merleau-Ponty's earliest discussion, in *SB*, of folds, hollows, and the temporality of structure (discussed below).

24 My thanks to Donald Beith for drawing my attention to the peculiarities of balance.

25 In Kant this is the problem of how concepts apply to intuitions, which leads to the schematism and the temporality of imagination. See note 40. On these issues in Plato, Kant, and Merleau-Ponty, see Dillon, "Apriority in Kant and Merleau-Ponty" and *Merleau-Ponty's Ontology*.

26 Bernhard Waldenfels, "The Paradox of Expression." On expression in Merleau-Ponty, also see Hass, *Merleau-Ponty's Philosophy*; Adams, "Expression"; and Landes, *Merleau-Ponty*.

27 Compare *IP* 246[188] on physical love as the flywheel that grounds sexual meaning and the point on *IP* 179[134] that my relations to others are not just a curse or weight, but the flywheel that gives my action meaning. My thanks to Don Landes for drawing my attention to the theme of weight in Merleau-Ponty.

28 Thanks to Shiloh Whitney for drawing this point about blurs to my attention.

29 On lags and temporality, see Waldenfels, "Time Lag."

30 In Merleau-Ponty's philosophy, gaps with this sort of structure are at work in the relation between activity and passivity, and in the relation between reversible terms in general. See Morris, "Reversibility and *Ereignis*."

31 There is an echo here of Aristotelian *epagogé*, induction.

32 The connection between meaning and temporality that we have excavated is already anticipated in Merleau-Ponty's point in the temporality chapter of *PP* that "beneath all of these uses of the word *sens* [to designate the meaningful], we find the same fundamental notion of a being oriented or polarized toward what he is not," and "this involves a relationship of active transcendence between the subject and the world," which is,

however, such that we discover that it is the *world* that is the "cradle of significations, direction of all directions [*sens de tous les sens*], and ground of all thoughts" (*PP* 493[454]). And this rootedness in the world rather than the heaven of ideas is because this "active transcendence" transcends via a "more" of temporality, which in fact requires a passive synthesis in which "we make our way into multiplicity," but "we do not synthesize it" (*PP* 490[451]) That is, we have to *wait* for synthesis to happen, in a process that anticipates the logic of institution here described.

33 Cf. Prigogine and Stengers, *The End of Certainty*.

34 Cf. note 13.

35 See note 16 on phenomenality.

36 Merleau-Ponty is here citing Hegel.

37 Note that this means that structure is an anticipation of field as that which is "total because it is partial" – which ontology is exemplified by time.

38 With regard to the theme of institution in Merleau-Ponty, note that the language of institution (especially in relation to language as inaugurating new worlds) is also at work in the 1951 "Philosopher and Sociology" (in *Signs*) and *The Prose of the World* and the 1952 "Indirect Language and the Voices of Silence," although these cannot be discussed here.

39 Our points from *Structure*, though, suggest that this temporality must also be "embodied." Above we noted that material balance would be impossible in a universe void of a temporality that carries the past over the present into the future. *Structure* suggests the converse: the temporality of institution, which leaves room for non-givenness, would be impossible in a universe in which temporality did not intersect with and become manifest in moving material structures. Temporality's "embodiment" – its being manifest in nature as moving matter, as it were – exerts a drag on the eventuation of temporality, preventing it from being manifest all at once. It is only in this way that temporality can take the time to be "clogged" with its past. Without matter, time is too quick to be meaningful.

40 There is an echo here of the temporality of Kantian imagination, transposed to the ontological level. The "Temporality" chapter of *PP* is perhaps more deeply influenced by the study of the temporality of Kantian imagination in Heidegger's *Kant and the Problem of Metaphysics* than it is by *Being and Time*, and this influence persists in Merleau-Ponty. (On this issue, see Kelly, "The Subject as Time.") This connection inflects temporality with a radical role in passive synthesis (see n32), which supports the point being made here, as does the connection between sense, fields, and time as total because partial. On the connection to Kantian imagination, also see Morris, "Reversibility and *Ereignis*."

41 I would like to thank Shiloh Whitney, Noah Moss Brender, Donald Beith, and Tristana Martin Rubio for their helpful comments on this chapter and them and Lisa Guenther for their contributions to my understanding of Merleau-Ponty on institution, without which this chapter would not have been possible. This chapter would also not be possible without John Russon's recent work on experience, meaning and temporality, and the work of Ed Casey, Bernhard Waldenfels, Len Lawlor, Susan Bredlau, Kym Maclaren, Maria Talero, and Kirsten Jacobson.

10 Implications of Merleau-Ponty's Account of Binocularity

ÖMER AYGÜN

In this chapter, I will first point out the increasing significance of binocular vision throughout Merleau-Ponty's philosophical career such that it becomes the prototype of the "chiasm" and the paradigm for understanding intersubjectivity, truth, and humanity in his later thought. To flesh out what it is about binocularity that leads Merleau-Ponty to attach so much meaning to it, I will then intertwine this question with a literary encounter of monocularity and binocularity – the one between Odysseus and Polyphemus the Cyclops in Homer's *Odyssey*. In this way we will see the implications of Merleau-Ponty's conception of binocular vision in the context of law, language, and love. The case of binocularity in Merleau-Ponty's work will also show us the special way in which phenomenology deals with examples – not merely as illustrations of the conclusion of a finished research, but also, and most specifically, as a very means of research, and even a guide to it.

I. Binocularity in Merleau-Ponty's Work

The central question of Maurice Merleau-Ponty's philosophy is perception. Before being a problem, perception is a mystery to him in that it seems to take place *at once* in the object *and* in the subject and cannot be explained away as the result of a juxtaposition of the two.[1] The mystery of perception is such that it requires, beyond the subject–object divide, a holistic view, since it undermines the very way of speaking of it as taking place in the object and in the subject, and immediately demands a critique of the very terms attempting to elucidate it: "*subject*," "*object*," "*place*," "*in*," and "*and*" ... Hence the "primacy of perception" – as he puts it in the title of a text from 1946 – is not to be understood in an exclusive way, in the sense that perception sets the boundaries of his work; rather, it provides him with a constant exemplary source of wonder, such that arguably in no other philosopher is perception more thoroughly ontological, political, erotic, linguistic, and artistic than in Merleau-Ponty. Thus, Merleau-Ponty's work on this mystery is neither confined to it nor attempts to overcome it as parasitic; he rather carries the mystery over to all other phenomena and keeps recognizing it beyond any exclusive urge for certainty. If Merleau-Ponty's philosophy can be characterized as a "philosophy of ambiguity," as Waelhens described it, it is because it stems from this mysterious character of perception.

Besides the paradigmatic character of perception itself, if one were to look for a recurrent exemplary case within perception that reiterates this mystery and ambiguity, binocular vision is perhaps the most significant and informative. For just as a phenomenological account of perception cannot reduce it to mere "impressions," "sensations," or "stimuli" beyond the first-person perspective, or to "thoughts," binocularity can be explained neither as the mere physical result of two superimposed self-sufficient monocular images nor as the act of superposition executed by a disincarnated mind. No wonder that, in clear opposition to Merleau-Ponty, one of the major philosophical figures of the mind/body divide and of the demystified search for epistemic certainty, René Descartes, approaches binocularity analytically as a mere superposition of pre-existing monocular images[2]:

> As, for example, if we see any creature come toward us, the light reflected from his body paints two images, one in each eye, and these two images beget two others by intercourse with the optic nerves in the interior superficies of the brain that looks towards its concavities. From thence, … and the motion which composes any point of one of these images tends to the same point of the kernel to which that motion tends that frames the point of the other image which represents, too, part of this creature; by which means the two images in the brain make up but one single one upon the kernel, which acting immediately against the soul, shows her the figure of that creature.[3]

This passage also indicates that, even before binocularity, Descartes applies his analytical approach to the monocular reception of retinal images: according to him, in the same way that the binocular image is a mere addition of monocular images by means of "animal spirits," the monocular image from the outset is itself a bundle of responses to local stimuli on distinct points of the retinal surface. Just as Descartes approaches binocular vision analytically, so does he construe monocular vision in a pointillistic or atomistic way. Thus, before we engage with Merleau-Ponty's approach to binocularity, it may be helpful to touch upon his non-pointillistic conception of the retinal image, which constitutes the first of the three stages of the history of the binocularity in his career.

1. *Retinal Image as Form in* The Structure of Behavior

In *The Structure of Behavior* (hereafter *SB*), in which Merleau-Ponty sets out to understand "the relations of consciousness and nature: organic, psychological or even social," he starts with reflex behaviour, which includes the reception of retinal stimuli.[4] In sharp contrast to the Cartesian analytic approach, he contends that vision cannot be reduced to a correlation between local stimuli on the retinal area and responses to those stimuli. To justify this claim, he engages in a *reductio* argument, pointing out that the loss of half of the retinal area does not result merely in a *diminishment* in the visual field of the subject, but also in a *deterioration* of the visual field as a whole. As he underscores in his quotation from Koffka, "*the quantity of space encompassed by our perception and the place of the zone of clear vision in the phenomenal field express certain modes of organization of the sensory field related to the objects presented to the eye much more than the geometrical projection of objects on the retina, and depend upon certain laws of equilibrium proper to the nervous system much more than upon anatomical structures*" (*SB* 42, italicized by Merleau-Ponty). Thus, the parts of the retinal area are not indifferent to one another and to the nature of the stimuli, as they would be in a strictly Euclidean space. For Merleau-Ponty, the parts of the retinal surface are not inert; rather, they are responsive to one another as much as they are responsive to external stimuli; in short, monocular vision must be accounted for not from an analytical viewpoint but from a holistic perspective.

While he argues that anatomical accounts are insufficient even for reflex behaviour, Merleau-Ponty carefully avoids falling into the other extreme position according to which the retinal stimuli would be merged with one another by an act of consciousness. According to him, if this were the case, this synthesis would not be reflex behaviour to begin with, and theoretically, the consciousness of the subject would be expected to be able to deliberately refrain from synthesizing stimuli on different parts of the retina and thereby see in a "cubistic" way, as it were, from two angles at once. Both purely anatomical and purely mental accounts of retinal phenomena fail to explain why the loss of half the retinal area does not simply result in the loss of half of the visual field. This is because both accounts deny an intrinsic relation between the parts of the retinal area.[5]

If both purely anatomical and purely mental accounts fail to explain the intrinsic relation of retinal points, how can one account for such an intrinsic relation? At this point in *The Structure of Behavior*, Merleau-Ponty proposes that we approach vision as a "physical system" or "form" in line with *Gestalt* psychology: "We will say that there is form whenever the properties of a system are modified by every change brought about in a single one of its parts and, on the contrary, are conserved when they all change while maintaining the same relationship among themselves" (*SB* 47). In this way, the concept of "form" will pave the way to a proper understanding of binocularity. One typical and informative example of "form" is a melody: changing one note in it modifies the whole (thus, the whole is not indifferent to its parts), whereas the melody remains the same when all of its notes are transposed to another key (thus, the whole is not reducible to the sum of its parts).

2. *Binocularity in* Phenomenology of Perception

The concept of "form" in *The Structure of Behavior* prefigures Merleau-Ponty's approach to binocularity in *Phenomenology of Perception*.[6] Merleau-Ponty's argument here is once again a *reductio* argument: If binocular vision were simply a superposition of monocular images, nothing in a monocular image taken analytically would let us infer any relation between that image and another monocular image, whether this relation is one of identity or difference, symmetry or dissymmetry, resemblance or dissemblance; in that case, we would have two monolithic, self-sufficient, atomic images without any possibility of communication or comparison between them. However much we clarified or analysed the two images, neither of them would present us with any hint to the other; furthermore, we would have no reason to view either as belonging to the same thing; rather, we would have two unrelated images belonging to no thing at all. To give an example, my left eye would be seeing the top, front, and left sides of a cube, while my right eye would be seeing its top, front, and right sides; yet I would have no reason to view the right side and the left side *as belonging to the same thing*; moreover, I would have no reason to view the two images of the top side or of the front side *as the same*. So what I would be seeing would not be a *cube*; it would not even be *one* thing. In a way, Cubist figures would come closer to normal perception than Cézanne's do; yet the point of Cubist painting is to *actualize* what remains *potential* in normal perception precisely in order to point out that potentiality – for instance, to project on the canvas a cube with an actual fourth side that, in normal vision, remains only potentially visible, on the "horizon." By contrast, Cézanne tilts planar perspectives not to *actualize* other *potential* aspects of his object, but precisely to suggest their *potentiality*.

So *having* binocular vision cannot be identical to *having* two unrelated and apparently unrelatable images. According to Merleau-Ponty, this impossibility is neither logical nor transcendental nor even physical or anatomical. Even if we assume that to see is to somehow *have* two unrelated and apparently unrelatable images, this does not account for why we *have* them in the first place. In other words, *how* the "animal spirits" effectuate the perceptual synthesis according to Descartes is as unclear as *why* they would do so. If there were no prior project, if there were no intention, there would be no monocular image to begin with, let alone binocular vision. As Merleau-Ponty quotes from Déjean: "We must 'look' in order to see" (*PP* 278[241]). Thus, binocularity rests not on a logical, transcendental, physical, or anatomic necessity, but on an *intentional* "necessity," on an existential project, on a "pre-*having*" and "looking-ahead." If Descartes's "animal spirits" had such an existential project, they just would be actual animals actually seeing – and we would have to explain how and why those animals see.

I have been italicizing the verb "to have" simply to point out that the issue at hand is related to the concept of *habitus* and ultimately that of *êthos*, *ethos*, and *hexis* and their original verbal form *ekhein* in Aristotle.[7] Mechanistic approaches tend to reduce the significance of "having" to the geometrical ideas of "containing" or "circumscribing," and to reduce potentiality to actuality. This discussion around the verb "having" is not foreign to Merleau-Ponty, given that in an ambivalent reference to Descartes, he says that the intricate character of the body/soul relation is such that the soul suffers within the body, as "when I say that I *have* a toothache."[8] *Having* a toothache requires a synthesis that can neither be performed by a transcendental Ego (since *my tooth* is aching), nor be reduced to an anatomical state of affairs (since *I* am having the toothache). The case of binocular vision is analogous to this:

> Has the "fusion of images" then been obtained through some innate mechanism in the nervous system, and do we mean that in the final analysis, if not at the periphery then at least at the center, we *have* only one single stimulation mediated by our two eyes? But the mere existence of a visual center cannot explain the unique object, since double vision sometimes occurs … If in normal vision we can understand double vision just as well as the unique object, this will not be through the anatomical organization of the visual apparatus, but rather through its functioning and through the psycho-physical subject's use of it. (*PP* 277[240], emphasis mine)

If, on the other hand, we adopt the intellectualist approach and assume that the transcendental Ego consciously manipulates the two images in order to superpose them and thereby infer the uniqueness of the object, we should ask why this operation takes place at all if indeed the Ego is truly transcendental. Why exactly would a truly *transcendental* Ego even care? After all, if this Ego has a worldly project and has already received the monocular images in the context of this project, then why not admit it is the "interested," worldly, bodily, desiring subject to begin with (*PP* 278[241])? So again, it is not in the context of anatomical or transcendental necessity, but in the context of an intentional "necessity," of an "existential" care, that the following sentences should be read: "The synthesis is not accomplished by the epistemological subject, but rather by the body when it tears itself away from its dispersion, gathers itself together, and carries itself through all of its resources toward a single term of its movement, and when a single intention is conceived within it through the phenomenon of synergy" (*PP* 279[241]). Thus, Merleau-Ponty attributes the binocular synthesis straightforwardly to the living body rather than to a transcendental subject or to "animal spirits."

Tracing Merleau-Ponty's career, we move from the *reflex* "synthesis" of the different parts of the retinal area in *The Structure of Behavior* to the *binocular* "synthesis" of monocular images in the *Phenomenology of Perception*; this latter work moves from binocular synthesis to the unity of senses – that is, to the intermodal *perceptual* "synthesis" as a whole, and then to intersensory perception (*PP* 271–2[234–5], 366ff[324ff]), linguistic experiences and, finally, to worldly ontology: "The monocular images wander vaguely *in front* of the things, they have no place in the world, and suddenly they pull back toward a certain place in the world and are absorbed into the world, just as ghosts return through the fissures of the earth from which they came when the day breaks" (*PP* 279[242], Merleau-Ponty's emphasis). Now let us turn to the third and last part of Merleau-Ponty's career, during which binocular vision becomes even more significant and exemplary.

3. *Binocularity in* The Visible and the Invisible

The *Phenomenology of Perception* foreshadows the extreme broadening and radicalization of the significance of binocularity in *The Visible and the Invisible.* These latter notes for an unfinished work are launched by the concept of binocularity as a paradigm of the relation between the body and the world along the lines of Déjean's distinction between looking and seeing:

> It is by *looking,* it is still with my eyes that I arrive at the true thing, with these same eyes that a moment ago gave me monocular images – now they simply function *together* and as though *for good* [*pour de bon*]. Thus the relation between things and my body is decidedly singular: it is what makes me sometimes remain in appearances, and it is also what sometimes brings me to the things themselves. (Merleau-Ponty, *VI* 23[8], Merleau-Ponty's emphasis)

The significance of binocularity is carried over to the relation between different senses (*PP* 270[242]ff) and is thematized in expressly ontological language: "The monocular images *are* not in the same sense that the thing perceived with both eyes *is.* They are phantoms and it is the real; they are pre-things and it is the thing: they vanish when we pass to normal vision and re-enter into the thing as into their daylight truth" (*VI* 22[7], Merleau-Ponty's emphasis). Binocularity is paradigmatic not only within mere vision or isolated intermodal perception, but in relation to being, reality, thingness, normality, and truth; furthermore, it is no longer a synthesis of monocular images, but is such that it "makes of my two eyes the channels of one sole Cyclopean vision" (*VI* 184[141]).[9] Even further, the issue of binocularity seems to have implications for the history of philosophy, since Merleau-Ponty talks about the "'strabism' of Western ontology in the context of Cartesian ontologies" and about "ontological dipoplia" (*VI 166*).

Exhibiting the raw and almost wild character of a draft, *The Visible and the Invisible* prefers the word "metamorphosis" to "synthesis" (*VI* 23[8], 184[141]), underlines "perceptual faith," and strengthens the wondrous character of the phenomenon of binocular vision by comparing it to a "miracle" and by employing an almost "teleological" language:

> It is not a *synthesis*; it is a metamorphosis by which the appearances are instantaneously stripped of a value they owed merely to the absence of a true perception. Thus in perception we witness the miracle of a totality that surpasses what one thinks to be its conditions or its parts, that from afar holds them under its power, as if they existed only on its threshold and were destined to lose themselves in it. (*VI* 23[8], Merleau-Ponty's emphasis)[10]

Whether a *synthesis* or a *metamorphosis*, binocular vision becomes the explicit paradigm of communication and of the fundamentally ambiguous character of truth:

> The communication makes us the witnesses of one sole world, as the synergy of our eyes suspends them on one unique thing. But in both cases, the certitude, entirely irresistible as it may be, remains absolutely obscure; we can live it, we can neither think it nor formulate it nor set it up in theses. Every attempt at elucidation brings us back to the dilemmas. (*VI* 27[11]; 265[216])

Finally, in Merleau-Ponty's last finished work, "Eye and Mind," binocular vision becomes a paradigm of reflection and humanity: "What if, like certain animals, we had lateral eyes with no cross blending of visual fields? Such a body would not reflect itself; it ... would not really be the body of a human being. There would be no humanity."[11]

So how are we to understand this conception of binocularity as a paradigm for the relation between untruth and truth, isolation and reflectivity, and as a distinctive feature, or even condition of possibility, of humanity? It could be the case that philosophy is too monocular to penetrate, as it were, the depth of this conception of binocularity, and that Merleau-Ponty's comparison of the monocular images to "ghosts" may be inviting us to answer our question by launching a certain binocularity between philosophy and literature, by observing a literary figure that may shed light on the philosophical significance Merleau-Ponty so insistently and increasingly invests in the difference between binocular and monocular vision.

II. Polyphemus, Odysseus ... and Galatea

If so, the most obvious literary figure of monocularity is indeed the Cyclops. Hence the most obvious confrontation between monocularity and binocularity is the famous encounter between Odysseus and

Polyphemus the Cyclops in the ninth book of Homer's *Odyssey*. In this section of the chapter, to flesh out the implications of the enormous significance given by Merleau-Ponty to binocular vision, I will analyse Polyphemus's relation to the realms of law, language, and love.

1. *Law*

The Cyclopes[12] are famously arrogant and lawless (Homer, *Odyssey*, 9.106, trans. Murray). Yet, according to the Homeric account, this is not because they were raised badly, or are innately evil or wicked, but rather because their island is so fertile that they need make no effort to survive: the Cyclopes inhabit an Eden, which the covetous Odysseus describes at length (9.107–39). There is no need for agriculture, deliberation, or legislation on the island, and each gives laws to his children and spouses (9.107–15), as Aristotle famously quotes in the *Politics*.[13] Aristotle adds that they live not a life of the *polis*, but an isolated life in caves. Odysseus's emphasis on the lack of concern and work on the island is unmistakable thanks to the wealth of privative adjectives in the Homeric text, and so is its deliberate contrast to the human condition "in the open": Cyclopes have no plough, no sowing, no hunting, *hence* no carpenters and no ships (9.125). No wonder that Odysseus, assuming the viewpoint of an entrepreneur or a colonizer, imagines how beautiful a city the Cyclopes would build if they had ships, and how easy an agriculture they would have because of the fertility of their island's soil (9.126–41).

It is well known that Odysseus is characterized in Homer by adjectives denoting plurality and multiplicity: having travelled and seen much, he is *polytropos*; having endured much, he is *polytlêmôn*; hence he is resourceful and always finds a way out of trouble (*polymêkhanos, polymêtis*). By contrast, Odysseus describes the Cyclopes' situation in almost exclusively negative terms: they have no clan (*aphrêtor*), no law (*athemistos*), and no homes (*anestios*); although they have tremendous strength, and although their island is naturally overabundant, or perhaps *because* of this, they have no agriculture, no ships, no visitors, no craftsmen, and little respect for gods: "Neither assemblies for council [*agorai boulêphoroi*] have they, nor appointed laws [*themistes*], but they dwell on the peaks of mountains in hollow caves, and each one is lawgiver to his children and his wives, and they have no regard for one another" (9.111–15; see also 9.210.). Note, however, that Homer's or Odysseus's account of the Cyclopean way of life is explicitly characterized not by a lack of vital natural resources, but, on the contrary, by self-sufficiency, and hence by a lack of concern and work. In short, by lacking human work, worship, and wandering, Cyclopean life is one of sheer positivity.

As for Polyphemus, he is described as even lonelier and more isolated than the other Cyclopes, for he is unmarried and has no children – thus he is not even a lawgiver to a wife and children. He is a lonesome shepherd. Yet, although he is not a lawgiver, he is a sort of king in the sense that he silently leads his flock without being accountable to anyone; he is a "shepherd-king" and a "leader" in the most literal sense. In any case, having no law at all, except perhaps for the implicit "law of the stronger," he has no familiarity with the "law of hospitality" (9.259–71); being the son of the sea god Poseidon, Polyphemus in fact *has* no gods, properly speaking (9.275–80). He is lawless not as a violator, a pirate, a thief, or a liar, but as someone who has not encountered any law to violate; he is impious not in the sense of denying gods, but solely to the extent that he is the son of one. Even his look distinguishes him from others: "He was fashioned a monstrous marvel, and was not like a man that lives by bread, but like a wooded peak of lofty mountains, which stands out to view alone, apart from the rest," says Odysseus about him, and then adds: "I bade the rest of my trusty comrades to remain there by the ship and to guard the ship, but I chose twelve of the best of my comrades and went my way" (9.189–95).

This transition from Polyphemus's solitude to Odysseus's own collective action is striking in that it moves from a life in mountaintop caves to a life in ships on the level of "open sea," that it steps from a world caught up in lawlessness and self-sufficiency into a world where the resourceful Odysseus engages in a task, and persuades and organizes his comrades by establishing a common goal based on common desires, a world in which resourcefulness and law implicate each other. It will not be long before Odysseus links Polyphemus's situation to his linguistic capacities.

2. *Language*

When Polyphemus first sees Odysseus in his cave and begins talking with him, he tries but fails to get his guest to tell him where his ship is. The famously cunning Odysseus recounts: "So he spoke, tempting me, but he trapped me not because of my great cunning; and I made answer again in crafty words: 'My Ship Poseidon, the earth-shaker, dashed to pieces'" (9.281–3). It is precisely then that Polyphemus makes a move to have Odysseus's comrades for dinner since, probably supposing that no one can be craftier than himself in speech, he is certain that Odysseus and his men are at his mercy. It is precisely at this point that Odysseus pays heed to language, appealing to his own openness to a life altogether foreign to himself by taking a look at the world through Polyphemus's round eye. Hence, besides his technical ability and indeed his commanding his fellow men in the fabrication of the spear (9.319–35), Odysseus makes, communicates, and executes his plan by means of language: the night before he blinds the Cyclops, he *speaks* to Polyphemus, while offering the good wine they purposefully brought with them, as if he were asking for mercy (9.347–52); and when in drunkenness Polyphemus *asks* his name (9.355–9), Odysseus famously *tells* him his name is "Nobody," thus beginning the process by which he will lead Polyphemus to his ruin (9.366).

So, as Odysseus predicted, when Polyphemus is blinded and tells the other Cyclopes that Nobody is slaying him (9.408), hoping to compensate for his blindness by organizing the eyes and speech of others, he takes "Nobody" for a proper name. The other Cyclopes, on the other hand, are unable to notice Polyphemus's shortcoming, immersed as they are in the literal sense of that name. Polyphemus has failed to attune himself not only to Odysseus's plans, but also to the other Cyclopes' way of thinking. The two sides understand the word "Nobody" unequivocally, as unambiguous, but, unfortunately, in different senses, precisely as Odysseus planned by using an ambiguous name. Cyclopes act as if words simply match beings, as if there is only one word for one being or one kind of being. Therefore, just as Polyphemus's life was marked by positivity such that he had no notion of law whatsoever, his view and usage of language is confined to a univocal, unambiguous language, one in which words have clear and distinct meanings and in which, by default, one expects certainty as a standard.

Thus Odysseus and his men escape right under the sheep caressed by the *doubly* blinded Polyphemus. Polyphemus is defeated by Odysseus when the latter defines himself as utter negativity, saying that he is "Nobody"; Polyphemus's downfall is thus a consequence of his lack of a sense of negativity, his sense that linguistic phenomena are univocal, atomic, self-given, and exempt from the necessary multivocity of, say, indefinite pronouns. Compare these linguistic failures to Schneider's case as analysed by Merleau-Ponty: Schneider's experience "never raises a question, and it never ceases to have this sort of evidentness and self-sufficiency of the real that stifles all interrogation, all reference to the possible, all wonder, and all improvisation" (*PP* 238[202]). Thus our intertwining of Merleau-Ponty's concept of binocularity with the literary figure of the Cyclops provides us with a strong connection between negativity, ambiguity, interrogation, possibility, and improvisation.

If so, then Polyphemus's monocularity in law and language is not simply a defect – it is the defect *of a defect*, a deficiency in confronting deficiency; it is his *pre-given* self-sufficiency, his lack of the sense of interrogation and possibility, in short, his lack of the sense of negativity and self-opposition. Thus, one guise of monocularity may be a certain interpretation of our interactions with the world and others solely in terms of needs and fulfilment, an interpretation whereby community, crafts, laws, language, love, and even gods are seen as fully actual and purely instrumental. According to this interpretation, Polyphemus's life was perfect in that all his needs seemed to be satisfied by the natural abundance of his environment; he never had to care about community, creativity, possibilities, and unexpected guests. Just as with monocularity, this Polyphemic interpretation of the world fails to be *one* precisely because of its monolithic or "panoptic" character. In his urge to return to Penelope in Ithaca, Odysseus is crafty by recognizing negativity as negativity, by being on his way from something to something; whereas, paradoxical as it may sound (but perhaps nothing is more paradoxical than perception in Merleau-Ponty), Polyphemic perfection is imperfect by being a *given* perfection, by not being exposed to the negativity of having-been "somewhere" and of having-to-be "somewhere," of both "pre-having" and "looking-ahead."

Are we then to conclude by simply matching Odysseus with binocularity and the sense of negativity, and Polyphemus with monocularity and full positivity? Hasn't Polyphemus ever been exposed to negativity as such, to an infinite need? Didn't Polyphemus ever think of risking the *pre-given* perfection of his life, or of improvising, of even giving up his unique eye for the sake of a true community with someone? In short, didn't Polyphemus ever fall in love?

3. *Love*

Apparently he did. Not in Homer, but in a prequel to the Homeric story, in an idyll written by the third-century BCE Sicilian Theocritus.[14] Here we see the poet recommending to his friend Nicias that he appeal to the Muses as a remedy for love, giving the example of our Polyphemus, who in his youth had fallen in love with the sea nymph Galatea and who sat on a rock and sang a poem to her instead of learning to swim: "O my white Galatea, why do you spurn your lover?" (Theocritus, *Idyll* 11, v. 19). This idyll shows the insufficiency of the apparent Homeric dilemma between grotesque monocular figures and cunning binocular ones; it shows us a way to interpret Polyphemus in the context of human law and language themselves, a way to detect the resurgence of the "ghosts" of monocularity as possibilities within binocularity itself. For beneath his self-sufficient, silent, irregular, lawless Edenic life, the young Polyphemus did in fact experience true frustration, the "hell" of "others," and negativity as such: "He loved, not with apples, roses, or curls of hair, / But in an outright frenzy. For him, nothing else existed" (v. 10–11).

The real comedy, if it is one, serves as a prequel to the Homeric episode; it shows us that Polyphemus was not living an exactly heavenly life before the fatal visit of Odysseus, and it places the Cyclops in a new contrast with the Greek hero famously awaited by Penelope and Telemachus. Being incapable of even herding his heavenly flock, which, being heavenly, went to pasture and came back to the cave on their own, Polyphemus sang:

> Burn away my life with fire – I could bear even that,
> And my single eye, my one dearest possession of all. (v. 52–3)

But it is important to note how this young Polyphemus interprets the reason for his frustration:

> I know, my beautiful girl, why you run from me:
> A shaggy brow spreads right across my face
> From ear to ear in one unbroken line. Below is a
> Single eye, and above my lip is set a broad flat nose.
> Such may be my looks, but ... (v. 30–4)

According to him, his love is frustrated because he is naturally ugly; he cannot learn to swim and join Galatea because he lacks gills (v. 54); but he thinks that the true cause of his frustration is his mother, Thoosa the Nereid:

> It's my mother who does me wrong; it's her alone I blame.
> She's not once spoken a gentle word to you about me,
> Although she sees me wasting away, day by day. (v. 67–9)

Indeed he can learn to swim instead of composing serenades to his beloved, but he is quickly distracted from this line of thought:

> It's not too late, my sweet, for me to learn to swim;
> If only some sailor [*xenos*] would sail here in his ship,
> Then I could fathom why you nymphs love life in the deep. (v. 60–2)

Thus, after blaming his physical appearance, his natural body, and his natural mother, Polyphemus oddly places all his hope for learning how to swim on the arrival of a helpful *xenos* – an ironic foreshadowing of the fatal Homeric story, indeed, added to the apparently "comedic" portrayal of Polyphemus.

Furthermore, this serenade exhibits not only his inability to take responsibility and action, but also his fundamental inability to comprehend the mindset, and thus the desires, of his beloved. The serenade itself, and not only its content, is provoked by his lack of action and synergy. Hence, in every attempt at persuasion, community, inspiration, expression, creativity, or improvisation, Polyphemus falls back onto his pre-given situation: He has no metaphors but the univocal names of the dull objects in his immediate environment, which, indeed, must be quite unlike that of a sea nymph:

> Whiter to look at than cream cheese, softer than a lamb,
> More playful than a calf, sleeker than the unripe grape. (v. 20–1)

His proposals to Galatea are clearly devoid of any concern for what a sea nymph would desire:

> All marked on their necks, and four bear cubs too.
> O please, come. You will see that life is just as good
> If you leave the grey-green sea behind to crash on the shore,
> And at night you will find more joy in this cave with me …
> Who could prefer waves and the sea to all this? ...
> I wish my mother had given me gills when I was born,
> Then I could have dived down and kissed your hand,
> If you denied me your mouth ... (vv. 41–4, 49, 54–6)

It seems that Theocritus or the narrator is suggesting to the reader that the young Polyphemus cannot help considering everything as *pre-given*, finished, perfect, fully actual objects – that he fails to set his body in motion, to crack his shell and assume someone else's perspective on the world.

But the most moving part of the serenade may be the lines that immediately follow. For here we are invited to go well beyond simply laughing at Polyphemus or pitying him. Polyphemus says:

> If you denied me your mouth, [I could have] brought you white
> Snowdrops or delicate poppies with their scarlet petals.
> One grows in summer and the other grows in winter,
> So you see I could not bring you both at once. (v. 56–9)

Right after promising snowdrops *or* poppies, what worries Polyphemus is not whether Galatea would want either of these, but that these two kinds of flowers do not bloom at the same time of the year so that actually he cannot bring them both at the same time. This is odd, at least because he did not promise both kinds of flowers at once, but one or the other. More importantly, he is so confined in univocity and so far from improvising that he does even think of hiding the inconsistency of his promises, of interpreting them metaphorically, or of finding a way to make them bloom at the same time of year; and he feels compelled to point this out to Galatea. Finally, it is odd that, before making promises to Galatea, he did not predict this problem, about which he now seems so concerned.

These verses are a parody of love poetry; they are somewhat awkward, even absurd, and perhaps "funny." Yet these very verses also go beyond the comedic and the laughable. For they show us how "honest" Polyphemus is in his own way, how "ashamed" he would be if he did not literally fulfil his promise. True, he forgot that the two flowers do not bloom at the same time of the year; once he notices this, he fails to find a way to cover up his mistake, or he refuses to cover it up; he does not even think that a sea nymph would have no idea when these flowers bloom to begin with. Again, he is the opposite of Odysseus. This is all true, but its impact goes beyond the comedic once we view Polyphemus's dream of giving Galatea the snowdrops and poppies at the same time as an act of love, honesty, and fidelity.

Hence the feeling of bitterness the reader feels at the end of the serenade:

> O Cyclops, Cyclops, where have your wits flown away?
> Show some sense, go and weave some baskets, collect

> Green shoots for your lambs. Milk the ewe
> At hand; why chase the one who runs away? Maybe
> You'll find another Galatea, and a prettier one too.
> I'm invited out for night-time play by lots of girls,
> And they giggle together as soon as they see I've heard.
> On land I too am clearly a man of some consequence. (v. 72–9)

Upon these closing words of Polyphemus's serenade, the narrator comes back to his advice to his love-struck friend Nicias and draws a somewhat empty moral:

> So by singing the Cyclops shepherded his love,
> And more relief it brought him than paying a large fee. (v. 80–1)

These moralizing verses – indeed the whole idyll – are probably satirizing Alexandrian love poetry[15]: the serenade form is no guarantee against solipsism or monocularity and constitutes no "cure" for love except for one who already wants this form to be its "cure." Yet one may also think that Theocritus's poem is not simply creating and ridiculing an "Other" in the form of a monocular or Cartesian monster. On the contrary, Theocritus may well be addressing a factual possibility (or even the very actuality) of human life in general. For besides the fact that we know nothing of Galatea's point of view, or whether she was forbidden to meet Polyphemus, it may have been the case that Galatea was dead. So in this sense, we are all Polyphemus. In pain and desperation, we are left with bitterness, mourning, or futile accusations. From this point of view, Polyphemus's story is a humane story of finitude, helplessness, and irretrievable loss. It does not simply invite the reader to laugh at, or pity, Polyphemus's clumsy serenade as a prequel to his legal and linguistic incompetence in the Homeric story; it is a story of the absolute opposition of winter and summer, a story of separation and sorrow. And in this sense, Polyphemus's story converges with the story of Odysseus, who, before returning to Penelope in Ithaca, was to come across his dead mother in Hades (*Odyssey*, 11.85–9; 11.152–224).

III. Concluding Remarks

In this chapter, we traced the significance of binocularity throughout Merleau-Ponty's work in his treatment of the retinal image as "form" in *The Structure of Behavior*; in his analysis of binocular vision in

Phenomenology of Perception, where he begins to adopt a more ontological terminology; and finally in his last works, *The Visible and the Invisible* and "Eye and Mind," in which binocular vision becomes explicitly paradigmatic for understanding intersubjectivity, truth, and humanity.

What then is the significance of the example of binocular vision for Merleau-Ponty? The significance seems to lie in the fact that, more clearly than other phenomena, binocularity illustrates that neither the "obvious" unity of the act of vision nor the "obvious" duality of our eyes are pre-given facts but are actually mediated and subtended by what Merleau-Ponty called a "form," a "synthesis," a existential "project," a "metamorphosis," or an "openness to being." But this example in Merleau-Ponty is also methodologically significant: for, as an example, binocular vision is less representative or illustrative than "heuristic," since it is not merely a sample of a pre-given doctrine, but a theme or a motif that drives the research further and widens and deepens its perspective. Binocularity is heuristic in that it immediately brings out the necessity for self-opposition, for the negativity of "looking," even in our merely "seeing" things, in our apparently immediate and unproblematic encounter with the world. Finally, our analysis of the figure of the Cyclops showed us the implications of Merleau-Ponty's account of binocularity in law, language, and love. These three are instances of negativity at work in that they all necessitate a synergic project with others, a sense of improvisation in light of unforeseen possibilities, irreducible ambiguities, and irretrievable loss.

Appendix: "The Cyclops' Serenade" by Theocritus, translated by Anthony Verity

"Nicias, there is no remedy for love, no liniment,
As I believe, nor any balm, except the Muses.
Theirs is a gentle, painless drug, and in men's power
To use; but it is hard to find. You know this well,
I think; you are a doctor, and one whom the nine
Muses love above all. This at any rate was the way
My countryman the Cyclops eased his pain,
Polyphemus long ago, when he loved Galatea,
When the down was fresh about his mouth and temples.
He loved, not with apples, roses, or curls of hair,
But in an outright frenzy. For him, nothing else existed.

Often his flocks would come of their own accord
Back from green pastures to the fold, while he, alone
On the weed-strewn shore, would sing of Galatea from
Break of day, wasting away with love. Deep inside he bore
A cruel wound, which mighty Cypris' dart had driven
Into his heart. But he found out the cure: he would sit
On some high rock, and gazing out to sea would sing:
'O my white Galatea, why do you spurn your lover?
Whiter to look at than cream cheese, softer than a lamb,
More playful than a calf, sleeker than the unripe grape.
Why do you only come just as sweet sleep claims me,
Why do you leave me just as sweet sleep lets me go,
Flying like a ewe at the sight of a grey wolf?
I fell in love with you, my sweet, when first you came
With my mother to gather flowers of hyacinth
On the mountain, and I was your guide. From the day
I set eyes on you up to this moment, I've loved you
Without a break; but you care nothing, nothing at all.
I know, my beautiful girl, why you run from me:
A shaggy brow spreads right across my face
From ear to ear in one unbroken line. Below is a
Single eye, and above my lip is set a broad flat nose.
Such may be my looks, but I pasture a thousand beasts,
And I drink the best of the milk I get from them.
Cheese too I have in abundance, in summer and autumn,
And even at winter's end; my racks are always laden.
And I can pipe better than any Cyclops here,
When I sing, my sweet pippin, deep in the night
Of you and me. For you I'm rearing eleven fawns,
All marked on their necks, and four bear cubs too.
O please, come. You will see that life is just as good
If you leave the grey-green sea behind to crash on the shore,
And at night you will find more joy in this cave with me.
Here there are bays, and here slender cypresses,
Here is sombre ivy, and here the vine's sweet fruit;
Here there is ice-cold water which dense-wooded Etna
Sends from its white snows – a drink fit for the gods.
Who could prefer waves and the sea to all this?
But if you think I'm a touch too hairy for you,
I have oak logs here, and under the ash unflagging fire.

Burn away my life with fire – I could bear even that,
And my single eye, my one dearest possession of all.
I wish my mother had given me gills when I was born,
Then I could have dived down and kissed your hand,
If you denied me your mouth, and brought you white
Snowdrops or delicate poppies with their scarlet petals.
One grows in summer and the other grows in winter,
So you see I could not bring you both at once.
It's not too late, my sweet, for me to learn to swim;
If only some mariner would sail here in his ship,
Then I could fathom why you nymphs love life in the deep.
Come out, Galatea, come out and forget your home,
Just as I sit here and forget to return to mine.
Follow the shepherd's life with me – milking,
And setting cheese with the rennet's pungent drops.
It's my mother who does me wrong; it's her alone I blame.
She's not once spoken a gentle word to you about me,
Although she sees me wasting away, day by day.
I'll see she knows how my head and feet throb with pain,
So that her torment will be equal to what I suffer.
O Cyclops, Cyclops, where have your wits flown away?
Show some sense, go and weave some baskets, collect
Green shoots for your lambs. Milk the ewe
At hand; why chase the one who runs away? Maybe
You'll find another Galatea, and a prettier one too.
I'm invited out for night-time play by lots of girls,
And they giggle together as soon as they see I've heard.
On land I too am clearly a man of some consequence.'
So by singing the Cyclops shepherded his love,
And more relief it brought him than paying a large fee."

NOTES

1 One of the recurrent expressions of this mystery is found at the beginning of *VI*: "We see the things themselves, the world is what we see" (*VI* 17[3]).

2 Merleau-Ponty's lifelong relation with Cartesian thought is indeed much more nuanced and interesting than that of mere opposition. See, for instance, the following note from 1 February 1960: "The Cartesian idea

of the human body as a human *non-closed*, open inasmuch as governed by thought – is perhaps the most profound idea of the union of the soul and the body" (*VI* 288[234]). See also, among other places, the 1947–48 lectures, as well as the numerous notes inspired by Descartes around March 1961, and the intricate discussions of Descartes in the 1959–61 lectures and in *The Eye and The Mind*.

3 Descartes, *Passions of the Soul*, Part I, 35th Article, trans. anonymous, London: A.C., 1650.

4 Merleau-Ponty, *The Structure of Behavior*, 3.

5 See also Merleau-Ponty, "The Film and the New Psychology," in *Sense and Non-sense*, 48–59.

6 Merleau-Ponty, *PP* 276[239].

7 Among other places, see especially Aristotle, *Nicomachean Ethics*, II, and *Physics*, VII.

8 Merleau-Ponty, *The World of Perception*, 64, emphasis mine.

9 I am not entirely sure as to the accuracy of the metaphor of "Cyclopean vision" that reappears in Béla Julesz's famous *Foundations of Cyclopean Perception*. For reasons that will be clearer in the third section of this paper, the Cyclops seems to me to be much better suited for a metaphor of monocularity, and not for one of synergic binocular vision that precisely is irreducible to an agglomeration of monocular images.

10 Merleau-Ponty explicitly distances himself from finalism or teleology in a raw, hectic, passionate, and confusing yet very exciting note from November 1960 titled "Activity: passivity – Teleology," which I must quote fully:

> What then is my situation with regard to *finalism*? I am not a finalist, because the interiority of the body (= conformity of the internal leaf with the external leaf, their folding back on one another) is not something *made, fabricated*, by the assemblage of the two leaves: they have never been apart –
>
> (I call the evolutionist perspective in question I replace it with a cosmology of the visible in the sense that, considering endotime and endospace, for me it is no longer a question of origins, nor limits, nor of a series of events going to a first cause, but one sole explosion of Being which is forever. Describe the world of the "rays of the world" beyond every serial-eternitarian or ideal alternative – Posit the existential eternity – the eternal body)
>
> I am not a finalist because there is dehiscence, and not positive production – through the finality of the body – of a man whose teleological organization our perception and our thought would prolong.

> Man is not the *end* of a body, nor the organized body the *end* of the components: but rather the subordinated each time slides into the void of a new dimension opened, the lower and the higher gravitate around one another, as *the high and the low* (variants of the side-other side relation) – Fundamentally I bring the high-low distinction into the vortex where it rejoins the side-other side distinction, where the two distinctions are integrated into a *universal dimensionality* which is Being (Heidegger)
>
> There is no other meaning than carnal, figure and ground – Meaning ≡ their dislocation, their gravitation (what I called "leakage" [*échappement*] in *Ph.P*). (*VI* 312–13[264–5])

11 Merleau-Ponty, "The Eye and the Mind," in *The Primacy of Perception*, 163.
12 These Homeric pastoral Cyclopes are to be distinguished from the heavenly Cyclopes and the builder Cyclopes (see Hesiod, *Theogony*, 139ff).
13 Aristotle, *Politics*, I, 1252b22–3. For a parallel analysis of the Cyclops in the context of the Aristotelian understanding of *logos*, see my concluding chapter in *The Middle Included*. That chapter is an elaboration of Sections II and III of this chapter in Aristotelian terms.
14 Theocritus, *Idylls*, pp. 33–5. Here I shall use Anthony Verity's translation and add it as an appendix to this chapter. See also Hunter's translation and notes in Theocritus, *A Selection*, pp. 86–91 and 208–18. I am grateful to Eric Sanday for pointing out this idyll to me.
15 See Legrand's nuanced and informative "notice" in *Bucoliques Grecs*, 70–73.

11 Alterity and Expression in Merleau-Ponty: A Response to Levinas

SCOTT MARRATTO

Especially in his later work, Merleau-Ponty attempts to free his account of the bond between ourselves and the world from the residue of subject–object metaphysics. Where Husserl never ceases to characterize this bond in terms of a paradoxical *transcendence-in-immanence*, Merleau-Ponty attempts to think transcendence *on its own terms*, affirming the metaphysical import of the painter Paul Klee's assertion, "I cannot be caught in immanence."[1] What is at issue, for Merleau-Ponty, is not an intentional correlation between ego and world, but a "dehiscence of being" (*OE* 85[187]), an "openness (*Offenheit*)" at the heart of being. This openness is a nexus in which the perceiver, along with the perceived, is always already caught up.[2] For much of modern philosophy the problem of perception has been to understand how a subject can accomplish an adequate mental, internal representation of an external (objective) world; according to Merleau-Ponty, by contrast, perception must first of all be understood as a form of *expressive* behaviour by which a living body responds to the affordances and solicitations of its environment. Rather than thinking of the subject as a kind of theatre of representations, Merleau-Ponty conceives of the subject as a living body intertwined with its world, as belonging to it.

How is it, we might ask, that an organ of my perceiving body – my hand, for example – can be the site of an opening onto a tangible world? "This can only happen," says Merleau-Ponty, "if my hand, while it is felt from within, is also accessible from without, itself tangible, for my other hand, for example, if it takes its place among the things it touches, is in a sense one of them, opens finally upon a tangible being *of which it is also a part*" (*VI* 176[133], emphasis mine). Between the hand touching and the hand touched, we would have a "dehiscence," a "fissuring" of being that would allow for a world of diversity and difference, but we would also have an "encroachment," "overlapping" (*VI* 165[123]), "reversal" (*VI* 252[199]), or "chiasm," allowing the perceiver to approach the perceivable precisely because both belong to the same event of being, to the same universal "flesh."

Emmanuel Levinas, however, claims (*contra* Merleau-Ponty) that there is no analogy to be made between touching my right hand with my left and *touching the hand of an other*.[3] The latter is a relation "imposed across a *radical separation* between the two hands."[4] In Levinas's view, Merleau-Ponty reduces otherness to the order of the same and thus misses the primarily *ethical* significance of the relation to the other. We will discuss two issues arising in connection with Levinas's critique of Merleau-Ponty. First, Levinas believes that Merleau-Ponty reduces the problem of otherness to the sphere of the problem of *knowledge* and thus remains within the enclosure of a philosophy of *consciousness* – knowledge, Levinas writes, "[by] joining the *known* immediately coincides with what may have been foreign to it" (*I* 58–9). This is apparently most evident in Merleau-Ponty's emphasis on *vision*, which according to Levinas has always been thought within philosophy as "*uncovering* par excellence, fully theoretical opening upon *being*, a fastening upon it in synthesis, [which] seizes and conceptualizes more being than hands could carry off" (*I* 66). What Merleau-Ponty fails to appreciate, argues Levinas, is that the "epiphany" of the other is not a matter of "sensation" but rather one of a "sentiment" by which I am, prior to any *knowledge*, put into relation with an absolute alterity of which a trace is borne in the face of the (human) other.[5] Second, Levinas claims that Merleau-Ponty makes the problem of *expression* unintelligible by neglecting its decisive orientation towards the (human) other. According to Levinas, Merleau-Ponty thinks of expression merely as an "incestuous disturbance" within being – whereas Levinas insists that it is only as an "address" to the other that expression can have genuine (which is to say, first and foremost, *ethical*) meaning.[6] We will consider these challenges, which concern the whole doctrine of chiasmic flesh, with reference to Merleau-Ponty's analysis of *expression* in his essays on painting. In particular, I will argue that Merleau-Ponty's mature account of expression aims to establish, on the one hand, the possibility of encountering otherness, and on the other hand, the possibility of recognizing the genuine *alterity* of the other. Merleau-Ponty implicitly challenges Levinas's claim that the encounter with the other must take place across a "radical separation."

The poet Robert Lowell, thinking of Vermeer, observes that "the painter's vision is not a lens, / it trembles to caress the light."[7] Merleau-Ponty, likewise, takes this lesson from the art of painting: "Quality, light, color, depth, which are there before us, are there only because they awaken an echo in our body and because the body welcomes them ... They arouse in me a carnal formula of their presence" (*OE* 22[164]). Merleau-Ponty often refers to painting because he believes that in examining the work of the great painters, like Cézanne and Klee, we can gain special insight into the nature of perception. According to Merleau-Ponty, seeing is more than mere *receptivity*, it is *looking*, and looking involves movement – for example, the movement of the eye or the head needed to get "a better look," to trace the patterns and contours within a visual field, or those subtle adjustments of each eye that yield a *binocular* vision of a *single* thing as it recedes or approaches. Accordingly, great painters are not merely trying to offer more accurate representations of the perceived world; rather they are, in a sense, trying to prolong the act of seeing into another medium. Painting is but a further reverberation of seeing itself, of a seeing that is already *expression*. As Merleau-Ponty writes, "it is the expressive operation of the body, begun by the least perception, that develops into painting and art" (*S* 112[70]). This is why he observes that "there is a little of [the painter] in every man" (*S* 104[64]).

As we have noted, Levinas believes that Merleau-Ponty fails to extricate himself from a tradition in which, as Heidegger had already argued, vision is taken to be the pre-eminent mode of intuition, and intuition is thought of in connection with the idea of *representation*. It is true that, especially in his later work, Merleau-Ponty pays special attention to vision as the means by which a subject is open to the world of perception – the last of his works published during his lifetime is, after all, titled *L'Oeil et l'esprit* ("Eye and Mind"). But his emphasis on vision and visibility can hardly be taken as a naive endorsement of the ocularcentrism of the Western metaphysical tradition. In fact, partly through his analysis of art, Merleau-Ponty's aim is to *decisively rethink* the nature of vision and the visible and the grounds on which vision's privilege has traditionally been established; in so doing he challenges the metaphysical tradition at its core.[8] Rather than privileging vision as the pre-eminent mode of representation, he shows how vision must be understood in connection with the whole body's behavioural interaction with its environment. He aims, for example, to establish the deep connection between vision and touch: "as ... every experience of the visible has always been given me within the context of the movements of the look, the visible spectacle belongs to the touch neither more nor less than do the 'tactile qualities'" (*VI* 176–7[134]). As in Lowell's poem, in which vision is spoken of as a *caress*, Merleau-Ponty speaks of vision as a kind of "palpation" (*VI* 177[134]). But Merleau-Ponty does not want simply to collapse the distinction between vision and touch. Vision has the special function of establishing a horizon of distance and depth; as Merleau-Ponty observes, "to see is to *have at a distance*" (*OE* 27[166]). However, according to Merleau-Ponty, it is because of the profound relation, a "difference without contradiction" (*VI* 179[135]), between vision and touch "that this distance is not the contrary of proximity" (*VI* 178[135]). It is partly because of the subtle movements of the eyes as they focus in on a thing – movements that are themselves kinaesthetically *felt* – that my hand is able to find its way precisely across the distance it has to traverse in order to touch the thing. Together, vision and touch are an opening onto a world of distance and depth in which I also find myself "caught up in the tissue of the things" (*VI* 179[135]). It is because, in perception, distance is not the contrary of proximity that we are able to encounter what is other while not collapsing that otherness into the self. The alternatives bequeathed to us by a philosophical tradition according to which vision must be *either* a passive receptivity *or* an active positing, are no longer adequate – this is what Merleau-Ponty's analysis of painting seeks, above all, to demonstrate.

Merleau-Ponty says that the "true meaning of painting ... is continually to question tradition."[9] Tradition here designates the sedimentation left from the decisions of painters and philosophers concerning the nature of vision and the visible. Painting is suspicious of this tradition (without, of course, having to be *knowingly* suspicious) because it wants to perform on its own terms the event of vision (*S* 91[56]). Regarding Cézanne, Merleau-Ponty writes: "He did not want to separate the stable things which we see and the shifting way in which they appear; he wanted to depict matter as it takes on form, the birth of order through spontaneous organization" (*SNS* 23[13]). This "spontaneous organization" is later referred to as "brute meaning" (*OE* 13[161]). We must, of course, be careful not to take this brute meaning as something simply *given*, like (for example) the sense-data of the empiricists. The burden of Merleau-Ponty's terminology is to express the truth of vision as, on one the hand, "a conceptless opening upon things" (*OE* 43[172]), and, on the other hand, a performance, a genesis of meaning that is always already under way. This genesis is enacted in the painter's vision; meaning proceeds out of an "'amorphous' perceptual world ... which contains no mode of expression and which nonetheless calls them forth and requires all of them and which arouses again with each new painter a new effort of expression" (*VI* 223[170]). The important thing to note here is that the conceptual dyads of activity and passivity, immanence and transcendence, form and matter, do not do justice to this "continued birth" that is the painter's vision (*OE* 32[168]).

In the first pages of "*Eye and Mind,*" Merleau-Ponty writes that "it is as if in the painters['] calling there were some urgency above all other claims on him" (*OE* 15[161]). I would suggest that this "calling" already bears an *ethical* significance – it designates a relation to alterity characterized by *responsibility* and by a kind of *kenosis* in favour of the otherness that the painter already encounters within herself. Merleau-Ponty writes that "immersed in the visible by his body, itself visible, the see-er does not appropriate what he sees; he merely approaches it by looking, he opens himself to the world" (*OE* 17–18[162]). This is the burden the painter must carry, it is a responsibility; his vision "does not *choose* either to be or not to be or to think this thing or that. It has to carry in its heart that heaviness, that dependence which cannot come to it by some intrusion from outside" (*OE* 51–2[175]). Again, these claims about the nature of the painter's vision are intended to reveal something about the nature of perception. Insofar as it is not merely representation but a kind of responsive behaviour by which a subject, so to speak, accommodates herself to the terms in which the visible manifests itself, there is something implicitly ethical – a kind of immanent normativity – in the act of perceiving. Merleau-Ponty often uses the image of pregnancy to speak of vision: "The pregnancy is what, in the visible, requires of me a *correct* focusing, defines its correctness. My body *obeys* the pregnancy, it 'responds' to it, it is what is suspended on it, flesh responding to flesh" (*VI* 262[209]). The figure of pregnancy captures the sense of a *genesis* of meaning, but it also expresses the sense of an alterity that is borne in the flesh of the same and that announces itself in the form of an irrecusable demand. Furthermore, it emphasizes that this bearing is not a modality of *knowledge*: art, says Merleau-Ponty, "rediscovers what articulates itself within us, unbeknown to us" (*VI* 261[208]).

We have already indicated the mutual dependence of the different perceptual modes – in this case vision and touch. This relation is characterized by reversibility. But in Merleau-Ponty's invocation of pregnancy in connection with the painter's look, we find a strange reversibility occurring along another axis: "The painter's vision is not a view upon the *outside*, a merely 'physical-optical' relation with the world.

The world no longer stands before him through representation; rather, it is the painter to whom the things of the world give birth by a sort of concentration or coming-to-be of the visible" (*OE* 69[181]). Vision is that "trembling to caress the light" of which Lowell's poem speaks, and which is already, at once, *the first presence of light* and the first stirring of *expression;* both the seer and the world's light are co-constituted in that trembling, each coming into the open through the other. Merleau-Ponty's provocative claim that the things at which we look also look at us (*OE* 31[167]) is thus not a poetic flourish, nor does it imply a pan-psychism; rather, it follows from his decisive refutation of a metaphysical tradition that must place the source of vision either in the subject or in the things themselves.

This is why Merleau-Ponty seems to constantly reverse the attributions of passivity and activity between perception and the perceived – he speaks of "[vision's] fundamental power of showing forth more than itself" (*OE* 59[178]), and later he says that "the eye accomplishes the prodigious work of opening the soul to what is not the soul" (*OE* 81[186]), but elsewhere he insists that "it is not we who perceive, it is the thing that perceives itself yonder" (*VI* 239[185]) and that "the things have us ... it is not we who have the things" (*VI* 247[194]). These reversals are of course not accidental. Vision, says Merleau-Ponty, "is question and response" (*VI* 173n[131n]); however, it is not possible to say once and for all who, or what, is questioning and who is responding (who is responsible?) without presuming the existence of two distinct entities: the visible and the seer. Merleau-Ponty's account of perception as a kind of reversible interrogation is meant to help us understand perception as a relation that is, in a sense, prior to its terms. On the one hand, it is the look that interrogates the things; on the other, "we are ourselves in question" (*VI* 140[103]). Nevertheless, the distance, across shifting axes, between question and response is the space of alterity; it is here conceived as an alterity that is already encountered in the body of the seer.[10]

How can we maintain that this "presence of the other in the same" is not a mere fusion or coincidence in the sense that Levinas would urge us to avoid? Merleau-Ponty writes that "we should have to return to this idea of proximity through distance, of intuition as auscultation or palpation in depth, of a view which is a view of self, and which calls 'coincidence' in question" (*VI* 170[128]). There is no proximity but through distance, no view of self that is not also non-coincidence. Reversibility is always incomplete, and necessarily so. In speaking of reversibility, Merleau-Ponty also speaks of "constitutive dissonance," "fundamental divergence" (*VI* 287[234]), "hiatus," "separation" (*VI* 195[148]). Between seeing and the seen, touching and touched, between the visual, the tactile, and the auditory, between one hand and the other hand, there is "an incessant escaping," an "impotency to superpose exactly upon one another ... They slip away at the very moment they are about to rejoin" (*VI* 194[148]); but, Merleau-Ponty adds, "this is not a failure" (*VI* 194[148]). These interstices or gaps are the "clearings" or "clear zones" in which perception can be an opening upon the world, in which the other can be borne, *as other*, in the flesh of the same. There is, for example, a difference between the visual and the tactile, just as there is a difference between the seeing and the touching; but it is precisely because, in the thing, the visible encroaches on the tactile, and vice versa, while never completely superposing, that the body achieves a provisional unity-in-difference through perception. The touching hand and the seeing eye meet each other, while preserving their difference, in the thing (*VI* 193[147], 21[7], 270[217]). It is, however, in the difference that is preserved that the thing can appear as something *other*; likewise, thanks to this difference, I can appear to myself as the other of myself.

In his account of perception, Merleau-Ponty is describing a responsibility that is not a *capacity* of a subject, a responsibility that can impose itself on a "consciousness" only because it precedes the conscious, because it is prior to any knowledge, calculation, or self-presence. Rather than a philosophy of coincidence between the knowing and the known, as Levinas would have it, Merleau-Ponty's is, in a sense, a philosophy of constitutive *un*knowing, where knowledge is always already a response to that which it cannot master, arising out of a space of divergence, difference, and alterity that it can never close up. The work of art puts these divergences into play, opens them up; it itself is never simply a kind of *reportage*, but an *event* – one into which the viewer is called to enter as a kind of respondent.

Which brings us to the last problem indicated by Levinas. He suggests that Merleau-Ponty's account of expression lacks the structure of an *"address" to the other* that can alone render expression ethically meaningful. In fact, as we have seen, the painting is already an address to the other even in the very act of painting it. To look, as we have argued, is already to enter into the relation of the other and the same within one's own skin. It is already to lend one's own body to that otherness, to dispossess oneself in favour of it. We ought not to overlook the ethical significance of this truth that is tacitly affirmed by the painter. Even the communication between the perceptual modes, with which we began our inquiry, their divergences and encroachments, suggests a kind of *sociality* (*VI* 271[217]). The two seeing eyes are open to each other only because they meet outside themselves, in an outside that is simultaneously an inside. Even in intermodal perception we find the secret of a common world.[11] As it is with the different sense modalities, so it is with persons: "It is in the world that we rejoin one another" (*VI* 26n[10n]). Indeed, this may have been glimpsed by the Greeks – in Homer's *Odyssey* the way of life of the cannibalistic Cyclopes is described thus: "They have no meeting place for council, no laws either, ... / ... each a law to himself, ruling his wives and children, / not a care in the world for any neighbour." Mythical prisoners of their monocularity, without the experience of a common vision in which the two eyes meet each other, the Cyclopes can have no shared, common world.[12]

The metaphysical prejudice in favour of vision as representation, and in favour of a self-identical, self-present subject, occludes this central mystery of the common world. But painting, perhaps, tentatively breaks the hold that such prejudices may have on us: "It summons one away from the already constructed reason in which 'cultured men' are content to shut themselves, towards a reason which contains its origins" (*SNS* 32[19]). The painting, on Merleau-Ponty's account, is not an object but an invitation to enter into the nexus of vision and visibility – this is why looking at a painting by Cézanne makes us feel that we have entered an "unfamiliar world" and perhaps even makes us somewhat "uncomfortable" (*SNS* 28[16]). Merleau-Ponty writes that "the accomplished work is ... not the work which exists in itself like a thing, but the work which reaches its viewer and invites him to take up the gesture which created it and, skipping the intermediaries, to rejoin, without any guide other than a movement of the invented line (an almost incorporeal trace), the silent world of the painter, henceforth uttered and accessible" (*S* 83[51]). No analytical work can accomplish this, "for when we analyse an object, we find only what we have put into it" (*S* 125[77]). An *object* would fail to invite the other to be other than herself, and to enter into the fecund relations that would be at play in the artwork – even if it were what is called an "*art* object," it would not, on Merleau-Ponty's account, be art.

So in a sense, the work of art is also an address to an audience, but not to one already extant: "The public [that the painter] aims at is precisely the one his oeuvre will elicit. The others he thinks of are not empirical 'others,' defined by what they expect of him at this moment ... No, his concern is with others who have become such that he is able to live with them" (*S* 119[74]). The artist, presumably, is unable to live with those "cultured men" who have shut themselves up in an "already constructed reason"; the artist's work cannot address itself to such as these, if only because their metaphysical prejudices will prevent them from being able to *see* the painting on the painting's own terms. The painter's concern, therefore, is with those who, in their encounter with the work, will have felt themselves to be the others of themselves; it is precisely this experience of the self-as-other that her artwork serves to elicit.

NOTES

1 Merleau-Ponty, "L'oeil et l'esprit" ("Eye and Mind") (hereafter *OE*), 87[188].
2 The language of "openness" is from Merleau-Ponty, *The Visible and the Invisible* (hereafter *VI*), 173n[131n], 238[185], 249[196].
3 See Merleau-Ponty, *Signs* (hereafter *S*), 168.
4 Levinas, "Intersubjectivity" (hereafter *I*)," 59.
5 Levinas, "Sensibility," 64.
6 Levinas, *Humanism of the Other*, 19.
7 Lowell, *Collected Poems*, 838.
8 Dastur, "World, Flesh, Vision," 41–2.
9 Merleau-Ponty, *Sense and Non-Sense* (hereafter *SNS*), 23[13].
10 Gary Brent Madison, "Flesh as Otherness," 31.
11 See Talero, "Intersubjectivity and Intermodal Perception."
12 Homer, *The Odyssey*, 215. The connection between Merleau-Ponty's account of monocularity and the mythical figure of the Cyclops is explored in detail by Ömer Aygün in chapter 10.

PART IV

Expression

12 Aesthetic Ideas: Developing the Phenomenology of Merleau-Ponty with the Art of Matta-Clark

MATTHEW J. GOODWIN

In this chapter I explore how a recent artist can be used to develop what Maurice Merleau-Ponty calls at the end of *The Visible and the Invisible*, "aesthetic ideas." These ideas are not contrary to the sensible but are "its lining and its depth." To articulate this relation, Merleau-Ponty employs the work of such near-contemporary artists as Paul Cézanne, Paul Claudel, and Marcel Proust. In the spirit of this collaboration between art and phenomenology, I turn to an artist who works in very different media with the hopes of highlighting other dimensions of these ideas. To do this I begin by describing Merleau-Ponty's appropriation of Leonardo da Vinci's "flexuous lines" and compare these with the "prosaic lines" of philosophy. The former line is that of a generative principle, the latter is that of an abstract definition. I then show how these two different kinds of lines motivate movements that establish the perceptual and spatial bearings of thought. In order to better understand these relations, I turn to Gordon Matta-Clark, a sculptural, performance-based artist who cuts elaborate holes in condemned buildings. Insofar as these building cuts follow the flexuous lines of development rather than the prosaic lines of abstraction, they are an artistic resistance to the second-order positivity of designed architectural space. Through his building cuts, Matta-Clark produces more aesthetic ideas of space that are the lining and depth of the sensible.

I. Merleau-Ponty and Artists

Maurice Merleau-Ponty is unique among early phenomenologists for his careful attention to artists and sensitive appropriation of ideas developed through their processes. These artists, many of whom were still working in his generation, were nevertheless born in a preceding century, and their ways of seeing and expressing themselves were unique to the late nineteenth and early twentieth centuries. The most prominent among these artists is Paul Cézanne, who was born in 1839 and passed away a little more than a year before Merleau-Ponty's birth in 1908. Cézanne's very name has become emblematic for *The Phenomenology of Perception,* bolstered by the non-historicist and non-psychologistic approach to studying the artist in "Cézanne's Doubt." But there are many other artists Merleau-Ponty turns to from his era. Pierre-Auguste Renoir, who appears in "Indirect Language and the Voices of Silence" (1952), passed away in 1922. Henri Matisse, who is perhaps the most current of the artists Merleau-Ponty turns to in the same publication, began painting as early as 1890 and died in 1954. Informing both *The Phenomenology of Perception* and *The Visible and the Invisible,* Marcel Proust's *À la recherche du temps perdu* was completed just before the novelist's death in 1922. And finally, poets Paul Valéry and Paul Claudel, who appear throughout Merleau-Ponty's works, but especially in the chapter on the "chiasm" in *The Visible and the Invisible,* died in 1945 and 1955 respectively.

Clearly, artists influenced the development of Merleau-Ponty's phenomenology. Indeed, the working notes to his final work projected a chapter transitioning into the study of art as "giving to the volume a 'definitive' character."[1] I propose that it is crucial that we look to more recent artists in order to continue Merleau-Ponty's project in a fresh way and to bring his thought into the twenty-first century. Artists today are no longer motivated by the same problems or in the same ways as Cézanne, and their tools, materials, and modes of expression have evolved tremendously. Furthermore, artists working today are studying perception and pressing the limits of communication as it is rooted in the specific time and place we share.

For these reasons I turn my attention to Gordon Matta-Clark, a sculptural/performance artist who cut large holes out of the floors, walls, and ceilings of an abandoned factory warehouse, office buildings, city apartments, and a suburban home. These holes begin as simple shapes, but when they are imposed upon planned architectural spaces they open enigmatic passages between rooms and floors, and into and out of the buildings themselves, ultimately undermining their stability and rendering them unusable. Each cut not only reveals physical layers of normally hidden materials and structural supports but also highlights presupposed experiences of lived space. Matta-Clark displays the cut-out sections of these structures in art galleries beside photographs of the spaces from which they have been cut, playing with the positive and negative spaces of doors, windows, holes, and passageways, evoking the experience of moving through these structures, which have since been demolished.

My goal of rendering Merleau-Ponty's phenomenology more contemporary may be undermined by choosing an artist who passed away in 1978; however, it is my position that Matta-Clark represents a generation that is still teaching and inspiring the artists who are working today. To do a phenomenology of our contemporary perception, we need to look a little closer to its immediate roots, if only because these are what today's artists must in some way either accept or reject. Another reason to turn to Matta-Clark is that he is one of those artists who, like Cézanne, left a wealth of articulate notes and interviews reflecting on the process of his art. He continues to inspire numerous publications and retrospectives, which celebrate a brief career that was impressive even if we consider only the sheer size and complexity of the building cuts. The physical scale of his works may be rivalled by that of other large-scale minimalist and earth art works of the era, such as those by Richard Serra, Christo and Jeanne-Claude, Robert Smithson, and Dennis Oppenheim, but comparisons with such artists often neglect the ways in which Matta-Clark's works awaken a visual, spatial, and intellectual interplay with the spaces and materials of intimately familiar structures. Furthermore, like many artists of the late twentieth century, Matta-Clark's works question the objectifying tendencies of the museum space by leaving us only with photographs, films, and parts salvaged from sites that no longer exist. Finally, he is an artist whose work is clearly concerned with perceptual experiences of depth and with the coming-into-being of the visible, both of which occupy so much of Merleau-Ponty's phenomenology. He is a powerful representative of art in the late twentieth century who can help move a phenomenology that is influenced by art into the twenty-first century, just as Cézanne and Proust did for Merleau-Ponty in the previous century.

In what follows I show that Gordon Matta-Clark demonstrates the same artistic development of aesthetic ideas that Merleau-Ponty finds in Marcel Proust, Paul Valéry, and Paul Claudel at the end of *The Visible and the Invisible*. I first discuss aesthetic ideas in terms of two related concepts: the flexuous line or generative principle described by Leonardo da Vinci, and the act of establishing perceptual bearings described by Claudel. I argue that Matta-Clark develops aesthetic ideas of lived space that resist the second-order positivity of planned architecture, and that he does this by following the flexuous lines of development and by establishing bearings within the buildings he cuts. The ideas of space generated in these buildings can never be purely conceptual, for they are inseparable from the time, place, material, and manner in which they are created. To show all of this I turn now to Merleau-Ponty's account of the flexuous line and of how establishing spatial bearings is essential for developing aesthetic ideas. Section III discusses Matta-Clark's concept of "anarchitecture," which is a starting point for developing his aesthetic ideas of space. Section IV shows how Matta-Clark develops these aesthetic ideas through the movements of establishing bearings around flexuous lines in his building cuts. I conclude in Section V with another movement that completes the earliest cuts even though the buildings that initiated them no longer exist.

II. Flexuous Lines and Establishing Bearings

In the chapter "The Intertwining – The Chiasm" of *The Visible and the Invisible*, Merleau-Ponty credits art with "describing an idea that is not the contrary of the sensible," but "is its lining and its depth."[2] Referring to Marcel Proust, he calls this an aesthetic idea that "cannot be detached from the sensible appearances and be erected into a second positivity."[3] More than just expressions of a particular object in a particular space and time, aesthetic ideas are communicable universals that are produced through the interaction of these dimensions.[4] He cites another example attributed to Paul Valéry, who says there is a "secret blackness of milk … accessible only through its whiteness."[5] This blackness, which comes from below, is not a simple empirical or symbolic association, but something generated "from beneath," in the depth of the white substance. These opposites, like the positive and negative spaces of shadows and passages through a building, are aesthetic ideas produced by the artist around a single generative principle. To make this clear requires an investigation of related concepts throughout Merleau-Ponty's works. There are two in particular I want to highlight that have received little attention: Merleau-Ponty's concept of the generative, flexuous line, and the corresponding operation of establishing perceptual bearings.

The flexuous line is a concept Merleau-Ponty adapts from Leonardo da Vinci's notebooks describing a principle of genesis: the lived experience of the coming-into-being of visible things.[6] The flexuous line constitutes both sides of the visible/invisible axis: both the active and the passive syntheses. Before anything is present as a consciously intended, thematic thing, it must come into being from the flesh of experience. It is around this generating axis that an artist develops a motif into a meaningful idea; it is never purely conceptual but always rooted in some material or location in space and time.[7] The flexuous line is better understood when contrasted with what Merleau-Ponty calls the "prosaic line," the abstracted, codified being that is taken out of lived experience and raised to a second positivity.

In "Eye and Mind," Merleau-Ponty identifies philosophy with a way of thinking about lines. He states that Cartesian philosophy is characterized by the prosaic line because it considers lines to be positive attributes of things.[8] The prosaic line determines the object once and for all like a defined term in already instituted speech, like an eidetic invariant that is never actually perceived. The prosaic line is not actually seen in the lived experience of the world, but I introduce it almost every time I attempt to define something, whether conceptually or visually. For example, the prosaic line is introduced into painting whenever I draw the outline of an object, such as an apple in a still life. However, such a line can only appear as a feature of the apple as long as I view it immobile against a background. The slightest movement effaces the line, giving way to the continuously variable curve of the apple as it is lived. A prosaic line is imputed to the object whenever I already have some concept of it as a definite thing. This concept originated within the lived experience of the thing as a whole, which is maintained through all the phases of my movements around it. But concepts lose the movement that is at their origin; they become static entities with which to prejudge things as if they have already become visible instead of observing them in their coming-into-being-as-visible. Merleau-Ponty finds this insight in Paul Cézanne, who removes from his paintings the prosaic lines of things in favour of the flexuous lines of their development.

The difference between the prosaic line and the flexuous line that I am describing is stated in *The Prose of the World* as the difference between prose and poetry, between informative speech regarding things as already instituted objects, and a creative speech that renders the visible in depth.[9] The flexuous line is the principle of development by which a thing becomes visible and comes into being. Citing Leonardo da Vinci: "The secret of the art of drawing is to discover in each object the particular way in which a certain flexuous line, which is, so to speak, its generating axis, is directed through its whole extent."[10] The idea here is not to draw an object according to a presumed external surface but to draw it according to whatever interior forces of development originally brought it into being; and it is by doing so that an artist brings something into being for the perceiver.

Artists seek the flexuous line of a thing's development corresponding with the lived coming-into-being of it in perception. The lived experience of the surface of a fruit does not form a line but blends with its surroundings in the continuous coming-into-being of its shape. The prosaic line defines the limits within which an object exists; the flexuous line is the *principle* of the thing, which always exceeds such boundaries. The flexuous line is both interior and exterior, both inner principle of development and outer definition of the whole experience. It is how a thing takes shape as visible and meaningful, combining its sensible, physical being and its non-sensible idea into an aesthetic idea. The prosaic line of the fruit defines it as approximately circular from a given perspective and with more or less uniform colour. The flexuous line accounts for the variations of shadows, colours, and reflected light that occur as the eye passes over the surface. But more than this, it also bears the whole story of the fruit's generation outward from the core until it reaches a certain size. At such a point one might pick it and eat it; or, if it is allowed to keep growing and become too heavy for the stem, it falls to the ground, where it eventually degrades and fertilizes its seed contents. This is only one possible story contained by the fruit, generated around a specific axis. Another axis with a completely different story is that of the forbidden fruit. But simply calling a fruit forbidden is prosaic, whereas creating a story that shows the nature of being forbidden is flexuous.

Everything in perceptual experience is given first as a flexuous line and only later limited by a prosaic line. I may point to certain lines that become visible in the world, but these are not properties of *things*; they are fragments of being abstracted from flesh.[11] I may, for example, identify a line around the circumference of the room created by the seam where the wall meets the floor or the ceiling; but the wall does not possess this line, and neither does the ceiling; what I call a line is formed by the relation of two separate elements plus my relative position to them.

Wherever I attend to a line I am immediately referred away from it to separate elements, neither of which possesses the line except in relation to the other elements, which change depending on my position. I interpret a line based on my movements and the horizon of my activity. If I were blindfolded and brought my fingers to rest on something, I could only infer that I have one thing based on the space separating my fingers. To get any more precise about what I am touching, I must move my fingers, possibly my whole hand, arm, and torso. I must take account of the moving angles of my arm, which are in turn related to my entire body and to the stance I have upon the ground. Far from defining a single prosaic line of an object, I am constantly torn away from it and introduced to other dimensions. I have discovered only the continual movement away from one surface to another as I try to bring something into view, establishing my position as I attempt to define things. What I have are dimensions generating about a common motif while I attempt to capture and define its initial appearance.

Merleau-Ponty's phenomenology is a philosophy of the generating, flexuous line rather than the prosaic line. By turning to artists he inserts himself within instituting expression when an expression first forms. The prosaic line accomplishes an important move of abstraction, one that allows speakers to step outside, to remove themselves from lived experiences and treat the matter with a degree of indifference. This movement allows speech to "detach itself from its material instruments" in ways that music and painting do not permit (*PP* 450[410]). This is why one can speak about speaking and write about writing but, according to Merleau-Ponty, one cannot paint about painting. Abstraction from lived experience permits a self-reflexive movement in which speech treats itself as an object. This removal from the given is essential for rational thought, but such thought is always after the fact. Focusing on artistic creativity returns one to the origin of thought. What artists do is an initial move in the direction of abstraction, slowed down as it were, in order to highlight the barest moments of the origin of meaning. The artist is initiating a movement towards meaning, a movement that will inevitably end in a prosaic conception with the declaration of meaning or historical significance. The artistic institution of meaning taken at the moment of motivation, however, is a direct encounter with the generative, flexuous line.[12]

Gordon Matta-Clark expresses the relation of the prosaic to the flexuous line when he describes his cutting activity as "a theatrical gesture that cleaves structural space."[13] Such cleavage does not cut randomly but follows particular guiding principles of development as well as specific qualities of the material being worked – just as cutting and shaping wood must work with the grain and other natural characteristics of the wood. Again, it is a "theatrical gesture," one that is done for affect and that only succeeds when it is reflected back in an interesting way – in other words, it need not be an identical reflection, but might in fact inspire further reflection and aesthetic modification. By following the flexuous line of seemingly arbitrary shapes imposed upon architectural space, Matta-Clark forces himself and his viewers to establish their spatial bearings, thereby producing the aesthetic idea of lived space within, through, and outside the structures he uses. But since these buildings are all going to be demolished, he has to somehow re-create this aesthetic idea apart from the building. He does this by removing the piece that is cut out of the building, such as a rectangular section of floor, which is cleanly excised complete with the linoleum or carpet covering and the plaster ceiling on the opposite side. He then places these artefacts on display next to photographs of the holes from which these pieces were cut. Finally, he develops the aesthetic idea a third time according to the same flexuous line of development, with photo montages of these structures carefully assembled and spliced into sprawling, maze-like images. These spliced photos are reminiscent of M.C. Escher drawings, in which architectural features flip and reverse back upon themselves, except that these are clearly photographs that carry more strongly "an odor of life."[14] Each of these building cuts, displays, and spliced photos awakens the need to orient oneself within a structure in order to determine whether one is looking through a window, or a door, or some other kind of passageway, and this requires that one constantly re-establish one's bearings. To establish bearings is to find some consistent relation between up/down, left/right, inside/outside, and empty/solid space. These are complicated everywhere by the ways in which these relations interact with light and shadow. These relations are not simple opposites, for they depend upon a flexuous line of their development through space and time. When one moves through an apartment, for example, a floor becomes a ceiling if one pays attention to the surfaces while moving through the different levels of the building. That a ceiling simultaneously implies a floor for an apartment above is easy to comprehend through our spatial orientation of the building. This is an aesthetic idea that evolves according to one's previous, current, and projected positions.

When he describes the element of flesh, Merleau-Ponty says it is midway between fact and meaning, adherent to a time and place, and the "inauguration of the *where* and *when*."[15] This means that lived experience is in the space between things and their instituted, prosaic meanings. Earlier in the same text he describes philosophy as the initial questioning of perceptual faith found in the act of establishing bearings in space and time.[16] His example comes from the poet Paul Claudel's *Art poétique*. Claudel says that "from time to time, a man lifts his head, sniffs, listens, considers, recognizes his position: he thinks, he sighs, and, drawing his watch from the pocket lodged against his chest, looks at the time. *Where am I?* and, *What time is it?* such is the inexhaustible question turning from us to the world."[17] To take one's bearings is to circumscribe a fragment of the world, such as this spot where I am standing. But by doing so I have transformed what I previously perceived, the general flesh of experience, into a secure foothold on the world. But this is a single, temporary "tacking-thread."[18] In a moment I will move away and forget this spot and it will no longer be mine. If I recall it later it will give me support from an altogether different direction. To establish bearings is to situate oneself in a fragment of being, whether in fact or in idea. Merleau-Ponty says that "there is no essence, no idea, that does not adhere to a domain of history and of geography," and perception entails continually situating oneself within a location.[19] This is due to the spontaneous exploration of the fragments of being in order to establish equilibrium for the whole experience of the flesh.

Although spontaneous, such exploration is not random, but purposefully continues a lead found from one fragment to the next; it is elicited by this place where I am standing, and it follows the flexuous lines of experience. It is this kind of questioning, of situating oneself in time and space, that Matta-Clark's building cuts initiate.

III. Gordon Matta-Clark's Aesthetic Ideas of Space

Gordon Matta-Clark, son of surrealist artists Anne Clark and Roberto Matta, received his architecture degree from Cornell University in 1968, but he resisted the formal training offered by his professors, preferring instead to pursue sculpture, performance art, and installation art.[20] Matta-Clark already seems to be interested in the flexuous line of lived space rather than the prosaic lines that form conceptually planned architectural space. The continuation of this flexuous line is an idea of space without a preconceived plan, one that has a principle of development that guides without predetermination. In other words, the development of space is not dictated by a particular principle of style or utility, but rather by the human perception of space.[21]

Matta-Clark's building cuts developed out of a group exhibition held by artists, friends, and activists called "Anarchitecture."[22] Some in this group had also opened a restaurant together called Food, the vision for which was to "restore the art of eating with love instead of fear"; this sometimes included live art performances as part of the menu.[23] This enterprise, intersecting with the start of Matta-Clark's artistic career, introduced an important motif of community and human relations that would continue throughout his later works, although this became less obvious and was easily eclipsed by the more impressive visual effects of buildings violently cut open, with gaping holes exposing their inner structures.

Anarchitecture, which combines the words anarchy and architecture, is described as "a simple manipulation of metaphoric ideas loosely related to a specific category, in this case architecture."[24] It is a reaction against some of the patterned ways in which architecture shapes human space, resulting in overlooked spaces such as back alleys, parking lots, and gutters, which often become the spaces of nefarious activities.

One of Matta-Clark's contributions to the group exhibit mentioned earlier was a monochromatic photograph of the recently constructed World Trade Center in New York. It was taken from the pedestrian's perspective on the ground looking up, unable to take in the entirety of the buildings so that neither the base nor the top of either was visible. From such an angle, one of the towers seems to lean in towards the other. The centre of the picture is the negative space between the towers, where only a sliver of sky shines between the structures. Yet with the buildings seemingly disconnected from the ground and apparently extending infinitely in each direction, the perspective easily shifts so that the buildings become the negative space and the sky becomes a positive space with dark, gaping slices taken from it. The impression is of imposing and inhospitable structures that are nevertheless precarious and inconstant. This project, a reaction against indifferent, fear-inspiring architectural forms, indicated the direction that Matta-Clark's work would take as he turned the violence these structures do to human space back upon the structures themselves. It also anticipated some playful reversals of positive and negative spaces that would come to characterize his building cuts.

The concept of anarchitecture is not purely destructive, as can be seen from one of Matta-Clark's notes:

> A RESPONSE TO COSMETIC DESIGN
> COMPLETION THROUGH REMOVAL
> COMPLETION THROUGH COLAPSE
> *COMPLETION IN EMPTINESS*[25]

Like the positive and negative spaces of his building cuts, removal, destruction, and emptiness are in a reversible relationship with completion.[26] Rather than total destruction and lawlessness, anarchitecture follows a principle of production guided by a sense of purpose and relevance. This is possible because the cuts follow the flexuous line of development from the original motive that begins within and around these structures.

The seemingly conflicting motifs of destruction and completion came together in Matta-Clark's building cuts to develop an idea of lived space that was destructive to buildings, rather than to people, yet completed the buildings. Each of his buildings was rendered into uninhabitable, unusable, but aesthetic spaces by his cutting actions. The living or working space was destroyed by holes and cuts in floors and ceilings. People could fall through, and outside elements could come inside, breeching the structures and inevitably destroying them. The very spaces that Matta-Clark saw as inhuman by design were rendered unusable, yet the essence of living/working space in its human relation was preserved.[27] Only by first upsetting, finding gaps, or calling into question one's expected relations and orientations within space does one find oneself – one's place, space, and time to live.

In one sense these works have not been completely destroyed because they are preserved by extensive photographic documentation, but I am pointing to something more: a preservation of an original motif, which continues from the cuts into the physical structures, to the cut-out pieces that are put on display in art galleries, and finally to the cut and spliced photographs of these sites later undertaken by Matta-Clark. Through these three separate movements, Matta-Clark's works destroy while simultaneously preserving – they destroy the space of planned architecture in favour of the lived space expressed by following flexuous lines. In what follows I review a selection of Matta-Clark's works in their temporal sequence so as to reveal the unfolding principle of that flexuous line as his ideas develop through his interaction with space and material. The next section deals with the first two movements of preserving while destroying; the third movement is addressed in the last section.

IV. Gordon Matta-Clark's Building Cuts

While working at Food, Matta-Clark took his first cut from a building, carefully cutting a rectangular hole from a section of the kitchen wall above the stove, thus creating a sandwich of plaster, wood, and steel building materials.[28] After this he began his first architectural cuts, called *Bronx Floors*. Trespassing into condemned apartments, Matta-Clark cut out "building sandwich walls," which he stood up and put on display in galleries together with photographs of the spaces from which they had been cut.

In these displays, Matta-Clark created the effect of walking through the space of the apartments through the relationship between the photographs and the cut-out pieces in the gallery space. This juxtaposition induced a strange feeling of vertigo: the physical space of the structure and the gallery space intertwined around the body as it attempted to orient itself with regard to the physical, cut-out object and the space from which it had been cut. In this display, a cut-out section of floor exposed structures that were likely similar to those currently beneath my feet; the worn textures of carpet, wallpaper, floorboards, plaster, and paint all gave clues to their rightful orientation as above, beside, or below, but these were still not easily placed – the object before me was still unrecognizable; in the photographs on the wall I could see similar shapes in the holes left in the floors, but these were misaligned from my perspective of the object, and the positive and negative spaces of the structures and the holes within them easily flipped into one another. Unable either to physically or imaginatively move these pieces into their matching holes, I resorted to walking around them, tilting my head and looking back and forth from one jagged edge of the object to an edge of the hole in the picture and back again to another edge of the object. The eye never seemed able to settle on any given surface or point that would satisfy the body's desire for a firm ground on which to stand. A piece of a building that was clearly part of a ceiling and that should have been horizontally laid out overhead was now standing perpendicular to the floor. Walking around it, I was confronted with a corresponding floor that, based on the previous logic of spatial orientation, should have been above the ceiling. But recognizing it as a floor simultaneously placed it beneath my feet; because it was on display vertically, this required an extra step in the imaginative bodily orientation of my corporeal schema to achieve this spatial arrangement.

This was disorienting, yet I found myself oriented precisely as it must feel to trespass into an abandoned apartment with holes cut out of its floors, ceilings, and walls. Each hole seemed to multiply as it interacted with other levels, each with its own holes – windows and doors created passages from room to room, from inside to outside. Each passage admitted a different light and colour and cast a different shadow that seemed to create new cuts dividing walls into false seams – each hole even produced a different air pressure and resonance, as one knows well when navigating a dark room looking for something like a door to a hallway.

So far I have shown two of the three spatial movements initiated by Matta-Clark's works. There is first the movement through the site where the physical cutting of floors has taken place. Only Matta-Clark and those friends who trespassed with him to assist in the cutting were able to experience this movement. The movement was initially guided by the architectural plan of the space, then by Matta-Clark's cutting motif, and finally by the structure again, insofar as load-bearing supports and other structural anomalies forced him to choose which material to cut and which should remain. The second movement was that which was open to observers in the art galleries where the cut-out pieces and photographs were on display. This movement was not identical to the first but was generated by it according to the flexuous line being followed by Matta-Clark.

After the success of *Bronx Floors* and other works, Matta-Clark began gaining permission to use properties slated for destruction. This meant he was no longer trespassing and could open the buildings themselves for viewers to experience the first spatial movement as he had. Unfortunately, since each of these buildings was slated for destruction and rendered unstable by his cuts, only a few viewers were ever able to experience them; the rest of us have only the exhibits of photographs and cut-out pieces.

One of Matta-Clark's most iconic works was *Splitting*, a typical two-storey suburban home that he cut completely in half by a single, narrow slice taken from the top of the roof all the way to the ground.[29] This might resemble the metaphor of a broken family that otherwise would have remained hidden by the superficial shell of normalcy – but I caution that such a reading would be to locate a prosaic line. After its exhibition and before its demolition, Matta-Clark undertook another cutting of the building: he removed each of the four upper corners of the house, complete with roofing shingles, framing, and siding. These corners were then displayed in a gallery in their original orientation, but with an open space where the house would have been. The original structure had been breeched by a relatively small split and no longer existed; now, in the space of a gallery, there were relatively small pieces of the house evoking the large gap where the house should have been. Walking between these four corners and within that gap, I could almost smell the familiar scent of a musty attic and grow dizzy from the imagined height of my position even though I was standing firmly on the art gallery floor.

After *Splitting*, Matta-Clark undertook a much more elaborate cut in *Conical Intersect*, using a building slated for destruction to make way for the Centre Pompidou in Paris. Here he began with the geometric shape of a cone and proceeded to carve this shape out of the interior of the building. The base of the cone began outside the outer wall, with the cone's axis pointing in and upward through the building, with the tip exiting out the roof. One assumes that most of a building is constituted by empty space enclosed within supporting walls, yet these cuts revealed an intricate network of structure that seemed to fill the space even though more material had been removed. All of the prosaic lines of the original building had now been overrun by a chorus of parabolic and elliptical curves created by following the flexuous line of the cone motif. The cone itself was a negative space hollowed out of the space in the building, outlined by the remaining walls, floors, and other structural pieces. Photographs of it from outside drew attention into the building and exposed the multiple levels of its inner floor plan. From inside, the hole became a telescopic window projecting outward and focusing on vehicles in the street, but this was the reverse of the actual cone's orientation, with its wide base outside and narrowing towards the tip as it entered deeper into the apartment. Inside and outside became reversible as the negative space of the cone cut into and gouged out the positive spaces of the rooms.

Office Baroque is another work that imposed a seemingly arbitrary shape on the planned architectural space of an office building. This time, Matta-Clark cut from the floor the circumferences of two giant overlapping circles, a design inspired by the stains imprinted on a napkin from the base of a coffee cup that has spilled over. Matta-Clark noticed this tiny, incidental detail, enlarged it, and cut into the abandoned office space with it.

Finally, Matta-Clark's last building cut, *Circus* – also known as *Caribbean Orange* – came from a brownstone slated for destruction to make way for the expanding Museum of Contemporary Art in Chicago. Like *Conical Intersect* and *Office Baroque*, *Circus* was formed by cutting out the space of a shape within the structure, this time the shapes of three spheres. The spheres were not hollowed out like the cone was in *Conical Intersect*; only a narrow band of space was cut around the circumference of each sphere, leaving the inner walls and floors of the building cut into a maze of seemingly random curves. The spheres themselves were oriented according to what in his plans Matta-Clark called the "generative axis," which ascended diagonally from the ground level at the front of the building to the roof at the back of the building. The first sphere cut into the ground in the basement, the second was suspended in the middle of the house, and the third exited out the roof. As the spheres went higher, the space around each increased and allowed more light. Matta-Clark described the experience of the interior space as "a kind of circular stage to look at and circulate through."[30] In other words, the work became a space that pulled one inward in a process of discovery that was the unfolding of the flexuous line. On the plan, this line was drawn as a straight diagonal, but it could not be discovered in the building because one experienced only the curves and spheres of space that had been generated from it.

V. Developing Ideas of Space along Flexuous Lines

So far I have shown two movements initiated by Matta-Clark's cuts – one through the space of the site guided by the cut structures, and the other through the gallery space guided by the cut-out objects with photographs of the holes from which they were cut. Matta-Clark later introduced a third type of spatial movement through manipulations of the photographs of the sites. These did not require literal movement through space and could be viewed in a book; but rather than documenting the building cuts, these photo assemblages re-created the lived experience of the cut buildings, and they did so according to the same flexuous line. To do this, Matta-Clark cut pieces of film much as he did the physical structures themselves: he followed some structural lines while cutting out others and rendering positive space into negative, and vice versa.[31] This film was then assembled and processed on photo paper to multiply perspectives into panoramas.

These cuttings-of-photographs-of-cuttings-of-buildings further subverted the tendency to raise the structure to a second-order positivity. They gave the impression that one was looking simultaneously from above and below the structure. Rather than a "view from nowhere" presupposed by the planned space of architecture, we retained a lived experience of the simultaneity of perspectives. This is shown by Merleau-Ponty in the way Cézanne paints soup bowls sitting on a table with both the inner surface and the profile visible from one perspective (*PP* 308–9[271]). Both are able to be intended at the same time, just as

I intend the contents of a bedroom upstairs while I am in the kitchen downstairs. Matta-Clark's cut and spliced photographs of his cut buildings exposed this simultaneity just as it would appear for someone entering the sites themselves. It was a disoriented space that awakened the viewer to find one's bearings, to establish and situate oneself with regard to the structure rather than be guided entirely by it.[32] In other words, I had to still move in accord with the structure, but I could still maintain my own generative axis within that structure. Rather than subvert the notion of structured space entirely, anarchitecture follows a flexuous line providing a principle of organization that grows from lived experience rather than a mathematical, ideal model of space. It is an aesthetic idea of space, generalized about all space, but it requires that I engage this thread of the flexuous line that leads through all of Matta-Clark's cuts.

VI. Conclusion

I have been focusing on the process of selection for Matta-Clark's cuts because these demonstrate the ways in which we think in space. We orient our thoughts according to up or down, before or after, just as we determine where rooms or exits are located in a building. Matta-Clark likewise oriented his thoughts around the structure at hand. He began with his motif of suspicion regarding the space created by hostile architectural plans. He then employed a technique of cutting and transferring positive and negative spaces that he had noticed within that planned space. He began with simple concepts such as a ring, a sphere, or a cone, but when enlarged and applied to such immovable structures, these became epochal moves and cuts. He often had to follow the lines and shapes of the structure itself, and the gaps transformed the space by forcing us to establish our own bearings within it. The result of Matta-Clark's cuts, whether one looks at the structures themselves, their remnants put on display in a gallery space, or the spliced photographs of the structures, is disorienting. In each case, one must work to find one's bearings in spaces that are clearly meaningful because they are demarcated by familiar prosaic lines – patterns of wallpaper, carpet, baseboard trim, and ceiling seams – but their orientation is continually upset by gaping holes and by displaced cut-outs. Matta-Clark's cuts suggest that one does not live in structures but one does live *through* them, through the holes we create that transform them into our own space. As stated previously, more than just expressions of a particular object in a particular space and time, aesthetic ideas are communicable universals that are produced by the active interaction of these dimensions. While prosaic lines lead to the abstract, ideal concepts of the positive sciences, flexuous lines return us to the grounded, aesthetic concepts of lived experiences.[33]

NOTES

1 Merleau-Ponty, *VI* 222[169].
2 Merleau-Ponty, *VI* 196[149].
3 Merleau-Ponty, *VI* 196[149].
4 Carbone, *The Thinking of the Sensible*, 39–47.
5 Merleau-Ponty, *VI* 197[150].
6 Merleau-Ponty, "Eye and Mind," 72[182–3].
7 Even conceptual artists are still rooted in this insofar as they provoke an event.
8 Merleau-Ponty, "Eye and Mind," 72[182–3].
9 Merleau-Ponty, *The Prose of the World*, 209[150–1]: "La perspective planimétrique nous donnait la finitude de notre perception, projetée, aplatie, devenue *prose* sous le regard d'un dieu, les moyens d'expression de l'enfant, quand ils auront été repris délibérément par un artiste dans un vrai geste créateur nous donneront au contraire la résonance secrète par laquelle notre finitude s'ouvre à l'être du monde et se fait poésie."
10 Merleau-Ponty, "Eye and Mind," 72[182–3].
11 Merleau-Ponty, *VI* 184[139–40]: "La chair n'est pas matière, n'est pas esprit, n'est pas substance. Il faudrait, pour la désigner, le vieux terme d''élément,' au sens où on l'employait pour parler de l'eau, de l'air, de la terre et du feu, c'est-à-dire au sens d'une *chose générale*, à mi-chemin de l'individu spatio-temporel et de l'idée, sorte de principe incarné qui importe un style d'être partout où il s'en trouve une parcelle. La chair est en ce sens un 'élément' de l'Être."
12 This is why "Cézanne's difficulties are those of the first word." It is up to him to give an expression its basis, to continue the movement first initiated by the mute visible. His doubt comes from the lack of certain delimitation that would be afforded by a prosaic line. "Cézanne's Doubt," 33[19]; cf. "Cézanne's Doubt," 30[17]: "Cézanne, selon ses propres paroles 'écrit en peintre ce qui n'est pas encore peint et le rend peinture absolument.'"
13 Simon, "Motion Pictures," 126n3: "The activity takes the form of a theatrical gesture that cleaves structural space. The dialectics involve my

dualistic habit of centering and removal (cutting away at the core of a structure); another socially relevant aspect of the activity then becomes clearer. Here I am directing my attention to the central void, to the gap which, among other things, could be between the self and the American Capitalist system. What I am talking about is a very real, carefully sustained mass schizophrenia in which our individual perceptions are constantly being subverted by industrially controlled media, markets, and corporate interests. The average individual is exposed to this barrage of half truths and monstrous untruths which all revolve around 'who runs his life' and how it is accomplished."

14 Merleau-Ponty, "Indirect Language," 70[56]. Merleau-Ponty says this with regard to abstract painting insofar as it still evokes geometrical forms.

15 Merleau-Ponty, *VI* 184[140]: "adherent to *location* and to the *now* … the inauguration of the *where* and the *when*, the possibility and exigency for the fact; in a word: facticity, what makes the fact be a fact. And, at the same time, what makes the facts have meaning, makes the fragmentary facts dispose themselves about 'something.'" See also Merleau-Ponty, *VI* 154[115].

16 Merleau-Ponty, *VI* 184[140].

17 Merleau-Ponty, *VI* 140[103], 161[121].

18 Merleau-Ponty, *VI* 160[119].

19 Merleau-Ponty, *VI* 154[115].

20 Owens, "Lessons Learned Well," 163–4.

21 Two motifs intertwine and form a flexuous line developed through Matta-Clark's works. One might be called negative and the other positive, but like the positive and negative spaces of his building cuts the two easily swap positions, so we will need to focus on the single flexuous chord that emerges rather than on any particular side of the dialectic. The first motif is the inhuman structuring of space given by architecture. This negative element is the material with which Matta-Clark works and to which the concept of anarchitecture responds in order to open up a space for the second, positive motif in his work: the human space of family, friendship, and community.

22 The group includes Suzanne Harris, Richard Landry, Tina Girouard, Jene Highstein, Bernard Kirschenbaum, Richard Nonas, and Laurie Anderson. Sussman, "The Mind Is Vast and Ever Present," 19.

23 Papapetros, "Oedipal and Edible," 79.

24 Sussman, "The Mind Is Vast and Ever Present," 23.

25 Ibid., 21.

26 Imposing structures, like the Twin Towers, leave only narrow spaces of

light and air, and their physical space, in turn, becomes gaps, the negative space within positive, lived space.

27 Papapetros, "Oedipal and Edible," 80. Papapetros draws this conclusion on the basis of cannibalism with reference to Freud's *Totem and Taboo*, but I will a draw a similar conclusion through Merleau-Ponty's concepts of flexuous lines and establishing bearings.

28 Lee, *Object to be Destroyed*, 72: "while we were putting food together … Gordon decided to cut himself a wall sandwich."

29 This work is also discussed in relationship to Merleau-Ponty's philosophy by Kirsten Jacobson in "A Developed Nature: A Phenomenological Account of the Experience of Home," *Continental Philosophy Review* 42 (2009): 355–73.

30 Fer, "Celluloid Circus," 137.

31 For details on this process, see ibid.

32 Sussman, "The Mind is Vast and Ever Present," 31: "There is collage and montaging. I like very much the idea of breaking – the same way I cut up buildings. I like the idea that the sacred photo framing process is equally 'violatable.'… I started out with an attempt to use multiple images to try and capture the 'all-around' experience of the piece. [They are] an approximation of this kind of ambulatory 'getting to know' what the space is about."

33 An earlier version of this essay was presented to the 2009 meeting of the International Merleau-Ponty Circle Conference in Starkville, Massachusetts. Many thanks go to all of the participants for their helpful comments. And special thanks to Kirsten Jacobson for introducing me to the work of Matta-Clark at the 2007 meeting of the International Merleau-Ponty Circle Conference in Memphis, Tennessee.

13 Flesh as the Space of Mourning: Maurice Merleau-Ponty Meets Ana Mendieta

STEFAN KRISTENSEN

Like Merleau-Ponty did himself, I intend to ask ontological questions in dialogue with works of contemporary art, an approach that is all the more relevant since Merleau-Ponty's phenomenological ideas have had a strong influence on recent art practices, and on "body art" in particular. I argue in this chapter that, since the body-subject is the invisible ground of perception, and since the content of perception is always already lost in the act of reflection, the structure of lived space always involves the process of mourning. The works of the artist Ana Mendieta (1948–1983) allow us both to understand better what is at stake in Merleau-Ponty's conception of phenomenal space and to understand the meaning of mourning as disruption of lived space.

I. The Problem of Space in the Late Merleau-Ponty

The aim of the ontological turn in the later work of Merleau-Ponty is no longer to rely on modern concepts such as subject–object, consciousness, intentionality, and so on. The ontology he heads for shows an analogy with the Heideggerian project of a fundamental ontology, but instead of posing being as the object of his investigation, he introduces the notion of "flesh," assuming that being as such actually must be understood as flesh, that is, the matter of sensibility. Contrary to Heidegger, his fundamental ontology is still a philosophy of perception; it is a way for Merleau-Ponty to ask the question of perception anew, and to overcome the distance between the subject and the world. When he died, he was addressing the same questions as in his earlier works: What is perception? How do the body and the world relate to each other? How do we describe the features and dynamics of pre-reflective experience? How do we define a more fundamental notion of time and space than the serial Cartesian one?

My question here pertains to the experience of space in this undertaking. Given that Merleau-Ponty's ontology of the flesh is aimed at exploring the structure of the pre-reflective perceived world, the very notion of space cannot be understood as the void extension between things, as we have seen in earlier chapters. Since things in the pre-reflective world are not separate beings, but differences in the perceptual field, the space in between them is not neutral: it is the very texture of their relations. As David Morris points out, space in the pre-reflective world involves the experience of movement, and this leads to the replacement of the notion of space by the notions of depth or thickness.[1] Depth is the unity of space and time, manifested by the phenomenon of movement, in the world of perception. According to a philosophy of the flesh, depth is a modulation of a fundamental proximity and even promiscuity of the perceiver and the perceived.[2] Understood as flesh, subject and object are both made of the same substance, and thus any measurable distance is abolished between them.

As Barbaras argued in 1993,

> "depth" is deeper than the distinction between the spatial and the temporal, and precedes indeed their opposition ... Because the perceived is exceeded, its distance is temporal as well as spatial: the object of desire, the pole of movement, is crossing space and time. Depth is indeed the third dimension, not within space, but beyond time and space; it is thus truly the first one ... Depth is the spatial figure of time, its proper way of presenting itself to us.[3]

We must then admit at least two notions of space, one resting upon the traditional distinction of consciousness and world, and opposed to the dimension of time, and a second, more fundamental notion identified as depth, or what I will call "phenomenal space," where space and time in the traditional sense are indiscernible, unified by the phenomenon of movement.[4] My aim is to describe the general structure of this phenomenal space, or depth, in particular its temporal features, in order to grasp the structure of the flesh as overlapping (*empiétement*), that is, as a space where things are not juxtaposed, but encroach on one another, just as Merleau-Ponty defines the time of perceptual experience as a "mythical time," a time that is not structured as the serial juxtaposition of mutually exclusive moments.[5] This temporal structure of phenomenal space might be clarified through a dialogue between the artist Ana Mendieta and the philosopher Maurice Merleau-Ponty.

II. The Archaic Immemorial Bodies of Ana Mendieta

Ana Mendieta was an artist of Cuban origin who grew up in the United States (more precisely in Iowa), where she attended art school. She was born in 1948 and died tragically in 1985, after falling from the thirty-fifth-floor window of her New York apartment. In the course of her short life, she produced an influential and now more and more recognized body of work. An exhibition with a catalogue organized by the Hirshhorn Museum in Washington in 2004 is a recent attempt to show her work to a larger audience.

She called her practice "Earth Body Art." Between 1972 and 1985, she created a great number of works involving most of the time the figure of a human female body. She went into nature, found places, and created anthropomorphic forms, made photographs, slides, or videotapes of them, and let them be in their natural context. There is an ambiguity in the very structure of this art work: Is the work the carving on the cliff, or the form on the sand, or is it the image of it taken by the artist herself? It could also be the interaction between the two. One of her more important works is the *Siluetas* series. To describe the *Siluetas*, imagine you are hiking along a river in Iowa, on a beach in Mexico, or in the Cuban countryside; at some moment you see a field, a marsh, or a fallen tree trunk that claims your attention. You get nearer and discover the figure of a human female body, a human shape committed to the variations of the weather and to the erosions of the wind and the sun. But of course you are actually in a museum, or in a university listening to a talk and watching the screening of those images. The art work here is complex: it is constituted by not only the shape in the landscape, but also the whole structure of its own presence and absence.

The *Siluetas* remind us of prehistoric paintings or carvings representing feminine divinities, but this aspect is not the only reason for their immemorial dimension,[6] which is manifest also because we cannot but imagine the erasing process of the *Silueta*. Sometimes Mendieta's work consists in a series of slides or a videotape of this very process. Our experience of Mendieta's work thus implies every time a mourning process, a fact that is underlined by some of her works that present themselves as actual tombs (*Tumbas*, 1977). In short, the immemorial dimension of her work is due to its temporal structure: the work is given as having already been destroyed – it bears witness to its own erasing. In more formal terms, the exhibition (or screening) structure puts up an after-effect (*après-coup / Nachträglichkeit*) that is constitutive of the work itself. By creating the immemorial structure of her figures herself, Mendieta renounces the search for something previously existent of which the works are traces. In presenting her works as precarious motifs in the aftermath of their destruction, she delineates a past or a space that was never present. It is remarkable that the motif by which she puts up the immemorial space is the body, both as object of mourning and as power of creation.

III. The Temporality of Depth

Merleau-Ponty was aware of the arts and sciences of his time. Let us imagine what interpretation he would have given to Mendieta's earth bodies. To do that, we must comment on some working notes from the 1950s, where he develops his theory of perceived space and time, stating that depth is the essential feature of transcendence. The central argument for this is the movement at work in the perceptual field such that things "slip into one another"; depth is responsible for the fact that "things have a flesh: that is, oppose to my inspection obstacles" (*VI* 272–3[219]). Movements of slipping and overlapping form the space of perception, and this is why Merleau-Ponty states that we have to use the same strategy for the problem of space as for the problem of time.[7] Not only are the problems of space and time parallel, but they are also intertwined inasmuch as space in the realm of flesh is defined as being "at the same time older than everything and 'of the first day'" (*VI* 264[210]), as he writes in the working note "Ontology," dated October 1959. The temporality of depth in the late Merleau-Ponty is a paradoxical notion, and it is my aim in the following pages to show some features of that paradoxical character.

In an unpublished working note transcribed by R. Barbaras and F. Robert, dated February 1959 and titled "OV" (*Origine de la vérité*), Merleau-Ponty writes that the "rediscovery of wild being" will become a "true intelligence of the movement of the same and the other," a dialectics of real movement and not a "proferred dialectics, a dialectics that has become thesis." The note ends with a strange idea: Merleau-Ponty writes that this "return to a living dialectics" will not be understood as a relativist or psychologistic turn, but as a "return to the monumental," this last word being apparently underlined. How is this term to be understood? It also appears in the published notes of *The Visible and the Invisible*, for example, in a note of April 1960 in which he speaks about perceptual life as "the 'monumental' life, the *Stiftung*, the initiation" (*VI* 296[243]). In other places, he uses terms such as "mythical," "monumental," or even "prehistorical" in order to signify the pre-reflective dimension of the flesh.[8] But those motifs actually imply a certain degree of sedimentation. What is at stake, then, is a certain structure of sense that is at the same time pre-reflective and nevertheless sedimented and transmissible. In other words, he has to give an account of the retroactive constitution of sense, the fact that when a signification appears, it appears as if it had always already been there. He writes in this respect in 1954–55 that "insight [in English] is reminiscence."[9] Insight, according to *Gestalt* theorists, is the categorial consciousness as a modulation of the perceptual consciousness. To understand is not to discover something pre-existing, but to form something that appears as having already been there. That is the structure of what Merleau-Ponty, using an expression from Bergson, also calls the "backwards movement of truth."[10]

In yet another working note from *The Visible and the Invisible*, dated 2 May 1959, Merleau-Ponty reflects on this peculiar temporality of perception. The note begins with two examples from his trip to Manchester the same year. More evidently than in the mother tongue, the understanding of a sentence quickly spoken with an unexpected accent comes all of a sudden, after a few seconds. One does not understand every word, but rather the totality of the sentence, afterwards (*après coup*). Merleau-Ponty writes that "first the meaning has to be given" (*VI* 243[189]), that is, an element in the sentence must act as an emblem and project itself on the structure of the whole. But this relation between the parts and the whole of the sentence cannot be made by inductions, since it is sudden and immediate. In this respect, understanding a sentence is analogous to perceiving a *Gestalt*. Merleau-Ponty seeks to show the conditions of the appearing of a meaning, the *Gestaltung* of what emerges in the field. The comparison he makes is the "recognition of someone according to a description, or of the event according to a schematic forecast." As with perception, where the body schema is the ground that allows the praxis to open up a perceptual field, the schematic form given by an emblematic sign, an element of the verbal chain or by a typical arrangement of the signifiers, stands for what is going to be grasped. The act of grasping itself, the moment of understanding, is thus a retrograde movement, a *Rückgestaltung*. Just as the body schema itself is not perceived, the level of the first perception, by which a field opens up and by which configurations of the field are possible, is necessarily unconscious. The perceiving body itself, as subject of perception and expression, stays necessarily in the background, and its representation, if it is to be rigorous, must be indirect, it cannot be immediate. It must incorporate the structure of the delay: when I perceive, I am late on myself. Merleau-Ponty concludes the working note with a paradox: "I do not perceive any more than I speak – Perception has me as has language – And as it is necessary that all the same I be there in order to speak, *I* must be there in order to perceive – But in what sense?" (*VI* 244[190]). At the moment when I become aware of my presence to the world, the perceiving I has already vanished, but is nevertheless present as having been there. The self has always to reconstitute its integrity, through and in spite of this splitting, that is, it is in danger of losing its orientation in space and constantly has to regain it. As Bernhard Waldenfels puts it, "a self is never a being who is just missing something or someone, it is a being who misses itself and who fails in the premoral sense of the word."[11] For this reason I am arguing for the permanence of the mourning work in the very activity of perception. The question is then to understand how the body-subject exists in this process of constantly mourning itself.

IV. The Schema of the Absent Body

In order to understand the body-subject as a process of mourning, we have to get back to Merleau-Ponty's conception of the body as a subject, which involves giving an account of his reception of Schilder's notion of the "body schema." In fact, this notion is central in his first course at the Collège de France, titled "The Sensible World and the World of Expression," from 1953. I will just pick out a few key aspects: Merleau-Ponty takes up the idea of a postural schema (coming from H. Head), that is, "the point where we are in a series of actions."[12] He also defines the body schema as "pre-objective spatiality," as what gives an intelligibility to the gestures of the body making the perception of moving objects possible (which is the same as perception *tout court*). The pre-established unity of the moving body is correlated to the possibilities of action of the body; the body schema itself is therefore latent as long as the body is resting, as long as it is in a position "where nothing is felt as figure."[13] Thus Merleau-Ponty defines it as the "ground of a praxis": its normativity is not a set of explicit organizational rules, but is rather that in opposition to which the visible appears. In other words, I cannot view my own body *as* subject, because as such, it is by definition invisible, undifferentiated. The differentiation, starting at the moment of perception, is nothing less than the very opening of depth, both temporal and spatial. According to Merleau-Ponty, the condition of possibility of lived/phenomenal space is the praxis of the body, that is, the movement as directed towards an actual or possible task. Praxis, in its turn, is organized by the body schema understood as the implicit norm for the action. As Merleau-Ponty writes in the lecture notes,

> the body schema is not perceived – It is a privileged norm or position in contrast to which the perceived body is defined. It is before explicit perception – It requires a rethinking of our notion of consciousness – Comparison of body schema with language: language expresses not significations, but differences of significations. In the same sense, body ≠ perceived things, but index of our preobjective relations with space where we are established by the body.[14]

As Maria Talero showed in chapter 2, if we are able to initiate a movement of projecting ourselves onto an action, a task, or a perception, it is because our body structures the world. This potential works at various levels (*gnosis, praxis, aisthesis*), and it consists in a transcendental condition of the constitution of a phenomenal field where figures detach themselves from a background. The symbolic, cultural level is also invested by this bodily power of motility; Merleau-Ponty writes that "the junction of the visible world and the world of expression is made through movement."[15] Thus Merleau-Ponty defines the symbol as "trace of a praxis" (*MSME* 119), which means that any symbolization, be it artistic or scientific, rests on the implicit normativity of the body, that is, its significant absence, as perceiving body, in the moment of conscious perception.

V. On the Phenomenology of Mourning

Somehow the motif of mourning haunts the philosophy of the late Merleau-Ponty. He never offers an explicit theory of mourning in any of his lectures or published texts, but the backwards structure of the temporality of perception, the experience of phantom limbs, and the status of the body-subject with regard to the process of reflection all point to the centrality of the work of mourning for properly understanding the structure of bodily subjectivity in Merleau-Ponty (and in general).

Before returning to the work of Mendieta, I will clarify some elements of a phenomenology of mourning, in order to distinguish mourning from other related notions, such as trauma, melancholia, and sorrow.

Mourning is a process of restructuring the body's spatiality, as we see in the case of phantom limbs: as Kirsten Jacobson demonstrated in chapter 5, the fact that the amputated subject still experiences sensations in the no longer existing parts of her limbs is the sign that the phenomenal space of her lived body no longer maps the objective space of the world. The process the subject must undergo is a process of restructuring her lived space, in exactly the same way as someone having lost a loved person has to restructure her affective space.[16] This situation of being lost in space, of not knowing how to situate oneself and thereby retreat into a confined space (literally or not), is something other than grief, sorrow, or sadness.[17] Mourning is the process that frees us from the seclusion of our affective life caused by a trauma, whereas melancholia is an existential state that inhibits the reconstructive capacity of mourning.[18]

The poems of Paul Celan underscore this tentative phenomenology of mourning. Celan's poetry often involves motifs of the disruption of cosmic order, the retreat of the sky and the soil giving way. Most of the time, one finds it together with the motifs of the gaze and the speech. For example, in *Das Wort vom Zur-Tiefe-Gehen* (GW 1, 212) –"weißt du, was sich in dein Aug schrieb, / vertieft uns die Tiefe" (Do you know what is written in your eyes, deepen our depth). And in *Zu Beiden Händen* (GW 1, 219), one observes the disruption in relation to intersubjectivity: "Du bist, / wo dein Aug ist, du bist / oben, bist / unten, ich / finde hinaus" (You are where your eye is, you are above, are below, I find my way out). The eye as the centre of the subject's perceived world does not work any more; no longer does it distribute the up and the down, the here and the there. The verdict concerning mourning (its impossibility or adjournment) comes in the poem *Die Schleuse* (GW 1, 222): "Über aller dieser deiner / Trauer: kein / zweiter Himmel" (Over all this mourning of yours: no second heaven). The only way to understand these texts is to read them from the idea of mourning as the restructuring of space and time for the subjects,[19] whence it becomes clear that Celan speaks of the impossibility of that very process in the case of catastrophic mourning.

Structurally, mourning is the process of regaining a presence to the present and freeing oneself from being stuck in the past. It is thus an experience in which time and space are indiscernible, just as in the paradoxical description Merleau-Ponty offers of our being in the present:

"Instead of saying that I am in time and in space, or that I am nowhere, why not rather say that I am everywhere, always, by being at this moment and at this place" (*VI* 152[113]). Where is the mourning subject? Everywhere or nowhere?

VI. "Where Is Ana Mendieta?"

One of the few books written on Mendieta bears the title *Where Is Ana Mendieta?*[20] This question points to the problème of the lack of recognition of women artists in the United States at the end of the twentieth century. The book focuses rightly on political and social issues such as feminism, colonialism, native art, and so on. But there is yet another way of understanding this uncertainty about the artist's location, and that is to see it as a feature of her work. Especially in the *Silueta* series, her presence is not limited to the spot shown on the picture, on the shore in Mexico or in the woods somewhere in Iowa; since the *Silueta* itself appears as the trace of a presence, at the moment when the spectator sees the art work in a gallery or in a museum, the body whose trace it is can be anywhere. Ana Mendieta, literally, "is everywhere by being at this moment in this place." Of course, if we look for her, she will never be where we expect her to be; the structure of her work engages us in a never-ending process of mourning her presence, a never-ending state of openness towards a not-yet-determined situation.

If we look once again for the structure of her work, we find that a constant doubling is taking place: the figures she draws in nature, and the performances she makes while videotaping herself, are always in some way depictions of herself (I should say depictions of her self, in two words). Then we have the artist showing her pieces in art places, which take on the status of the author. Since Mendieta's work actively encompasses the very structure of the exhibition, I would maintain that there are always two figures in her work, that her work actually is constituted by the interplay between the immemorial archaic body figure and the figure of the artist calling upon this ever-lost dimension. The artist is in that sense the witness of her own living, perceiving body, and in this very gesture, she lays bare the structure of reflection as witnessing in the name of the one who is no more there, of a past presence that has never been present. The perceiving subject is dispersed in that immemorial past and the reflecting/mourning subject's task is to institute a present of which it is the past. The mourning subject is precisely in this paradoxical place that only presents itself as past, that is, as lost.

Any act of conscious perception thus implies a process of mourning as a process of stabilizing the perceived and bringing the perceiving self (the lost one) and the perceived self into correspondence. To say that the mourning subject is "everywhere by being at this moment in this time" is to say that it is both lost and situated, because those two "moments," the mourning and the mourned, do not follow each other, but are simultaneous yet distinct. This implies a notion of space and time other than the serial successive one, a conception where simultaneity admits an extension, where the instant is extended. At this point, we can think bodily subjectivity and the unconscious together.

NOTES

1 Morris, *The Sense of Space*, ch. 4.

2 Emmanuel de Saint Aubert develops the notion of promiscuity, in particular concerning Merleau-Ponty's relation to psychoanalysis in his 2006 article "La 'promiscuité.'"

3 Barbaras, "L'espace et le mouvement vivant," 28.

4 For a detailed reading of the notion of depth in the whole work of Merleau-Ponty, see the first part of Cataldi, *Emotion, Depth, and Flesh*, esp. chs. 3 and 4.

5 Cf. for example the working note dated April 1960, "Indestructible past and intentional analytics," in Merleau-Ponty, *VI* 296–8[243–4].

6 She was indeed searching for archaic forms in the first sense of this term, and one should not underestimate that aspect of her work. It also expresses her belonging to a movement (feminism) and a time (the 1970s) when the reference to an archaic time had an evident political dimension, a time when the subjection of women would not exist and when the matriarcate and mother goddesses would reign.

7 Cf. *VI* 284[231]: "Apply to the perception of space what I said about the perception of time (in Husserl)"; and, *VI* 248[195]: "For in fact space does not comprise *points, lines* any more than time does."

8 *Le Problème de la Parole*, unpublished lecture at the Collège de France, 1953–54, 78.

9 *L'institution dans l'histoire personnelle et publique*, 93. Hereafter cited as *NC 54–55.*

10 Cf. for example, the final pages of the manuscript of *VI*, where Merleau-Ponty compares the reversibility of the viewer and the visible with the reversibility of speech and signification (*VI* 202[154]). See also the working

note dated 2 May 1959, where Merleau-Ponty defines the "backwards movement of truth" (Lingis trans: "retrograde movement of the true") in relation to the movement of institution, in particular to the fact that one cannot undo what has once been thought (*VI* 243[189]).

11 Waldenfels, *Bruchlinien der Erfahrung*, 205.

12 "Repérage de positions, du point *où nous en sommes* d'une série d'actions," *Le monde sensible et le monde de l'expression. Cours au Collège de France*, 138; my translation. Hereafter referred to as *MSME*.

13 *MSME*, 143.

14 *MSME*, 143: "Le schéma corporel n'est pas perçu- Il est norme ou position privilégiée par opposition à laquelle se définit le corps perçu. Il est *avant* la perception explicite- Il exige refonte de notre notion de la conscience- Comparaison du schéma corporel et du langage: langage exprime non significations, mais différences de significations. De même corps ≠ choses perçues, mais index de nos rapports préthétiques avec espace où nous sommes établis par lui."

15 *MSME*, 149: "C'est par le mouvement que se fait la jonction du monde visible et du monde de l'expression."

16 On this point see Talero, "Merleau-Ponty and the Bodily Subject."

17 One could even say it is the impossibility of experiencing emotions; because of the intimate link between emotions and spatiality, mourning as loss of lived space is also the blocking of emotional life; see Cataldi, *Emotion, Depth and Flesh*, esp. ch. 6.

18 As Freud remarks, melancholia is characterized by a lack of self-esteem: "In mourning, the world has become poor and void, in melancholia, it is the self itself" (*Metapsychology*, French transl., 1987, p. 150).

19 A similar idea is to be found in the first lines of Binswanger's essay "Dream and Existence."

20 Blocker, *Where Is Ana Mendieta?*

14 Phenomenology and the Body Politic: Merleau-Ponty, Cézanne, and Democracy

PETER COSTELLO

This chapter argues that the concept of a democratic citizen both appears and is challenged to develop itself further in the work of Merleau-Ponty. In particular, it explores the link between Merleau-Ponty's discussion of the flesh and his politically "evocative suggestion"[1] regarding how (Cézanne's) painting works in "Cézanne's Doubt," "Indirect Language and the Voices of Silence," and "Eye and Mind."[2] Within this chapter's exploration of this link, democratic politics comes to the fore as the juncture of reflection and anonymity, embodiment and flesh, spontaneity and support. In its attempt to argue for the character of Merleau-Ponty's politics and its reflection in his aesthetics, this chapter seeks to further the work of Diana Coole, who in her recent book *Merleau-Ponty and Modern Politics after Anti-Humanism* and in her earlier article "Thinking Politically with Merleau-Ponty" describes how Merleau-Ponty is, throughout his corpus, engaged in "a return to ontology, where the primordial relationship between meaning and material existence is grasped."[3] Following along with Coole, I provide more evidence that Merleau-Ponty's politics derive from his ontology, particularly his ontological description of bodily coexistence. However, I do this by looking further into Merleau-Ponty's aesthetic descriptions, descriptions that Coole acknowledges as important to constructing "the flesh of the political" but that still have not received their due in that regard.[4]

I. Preparation – Aristotle and Winnicott

Aristotle's *Politics* discusses the virtuous citizen as one who knows both how to rule and how to be ruled: "he should know how to govern like a freeman, and how to obey like a freeman – these are the excellences of a citizen."[5] Especially in a democracy, this principle of knowing, of seeing both sides of what it means to govern, or of coming to terms with the implications of coexistence, must be a main requirement for entering political life: "One principle of liberty [within democracy] is for all to rule and be ruled in turn."[6] That is, in a democracy, what is required is a kind of mutual recognition in which each citizen must be able to see and to will every other citizen's legitimate claims – especially since, when she is no longer "in power," she will be ruled in turn.

D.W. Winnicott, in *The Family and Individual Development*, describes a child's growing capacity to draw figures on paper as the initial instantiation of the concept of democracy: "There comes a balance of objects and of movements ... the child has shown a developing capacity to retain spontaneity while respecting form and all the other controls. This is the democratic idea in miniature."[7] For Winnicott, however, this miniature democratic idea is not fleshed out immediately. Instead, the idea of democracy becomes personally, and more fully, established after the child breaks from and diffuses the guidance of an external person, who had previously supported the child's capacity to draw: "he or she has to be able to supply *from within* this person in relation to whom, externally, the early artistry was so richly shown."[8] Winnicott thus sees in artistic endeavour the example of the process of moving from a necessary, familial autocracy and from the relative anonymity of one's place in that family, to another, more sophisticated, creative, and reflective stance of self-governing mutuality.[9]

Like Winnicott, I would like to establish a link between art work and democracy, to argue that democracy arises "from within" through the introduction and diffusion of personal governance and spontaneity into form, line, and colour. But instead of speaking of how democracy can arise as an idea or a project within the life of the individual artist, I would like to speak about how democracy can arise within the art work itself and within those who view it, thereby bolstering their ability to rule, as Aristotle says, in turns. That is, I would like to argue that democracy is transmitted, in part, because our roles as citizens, our struggles to be free, can take flesh aesthetically, and that a painting can promote an open-ended reflection on what is at stake in the intertwining of the aesthetic image and one's own experience of relations and power.

II. Embodiment and Flesh

For Merleau-Ponty, in order to talk meaningfully about either politics or painting, one must first clarify the ontology of embodiment, of the bodies that view and govern. It is with our bodies that we encounter the demands and the gazes of others. It is as bodily indices and interpretations that paintings refer to and move us. That is, a painting is a network and field of the perceptual and artistic motions that created it, of the complementary motions and emotions it draws forth from the viewer, and of the shifting set of relations it maintains with other works in the history of painting.[10] And we can recognize that others demand from us, that paintings move us, because our own bodies are such networks, such fields, that is, our bodies are historical openings always already inserted into the world as both seeing and being seen,[11] as both being governed and as governing – in short, as initiating new habits of interaction.

In the dual insertion of our bodies into the world – as both seeing and being seen – our bodies are not static things. On the one hand, as that which sees, our bodies are the very manners in which our consciousness flows into, connects with, sediments the traces of, and flees from others and the world: "Is my body a thing? Is it an idea? It is neither, being the measurant of things."[12] Our bodies are thus immediately identified with our consciousnesses, and our bodies as "measurants" continually reveal the significance of the world. On the other hand, as these "measurants," our embodiment is also that which is seen, and our bodies are therefore an experience that stretches beyond self-experience, beyond the grasp of our *own* bodies. Our bodies thus retain some connection to thinghood, even if not to the static kind.

As the particular kind of dynamic thing, as a measurant that is also measured, embodiment reveals itself to us as the dual structure of insertion/action only insofar as we also discover more about how we are always already with *other* bodies. To be a body is not simply to grasp things as pointing back to us. To be a body is not only to grasp in the abstract the mere possibility of our being seen; to be a body is also to have to come to terms with the concrete, actual *ways* in which these or those actual others' acts of seeing work with me to form my own habits of seeing myself. That is, to be an experiencing body is to be part of a network of other bodies that experience me; to be a body is to be intercorporeal and thus shot through with the effects of anonymous others who take a stance on me.[13]

Such a description of the body, as both seeing and seen, as both the process and the site of mutual recognition, is what motivates Merleau-Ponty to ask after the possibility, support, and goal of intercorporeality and to discover "flesh." As he describes it particularly in *The Visible and the Invisible*, flesh is the "formative medium of the object and subject."[14] It is that which is prior to the distinction between subject and subject, between subject and object.

As this prior, formative medium, flesh supports an explicit experience of anonymity, in particular an experience of *the visible itself.* Even the fruit and the tablecloth could be experienced as looking, perhaps right back at me, because of the flesh that I am: "It is not *I* who sees, not *he* who sees, because an anonymous visibility inhabits both of us ... in virtue of that primordial property that belongs to the flesh, being here and now, radiating everywhere and forever, being an individual, of being *also a dimension and a universal.*"[15] The "anonymous visibility" of the visible itself, of the entire visible world, and my participation in it, is the source of my conceptual and perceptual grasping of what is. It is because I am part of the anonymous visible that I am able to return to myself as an individual, cutting away from the universality of the flesh through a kind of phenomenological reduction. Or, to put it another way, it is as flesh that reflects itself into a subject who lives or exists its body that I acquire and maintain particular acts of bodily perceiving.

Furthermore, the flesh that I am supports not only the experience of anonymity or of visibility as such. Flesh also supports the experience of our bodies, as particular experiencers, passing into one another, as tending towards anonymity here and now:

> for me to have not an idea, an image, nor a representation, but as it were an imminent experience of them [i.e., colours, forms as they appear to the other person], it suffices that I look at a landscape, that I speak of it with someone. Then, through the concordant operations of his body and my own, what I see *passes into him,* this individual green of the meadow under my eyes invades his vision without quitting my own, I recognize in my green his green.[16]

It is possible, Merleau-Ponty claims here, that my own vision, which appears to be quite private, bears and bleeds – "without quitting my own" – into the eyes and objects of this or that other viewer.

Finally, the flesh that reflects itself into and out of anonymity can even be experienced within one's own body. It is thus that one experiences a tendency to "reversibility,"[17] one that is always almost achieved with explicit evidence yet without the necessary "coincidence" that would guarantee it. My act of touching in my right hand can almost be "reversed" by being touched by my left. My act of vocalizing can almost be heard and, as it were, voiced. Instead of touching (or seeing, or voicing) simply by turns, there is almost the sensation of touching together; there is almost a reversibility of touching, of the very turning from touching to touched.

The almost-experienced reversibility of my own body, the tendency towards anonymity in passing into others, the viewing power of the visible itself – these are what the flesh sustains. These are the marks of its ontological character. My experience of subjects and objects, my experience of my body within my lived experience, then, points to experiences at the edges, to experiences of an opaque but nevertheless delimited anonymity: "My flesh and that of the world therefore involve clear zones, clearings, about which pivot their opaque zones, and the primary visibility, that of the *quale* and of the things, does not come without a secondary visibility, that of the lines of force and of dimensions, the massive flesh without a rarefied flesh, the momentary body without a glorified body."[18] There is, then, in my lived experience of (subjective) bodily life, evidence that I tend towards (and out of) an anonymous and secondary visibility.

However, this evidence of secondary visibility, of anonymity is not complete. It is not enough to grant me certainty. The evidence does not serve to mark out flesh sufficiently for me to master it. If the evidence for its "lines of force" were sufficient, I would be able to inhabit and review the very turn to anonymity. I would be able to witness reversibility at the very moment of the shift from touching to touched, from voicing to voiced. I would be able, in short, to coincide with my origin in and departure from anonymity. But I cannot so coincide.

There is a gap at the heart of my relation to flesh, one that conserves the character of my experiences of flesh as "tendencies." However, such a gap is not indicative of a "failure" on my part to be my body and its relations to flesh and to the world. Rather, the non-coincidence of my lived body to itself, the non-coincidence of my relation to anonymity, is "spanned by the total being of my body, and that of the world."[19] I *am* the gap between my touching and touched, between anonymity and personal experience, and the flesh of the world supports the being of my body with its own.

Flesh, by simultaneously being what I am and what I differentiate myself from, allows the almost coincident to show itself. Flesh allows the "tendency" or "transition" from touching to touched, from self to other, from vision to visibility, to appear as a human experience.[20] And in turn, this non-coincident evidence is sufficient for me to sketch out for myself and others the whole of flesh without the sketch being sufficient or exhaustive. The non-coincidence that flesh brings to view is what allows a particular, reflective human being to paint flesh as it undulates, throwing up new forms for review in a manner that allows flesh to remain at a distance.

III. The Political Space between Embodiment and Flesh

This very complicated way in which I exist my body, as lived body and as flesh, imposes on me a political task – namely, stewardship. I need to care for the whole that supports me, in which I exist and to which I return more directly and dramatically in dreams, in death, in moments of pre-reflective dispersion. I need to care for this whole so that, whenever I do turn from (or return to live and govern in) my embodiment, I make visible to all the anonymous viewers, who always already include myself, how the whole might concretize itself more effectively and justly.[21]

Visibility, so far as I live it in my own body as both seeing and being seen, is a kind of public space, which is unable to be carved out unproblematically into private property. Concretely, this means two things: first, whatever I do, say, or see is immediately seen or absorbed by the whole world, and the world is thereby empowered to reflect my visibility back to me, if it ever does, so as to allow for further review.[22] And second, this means that whatever I see, whatever I reflect, is always already given to me *implicitly* by virtue of my participation in anonymity and requires that I take up an attitude of making its anonymous lineage more *explicit*.

For Merleau-Ponty, to be part of (and to make explicit) an anonymous visibility is neither to experience my own agency, my own acts of seeing, as worthless, nor to experience them as self-founding.[23] Rather, my task is to situate my seeing, to draw out its origin, support, and goal. How did I come to this experience of a crowd as pleasant or frightening? How is my act of reading a novel given to me as a certain set of presuppositions gained from others? And in witnessing to this lineage, to the anonymity that inhabits my own vision, I discover that my participation in the visible, in flesh, is the foundation of my experience of responsibility.[24]

Our bodies in their very structure as flesh put us into the situation of needing to be responsible for one another, for continually having to reconcile how our visibility to others maps onto their visibility for us. To incorporate an immigrant, a newborn child, a soldier returning home from a war – to have these particular people enter or re-enter the community – is to be compelled to adopt new habits of seeing and being seen. That is, at their entry, the flesh of the world turns over onto us in the eyes of this immigrant, this newborn, and this soldier.[25] In the soldier, the war brings itself home. In the infant, the act of reproduction touches us again. In the immigrant, liberty falls upon our land, clinging to a torch and exhausted.

Given their entry, and given that the immigrant, the newborn, and the soldier are *always* entering and emerging from our shared anonymity, one's participation in the visible entails a continuous witnessing, a continuous revision of self-awareness, a continuous researching and reappraising of the state of one's embodiment. And indeed, the fact of the incipient visibility of our very acts of witnessing, of our reflective, lived efforts to make way (or to inhibit), will not let us rest but gives these efforts over, again and again, to the others that inhabit the anonymous flesh that lands again and again as already claiming community with us.

As we are pressed into this continuous, reflective research by virtue of the ever-renewed anonymity that is our shared flesh, our bodies compel us towards more and other interpretations, towards new images and political relationships. But it is not simply that we must have *new* images, new forms. Even the ones we already have urge us forward. For we cannot come to terms with this urgent, renewed, and anonymous visibility without having *explicitly* to put the entire process of "coming to terms," to sediment the images and relationships such as we live them at the moment, further into our bodies and into the world.

One example might be how we attempt to put up more reflective signs to the anonymous: "No Trespassing," "Welcome Home," and so on. For it is in signs like these that we attempt to stabilize, harmonize, and make more explicit the intertwining of our bodies. It is in these images and relationships, deliberately erected, that we attempt to mark out the world as significant, by pointing to indications or to indices of how we see and are seen by one another.

Again, however, at the same moment that we concretize the flesh and take a stand on it by erecting such signs, by making these reflective moves, we also unavoidably return to the anonymity of the flesh. Our reflection, our stances are those that necessarily and uncontrollably fold over onto the others. Our stances become immediately claimed by anonymity – by those whom we did not intend to welcome or ward off as well as by those we did so intend. And our stances roll us over by means of the others who take them up into a style, a culture, a history, and, ultimately, a life-world.[26]

The scholarly creation of art and politics as further research[27] on our intercorporeality is, I would argue, just a more sophisticated extension or development of the idea of signs of welcome or warning. Art and politics, just as surely as a "Welcome Home" sign, operate within the space between embodiment and flesh. And we bridge this space, without coinciding with it, without collapsing it, by virtue of the support of the world.

In the case of art, and of painting more specifically, a painting is a particular way of making explicit what we always already do whenever we perceive a visible object. According to Merleau-Ponty, perception by definition is "this bursting forth of the mass of the body toward the things, which makes a vibration of my skin become the sleek and the rough, makes me follow with my eyes the movements and the contours of the things themselves, this magical relation, this pact between them and me according to which *I lend them my body* in order that they *inscribe upon it* and *give me their resemblance*."[28]

But of course this "bursting forth," this "following the contours," what is this but painting? In interacting with things, with brushes, paints, canvas, objects, and viewers, the painter seeks out their mediation. But he or she does so as one who bears some community with each of them. The painter lends to things her body; and we, the viewers in the museum, echo her effort by lending our eyes.

As painting requires that the painter and the viewer lend eyes and body to the world, politics might be said to require something similar. For what is the formation of a constitution but the act of a people contending with anonymity, with the future generations that would come to take up that original decision, in order that the people continue to demonstrate to itself how it might "lend" the bodies of its citizens to a form of government? And what is the ongoing renewal of that constitution but the effort to see according to it, in order that that form of government "inscribe itself upon them" and also "give them back its resemblance"?

For Merleau-Ponty, a painting and a government is thus how we pursue the visible's act of coiling back upon itself. A painting is our attempt to pursue the visible within the visible, a research whose form and content are as closely intertwined and as (almost) reversible as our touching and touched hands. The question becomes, then, given that we can pursue the relation of anonymity and reflection, flesh and body – that is, given these pursuits – whether we can in fact paint or govern in a way that concretizes those relations into lasting forms of art and politics. Can we paint flesh and its coming to presence in lived, reflective structures? Can we govern with a constitution that insists on the anonymous source of all community as the source of laws? The very gaps that do not coincide, and the opacity (e.g., of future viewers or generations), which founds artistic and political stances, make art and politics both possible and difficult.

However, when we find a painting or government compelling, when it succeeds, it succeeds momentously, since, in viewing and participating with it, we can come to see and to extend one another and ourselves through it. That is to say, when it is compelling, a painting extends the visible, concretizes the flesh, and makes it come alive and pass between us as a shared vision. And when it is sophisticated, a political system allows for the creation of a particular kind of human relation, a particular kind of concord or friendship, in Aristotle's terms: "therefore while in tyrannies friendship and justice hardly exist, in democracies they exist more fully; for where citizens are equal they have much in common."[29]

Unfortunately and fortunately, there is never just one successful painting. Or at least a painting's success is never total. In our very attraction to a successful painting, in our committing it to the canon of great works, our bodies are disappointed. In the very act of extending ourselves to the painting, we discover therein that our embodiment is never fully comprehended. Before the painting, or on the way back from the museum, or in an attempt to paint it again, we recognize (or at least some anonymous viewer discovers) that something is missing. We begin to feel that here too we have never thoroughly felt and communed with the visible, or with one another.

In the act of appreciation, in the analysis of our research, then, we grow restless. Our embodiment outstrips this latest attempt to formalize its logic, and in our growing restlessness the way in which colours arise together, the way of the painter, changes.

A *succession* of paintings and painters then happens. And indeed such a succession in the history of painting carries political ramifications, much as a succession of elected representatives does, for what the painters and the viewers discover together is the following: that there is more to say; that the use of colour must adapt and reappraise itself in its very coming to visibility; that the sight of one another dims and reilluminates elsewhere within an infinitely renewable world. Painting like politics must find itself concerned with its own reproduction and with its own medium; the citizens and viewers who vote and see today must be prepared in the context of government and art to take on these disciplines for themselves insofar as they give themselves over to the anonymous traditions of art and politics.

In order to continue to determine which paintings and governments are most appropriate, then, we must continually reacquaint ourselves with our embodiment, with this bodily space that is intercorporeal and (perhaps even more importantly) this bodily time that is self-transcending.

Our very bodies press us to strive to select paintings and government that move us towards greater capacities of self-governance, greater self-comprehension as these bodies that we are. The very participation of our bodies in the visible, in flesh, means that "the visible body provides for the hollow whence a vision *will* come"[30] just as much as our participation means that our past acts of seeing have become part of the visible world. The painter and the politician, then, who are most successful at explicating our embodiment will succeed in painting or governing *both* the way that we see here and now *and* the way we will see after encountering their work and having that open us towards our future encounters with others. More, the successful painter or politician will allow us to develop a particular take on the relationship between the past and future seeing. He or she will make it possible for us to make explicit to ourselves what our seeing *means*.[31]

IV. Cézanne the Democrat

According to Merleau-Ponty, Cézanne painted against the Impressionists and the way their painting kept an external guide, a sort of tyranny over colour, in the form of the outline. He gave up the outline, and according to Merleau-Ponty, "abandon[ed] himself to the chaos of sensations."[32] For Cézanne, the order of the individual colours had to be more organic, more within the unity they already occupied from within the object. The outline could not be imposed from without, by the painter, as if he or she were a dictator. The painter had to learn how the whole, the object, is a spontaneous *process* of unification: "He did not want to separate the stable things which we see and the shifting way in which they appear; he wanted to depict matter as it takes on form, the birth of the order through *spontaneous organization*."[33] Cézanne made pictures in such a way that, when one viewed them globally, one saw that "perspectival distortions are no longer visible in their own right but rather contribute, as they do in natural vision, to the impression of an emerging order, of an object in the act of appearing, organizing itself before our eyes."[34] That is, for Cézanne, the individual perspective, the viewer's "distortion," perhaps even the individual colour, retained their meaning by "contributing" to an "order" that transcended it without violating it.[35] "Natural" vision and aesthetic vision were superimposed in Cézanne's paintings – and this superimposition was important, Merleau-Ponty argues, because it demonstrated that Cézanne painted in order to show us what our vision was.[36]

For Merleau-Ponty, then, Cézanne's main accomplishment was not that he could, on his own, organize colours differently than the Impressionists. It was that he *experienced* differently than they did, according to the implicit logic of vision/visibility that is the "flesh." For Cézanne saw that colours organized themselves "before his eyes," and he painted the *relation and intertwining* of eyes and body with the world. Cézanne focused through the colours and with them onto the object: "Cézanne follows the swelling of the object in modulated colors and indicates *several outlines* in blue. Rebounding among these, one's glance captures a shape that emerges from among them all, just as it does in perception."[37] If we are like those multiple outlines and colours, if the painter gives us to understand ourselves and our bodily coexistences through both form and content, then Cézanne could also show, through his aesthetic efforts, that politically, it is not that we can abstractly give the law to our shared life but rather that our life together, in its natural patterns of interrelationship, shows the law that strengthens and furthers that sharing: "The outline should therefore be a *result* of the colors if the world is to be given its true density."[38] The question of embodiment and painting, then, is not whether wishes are horses, but whether colours are bodies.

That Cézanne *did* in fact give us to notice our intercorporeality and our politics through the method and content of his painting, or that we *are* like self-governing colours that tend towards stable projects, is something Merleau-Ponty begins to suggest in his description and defence of Cézanne as a philosophical exemplar. Similarly to how Merleau-Ponty retained his philosophical relationship with the phenomenology of Husserl throughout his own works, he notes that Cézanne enacted painting as a relationship that was predicated on learning, and then *forgetting*, the classical (and the Impressionist) rules of perspective, design, and anatomy.

On the one hand, "the rules of anatomy and design are present in each stroke of his brush just as the rules of the game underlie each stroke of a tennis match"[39]; on the other, "the task before him was, first to *forget* all he had ever learned from science, and second *through* these sciences to recapture the structure of the landscape as an emerging organism."[40]

This balancing of memorializing and forgetting of tradition and science is something Merleau-Ponty relates explicitly to bodily effort, to a tennis match. The painter Cézanne thus forms an example not simply of aesthetics but of human bodily structure in general. Cézanne simply makes such bodily structure explicit and thereby seems also to make explicit, or at least to make more accessible to discovery, the bodily sources for the development of an honest, responsive democracy.

Like Cézanne's relationship with his ancient, classical sources, one should, I would argue, after reading Merleau-Ponty's phenomenology in general and his aesthetic essays in particular, move back towards and reappraise the worth of Aristotle's exploration of the democratic citizen and his argument from nature about the human as a political animal – that is, one must *see oneself according to those terms* – but one must also move forward. Forgetting Aristotle, one must move towards a recapturing of the political landscape as itself bodily, as not only "organism" – a concept that has inspired a less than sufficient politics when used as a model – but also "flesh." As an expression of flesh, as itself flesh, the political landscape, the body politic would not be made to stand ossified once and for all, would not simply submerge individuals, but would reach towards the more organic politics that humans' intercorporeality and situatedness in relation to objects and one another reveal and demand.

As, Merleau-Ponty saw, Cézanne, like a good phenomenologist, bracketed the epistemological stances implicit in the classical traditions in order to hear the other voices, the other views, those buried within the tradition and those of the ones yet to come.[41] In the same way that a good democrat would "lend" or put her body in service to others, would allow the whole to be born in her speech, her actions, Cézanne allows the landscape to think itself in him. Like his paintings, a good democracy too reveals that its purpose and patterns are developed from within an intimate challenge and relationship with tradition and with those who are its citizens.

Merleau-Ponty argues that Cézanne begins a new series of experiences, relations, rational acts. Cézanne, like a child, or like a foreigner who has just been naturalized, looks at what is most familiar and expresses surprise or demands an account. Like the child or the foreigner, Cézanne awakens us to something: "It is not enough for a painter like Cézanne, an artist, or a philosopher, to create and express an idea; they must also awaken the experiences which will make their idea take root in the consciousness of others."[42] Cézanne awakens us to a new idea or to a new interpretation of an old idea, and this means that he opens a gap between us and our tradition. By means of this gap, by means of this awakening, Cézanne shocks us. But he not only shocks; he also supports.

Cézanne takes on the role of the flesh. And insofar as he is concerned to awaken us to experiences that confirm his painting, he forms a support and a bridge to further evidence. He makes arguments by making experiences possible, by showing the path through tradition that leads to new insight. He pushes us towards that which is "secondary visibility" for us.

In all of his awakening, support, and bridging, however, Cézanne's painting does not wield authoritarian power, as is clear from the writings of his contemporaries who descried it. Cézanne does not wield but awakens, much as one of our bodies need not use force to awaken another to desire, fear, love, hatred, and so on. In Cézanne's contemporaries and their rejections, however, Merelau-Ponty sees a testament to Cézanne's strength, a fitness for exemplarity. For Merleau-Ponty, the good painter, like the good leader,

> can do no more than construct an image; he must wait for the image to come to life for other people. When it does, the work of art will have united these separate lives; it will no longer exist in only one of them like a stubborn dream or a persistent delirium, nor will it exist only in space as a colored piece of canvas. It will dwell undivided in several minds, with a claim on every possible mind like a perennial acquisition.[43]

The good painting, if it is to reveal the ontology of our embodiment and thereby reflect us towards one another, must appeal to our own nature, to our own experience, but it must do so through an appeal to what we are not yet explicitly for ourselves. That is, the painting must give us the experiences to continue moving towards seeing ourselves through its reflected light, towards becoming what the painter has revealed us already to be and to see in one another. Painters do not just re-create the embodiment of the past – they anticipate the way our embodiment pushes into the future on the basis of our histories and our commitments.

For Merleau-Ponty, painters like Cézanne in their manner of anticipation redefine what a work means: "the accomplished work is thus not the work which exists in itself like a thing, but the work which *reaches its viewer* and invites him to *take up the gesture which created it*, skipping the intermediaries."[44] Such painting is not the creation of commodities for the market, works of art in the objectified sense, but the elucidation of the viewer's perceptions, the creation of an experience and gesture that allows for a community between the world of the painter and the experience of the viewer.

Cézanne's painting, according to Merleau-Ponty, is an invitation to bodily movement, to "gestures." It is mediation, a form, which calls person to person, body to body, by allowing itself to fade from view. It is a thing, Cézanne's painting, that immediately enacts the flesh, a thing that is at once the inclination to grow in the recognition of the meaning of embodiment. As such, his painting is more the instigation towards self-governance than it is a thing.

V. Cézanne Cannot Paint Again: Long Live Cézanne

Cézanne's art indicates to us the role of ourselves as viewers and perceivers and the role of ourselves as caught up in an anonymous web of the visible. It allows us to emerge as critical subjects, to gain finer purchase on our experience of shape and colour, and also to recognize that we are located by a field of perception, art, and industry that we cannot comprehend or control. That is, Cézanne returns us in a visceral way to the fact that all logic, all motivation for thought, derives from intercorporeality, from the perceptual experience of embodiment and flesh.

This double-placement of the viewer by Cézanne's art, this putting us in play as both personal subjects and anonymous members of a field, calls to mind the experience of the democratic citizen. The democratic citizen cannot ever hope to exchange places with every other citizen; no one citizen can be assured of ruling at any one time. Furthermore, the anonymity that sustains and furthers the emergence of individual subjects is far too complicated (because implicit and total) to be grasped by the subjects who emerge out of (and back into) it. The business, then, of taking turns in ruling, the business of emerging and re-emerging, is just, as Derrida might claim, the impossible.[45]

Although a democratic politics appears as the impossible, however, we are still capable of pursuing this politics by means of the kinds of bodies that we are. What decides whether we can pursue this impossibility is the manner in which we interrogate what we are as agents, as perceivers. If we, as Cézanne did for Merleau-Ponty, interrogate our body as flesh in a rigorous manner, we may find that we have an ability to impart flesh to politics, to impart politics to flesh, without ever giving up the need for more bodily and political work.[46]

Again we turn to the character of the body as both ruling and being ruled. The body such as we live it is ruling, in the midst of the world, and it brings things close by tearing itself away from them. The body such as we live it is also ruled: "It is caught in the fabric of the world, and its cohesion is that of a thing."[47] To be a body is thus to live (without necessarily knowing) both sides of ruling and being ruled at the same time. To be a body is to be that which occurs when "between the see-er and the visible, between touching and touched, between one eye and the other, between hand and hand a kind of crossover occurs."[48] To be a body is to be between – to be intersubjective, to be intercorporeal.[49] To be a body is to be a crossover.

As a crossover, our body establishes intentional structures that surpass it. One hand crosses over into the other hand. One hand does not stay locked in itself. The viewer passes into the painting ... and vice versa. The viewer does not stay at home, behind her eyes. Rather, the body's openings to the world immediately reveal a shared exercise, a mutual calling forth of higher levels of interaction: "Quality, light, color, depth, which are there before us, are there only because they awaken an echo in our bodies and because the body welcomes them."[50] We are ruled – echoes are awakened before we are awake to them. We rule – we welcome them, these colours, this world, and we respond to them and create something important within the interstices we occupy. Politics, the working out of what these qualities and their echoes mean and what overarching unity lies implicit within them, is an inescapable component of bodily life in its enigmatic space of "between" and its time of "crossover."

One way to see the political implication of living one's body as "crossover" is to examine painting as Merleau-Ponty does. As he describes the work of Cézanne, we begin to see in painting a posture that expresses our own bodily structure as political. For the painter lends[51] his body to the world, and in doing so, he allows himself to be ruled by it. The painter submits himself to rule, however, in order to rule in turn, in order to change that world and that body by making world and body attend to themselves.

The painter paints, then, because of a fundamental and "extraordinary overlapping"[52] of the visible world and her motor world, the overlaying of the eyes and the power of motion, the overlaying of her flesh and the flesh of the world. Painting is possible, as is any perception, because of "the fact that my body simultaneously sees and is seen. That which looks at all things can also look at itself and recognize, in what it sees, the reversibility, the 'other side' of its power of looking."[53] Painting is the possibility, one of the most sophisticated possibilities, that the very structure of the body was calling for, since painting uses this enigmatic structure in order to re-present *that same structure*, to make it more explicit, to extend it and to learn from it.

This logic of the body, and its self-enactment in a certain kind of painting, should be what compels us to seek democracy as the best form of government. First, the character of my body as both seeing and being seen appears to demand a governmental structure that is adequate to it, namely, one in which I am both governing and being governed. And second, the character of my body as one of reproductive and finite life demands a process of succession, inasmuch as I must pass on the power of vision and governance to others.

Merleau-Ponty shows how this second point, that of the necessity of succession, is part of the art of painting when he describes how painting in general requires a succession of painters:

> The domination of the many by the one in the history of painting, *like that domination which we have encountered in the functioning of the perceiving body*, does not swallow up succession into an eternity. On the contrary it *insists upon succession*; it needs it at the same time that it establishes it in meaning. And there is more than just an analogy between the two problems: it is the expressive operation of the body, begun by the least perception, that develops into painting and art.[54]

It is because a notion of succession occurs in bodily life, in passing from birth to procreation to death, and in the very activity of perception as it frees an object from the horizon and allows it to fall back there again, that painting itself, that bodily process of bodily recognition and representation, must also be a succession. A painter can be imitated, her paintings can be written about; and thus she can and must be surpassed by those who understood what she was doing better than she did.

In the tradition of democracy, like that of painting, those who rule are to sediment themselves, must will that sedimentation,[55] must will their own eventual overcoming and domination, in order for this meaning that is rooted in the very structure of perceptual embodiment to have its effect, in order for flesh to come into view. As a child learns to hold its head upright and to pull itself up by its arms to stand and then to walk, as we naturally synthesize multiple perspectives and multiple sense organs into a single, many-layered experience of the same thing, the painter and the democratic citizen *must* will that the organizational gestures they inaugurate become the embodied habits of the communities they inaugurate. If such is not possible, if the future painters and the future citizens do not act according to and as supporting what they have opened up, then they have not painted or ruled well.

VI. The Painter and Politician

Merelau-Ponty's account of the painter, who is exemplified in Cézanne, remains cautious in its politics. Speaking for – or as one might also say *representing* – the painter, the philosopher who governs says that what the painter meant was that

> others will judge what I have done, because I painted in the realm of the visible and spoke for those who have ears – but neither art nor politics consists in pleasing or flattering them. What they expect of the artist or of the politician is that he draw them toward values in which they will only later recognize their values. The painter or the politician moulds others much more often than he follows them ... No his concern is with others who have become such that he is able to *live with them*.[56]

In these words, in this speaking for the artist, Merleau-Ponty seems to know, in his descriptions of aesthetic politics, that a phenomenological democracy would be difficult, since, like the decision of a philosopher to speak on behalf of a painter, and like painting itself, a just government "simply adds to my obligations as a solitary person to understand situations other than my own and to create a path between my life and that of others, that is, to express myself."[57] My embodiment puts me not in the position of one who can rule absolutely, since my body in its structure belies this possibility, but of one who can at best create situations that do something meaningful with embodiment.

The best democracy, in terms of the citizens who know well the demands of both ruling and being ruled, remembers always the silent, concealed voices who are not yet able to rule. Democracy when it is done well never removes itself from the silence of the others. Just as our representatives are required to remain tied to us and to our speech that is not spoken and not voted, so too "no language ever wholly frees itself from the precariousness of the silent forms of expression, reabsorbs its own contingency, and melts away to make the things themselves appear."[58] Our politics would be less contradictory and more truly democratic if our speech bore within it the signs of our silent modes of expression, our paintings, and our literature.

The painter who gives her life to the world, who lends her body to the act of intersection with others, knows that the logic of perception, that which enables us to see depth and possibility, is thus the way things call to us as each having something like rights, having an intertwined interdependence. Cézanne painted according to this logic, painted our intimacy with things and with one another as the very possibility of each thing to come to visibility. If Cézanne painted this logic, since it is what the things naturally demand of us in our relation to them, surely a politics which did that would also be beautiful?

Aristotle in the *Politics* says that the beautiful state is the one that "combines magnitude with good order."[59] And this divine power, this combination of the many with the one,[60] which Aristotle borrows from aesthetics, which Aristotle uses to link politics to aesthetics, is this not the power that lives within and gives us over to our bodies and their intersection with the world? Is not that which most beautifully combines ruling and being ruled, magnitude and order, the body itself in its flesh and reflection, in its intersubjectivity and intercorporeality? Is not the model of good order that which does what is natural, what is divinely inspired in the very intertwining of seeing and being seen?[61]

We can only do or speak what we *are*. And the only way to live more politically, to live more justly, is to become more fully what we are; that is, in terms of phenomenology, to be who we are means to be open to experiencing differently the tension that is embodied life.[62]

Conclusion

Merleau-Ponty, in a review of Sartre's *The Flies*, asks: "How can it be that the work itself is able to draw a public that the critic would like to turn away?"[63] That which lived experience, lived bodies, artists and politicians, can accomplish, even with the best of intentions, is finite. And these finite accomplishments must be offered to anonymity and the dangers that anonymity holds for succession, regeneration, permanence. There is nothing certain about a politics that arises from an intertwining of anonymity and reflection, flesh and body. There is nothing certain (nor necessarily pleasant) about being immersed together with anonymous others whom one must will as interchangeable with oneself when it comes to power – both in ruling and in expressing. After all, it is never just one newborn, one immigrant, one soldier at a time. There are innumerable ones, and their emergence takes place both as a group and as individuals. There are always too many places, too many orientations, too many exchanges for ruling to take place, for being ruled to be possible. Yet the impossible demands of exchange are what democracy mirrors when it mirrors the structure of intertwined flesh, of flesh and lived bodies.

In the same review of Sartre's play, Merleau-Ponty further notes that "the onlooker who gives himself up to the drama can 'perceive' the greatness of a theme and grasp the author's intentions in one deft move."[64] The power to "give oneself up to," to agree to be ruled so that one may rule, may identify, so that one may draw forth the moving line, the overarching theme – this is the power that flesh possesses, the bleeding into and out of the play or the painting or the governance. The very discomfiture of the flesh, then, which never loses its nodes of lived bodies and never fully releases them, is the very possibility of stabilizing it. The very *écart* is the hope for one's stances gaining purchase when addressed appropriately to the others with whom one lives but who remain, for the most part, only peripherally visible.

It is to those on the periphery, and here one might recall Winnicott's discussion of the child's burgeoning drawings, that democratic politics demands to be addressed. For democratic politics is about turning the periphery into the ruling members, turning the masses into educated leaders. And there is already something, even in the drawing of the child, of a "deft move."

NOTES

1 Michael Smith argues that "we often find in Merleau-Ponty a more slipping grasp – argument by persuasion, by evocative suggestion" (Smith, "Merleau-Ponty's Aesthetics," 211).

2 It is in these pieces on art that I see Merleau-Ponty claiming, as Thomas Busch does, that "reason is inseparable from a call to fraternity imbedded within body and language themselves" and that "ethics and politics are grounded in the expressive, communicative self" (Busch, "Husserl and Merleau-Ponty," 97).

3 Coole, "Thinking Politically," 23. Coole also argues in this paper that for Merleau-Ponty "the radical challenge was to rethink the political in terms of *intersubjectivity*. This must entail something far more fundamental than placing rational individuals within a communicative situation: what is

needed is an ontology of this interworld, in order to grasp the way rational forms are engendered within the thick, adverse space between subjects (25). The "interworld" and the "thick, adverse space" Coole mentions are, I believe, those of flesh, of intercorporeality, and it is the purpose of this chapter to show how the body is the source of political efficacy.

4 That Merleau-Ponty performs this ontology and this political development of the logic of intersubjectivity and intercorporeality within *aesthetic* analyses is something that Coole has seen and briefly mentioned even in her earlier article: "The phenomenologist who reconstructs these lived meanings from the ambiguities of collective life is not therefore locked in gratuitous imaginings and relativism; nor is she aiming for a true representation. Rather, she composes them 'as an experienced pianist deciphers an unknown piece of music' through communicating with its mode of being" (Coole, "Thinking Politically," 27). In her more recent book, particularly in the final chapter, Coole does comment specifically on Merleau-Ponty's treatment of Cézanne. See especially Coole, *Merleau-Ponty and Modern Politics*, 227ff.

5 Aristotle, "Politics," 1277b15.

6 Ibid., 1317b1.

7 Winnicott, *The Family*, 23.

8 Ibid., 23.

9 McBride maintains that Sartre attributes Merleau-Ponty's ontology, and its emphasis on "perceptual faith," intersubjectivity, and intercorporeality, to the fact that Merleau-Ponty "never recovered from his childhood" (McBride, "Merleau-Ponty and Sartre," 65). It seems that for Sartre, Merleau-Ponty never broke from or diffused the contingent happiness of his childhood – or at least did not do so enough.

10 Or, perhaps more accurately, within the painting lies, fully preserved, the appeal and networks of a bodily life that calls forth the bodily structure of the living viewers to itself.

11 I take visibility as the most relevant sense to speak about when talking about painting. But I believe that Merleau-Ponty has in mind all five senses as revealing the lived-body and flesh as intertwined. On this point, Maxine Sheets-Johnstone in *Primacy of Movement* comments on how Merleau-Ponty's account of Cézanne as "thinking in painting" in "Eye and Mind" entails not just perception (or vision) but also movement: "perception is interlaced with movement, and to the point, we might add, where it is impossible to separate out where perception begins and movement ends or where movement begins and perception ends" (Sheets-Johnstone, *Primacy of Movement*, 494).

12 Merleau-Ponty, *VI* 199[152].
13 In the section titled "Others and the Human World," Merleau-Ponty claims this point as follows: "just as the parts of my body together form a system, the other's body and my own are a single whole" (*PP* 410[370]).
14 Merleau-Ponty, *VI* 193[147].
15 Merleau-Ponty, *VI* 187–8[142].
16 Merleau-Ponty, *VI* 187[142].
17 Gary Madison notes that the vision of the "flesh" as reversibility of viewed and viewer, of touched and touching, grounds Merleau-Ponty's ethics and politics: "The 'ground' of Merleau-Ponty's universalist ethics is that most remarkable feature of the flesh (which in fact serves to define it) that he referred to as 'reversibility'" (Madison, "Ethics and Politics," 164). This reversibility implies a kind of standing-in-for-one-another. And if I am to involve myself in a government that does justice to my role as the location in which the world sees itself seeing itself, as the lived reversibility of self with self and self with other, then I ought to involve myself in democracy. As Madison argues, "Merleau-Ponty's politics would almost certainly have amounted to a theoretical defense of democratic praxis" (173–4).
18 Merleau-Ponty, *VI* 195[148].
19 Merleau-Ponty, *VI* 195[148].
20 Merleau-Ponty, like Husserl before him in the Fifth Cartesian Meditation, calls attention to transition as an experienceable relation: "I experience – and as often as I wish – the transition and the metamorphosis of the one experience into the other, and it is only *as though* the hinge between them, solid, unshakeable, remained irremediably hidden from me" (Merleau-Ponty, *VI* 194–5[148]).
21 Kerry Whiteside argues that Merleau-Ponty's emphasis on dialogue and the interrogative mode of discourse serves "to make them recognize that universality and particularity, determinism and choice, non-sense and sense are all intrinsic to human existence. The challenge we face is then to devise a political theory of existence that comprehends these dichotomies rather than denies them" (Whiteside, *Merleau-Ponty and the Foundation*, 306–7).
22 Bernard Flynn argues that Merleau-Ponty sees the agency of the world as an interrogative function: "Merleau-Ponty proposes to interrogate a world which is thought neither as the 'true world' nor as the debris left by its having been turned into a fable, but rather as a world which itself exists *in the mode of interrogation*" (Flynn, "Merleau-Ponty and Nietzsche," 14).
23 Coole argues similarly: "what saves Merleau-Ponty's selves from fragmenting like Lyotard's postmodern ciphers is that within this mobile

field … there are also lived experiences that sediment over time to sustain visible forms whose memories and practices congeal into the enduring styles that are coiled over themselves" (Coole, *Merleau-Ponty and Modern Politics*, 248).

24 Coole notes that the flesh is too "tender" to sustain sufficient political weight, so she proposes to enlarge the flesh to be a field of forces, as Foucault and even Merleau-Ponty might do. At stake in surpassing flesh for a field of forces is the sustenance of subjectivity: "if flesh nurtures emergent singularities, the field sustains their liberties within its open horizons" (Coole, *Merleau-Ponty and Modern Politics*, 234). Nevertheless, it must be emphasized that flesh for Coole is the complement of force and is, flesh itself is, quite political: "For in politics, the tenderness, vulnerability, and mortality of the flesh is the very stuff of material power relations and it invites the philosopher, as well as the actor, to plunge into their analysis, judgment and transformation" (Coole, *Merleau-Ponty and Modern Politics*, 229).

25 Simone de Beauvoir claims that Maman "clung with her eyes to the world" (de Beauvoir, *A Very Easy Death*, 69).

26 I have argued in "The Life of the Life-World" that Husserl's conception of the transcendental ego is one of anonymous subjectivity whose flesh *is* the life-world. I see Merleau-Ponty as doing something similar in his connection of lived body and flesh.

27 Art and politics and philosophy must take up human togetherness, must take up any given structure of perception or of history or of political community, as a reflection on a text that is neither fully given nor fully exhausted. We rule only by preparing to rule, by investigating the given structures for actual and possible interpretative stances, by submitting to the task of entering into previous conversations so as to understand them and to comment on, ignore, or reorient them. Research thus is the way in which I hold off having something to say until I actually must and do. Research is learning what I intend to claim by working through and working with the others with whom I share the structure.

28 Merleau-Ponty, *VI* 192[146].

29 Aristotle, *Nicomachean Ethics*, 1161b10.

30 Merleau-Ponty, *VI* 193[147].

31 "For Merleau-Ponty, the question 'What does it mean to see?' is the fundamental philosophical question; he poses it even when the ostensible subject of discussion is language, thought, history, or politics … Painting, as the visual rather than conceptual interrogation of vision, is for him a guide to the re-orientation of thought" (Fóti, "The Evidences of Paintings," 137).

32 Merleau-Ponty, "Cézanne's Doubt," 12.

33 Ibid., 13.
34 Ibid., 14.
35 Olivier Mongin notes that "Merleau-Ponty attempts to conceive of an active temporality in which the one and the other, the same and the other, do not cancel one another out. A temporality in which coexistence would be inseparable from dissonance: neither submission to the one, nor dispersal, scattering … which always returns to the same" (Mongin, "Since Lascaux," 253). Painting, which assumes a different temporality, can disagree with itself, with its tradition, with us. Painting can affront us, yet still it can include us. How can we take this structure into our way of seeing the freedom of speech? How can we educate our citizens to speak from such a balanced, tenuous view?
36 Jacques Derrida's *The Truth in Painting* begins by attempting to interrogate a comment by Cézanne: "I owe you the truth in painting and I will tell it to you" (2). Its beginning is one that is shrouded in conditions: "I cannot dominate the situation, or translate it, or describe it … I would always have to renew, reproduce, and reintroduce into the formalizing economy of my tale – overloaded each time with some supplement – the very indecision which I was trying to reduce" (2). This reintroduction of indecision, this inability to state what painting is, what this painting is about, once and for all, is a way of representing, perhaps, the democracy-to-come that Derrida speaks about in *Rogues* and other works. Democracy is the situation of a formalizing economy of meaning that can never dominate the situation it necessarily seeks to delimit – and has given up seeking dominance as far as possible.
37 Merleau-Ponty, "Cézanne's Doubt," 15.
38 Ibid., 15.
39 Ibid., 17.
40 Ibid., 17.
41 Wayne J. Froman links Merleau-Ponty's aesthetics and politics around the notion of "flesh" and natality and argues as follows: "The issue of natality is critical for Merleau-Ponty specifically because his effort was directed to the question of *how the self can speak, but also what it may mean for the self to do without doing violence to the other*, without infringing upon the other or without letting the other infringe upon the self" (Froman, "At the Limits," 25).
42 Merleau-Ponty, "Cézanne's Doubt," 19.
43 Ibid., 20.
44 Merleau-Ponty, "Indirect Language," 88.
45 "If *correspondence* is another name for an *indivisible* community of the soul between lovers, why should it harbor this taste of death, of the impossible, of the aporia?" (Derrida, *Politics of Friendship*, 179).

46 It must still be the case, as Coole argues, that Merleau-Ponty reveals "a phenomenology of agentic capacities that explains experiential motivation and thereby imparts more flesh to everyday politics" (Coole, *Merleau-Ponty and Modern Politics*, 238).
47 Merleau-Ponty, "Eye and Mind," 125.
48 Ibid., 127. See also Hugh Silverman: "The domain in which he [Cézanne] operates is the space of difference between Being as a fullness and Being as sheer multiplicity" (Silverman, "Cézanne's Mirror Stage," 269). Between the one and the many, democracy operates.
49 Merleau-Ponty argues this as follows: "Hence my body can include elements drawn from the body of another, just as my substance passes into them; man is a mirror for man" (Merleau-Ponty, "Eye and Mind," 130). We live as reflections of one another, drawing our meaning and our significance from one another. And painting is simply the expression of this intercorporeality, this intersubjectivity.
50 Merleau-Ponty, "Eye and Mind," 125.
51 Hugh Silverman speaks about this notion of lending: "by lending his body to it, standing before it with his easel and palette, Cézanne would lean forward toward his canvas and render visible what the profane eye would not see" (Silverman, "Cézanne's Mirror Stage," 269). Lending – and not at interest – is this not what we do with our bodies when we speak on behalf of others? Do we not lend them our ears?
52 See Jacques Taminaux's argument: "In addition to the overlapping of the particular and the general, the perceived attests to a surprising overlapping of our fellow beings and the 'I,' a pluralistic interweaving of subjects" (Taminaux, "The Thinker and Painter," 281).
53 Merleau-Ponty, "Eye and Mind," 124.
54 Merleau-Ponty, "Indirect Language," 106–7.
55 I have in mind here Husserl's references to sedimentation in the *Crisis of the European Sciences* and elsewhere. The layers of meaning, which citizens and painters form by virtue of their acts of governance and painting, must pass into the geological formation of an era. They must become part of a whole that, from further up, looks much more like a general style than an individual. Nevertheless, the impact of their individual efforts, their names and memory, can also act as a kind of pressure, causing tectonic shifts, etc.
56 Merleau-Ponty, "Indirect Language," 110–1.
57 Ibid., 112.
58 Ibid., 115.
59 Aristotle, *Politics*, 1326a24.

60 "In the perceived realm, the unity is not heterogeneous to multiplicity; rather it is folded within the multiplicity of the thing and is even required by it" (Taminaux, "The Thinker and Painter," 281). If our perception works this way, and if we are compelled to enact the best we can what we most clearly *are*, then how can our politics not strive to be like our perception, to be like the most sophisticated unity of wholes and parts that we can possibly attain? Another way of saying this: we already are more sophisticated and more democratic in our very life's unity with itself and with the others within the world than any previous politics has been. The need is to move towards that which we already are.

61 For Marjorie Grene, painting shows "the single, equivocal unity of the person" (Grene, "The Aesthetic Dialogue," 224).

62 See Grene, who says that "in painting we have, visible and incarnate, the concrete expression of this tension, this reverberation between sign and signified, meaning and what is meant. This is intentionality, not caught between two unattainable abstractions but *at home*" (Grene, "The Aesthetic Dialogue," 223). Our tension, our embodiment, between ruling and being ruled, is not ultimately some slavery we must bend our nature under but our very system of living. It is natural. It is home.

63 Merleau-Ponty, "On Sartre's *The Flies*," 117.

64 Ibid., 117.

15 Phenomenology as First-Order Perception: Speech, Vision, and Reflection in Merleau-Ponty

LAURA MCMAHON

In *Politics* II.2, Aristotle distinguishes *logos* or speech – nature's gift to human beings – from the cries of animals. He writes:

> Nature, as we often say, makes nothing in vain, and man is the only animal whom she has endowed with the gift of speech. And whereas mere voice is but an indication of pleasure or pain, and is therefore found in other animals (for their nature attains to the perception of pleasure and pain and the intimation of them to one another, and no further), the power of speech is intended to set forth the expedient and the inexpedient, and therefore likewise the just and the unjust. And it is characteristic of man that he alone has any sense of good and evil, of just and unjust, and the like, and the association of living beings who have this sense makes a family and a state.[1]

This passage points us to the awkward manner in which human beings fit into the world of nature. On the one hand, human beings are, like other animals, *of* nature, and it is our biological body – a body that must be maintained and reproduced through nutrition, sleep, and sex – that first perceptually opens us to the surrounding world of nature. On the other hand, human beings have *logos*, which is to say they *take account* of the physical world in which they find themselves in ways that *transform* this physical world in remarkably variable ways.[2] This taking of account does not occur only in practices of explicit reasoning and debate. Rather, as Maurice Merleau-Ponty argues, human behaviour, from its simplest gestures to its most sophisticated artistic and intellectual expressions, "superimposes a virtual or human space over physical space," thus projecting around itself a moral, cultural, and political world.[3]

In this chapter, I explore the essentially *expressive* nature of human existence through a close engagement with Merleau-Ponty's discussions of the nature of expression, perception, and reflection, primarily in his *Phenomenology of Perception*. A central insight of Merleau-Ponty's philosophy is that the manner in which human beings take account of the world of experience – and the manner in which they bring to voice possibilities that remain only latent or "still mute" therein – takes a definitively *embodied* form.[4] By way of our natural bodies, and through such physical bodies of sound, stone, paint, and ink, we transcend our biological existence in order to articulate a meaningful world in dialogue with past and present others.[5] There is something miraculous about this human gift, but it is a miracle, and a gift, that we typically take for granted. For the most part, we think of reality as definitively indifferent to our presence within it, and of our own identities as distinct from the world of things in which we find ourselves. The miraculous nature of expression, as well as our tendency to lose sight of this, is a central concern in Merleau-Ponty's study of the nature of language in the chapter of *Phenomenology of Perception* titled "The Body as Expression, and Speech." Section I of this chapter explores the distinction Merleau-Ponty draws there between "first-" and "second-order speech." First-order speech is expression that is alive to its own powers to initiate new domains of significance – new "worlds" – within the natural and cultural world in which it finds itself. Second-order speech, by contrast, covers over this fact, taking itself to be operating in a world already "spoken" (*PP* 224[189]). In Section II, I engage primarily with the Introduction to *Phenomenology of Perception* in order to argue that perception itself is already a "nascent *logos*": from the moment we open our eyes, we are engaged in a creative, albeit typically unnoticed, taking account of the world.[6] I argue that, thus, the distinction between first- and second-order speech is at play at the level of perception itself, and that by making ourselves alive to the creative nature of our own perception, we can effect different ways of seeing the world and our own implication within it. In Section III, I argue that such "first-order perception" is the practice of phenomenology itself. Engaging primarily with the Preface to *Phenomenology of Perception,* I discuss the power of what Merleau-Ponty calls "radical reflection" to take us back to the roots of our own reflective activity in the world of experience itself. I conclude with a discussion of the nature of a properly phenomenological – a "first-order" – hermeneutical engagement with the history of philosophy.

I. Speech

In "The Body as Expression, and Speech," Merleau-Ponty argues that the phenomenon of speech is neither merely physiological or biological – like the animal's cry of pleasure or pain – nor purely intellectual, as if it were merely the transparent "clothing" of the mind's thinking to which it gives voice.[7] Against either such view, Merleau-Ponty argues that speech is indeed a bodily, material phenomenon, but one that is the very vehicle in which thinking is accomplished. [8] To grasp the sense of this claim, let us consider the phenomenon of writing. In sitting down to write a poem, a meaningful letter to a friend, or a philosophical essay, one will likely feel a strong urge to express something important and to express it well, but without knowing exactly what one is going to say. Merleau-Ponty writes: "The thinking subject is in a sort of ignorance of his thoughts so long as he has not formulated them for himself, or even spoken or written them, as is shown through the example of so many writers who begin a book without knowing just what they are going to include" (*PP* 216–17[183]).

Even if one has drawn up a detailed plan of execution, one can find that one nevertheless does not quite "catch on" in one's words to the proper embodiment and direction of one's urgent, but still indeterminate, thought.[9] Alternatively, one can feel oneself caught up in the perhaps surprising movement of the expression itself, finding oneself rushing to keep up with the developing "organism of words" that seems, as if with a life of its own, to at once capture and to reveal what it is that one is trying to say (*PP* 222[188]). In either case, we see that the thought does not already exist somewhere prior to being expressed, but struggles to come out in the words that will be its body if it is to exist at all.

We can observe something similar in the phenomenon of reading a difficult text, that is, a text for which we do not already possess all the terms needed to understand it. In our attempts to understand what the text is trying to say, we begin by attempting to "feel" our way into it, seeking the moment when we will be "let in," so to speak, and swept up in the meaning and direction of the words themselves. Merleau-Ponty writes:

> Each word of a difficult text awakens thoughts in us that belonged to us in advance, but these significations sometimes combine into a new thought that reworks them all, and we are transported to the heart of the book and connect with the source ... In understanding others, the problem is

> always indeterminate, because only the solution to the problem will make the givens retroactively appear as convergent, and only the central motive of a philosophy, once understood, gives the philosopher's texts the value of adequate signs. (*PP* 218[184])

In seeking to understand another's thought, we must give ourselves over to the words themselves, preparing ourselves through persistent labour to the *Gestalt* shift that will "rework" the disparate words of the text, and the disparate thoughts they invoke in us, into a meaningful whole that allows us to see things, as it were, with new eyes.[10] As Merleau-Ponty argues, the successful operation of expression "instills [its] signification in the writer or the reader like a new sense organ, and it opens a new dimension or a new field to our experience" (*PP* 222–3[188]).

These descriptions of writing and reading point us to the deep kinship of linguistic expressions with the emotional expressions of art. While we might initially think that a thought or an idea can be separated from the words in which it is expressed, or translated without remainder into other words, we can be under no such illusions with a piece of music or a painting. Merleau-Ponty writes: "The musical signification of the sonata is inseparable from the sounds that carry it: prior to having heard it, no analysis allows us to anticipate it … During the performance, the sounds are not merely the 'signs' of the sonata; rather, the sonata is there through them and descends into them" (*PP* 223[188]). Merleau-Ponty argues that thought does not exist prior to its expression any more than the sonata exists prior to its sounds; what we mean to say comes to life only in the act of expression itself, and it is thus an *attempt* and a *gesture* – something to be accomplished – rather than a fully determinate reality that exists prior to being expressed. Furthermore, even after it has successfully come into its own in embodied form, the meaning of a piece of writing cannot be fully excised from its expression or simply translated without remainder, as is demonstrated by the difficulties with translating a poem or a work of philosophy from one language to another.[11]

It is in an emotional, gestural, and creative sense that Merleau-Ponty argues we should seek the origins of language. Reverberating with the passage from Aristotle's *Politics* quoted in the Introduction above, Merleau-Ponty argues that "speech is the excess of our existence beyond natural being" (*PP* 239[203]). He argues that it is the lived body which is the first and most basic vehicle of expression, and which cannot *but* be expressive and communicative in each of its words, gestures, and behaviours. He writes:

> For man, everything is constructed and everything is natural, in the sense that there is no single word or behavior that does not owe something to mere biological being – and, at the same time, there is no word or behavior that does not break free from animal life, that does not deflect vital behaviors from their direction [*sens*] through a sort of *escape* and a genius for ambiguity that might well serve to define man. (*PP* 230[195])

A few basic phenomena of bodily expressiveness will serve to illustrate this definitive "genius for ambiguity."[12]

First, we can observe that speech is simultaneously a motor function and, miraculously, in the meanings it expresses, irreducible *to* this motor functioning.[13] As Merleau-Ponty writes, "the contraction of the throat, the sibilant emission of air between the tongue and the teeth, a certain manner of playing with our body suddenly allows itself to be invested with a *figurative sense* and signifies this externally" (*PP* 235[200]). When we hear another speak, we are not attuned to the bodily changes in her throat and mouth, and we do not hear the material sound of her words as such; rather, we are transported through these changes and these sounds to the worldly meanings she intends. More originally than it expresses this thought or that, speech has a *gestural* significance: it makes use of the body and of sound to initiate a world of human meaning.[14]

Second, we can observe our "genius for ambiguity" in the apparently simple act of pointing. Pointing, which is intimately tied up with early childhood language acquisition, uses a finger or other body part, such as the head, to designate something of interest in the external world to another, and thus opens up a new dimension in the shared world.[15] In "An Unpublished Text by Merleau-Ponty: A Prospectus of His Work," Merleau-Ponty writes: "This insertion of our factual situation as a particular case within the system of other possible situations begins as soon as we *designate* a point in space with our finger. For this pointing gesture, which animals do not understand, supposes that we are already installed in virtual space – at the end of the line prolonging our finger in centrifugal and cultural space."[16] When someone points something out, her interlocutor looks not at the pointing finger but at the thing pointed at, such that the sign – like the sound of "the sibilant emission of air between the tongue and the teeth" in speech – "disappears" in favour of the thing signified. Pointing is a phenomenon that presumes the capacity for communication and for objectivity, in that the one pointing must tacitly assume the stance and viewpoint of her interlocutor in order to point something out to him, and the interlocutor must in turn see the pointing gesture *as* a meaningful gesture intended to show something to him.

A third bodily phenomenon that reveals our "genius for ambiguity" is that of the expression of emotion. In the reddening of a friend's face or the shrillness of his voice, I am in the presence not of expanding capillaries or "the sibilant emission of air between tongue and teeth," but of his anger, yet the anger is expressed nowhere *but* in and through these embodied changes.[17] While we might think of such emotional gestures as merely "natural" signs, as if, as Merleau-Ponty writes, "the anatomical organization of our body made definite gestures correspond to specific 'states of consciousness,'" personal and cultural differences in the expression of emotions should reveal to us that "there are no natural signs for man" (*PP* 229[194]). Merleau-Ponty writes:

> When angry, the Japanese person smiles, whereas the Westerner turns red and stamps his foot, or even turns pale and speaks with a shrill voice. Having the same sense organs and the same nervous system is not sufficient for the same emotions to take on the same signs in two different conscious subjects. What matters is the manner in which they make use of their body, the simultaneous articulation of their body and their world in the emotion. (*PP* 230[195])

Like speech and like pointing, emotional gestures are ways of projecting on the outside an interpersonal and a cultural world. Thus speech, pointing, and emotional gesticulation are all forms of bodily transcendence and freedom with respect to our natural being.[18]

Finding the roots of language in the bodily life of speech, gesture, and emotion compels us to notice the essentially contingent, and hence essentially creative, nature of human expression. As we will see further in Section III, certain expressions, once expressed, are lived with all the weight of necessity, even though they never *had* to come into being.[19] The contingency of any *given* expression, however, points us to the deeper contingency – and the deeper "miracle" – that there *is* contingent and creative expression at all (*PP* 239[204]). Merleau-Ponty writes: "We must recognize as an ultimate fact this open and indefinite power of signifying – that is, of simultaneously grasping and communicating a sense – by which man transcends himself through his body and his speech toward a new behavior, toward others, or toward his own thought" (*PP* 236[200]). By some "irrational power," there are animals whose movements and speech, while always rooted in nature, can never be fully enclosed *by* this natural being, but rather *take account* of the world in bodily, creative, and intellectual expression (*PP* 231[195]).

While we ought to be struck by a certain wonder at the miraculousness of the fact that we are beings capable of "simultaneously grasping and communicating a sense," everyday language works precisely to cover over the primordial opening in being that is human bodily expression. Merleau-Ponty lays out the distinction between first- and second-order speech in a footnote in "The Body as Expression, and Speech," where he writes: "Of course, there are reasons to distinguish between an authentic speech, which formulates for the first time, and a second-order expression, a speech about speech that makes up the usual basis of empirical language. Only the first is identical with thought" (*PP* 217–18n2[530n6], translation modified).[20]

Second-order speech deals in ready-made, banal meanings, and in the process covers over the fact that it is itself a gesture and a manner of projecting around itself, whether it knows it or not, "the world according to man" (*PP* 229[194]). Merleau-Ponty writes in the Preface to *Phenomenology of Perception*:

> There is not a single word or human gesture – not even those habitual or distracted ones – that does not have a signification. I believed I was keeping quiet due to fatigue, or some politician believed he had merely uttered a platitude, and just like that my silence or his utterance take on a sense, because my weariness or his recourse to some ready-made formula are not accidental: they express a certain disinterest and thus are still a certain taking up of a position with regard to the situation. (*PP* 19[lxxxiii])

While second-order speech does not take itself to properly *do* anything, first-order speech – be it the first words of a child, or of the lover who finds words for her emotion, or an unprecedented artistic or philosophical work – is alive to the manner in which it opens a new field or "world" within being, and thus bears witness to the marvel *that* we speak, and that there is a world of indeterminate and unfinished meaning, to begin with. First-order speech struggles to say something for which there are not yet words and thus bears witness to the miraculous nature of expressive life as such, which breaks the "primordial silence" that continuously persists beneath "the noise of words" (*PP* 224[190]).

We can take as an example of first-order speech the efforts at expression of the painter Paul Cézanne, which Merleau-Ponty explores in his essay "Cézanne's Doubt." Merleau-Ponty argues here that Cézanne, although educated and practised in techniques of perspective and colour and thus drawing on an entire history of painting, "speaks as the first man spoke and paints as if no one had ever painted before."[21] Cézanne thus "modulates upon this keyboard of acquired significations" in order to create an unprecedented vision of things in colour on canvas (*PP* 227[192]).[22] What is this experience like for the painter? Echoing our description above of the writer chasing after her words, Merleau-Ponty writes: "'Conception' cannot precede 'execution.' Before expression, there is nothing but a vague fever, and only the work itself, completed and understood, is proof that there is *something* rather than *nothing* to be said" (*CD* 24–5[19], translation modified).

The success of the work retroactively brings together and thereby justifies the first tentative words composed or brush strokes ventured; a new "world" has appeared, from a sea of indeterminacy, in determinate, bodily form.[23] Merleau-Ponty writes:

> Because he returns to the source of silent and solitary experience on which culture and the exchange of ideas have been built in order to know it, the artist launches his work just as a man once launched the first word, not knowing whether it will be anything more than a shout, whether it can detach itself from the flow of individual life in which it originates and give the independent existence of an identifiable *meaning*. (*CD* 25[19]).

It is only in their successful, although ultimately contingent, transformation of an indeterminate material existence into meaningful, original figures that the cries of animal life become words, and that nascent thoughts or conceptions can take on a life of their own – and thus a life for present and future others – in shared existence.[24]

But in time, the most original emotional, artistic, and intellectual expressions become sedimented in an unsurprising storehouse of acquired cultural meanings. Merleau-Ponty writes:

> We live in a world where speech is already *instituted*. We possess in ourselves already formed significations for all of these banal words. They only give rise in us to second-order thoughts, which are in turn translated into other words that require no genuine effort of expression from us, and that will demand no effort of comprehension from our listeners ... The linguistic

> and intersubjective world no longer causes us any wonder, we no longer distinguish it from the world itself, and we reflect within a world already spoken and speaking ... Constituted speech, such as it plays out in everyday life, assumes that the decisive step of expression has been accomplished. (*PP* 224[189–90])

Original paintings become so many mass-produced images, penetrating philosophical insights become chess pieces in "intellectual" competitions, and both the first-order expressions that these things *were*, and our own responsibility *as* expressive beings, are forgotten.

We will further explore the nature of such sedimentation and the "second-order thoughts" to which it gives rise in Section III. But first, let us turn to the manner in which perception is already a primordial kind of expression, and the manner in which Merleau-Ponty's distinction between first- and second-order at speech is already at play in the manner in which we come to look at things.

II. Perception

In Section I we discussed the miraculous nature of human *logos*, which transforms silence into speech and lets it be the case that there was something, rather than nothing, to be said. Next we will see that "the miracle of expression" is not just a gift enjoyed by speaking human beings; it is also at play in the expressive nature of the things themselves. Merleau-Ponty writes in the chapter of *Phenomenology of Perception* titled "The Thing and the Natural World" that "prior to and independently of other people, the thing achieves that miracle of expression: an inner reality which reveals itself externally, a significance which descends into the world and begins its existence there, and which can be fully understood only when the eyes seek it in its own location" (*PP* 369[373]).[25]

We also saw in Section I that no human gesture or word can be understood as merely a natural function; rather, in gesture and in speech the human being transcends herself through her body to project around herself "the world according to man." Here we will see that the situation is analogous for human perception. While it might seem that perception is merely passive, the phenomenology of perception reveals that perception in truth takes the form of a creative dialogue with the things of the world that, as a "nascent *logos*," it projects around itself. Perception, like expression, *does* something and is thus itself already a kind of "language" confronted with the task of meaningfully articulating the world, and, in the process, meaningfully articulating its own creative powers. As James Elkins writes in *The Object Stares Back*, "seeing alters the thing that is seen and transforms the seer. Seeing is metamorphosis, not mechanism."[26]

We can see how this is so by turning to a basic descriptive premise of *Gestalt* psychology and of *Phenomenology of Perception* – namely, that the most basic "unit" of perception is a figure against a background.[27] What we see, touch, taste, hear, and smell is not mere sense data, which must subsequently – and problematically – be constructed into meaningful wholes, as empiricist accounts of perception hold.[28] Neither, however, is what we see, touch, taste, hear, and smell merely our invariable – our clear and distinct – intellectual representations of things in the world, as intellectualist or rationalist accounts of perception hold.[29] Rather, we perceive things as meaningful "wholes" – as *Gestalten* – whose unities allow us only retrospectively to make sense of the "parts" of which they are constructed – parts that are what they are by virtue of their belonging to a meaningful whole. Merleau-Ponty's description of approaching a ship on the beach captures the manner in which things "take shape" before our eyes in a kind of "dialogue" between the perceiving subject and the perceived object within the indeterminate horizons of the perceptual field.[30] He writes:

> If I am walking on a beach toward a boat that has run aground, and if the funnel or mast merges with the forest that borders the dune, then there will be a moment in which these details suddenly reunite with the boat and become welded to it. As I approached, I did not perceive the resemblances or the proximities that were, in the end, able to reunite with the superstructure of the ship in an unbroken picture. I merely felt that the appearance was about to change, that something was imminent in this tension, as the storm is imminent in the clouds. The spectacle was suddenly reorganized, satisfying my vague expectation. (*PP* 40[17–18])

In the "vague fever" that preceded Cézanne's act of expression, a felt tension called for resolution in the "execution" of the painting, and it is only the (still uncertain) success of this execution that will retroactively bring the "conception" of the painting into existence. In a parallel manner, the perceiving subject discovers what was in front of him all along through the satisfaction of a "vague expectation," which puts the "imminent tension" in the landscape to rest, allowing the funnel and mast to "become welded" to the boat to which they had in fact always belonged.[31] Figures are always suggesting themselves as *something* rather than *nothing* to be seen, but they are only grasped *as* the figures that they are through the approach and perceptual interrogation of a perceiving subject, whose activity renders them determinate within an always *in*determinate – an always "shifting" [*bougé*] and receding – field of perception.[32]

Perception not only engages in an expressive and transformative manner with things in the perceptual field, but simultaneously transforms the perceiver's own capacities for seeing. In our discussion of writing in Section I, we saw the manner in which an "organism" of words takes on a life of its own, calling forth what it is appropriate to say next; and in our discussion of reading, we saw how we must feel our way into the overall movement and direction of the ideas we seek to understand. In each of these cases, understanding is an experience of learning, in that new fields are opened up within our experience, and what it becomes possible for we ourselves to say and to hear is itself transformed. In perception, likewise, what the perceiver is capable of seeing – what she is capable of perceptually "pointing to" in the process of rendering determinate an indeterminate world – is a matter of perceptual *education*.[33] Elkins offers an example of city dwellers in the forest that brings out this point. He writes:

> If a person who has grown up in the city takes a walk in the forest, she will not see very much. I have been told that inner-city children who are taken on trips to the rain forest tend to huddle together: they know that the jungle is full of things, but they can't tell them apart. For all they know, a stinging plant might be right in front of them, or a snake just underfoot. An average city person can certainly enjoy the outdoors; the national parks are jammed with people from large cities. But what do they see? If they can't tell the plants apart and if they don't know the animals and don't recognize geological formations, then they can see only general categories: bird, mountain, stream. Vast amounts will pass them by.[34]

Perceiving or, so to speak, "reading" the diverse figures and rich differences at play in the landscape does not happen automatically. Rather, it is an accomplishment: something that must be learned through educative experiences that open up a "world" of possible things to perceive, be this the "world" of the botanist, the zoologist, the geologist, or the one who has grown up in and become intimately familiar with the flora, fauna, and secret pathways and hiding places of the forest.[35] Through such perceptual accomplishments, the perceiver can see "at a glance" what the uninitiated would grasp not at all or only through deliberate effort.[36] As we learn, our powers of perception are made more subtle and more discriminating, allowing us to see – as with the example of the ship on the beach – figures that were nascently there to be seen all along, or possibilities with which the landscape was formerly only "pregnant."[37]

In its mutually transformative dialogue with the world, perception is thus at once responsive and creative; it is, as Merleau-Ponty writes in *The Visible and the Invisible*, an "inspired exegesis" (*VI* 173[133]). The senses that things have are not imperiously created *by* perception, any more than the successful writer or painter creates by imposing a ready-made plan. Rather, we say that a person *has vision* – or is even a vision-*ary* – when the senses that things themselves have are realized *in* his perception. Echoing his description of reading, Merleau-Ponty writes of perception: "Here the givens of the problem do not exist prior to its solution, and perception is precisely this act that creates, all at once, out of the constellation of the givens, the sense that ties them together. Perception does not merely discover the sense *they have*, but rather, sees to it *that they have a sense*" (*PP* 61[38]).

Perception, then, is a kind of interpretive or hermeneutical work.[38] Its preparation for seeing well requires that, like the textual interpreter, perception be open and alive to the diverse range of meanings already clamouring for recognition in the visual scene, such that, as Merleau-Ponty writes, "finally one cannot say if it is the look or if it is the things that command" (*VI* 173[133]). By the same token, the perceiver finds herself reflected back to herself in what she is able to see in the world of perception: the city dweller finds himself *as* a city dweller in the familiar busy streets, neighbourhoods, and businesses with which he surrounds himself, just as the botanist finds herself *as* a botanist in the diversity of plants, flowers, and trees that stand out to her against the background of the forest and meadow.

We saw in Section I that meaningful thoughts, emotions, and ideas only ever occur in and through embodied expression, and that they are, thus, necessarily characterized by a certain contingency: these expressions did not need to come about, or the nascent thought, emotion, or idea might have found its way into existence in a different bodily form. From this recognition, we arrived at the recognition of the contingency of the sheer fact – the miracle – of expression in general. Now, we can see that the same movement is at play in perception itself. There is a contingency to the rendering determinate of *this* "something" rather than *that* "something" in one and the same indeterminate perceptual field; one's personal and one's cultural perception of things could, as a result of different accidents or with a different history, be otherwise.[39] However, as in the case of expression, the contingency of any given act of perception points to the deeper contingency, and the deeper miracle, of the *fact of* perception itself. Perception is not, any more than expression, a fact that can be accounted for by the natural sciences without begging the question, for the natural sciences are already a way of perceiving or, as Martin Heidegger says, of interpretively "enframing" the world.[40] Merleau-Ponty writes: "There can be no question of describing perception itself as one of the facts that happens in the world, for we can never efface from the picture of the world this lacuna that we are and by which the world itself comes to exist for someone, since perception is the 'flaw' in this 'great diamond'" (*PP* 251–2[215], translation modified). If the world were a closed system, replete in its meanings, there would be no place for the revelatory and creative play of perception *within* the world, which lets there be a world *as such* to begin with.

The perceiver is thus, as Merleau-Ponty argues, a "hollow" or a "fold" in being "that was made and can be unmade" (*PP* 260[223]). From in the midst of the sensible, a power of sensibility – a power to open up new meaningful spaces within the sensible in which the things can be grasped *as* the things that they are – is born.[41] While this miraculous fact of perception ought to fill us with wonder, in the expedience of everyday life we tend, as in the case of language, to forget this originary miracle. Merleau-Ponty writes: "Perception is an *originary* knowledge. There is an empirical or second-order perception – the one that we exercise at each moment – that, because it is chock-full of previous acquisitions and plays out, so to speak, on the surface of being, hides this fundamental phenomenon from us" (*PP* 69[45]).

We by and large dwell within a world of already accomplished, stereotyped meanings, like the city dwellers who see only the general types "mountain" or "stream" in the forest, and we thus fail to see our own revelatory and creative power *within* the world of perception. Second-order perception is a natural consequence of the paradoxical, "folded" nature of our being as at once bodies within the world and perspectives on the world, for to perceive the world as *real* is to see it as definitively not in need of our perception in order to exist.[42] In this natural attitude, the "objective" world presents itself to us as preceding and exceeding our "subjective" experience *of* it, and as thus impervious in its being to the various ways we might look at it.

By contrast to second-order perception, what we can appropriately call "first-order perception" is alive to its power to see things as if for the first time, and thus to its own operation as a primordial *revelation* of reality *qua* reality. Merleau-Ponty writes:

> When I contemplate an object with the sole concern of watching it exist and unfold its riches before my eyes, it ceases to be an allusion to a general type and I become aware that each perception, and not merely that of sights that I discover for the first time, begins anew on its own account the birth of intelligence and has something of a creative genius about it: in order that I may recognize the tree as a tree, it is necessary that, beneath this acquired signification, the momentary arrangement of the sensible spectacle should begin anew, as on the very first day of the vegetable kingdom, to sketch out the individual idea of the tree. (*PP* 69[45–6], translation modified)

First-order speech, we saw, comprehends itself *as* speech; that is, it grasps itself as opening new dimensions of experience that surpass any simply natural or unreflective experience. By the same token, first-order perception comprehends itself *as* perception; it is, to adapt a phrase from *The Visible and the Invisible*, a veritable perception of perception, and thus of the very fact of appearing – "the momentary arrangement of the sensible spectacle" – that is born and reborn in each new moment.[43] First-order perception accomplishes a way of seeing that addresses itself to the irreducible reversibility between seer and seen, touching and touched – a reversibility that is, Merleau-Ponty argues, "the ultimate truth" (*VI* 201[155]). It is grasping and describing this originary birth of meaning that is, as we will argue in Section III, the proper object and style of phenomenological reflection.

III. Reflection

I would like to argue now that "first-order perception" is phenomenology itself. Phenomenology is the rigorous description of experience as it is lived, and describes what must be the case – what must already be under way – for experience to take the forms that it does.[44] When I watch a television show at the end of a long day, or when I am concentrated on a practical project such as doing the dishes or getting to work on time, I can take up my experience in two different kinds of ways. In the first, I am simply absorbed in the perceptual objects: my experience is "outside" of myself, involved with a practical world of on-screen characters, dishes, cars, and roads. However, I can, at any moment, shift my attention from the objects that absorb my attention to the *fact* of my attention – of my inalienable *taking account* – itself. In other words, as we saw in our discussion of first-order perception in Section II, I can see not things but, so to speak, my own seeing *of* things. In doing this, I bear witness not merely to my own private, interior experience as a "subject," but to the originary perceptual happening of meaning itself – an original happening from which "subject" and "object" are only subsequently distinguished.[45] It is this "reduced" sphere of lived experience, where all appearance of things originarily happens, that phenomenology is devoted to elucidating.

Merleau-Ponty argues that the kind of reflection proper to a phenomenological method – what he calls "radical reflection" – is one that is devoted to uncovering its own roots – and the roots of all perceptual and expressive life – in this "reduced" world of experience or, as Edmund Husserl says, this delimited "sphere of givenness."[46] Merleau-Ponty writes in the Preface to *Phenomenology of Perception*: "Reflection does not withdraw from the world toward the unity of consciousness as the foundation of the world; rather, it steps back in order to see transcendences spring forth and it loosens the intentional threads that connect us to the world in order to make them appear; it alone is consciousness of the world because it reveals the world as strange and paradoxical" (*PP* 14[lxxvii]). It is in the midst of this "strange and paradoxical" world of perception that the indeterminate, open-ended identities of perceived objects and perceiving subjects are simultaneously born, as the city dweller is born and reborn in his acts of perceptually "pointing out" the subtle aspects of what there is to be seen in the city in which he lives. Merleau-Ponty argues that the "entire effort" of phenomenological philosophy "is to rediscover this naïve contact with the world in order to finally endow it with a philosophical status" (*PP* 7[lxx], translation modified).

However, it is precisely this "naïve contact" with the world of all experience, including the experience of scientific and philosophical reflection, that is covered over in second-order expression, second-order perception, and, as we will now see, "second-order reflection" (*PP* 9[lxxii]). In our reflective life, we typically take reflection to be more or less accurately mirroring, as its name would suggest, the nature of things in the objective world "out there" – an objective world that, as we saw in Section II, we typically experience as indifferent to our perceptions of it.

In the process, we lose sight of the primordial experience of the world from which our reflective life emerges. The kind of knowledge typical of the empirical sciences, for example, does not regard with wonder the miracle that *there is* a meaningful world of experience to begin with; rather, it seeks accurate knowledge of the workings of objects *within* the world of experience. As Merleau-Ponty writes in *The Visible and the Invisible*, this kind of reflection "recuperates everything except itself as an effort of recuperation, it clarifies everything except its own role" (*VI* 54[33]). Like second-order expression and second-order perception, second-order reflection fails to take itself to *do* anything, even as it is busy "enframing" the ways in which it is possible for us to perceive and to understand the world, and thus everything that we can make correct or incorrect statements about.[47]

Radical or phenomenological reflection, by contrast, seeks the things themselves within the world of experience wherein they originally show themselves, and wherein all scientific and philosophical reflection is itself born. Merleau-Ponty writes: "To return to the things themselves is to return to this world prior to knowledge, this world of which knowledge always *speaks*, and this world with regard to which every scientific determination is abstract, signitive, and dependent, like geography with regard to the landscape where we first learned what a forest, a meadow, or a river is" (*PP* lxxii[9]). As the original appearance of the things themselves, this "world prior to knowledge" cannot be "constructed," but only rigorously "described" (*PP* 10[lxxiii]). This is so because any of the terms that one might use to "construct" a theoretical model of the world of experience would necessarily be drawn *from* the more original experience of this world itself, and would thus, like attempts to "naturalize" perception, beg the question. Radical reflection can only commit itself to rigorously describing the things themselves, precisely in the terms in which they appear. A number of things follow from this.

First, no ultimately complete reduction – no reduction to end all reductions – is ever possible, because the world of experience, and the activity of reflection, is always already under way as soon as one attempts to "catch" or "freeze" it in the advent of its appearance.[48] Merleau-Ponty writes: "Radical reflection is the reflection that again takes hold of me while I am in the process of forming and formulating the idea of the subject and that of the object; it reveals the source of these two idea and it is a reflection that is not merely operating, but moreover is conscious of its own operation" (*PP* 264[227]). As a veritable perception of perception, radical reflection *almost* – but never *quite* – catches itself at the very advent of its own emergence, and *almost* – but never *quite* – catches the "the momentary arrangement of the sensible spectacle" in its ever-new beginning. Since it never quite catches up with its own activity or with the advent of appearance *qua* appearance, radical reflection's efforts to give voice to this birth and rebirth of the world of appearance will be a never-ending project.[49] Since the phenomenal field – the very scene of appearance from and upon which radical reflection reflects – "resists in principle being directly and completely made explicit," as Merleau-Ponty writes, radical reflection arrives not at the final transparency of experience but at the ultimate obscurity, and the ultimate miraculousness, of "the unmotivated springing forth of the world" (*PP* 14[lxxvii]).

Second, phenomenological description is in an important sense akin more to painting or to literature than it is to a science, which claims to offer transparent "translations" of things in the world.[50] We saw in Section II that perception takes the form of a kind of "pointing out." Here, we might say that phenomenological reflection is a kind of pointing out *par excellence*, in that it points, not to this or that meaningful figure *within* the world of experience, but to the miraculous *fact of* the world of experience. Merleau-Ponty writes in his essay "Metaphysics and the Novel": "When one is concerned with giving voice to the experience of the world ... one can no longer credit oneself with attaining a perfect clarity of expression, if the world is such that it cannot be expressed except in 'stories' and, as it were, pointed at [*montré du doigt*]."[51] Like Cézanne, in whose paintings "frozen objects hesitate as at the beginning of the world," or like Marcel Proust, in whose novels "the past is involved in the present and in the presence of times gone by," the phenomenologist seeks to give voice to the texture of experience in the very process of its happening (*CD* 22[16]; *MN* 34[26]).

Third, the truths of experience revealed by phenomenological description can only be accessed in the first person, that is, by the reader or the interlocutor who is engaged *for herself* with the phenomena these descriptions elucidate. Phenomenology *explains* nothing to the suspicious outside observer. Rather, it offers careful descriptions of the world of experience to the honest and engaged reader, who can test their truth and their power only by interrogating her *own* experience and finding the manners in which these descriptions – like Cézanne's paintings or

Proust's novels – do or do not illuminate and clarify this experience. Merleau-Ponty writes:

> It is in we ourselves that we find the unity of phenomenology and its true sense [*sens*]. It is less a question of counting up citations than of determining and expressing this *phenomenology for us* which has caused many of our contemporaries, upon reading Husserl or Heidegger, to have had the feeling much less of encountering a new philosophy than of recognizing what they had been waiting for. (*PP* 8[lxxi])[52]

As the botanist finds herself in the world of plants, which are in turn illuminated in their detailed aspects in her educated perception of them, so must we recognize ourselves in phenomenology, which in turn finds its voice only in us.

Fourth and finally, radical reflection does not simply mirror the world of experience, but effects a transformation *of* this world. Merleau-Ponty writes: "Reflection is only truly reflection if it does not carry itself outside of itself, if it knows itself as *reflection-upon-an-unreflected*, and consequently as a change in the structure of our existence" (*PP* 90[63]). As we saw in Section II, the ways in which we look at things effect a transformation in both the object and the subject of experience. When we "rupture our familiarity" with things with which we are normally engaged – and when, in this rendering strange, we "*stand ... in wonder*" before those things – the texture of the world of experience is itself transformed (*PP* lxxvii[14]).[53] We saw above that second-order reflection is not alive to its own activity *as* reflection, and thus to its own effective power to *shape* the manner in which we are able to see things. By contrast, radical reflection requires that we be alive to our own implication – and hence our own responsibility – within the world upon which we reflect. Merleau-Ponty writes: "We must not merely practice philosophy, but also become aware of the transformation that it brings with it in the spectacle of the world and in our existence" (*PP* 89[63]). From this perspective, truth does not amount to correct statements about existing states of affairs, but is rather the simultaneous illumination and transformation of the world of experience as such.[54]

Indeed, this understanding of truth speaks not so much to the special status of phenomenology as to the nature of philosophical expression as such. Merleau-Ponty writes: "Philosophy is not the reflection of a prior truth, but rather, like art, the realization of a truth" (*PP* 21[lxxxiv], translation modified). All enduring philosophies, like all individual lives, begin at the beginning and are, as Merleau-Ponty argues, "total undertakings" if they are to endure at all.[55] The philosopher engages her entire being in expressing a way of seeing, and a concomitant way of conceptualizing, what is implicit in the unreflected life by means of which her reason develops and that her reason, in turn, elucidates and transforms.[56] For this reason, a philosopher's work will be given as a certain embodied *style* before it is given as a set of theses detached from the world of experience.[57] Merleau-Ponty writes in "The Body as Expression, and Speech" that "just as, when in a foreign country, I begin to understand the sense of words by their place in a context of action and by participating in everyday life, so too a philosophical text that remains poorly understood nevertheless reveals to me at least a certain 'style' – whether Spinozistic, critical, or phenomenological – which is the first sketch of its sense" (*PP* 219[184]). As we saw in our discussion of reading in Section I, we learn only by "catching on" to the general movement of an expression. This is as true of difficult philosophical texts – and the philosophical truths they express – as it is with works of art or the expression of an emotion: we arrive at their truths by feeling our way into their singular styles.

An objection might be raised here. Are there not, in fact, certain ideal truths – the truths of mathematics or, perhaps, of philosophy – that are precisely indifferent to the world of experience in which they were born and to the particular, bodily situations in which they are incidentally expressed and received? Relatedly, are there not ideal truths that can be, in opposition to what we said in Section I, separated from the material marks in which they are expressed and translated without remainder into other "languages"? Merleau-Ponty speaks to such an objection in the chapter of *Phenomenology of Perception* titled "The *Cogito*." He writes:

> What we call an "idea" is necessarily linked to an act of expression and owes its autonomy to this act. It is a cultural object, like the church, the street, the pencil, or the Ninth Symphony. The objection will be that the church can burn, the street and the pencil can be destroyed, and that, if all the scores of the Ninth Symphony and all musical instruments were reduced to ashes, then it would no longer exist apart from a few brief years in the memory of those who heard it, whereas, on the contrary, the idea of the triangle and its properties are imperishable. In fact, the idea of the triangle along with its properties and the idea of the quadratic equation have their historical and geographical regions, and if the tradition from which we receive them and the cultural instruments that carry them were

> destroyed, then new acts of creation would be required to bring them into the world ... Ideas endure or pass away, and the intelligible sky subtly changes color. (*PP* 450–1[410])[58]

One of the wonders of expression is that it can, precisely, point to truths that transcend the time and place of their utterance and that thus give the illusion of having no need of being expressed in order to exist. Merleau-Ponty argues in "The Body as Expression, and Speech" that there is, thus, "a privileged place for Reason," for language itself points to "the ideal of a thought without speech, whereas the idea of a piece of music without sound is absurd" (*PP* 231[196]). However, as we saw in our discussion of the accomplishment of thought in writing and reading in Section I, the truths of reason nevertheless come into their own only by being expressed and received by individuals in specific cultural situations, and their life is maintained so long as they are continuously "reawaked," as Husserl says in "The Origin of Geometry."[59] Furthermore, such ideal truths do not leave the world of experience in which they are born, and which they in turn elucidate, untouched; rather, through their expression and reception "the intelligible sky subtly changes color."

A certain hermeneutics, I would like to suggest, emerges from the distinction between first- and second-order expression, perception, and reflection that has been at play throughout this chapter. We saw in Section I how what were once first-order expressions, be they works of art, philosophy, or, we can now add, mathematics, become sedimented in the storehouse of ready-made, second-order cultural meanings. Things that once *spoke*, discovering in the world new possibilities for vision and reflection, become buried – spok*en* – in the "naturalized" world of culture. In the academic discipline of philosophy, a burial of this sort happens when we treat past philosophical works as so many second-order entries in a chronological history of thought, rather than as living expressions that demand our engagement with the phenomena they promise to enable us to see anew. By contrast, we can reawaken the text's originary power through the kind of first-person engagement that lets the text speak in its own voice again, as the unprecedented, creative gesture that at its inception it was; the text can live only if we are alive *to* it.

This voice is not the *same* historical voice in which the text spoke when it first came to expression in vocal utterance or ink. Nevertheless, the manner in which the text is enabled to speak in the present situation in which it is reawakened is among the indefinite possibilities that have belonged to the text from its very beginning. In "Eye and Mind," Merleau-Ponty draws a parallel between the abilities of great art works to continue issuing new meanings and endlessly interpretable, transformative political events like the French Revolution. He writes:

> In a sense everything that could have been said and that will be said about the French Revolution has always been and is henceforth within it, in that wave which arched itself out of a roil of discrete facts, with its froth of the past and its crest of the future. And it is always by looking more deeply into *how it came about* that we give and will go on giving new representations of it. As for the history of work of art works, if they are great, the sense we give to them later on has issued from them. It is the work itself which has opened the field from which it appears in another light. It changes *itself* and *becomes* what follows; the interminable reinterpretations to which it is *legitimately* susceptible change it only in itself.[60]

The same can be said of great philosophical works: if, in the manner of first-order perception, we can "point out" its original and originary meanings anew, and enable it, via its ongoing transformation in historical interpretation, to once again achieve the miracle of expression.

The historical work, then, continues to speak to the extent that we meet it, in *its* own location, from the world of *our* own concerns.[61] Merleau-Ponty writes: "We find in texts only what we have put into them" (*PP* 8[lxxi]). This claim does not say that we imperiously "project" our own meaning onto historical texts, but rather that a philosophical text has something to say to us to the extent that we let its terms be our terms and our terms its. In this sense, the study of a past thinker resembles a conversation; if we have the philosophical eyes and ears for it, the text's perspective and our own "slip into each other," as Merleau-Ponty writes in his discussion of dialogue in the chapter of *Phenomenology of Perception* titled "Others and the Human World" (*PP* 412[370–1]). Merleau-Ponty writes in his essay "On the Phenomenology of Language": "When I speak or understand, I experience that presence of others in myself or of myself in others … To the extent that what I say has meaning, I am a different 'other' for myself when I am speaking; and to the extent that I understand, I no longer know who is speaking and who is listening."[62]

To understand a past work is to allow its thoughts to speak through me so that they resound not as his or mine alone, but as a creative and truthful *taking of account* within the horizons of a shared phenomenal field that stretches between historical and cultural periods. It is in my current situation that I may reawaken the creative truths of past presents sedimented in my own, and, as Merleau-Ponty writes, "it is in the actual practice of speaking that I learn to understand" (*PL* 22[97]). Rainer Maria Rilke's advice to the young poet comes to mind: "Read the lines as though they were someone else's, and you will feel deep within you how much they are your own."[63]

As students and teachers of the history of philosophy, we are dealing not with a chronology of ready-made ideas or competing opinions about the nature of reality; the history of philosophy is not the history of second-order expressions. Rather, we are dealing with first-order attempts to bring to language what is implicit – what is already under way – in the world of experience itself; we are dealing with insights that have, in their time and for our own, subtly changed the colour of the intelligible sky. In "Eye and Mind," Merleau-Ponty argues that "the very first painting in some sense went to the farthest reach of the future," and that we can see in the cave paintings of Lascaux the traces of such an originary breaking of the silence – a breaking of the silence that is given testimony to in every original effort of painting to this day (*EM* 92[190]). A parallel claim can be made about the history of philosophical expression. In *In Praise of Philosophy*, Merleau-Ponty argues that it is the figure of Socrates – the philosopher for whom philosophy was not "an idol of which he would be the guardian" but that existed only "in its living relevance to the Athenians" – that most originally shows us the paradoxical tension between the speaking individual and the world of accepted meanings in which she finds herself.[64] The original figure of the philosopher seeks in the world of experience truths that are born in, but that transcend and transform, this very world. It is this originary gesture – the gesture proper to the kind of beings that take account of things – that is given testament to in the history of philosophy, and this gesture that a truly philosophical study of the history of philosophy must recognize, preserve, and carry forward in its own voice.

NOTES

1 Aristotle, *Politics*, 1253a7–17.

2 On the human being as the animal with *logos*, see Aristotle, *Nicomachean Ethics* I.7 and I.13. While the *zoon logon echon* is often translated as the "rational animal," John Russon makes the case for understanding *logos*

as a "taking account" that precedes, and is necessary for, human reason (*Bearing Witness to Epiphany*, 4). For a further discussion of the meaning of *logos* in Aristotle, see Francis Sparshott, *Taking Life Seriously*, 45–8, esp. 47: "To see what the implications of Aristotle's emphasis on *logos* are, we should ask ourselves his question: what, in fact, is the characteristic way of life for humans? One answer is that, unlike those of other animals, human life patterns vary from society to society: what is human is precisely this variability, the very fact that the way of life in a society is determined by its culture, its symbol system and the way that symbol system is used … The task of discovering what the human way of life in general is can only be the task of discovering the dimensions of and limits to this variability." Although this is not the place to explore it, I think that Merleau-Ponty's philosophy from *The Structure of Behavior* can be seen to be descriptively engaged in such a task of finding what is common to human behaviour and experience across its diverse historical and cultural manifestations.

3 Merleau-Ponty, *PP* 142[114].

4 In my reference to the "still mute" world that human *logos* brings to voice, I am alluding to Maurice Merleau-Ponty's numerous references throughout his career to Edmund Husserl's idea of phenomenology as bringing a "still mute experience that must be brought to the pure expression of its own sense" (*PP* 15[lxxix]). See also Husserl, *Cartesian Meditations*, §16; *PP* 264[228]; Merleau-Ponty, *Les aventures de la dialectique*, 192–3n1 (*Adventures of the Dialectic*, 138n78); and Merleau-Ponty, *VI* 169[129]. For discussions of this passage in Merleau-Ponty's philosophy, see Waldenfels, "The Paradox of Expression"; and Landes, *Merleau-Ponty*, 16–22.

5 See *PP* 197[162]: "Biological existence gears into human existence and is never indifferent to its particular rhythm. This, we will now add, does not prevent 'living' (*leben*) from being a primordial operation from which it becomes possible to 'live' (*erleben*) such and such a world, nor does it keep us from having to eat and breathe prior to perceiving and reaching a relational life, nor of having to be directed toward color and light through vision, toward sounds through hearing, and toward the other person's body through sexuality, prior to reaching the life of human relations."

6 Merleau-Ponty argues that perception is a nascent *logos* in "Le primat de la perception," 133 ("The Primacy of Perception," 25). Hereafter cited as *PrP*, with the French pagination first and the English second.

7 For Merleau-Ponty's criticism of empiricist and intellectualist approaches to language, see *PP* 213–16[179–82].

8 See *PP* 217[183], where Merleau-Ponty argues that "speech does not

translate a ready-made thought; rather, speech accomplishes thought."

9 Merleau-Ponty speaks of the manner in which a book "catches" (*prenne*) like a fire in *La prose du monde*, 18 (*The Prose of the World*, 11). See also his discussion of how children catch on to language by "playing at speaking" in "La conscience et l'acquisition du langage," p. 15 ("Consciousness and Language Acquisition," 8).

10 On learning as a *Gestalt* shift, see Russon, "Aristotle's Animative Epistemology," 247–8: "'The penny drops,' we say, that is, one experiences what is essentially a '*Gestalt* shift' and quite suddenly 'you get it,' and what were formerly disparate elements struggling to be synthesized transform their appearance and work together as a whole … What one does is *prepare*, and *await synthesis*, that is, we wait for the act of understanding to essentially bring itself into being, and as it were 'pull us up' to its level." See also Merleau-Ponty's discussion of the so-called "learner's paradox" in Plato's *Meno* at *PP* 52[30]: "Empiricism does not see that we need to know what we are looking for, otherwise we would not go looking for it; intellectualism does not see that we need to be ignorant of what we are looking for, or again we would not go looking for it. They are in accord in that neither grasps consciousness *in the act of learning*." Dillon begins his study of Merleau-Ponty's philosophy with an account of how Merleau-Ponty offers a phenomenological response to this apparent paradox (see *Merleau-Ponty's Ontology*, 1–6). See also Scott Marratto's discussion of learning in *The Intercorporeal Self*, 45, 66–77.

11 On the difficulty of translation, and the way in which natural languages are "several ways for the human body to celebrate the world and finally to live it," see *PP* 228[193].

12 On different senses of ambiguity in Merleau-Ponty, see Weiss, "Ambiguity."

13 See also *PP* 236[200]: "Speech … is entirely motricity and entirely intelligence."

14 See *PP* 224[190]: "Speech is a gesture, and its signification is a world."

15 For discussions of the gesture of pointing, see Simms, "Egocentric Language and the Upheaval of Speech," 296–9. See also Kym Maclaren's discussion of how we are swept up in another's intentionality in "Embodied Perceptions," 79–80: "Her intentionality is, in itself, not an object of perception so much as a *self-effacing directive*: 'look over there; pay attention to that; take up this attitude towards that thing …' it says, while also making this solicitation not a thematic object but a guiding directive to our consciousness."

16 Merleau-Ponty, "Un inédit de Maurice Merleau-Ponty," 405; "An

Unpublished Text by Maurice Merleau-Ponty," 7. See also Merleau-Ponty's discussion of "abstract behavior" in the chapter of *PP* titled "The Spatiality of One's Own Body, and Motricity," *PP* 137–43[109–15].

17 See *PP* 225[190]: "The gesture does not *make me think* of anger, it is the anger itself."

18 Merleau-Ponty writes in the chapter of *PP* titled "The Body as a Sexed Being": "'Transcendence' is the name we shall give to this movement by which existence takes up for itself and transforms a *de facto* situation," and "freedom resides in the power for equivocation" (*PP* 208[172–3]; *PP* 212n[177n]). For a further discussion of Merleau-Ponty's view that it is the nature of embodied human existence to transcend itself towards others, see Maclaren, "Merleau-Ponty's Embodied Ethics," which argues that the ethics to be garnered from Merleau-Ponty's philosophy bring together crucial insights from both Aristotelian ethics and Kantian ethics.

19 See *PP* 209[174]: "Human existence will lead us to revisit our usual notion of necessity and contingency, because human existence is the change of contingency into necessity through the act of taking up."

20 See also Merleau-Ponty's discussions of this distinction at *PP* 224[189–90], *PP* 218n1[530n7], and at *PP* 449[409], and Landes's discussion of the distinction in *Merleau-Ponty and the Paradoxes of Expression*, 14. See also Heidegger's discussion of "they-speak" or "idle chatter" in *Being and Time*, §35.

21 Merleau-Ponty, "Le doute de Cézanne," 24 ("Cézanne's Doubt," 19). Hereafter cited as *CD*, with the French pagination first and the English second. See also Véronique Fóti, *Tracing Expression in Merleau-Ponty*, ch. 1, "Primordial Perception and Artistic Expression: Merleau-Ponty and Cézanne."

22 See also Merleau-Ponty's discussion of "coherent deformation" in "Le langage indirect et les voix du silence," 87 ("Indirect Language and the Voices of Silence," 54). I discuss this concept further in relation to artistic and literary expression in "'Thinking According to Others.'" See also Waldenfels's discussion of expression as opening a new world between the relatively old and the relatively new ("The Paradox of Expression," 95); and Don Landes's discussion of expression as establishing new "metastable" equilibriums (*Merleau-Ponty and the Paradoxes of Expression*, 22–7).

23 See also Waldenfels's discussion of the event of expression as preceding itself ("The Paradox of Expression," 96); and Henri Bergson's discussion of how acts retroactively produce their own antecedents (*Time and Free Will*, 190).

24 See John Dewey on the conversion of emotional discharge into aesthetic expression by way of a transformation of external material (*Art as Experience*, ch. 4, "The Act of Expression," esp. 63–9).

25 Merleau-Ponty says something similar in the final pages of "The Body as Expression, and Speech," where he writes: "The revelation of an immanent or nascent meaning [*sens*] in the living body extends, as we will see, to the entire sensible world, and our gaze, informed by the experience of one's own body, will discover the miracle of expression in all other 'objects'" (*PP* 239[204]).

26 Elkins, *The Object Stares Back*, 12.

27 On the figure–background structure, see the Introduction to *PP*, esp. *PP* 26–8/[4–7] and 39–41[16–18]. On Merleau-Ponty's relationship to *Gestalt* psychology, see Heinämaa, "Phenomenological Responses to Gestalt Psychology"; Toadvine, *Merleau-Ponty's Philosophy of Nature*, ch. 1, "Nature as Gestalt and Melody"; and Dillon, *Merleau-Ponty's Ontology*, ch. 4, "Ontological Implications of Gestalt Theory."

28 For Merleau-Ponty's criticism of such "empiricist" accounts of perception, see the first two chapters of the Introduction to *PP*, "Sensation" and "'Association' and 'The Projection of Memories.'"

29 For Merleau-Ponty's criticism of "intellectualist" accounts of perception, see the third chapter of the Introduction to *PP*, "Attention and Judgment."

30 On perception as dialogue, see Evans and Lawlor: "Like a dialogue, perception leads the subject to draw together the sense diffused throughout the object while, simultaneously, the object solicits and unifies the intentions of the subject ... In other words, this dialogue provides a direction for the becoming of both subjects and objects and yet retains the degree of indeterminacy or ambiguity required for the creative contributions of subjects and for the surprises that the world harbors" ("The Value of Flesh," 4).

31 Landes also draws attention to the resonances between the description of the ship on the beach and Cézanne's "vague fever" (*Merleau-Ponty and the Paradoxes of Expression*, 81, 193n1). See also Husserl on "retroactive crossing out" in his *Analyses*, §7.

32 See *PP* 34[11]: "The nature of the perceived is to tolerate a certain ambiguity, a certain 'shifting' [*bougé*], and to allow itself to be shaped by the context" (translation modified). On the manner in which perception always occurs within the indeterminate horizons of a field, see the chapter of *PP* titled "The Phenomenal Field."

33 On perception as a kind of "pointing" and hence a kind of language, see Russon, *Reading Hegel's* Phenomenology of Spirit, 20–1.

34 Elkins, *The Object Stares Back*, 56. See also Bredlau, "Learning to See."

35 See Dewey's argument that a person's "genuine environment" – what we are calling, with Merleau-Ponty, his "world" – is "the things with which a man *varies*" (*Democracy and Education*, 11). Dewey writes: "Thus the activities of the astronomer vary with the stars at which he gazes or about which he calculates. Of his immediate surroundings, his telescope is most intimately his environment. The environment of an antiquarian, as an antiquarian, consists of the remote epoch of human life with which he is concerned, and the relics, inscriptions, etc., by which he establishes connections with that period" (*Democracy and Education*, 11). On such cultivated familiarities as the ways in which we are originally "at home" in the world, see Jacobson, "A Developed Nature" and "The Experience of Home."

36 I am taking this phrase from Casey, *The World at a Glance*.

37 See *PP* 344[304]: "we much acknowledge the symbolic 'pregnancy' of form in content as prior to the subsumption of content under form." On the relationship between Merleau-Ponty's concept of intentionality and this way of interpreting insights from *Gestalt* psychology, see Dillon, "Gestalt Theory"; and Reuter, "Merleau-Ponty's Notion," esp. 77–82.

38 On perception as interpretation, see Russon, *Human Experience*, pt 1, esp. ch. 1, "Interpretation."

39 As so contingent and partial, there is thus a certain violence or transgression (*impiètement*) to the act of perception, in that it projects in each of its visions an entire perceptual trajectory or future at the expense of, or perhaps in conflict with, other ways of seeing. See *PP* 419–20[378–9] on "the violent act that is perception itself." See also Waldenfels's argument that the "violence of perception is the reverse side of its contingency" ("The Paradox of Expression," 98).

40 Merleau-Ponty refers to this begging of the question with regard to perception, which tries to build perception out of the perceived, "the experience error" (*PP* 27[5]). On the primacy of perception, see *PP* 40[17] and "The Primacy of Perception." On "enframing," see Martin Heidegger, "The Question Concerning Technology," 324–6.

41 See Merleau-Ponty's discussion of "the flesh of the world" in the chapter of *VI* titled "L'entrelacs – le chiasme" ("The Intertwining – The Chiasm"), esp. 174[133]: "Between the exploration and what it will teach me, between my movements and what I touch, there must be some relationship by principle, some kinship, according to which they are not only, like the pseudopods of the amoeba, vague and ephemeral deformations of the corporeal space, but the initiation to and opening upon a tactile world";

and *VI* 176[135]: "The thickness of flesh between the seer and the thing seen is constitutive for the thing of its visibility as for the seer of his corporeity; it is not an obstacle between them, it is the means of their communication."

42 For example, see *PP* 191[156]: "Indeed, the natural world is given as existing in itself beyond its existence for me, the act of transcendence by which the subject opens to the natural world carries itself along and we find ourselves in the presence of a nature that has no need of being perceived in order to exist."

43 In his experiments with touching one hand with the other, Merleau-Ponty writes that the touching hand can *almost* coincide with the power of touch in the touched hand, such that there is "a veritable touching of the touch" (*VI* 174[133]).

44 See Russon, "Haunted by History," 81.

45 On the situation or the "event of meaning" as "a subject-object pair, see Russon, *Human Experience*, 20. On perception as the negotiation of boundaries between self and other from a more primary intertwining, see Maclaren, "Embodied Perceptions," 68–9.

46 See Husserl, *Ideas 1*, §46. On "radical reflection," see, for example *PP* 14[lxxviii], *PP* 90[63], and *PP* 264[227]. See also the chapter of *VI* titled "Reflection and Interrogation."

47 On the distinction between correct statement, which "fixes upon something pertinent to what is under consideration," and truth as a primordial "uncovering" or *aletheia*, see Heidegger, "The Question Concerning Technology," 313. See also *Being and Time*, §44.

48 In the "Preface" to *PP*, Merleau-Ponty writes: "The most important lesson of the reduction is the impossibility of a complete reduction" (*PP* 14[lxxvii]).

49 See also *PP* 14[lxxviii], where Merleau-Ponty argues that the philosopher is "a perpetual beginner," and argues: "This means that he accepts nothing as established from what men or scientists believe they know. This also means that philosophy itself must not take itself as established in the truths it has managed to utter, that philosophy is an ever-renewed experiment in its own beginning, and finally, that radical reflection is conscious of its own dependence on an unreflected life that is its initial, constant, and final situation."

50 See *PP* 22[lxxxv]: "Phenomenology is as painstaking as the works of Balzac, Proust, Valéry, or Cézanne – through the same kind of wonder, the same demand for awareness, the same will to grasp the sense of the world or of history in its nascent state." See also Joe Sachs, when he writes

that if there is "some sort of knowing that you seek without guarantees that it exists and for no reason other than for its own sake, then the best explanation available is a description that is adequate and truthful. It is likely that, no matter how much you reflect on what you are seeking, some obscurity will remain in your conception of it. You are stretching yourself to understand something higher, not reducing it to something lower and already understood" ("Introduction," 14).

51 Merleau-Ponty, "Le roman et la métaphysique," 36–7 ("Metaphysics and the novel," 28). Hereafter cited as *MN*, with the French pagination first and the English second.

52 Compare to Dewey, *Art as Experience*, 109: "Those who are moved feel, as Tolstoi says, that what the work expresses is as if it were something that one had oneself been longing to express."

53 Compare to Heidegger's discussion of the uncanny (*unheimlich*) in *Being and Time*, §40. Although I can only suggest this connection here, it is worth noting the ways in which both the attitude of anxiety and the attitude of wonder reveal to us our personal implication in the meaning of things, and thus our responsibility with regard to this meaning.

54 See Waldenfels's argument that the truth of a thought can be grasped and assessed not according to its correspondence to its external reality but according to the extent to which its expression has, as we say, "hit the point" or "struck a nerve" ("Verité à Faire," 190).

55 Merleau-Ponty, "Partout et nulle part," 207 ("Everywhere and Nowhere," 128).

56 See Taminiaux's argument that, against a philosophical tradition that has long pitted perceptual life – with all its perspectival "distortions" – against clarity of thought, "to think, for Merleau-Ponty, does not mean to turn away from the perceived; rather it means to grant it the status of first ground, to dwell within its boundaries, to listen to its echoes, to interrogate it, to always go back to it" ("The Thinker and the Painter," 280).

57 On the notion of style as a kind of dynamic essence, see Singer, "Merleau-Ponty and the Concept of Style." See also Marratto, *The Intercorporeal Self*, 102: "We are not able to define a style, the style of a writer or painter, because precisely what is stylized in our experience is a certain singularity. I cannot really define Merleau-Ponty's style of philosophizing by saying it is like, or unlike, someone else's style, nor can I do so by itemizing his persistent themes and concepts, or his preferred phrasings – I can only read it, let myself adhere to its unique demands."

58 See also *PrP* 128[20]: "When I think of the Pythagorean theorem and recognize it as true, it is clear that this truth is not for this moment only.

Nevertheless later progress in knowledge will show that it is not yet a final, unconditioned evidence and that, if the Pythagorean theorem and the Euclidean system once appeared as final, unconditioned evidences, that is itself the mark of a certain cultural epoch. Later developments would not annul the Pythagorean theorem but would put it back in its place as a partial, and also an abstract, truth. Thus here also we do not have a timeless truth but rather the recovery of one time by another time."

59 Husserl, "The Origin of Geometry," 359. See also Hass and Hass, "Merleau-Ponty and the Origin of Geometry."

60 Merleau-Ponty, *L'Œil et l'esprit*, 62 ("Eye and Mind," 179). Cf. Merleau-Ponty's claim in "The Body as Expression, and Speech" that a difficult painting or piece of music "creates its own public ... by secreting its own signification" (*PP* 219[185]); also cf. Dewey's claim that "if the time span be extended, it is true that no man is eloquent save when someone is moved as he listens" (*Art as Experience*, 109).

61 See Landes's complementary argument for a "practice of reading" inspired by Merleau-Ponty's philosophy of expression (*Merleau-Ponty and the Paradoxes of Expression*, 37–9).

62 Merleau-Ponty, "Sur la phénoménologie du langage," 158 ("On the Phenomenology of Language," 97).

63 Rilke, *Letters to a Young Poet*, 40.

64 Merleau-Ponty, *Éloge de la philosophie et autres essais*, 41 (*In Praise of Philosophy and Other Essays*, 36).

Bibliography

Cited Works by Merleau-Ponty

Adventures of the Dialectic, trans. Joseph Bien. Evanston: Northwestern University Press, 1973.

Les Aventures de la dialectique. Paris: Galimard, 1955.

"Cézanne's Doubt." In *The Merleau-Ponty Aesthetics Reader*, ed. Galen A. Johnson, trans. Michael B. Smith., 59–75. Evanston: Northwestern University Press, 1993.

"The Child's Relations with Others." In *Primacy of Perception*, ed. James M. Edie, trans. William Cobb, 96–155. Evanston: Northwestern University Press, 1964.

"The Concept of Nature, 1956–57." In *Nature: Course Notes from the Collège de France*, trans. Robert Vallier. Evanston: Northwestern University Press, 2003.

"La Conscience et l'acquisition du language." In *Merleau-Ponty à la Sorbonne: résumé de cours 1949–1952*. Grenoble: Editions Cynara, 1988.

"La conscience et l'acquisition du langage." In *Psychologie et pédagogie de l'enfant: course de Sorbonne 1949–1952*. Lagrasse: Verdier, 2001.

Consciousness and the Acquisition of Language, trans. Hugh J. Silverman. Evanston: Northwestern University Press, 1973.

"Consciousness and Language Acquisition," trans. Talia Welsh. In *Child Psychology and Pedagogy: The Sorbonne Lectures 1949–1952*, 3–67. Evanston: Northwestern University Press, 2010.

"Le doute de Cézanne." *Sens et non-sens*, 13–33. Paris: Gallimard, 1961, 1996.

Éloge de la philosophie et autres essais. Paris: Gallimard, 1960.

"L'entrelacs – le chiasme." In *Le visible et l'invisible*, ed. Alphonso Lingis, 178–95. Paris: Gallimard, 1964.

"Everywhere and Nowhere." In *Signs*, trans. Richard C. McCleary, 126–58. Evanston: Northwestern University Press, 1964.

"Eye and Mind." In *The Merleau-Ponty Aesthetics Reader*, ed. Galen A. Johnson, trans. Michael B. Smith, 121–50. Evanston: Northwestern University Press, 1993.

"Eye and Mind." In *The Primacy of Perception*, ed. James M. Edie, trans. Carleton Dallery, 159–90. Evanston: Northwestern University Press, 1964.

Husserl at the Limits of Phenomenology, trans. Leonard Lawlor. Evanston: Northwestern University Press, 2002.

The Incarnate Subject: Malebranche, Biran, and Bergson on the Union of Body and Soul, trans. Paul B. Milan. Amherst: Humanity Books, 2002.

"Indirect Language and the Voices of Silence." In *The Merleau-Ponty Aesthetics Reader*, ed. Galen A. Johnson, trans. Michael B. Smith, 76–120. Evanston: Northwestern University Press, 1993.

"Indirect Language and the Voices of Silence," trans. Richard C. McCleary. In *Signs*, trans. Richard C. McCleary, 39–83. Evanston: Northwestern University Press, 1964.

"Un inédit de Maurice Merleau-Ponty." *Revue de Metaphysique et de Morale* 67, no. 4 (1962): 401–9.

In Praise of Philosophy and Other Essays, trans. John Wild, John O'Neill, and James Edie. Evanston: Northwestern University Press, 1963.

Institution and Passivity: Course Notes from the Collège de France (1954–55), trans. Leonard Lawlor and Heath Massey. Evanston: Northwestern University Press, 2010.

L'Institution dans l'Histoire Personnelle et Publique: Le Problème de la Passivité, le Sommeil, l'Inconscient, la Mémoire. Notes de Cours au Collège de France (1954–1955), ed. by S. Ménasé, D. Darmaillac, and C. Lefort. Paris: Belin, 2003.

"Institution in Personal and Public History." In *Institution and Passivity: Course Notes from the Collège de France (1954–1955)*, trans. Leonard Lawlor and Heath Massey. Evanston: Northwestern University Press, 2010.

L'institution, la passivité: Notes de cours au Collège de France, 1954–1955, ed. Claude Lefort. Paris: Belin, 2003.

"Intertwining – the Chiasm," trans. Alphonso Lingis. In *The Visible and the Invisible*, 135–49. Evanston: Northwestern University Press, 1968.

"Le langage indirect et les Voix du silence." In *Signes*, 63–135. Paris: Gallimard, 1960.

The Merleau-Ponty Reader, ed. Ted Toadvine and Leonard Lawlor. Evanston: Northwestern University Press, 2007.

"Metaphysics and the Novel." In *Sense and Non-Sense*, trans. Hubert L. Dreyfus and Patricia Allen Dreyfus, 26–40. Evanston: Northwestern University Press, 1964.

Le monde sensible et le monde de l'expression. Cours au Collège de France, 1953, ed.

E. de Saint Aubert and S. Kristensen. Geneva: Metis Presses, 2011.
Nature: Course Notes from the Collège de France, trans. Robert Vallier. Evanston: Northwestern University Press, 2003.
La nature: Notes, cours du Collège de France. Paris: Seuil, 1994.
L'oeil et l'esprit. Paris: Gallimard, 1964.
"On the Phenomenology of Language." In *Signs*, trans. Richard C. McCleary, 84–97. Evanston: Northwestern University Press, 1964.
Le Problème de la Parole (lecture at the Collège de France, 1953–54). Unpublished manuscript.
"On Sartre's *The Flies*." In *Texts and Dialogues: On Philosophy, Politics, and Culture*, ed. Hugh J. Silverman and James Barry, Jr., 115–18. New York: Humanity Books, 1992.
Parcours deux: 1951–1961. Paris: Éditions Verdier, 2000.
"Partout et nulle part." In *Signes*, 203–58. Paris: Gallimard, 1960.
Phénoménologie de la perception. Saint Amand: Gallimard, 2005.
Phenomenology of Perception, trans. Don Landes. New York: Routledge, 2012.
"The Primacy of Perception and Its Philosophical Consequences." In *The Primacy of Perception and Other Essays on Phenomenological Psychology, the Philosophy of Art, History and Politics*, ed. James M. Edie, trans. James M. Edie, 12–42. Evanston: Northwestern University Press, 1964.
"Le primat de la perception et ses consequences philosophiques." In *Le primat de la perception et ses consequences philosophiques*, ed. Jacques Prunair. Lagrasse: Verdier, 1996.
The Prose of the World, trans. John O'Neill. Evanston: Northwestern University Press, 1973.
La prose du monde. Paris: Gallimard, 1969.
Les relations avec autrui chez l'enfant. Paris: Centre de Documentation Universitaire, 1969.
"Le roman et la métaphysique." In *Sens et non-sens*, 34–52. Paris: Gallimard, 1996.
Sense and Non-Sense, trans. L. Dreyfus and Patricia Allen Dreyfus. Evanston: Northwestern University Press, 1964.
Signs, trans. Richard C. McCleary. Evanston: Northwestern University Press, 1964.
Las structure du comportement. Paris: Presses Universitaires de France, 1972, 2006.
The Structure of Behavior, trans. Alden Fisher. Pittsburgh: Duquesne University Press, 1963.
"Sur la phénoménologie du langage." In *Signes*, 136–58. Paris: Gallimard, 1960.
"An Unpublished Text by Merleau-Ponty: A Prospectus of His Work." In *The Primacy of Perception*, ed. James M. Edie, trans. Arleen B. Dallery, 3–11. Evanston: Northwestern University Press, 1964.

The Visible and the Invisible, Followed by Working Notes, trans. and ed. Alphonso Lingis, ed. Claude Lefort. Evanston: Northwestern University Press, 1968.
Le visible et l'invisible, ed. Claude Lefort. Paris: Gallimard, 1964.
The World of Perception, trans. Oliver Davis. London and New York: Routledge, 2004.

Other Sources

Adams, Harry. "Expression." In *Merleau-Ponty: Key Concepts*, ed. Rosalyn Diprose and Jack Reynolds, 152–62. Stocksfield: Acumen Publishing, 2008.
Adams, Marilyn Jager. *Beginning to Read: Thinking and Learning about Print*. Cambridge, MA: MIT Press, 1994.
Adamson, Lauren, and Janet E. Frick. "The Still Face: A History of a Shared Experimental Paradigm." *Infancy* 4, no. 4 (2003): 451–73. http://dx.doi.org/10.1207/S15327078IN0404_01.
Al-Saji, Alia. "'A Past Which Has Never Been Present': Bergsonian Dimensions in Merleau-Ponty's Theory of the Prepersonal." *Research in Phenomenology* 38, no. 1 (2008): 41–71. http://dx.doi.org/10.1163/156916408X258942.
– "The Temporality of Life: Merleau-Ponty, Bergson, and the Immemorial Past." *Southern Journal of Philosophy* 45 (2007): 177–206.
Anderson, John R. "Problem Solving and Learning." *American Psychologist* 48, no. 1 (1993): 35–44. http://dx.doi.org/10.1037/0003-066X.48.1.35.
Aristotle. "The Movement of Animals." In *The Complete Works of Aristotle*, ed. Jonathan Barnes. Princeton: Princeton University Press, 1971.
– "Nicomachean Ethics." In *Introduction to Aristotle*, ed. Richard McKeon. New York: Modern Library, 1947.
– *Nicomachean Ethics*. In *The Complete Works of Aristotle: The Revised Oxford Translation*, vol. 2, ed. Jonathan Barnes, 1729–867. Princeton: Princeton University Press, 1995.
– *Physics*. In *The Complete Works of Aristotle: The Revised Oxford Translation*, vol. 1, ed. Jonathan Barnes, 1729–867.
– "Politics." In *Introduction to Aristotle*, ed. Richard McKeon. New York: Modern Library, 1947.
– "Politics." In *The Complete Works of Aristotle: The Revised Oxford Translation*, vol. 2, ed. Jonathan Barnes, 1986–2129. Princeton: Princeton University Press, 1995.
Arvidson, P. Sven. "Toward a Phenomenology of Attention." *Human Studies* 19, no. 1 (1996): 71–84. http://dx.doi.org/10.1007/BF00142856.
Atlan, Henri, and Irun R. Cohen. "Immune Information, Self-Organization, and Meaning." *International Immunology* 10, no. 6 (1998): 711–17. http://

dx.doi.org/10.1093/intimm/10.6.711.

Aygün, Ömer. *The Middle Included: Logos in Aristotle*. Evanston: Northwestern University Press, 2016.

Barbaras, Renaud. *The Being of the Phenomenon*, trans. Ted Toadvine and Leonard Lawlor. Bloomington: Indiana University Press, 1991, 2004.

– *Le Désir et la Distance. Introduction à Une Phénoménologie de la Perception*. Paris: J. Vrin, 1999.

– "L'Espace et le Mouvement Vivant." *Alter* 2 (1996): 11–29.

– "Merleau-Ponty and Nature." *Research in Phenomenology* 31, no. 1 (2001): 22–38. http://dx.doi.org/10.1163/15691640160048540.

– "The Movement of the Living as the Originary Foundation of Perceptual Intentionality." In *Naturalizing Phenomenology: Issues in Contemporary Phenomenology and Cognitive Science*, ed. Jean Petitot, Francisco J. Varela, Bernard Pachoud, et al., 525–38. Stanford: Stanford University Press, 1999.

– "Perception and Movement: The End of the Metaphysical Approach." In *Chiasms: Merleau-Ponty's Notion of Flesh*, ed. Fred Evans and Leonard Lawlor, 77–87. Albany: SUNY Press, 2000.

Behrmann, Marlene, Patricia Ebert, and Sandra E. Black. "Hemispatial Neglect and Visual Search: A Large Scale Analysis." *Cortex* 40, no. 2 (2004): 247–63. http://dx.doi.org/10.1016/S0010-9452(08)70120-5.

Bergo, Bettina. "Radical Passivity in Levinas and Merleau-Ponty (Lectures of 1954)." In *Radical Passivity: Rethinking Ethical Agency in Levinas*, ed. Benda Hofmeyr, 31–52. Netherlands: Springer, 2009. http://dx.doi.org/10.1007/978-1-4020-9347-0_3.

Bergson, Henri. *Time and Free Will: An Essay on the Immediate Data of Consciousness*, trans. F.L. Pogson. Mineola: Dover Publications, 2001.

Bernet, Rudolf. "The Subject in Nature: Reflections on Merleau-Ponty's Phenomenology of Perception." In *Merleau-Ponty in Contemporary Perspective*, ed. Patrick Burke and Jan Van der Veken. The Hague: Kluwer, 1993. http://dx.doi.org/10.1007/978-94-011-1751-7_5.

Binswanger, Ludwig. *Dream and Existence*, ed. K. Hoeller. New York: Humanities Press, 1993.

Blocker, Jane. *Where Is Ana Mendieta? Identity, Performativity, and Exile*. Durham: Duke University Press, 1999.

Bowen, Audrey, Kate McKenna, and Raymond C. Tallis. "Reasons for Variability in the Reported Rate of Occurrence of Unilateral Spatial Neglect after Stroke." *Stroke* 30, no. 6 (1999): 1196–202. http://dx.doi.org/10.1161/01.STR.30.6.1196.

Brainard, Paul P. "The Mentality of a Child Compared with That of Apes."

Pedagogical Seminary and Journal of Genetic Psychology 37, no. 2 (1930): 268–93. http://dx.doi.org/10.1080/08856559.1930.10532238.

Brazelton, T. Berry. "Joint Regulation of Neonate-Parent Behavior." In *Social Interchange in Infancy: Affect, Cognition, and Communication*, ed. Edward Z. Tronick. Baltimore: University Park Press, 1982.

Brazelton, T. Berry, Barbara Koslowski, and Mary Main. "The Origins of Reciprocity: The Early Mother–Infant Interaction." In *The Effect of the Infant on Its Caregiver*, ed. Michael Lewis and Leonard Rosenblum. Toronto: John Wiley and Sons, 1974.

Bredlau, Susan. "Husserl's 'Pairing' Relation and the Role of Others in Infant Perception." *Journal of Consciousness Studies* 23 (2016): 8–30.

– "Learning to See: Merleau-Ponty and the Navigation of 'Terrains.'" *Chiasmi International* 8 (2006): 191–8. http://dx.doi.org/10.5840/chiasmi2006828.

– "Monstrous Faces and a World Transformed: Merleau-Ponty, Dolezal, and the Enactive Approach on Vision without Inversion of the Retinal Image." *Phenomenology and the Cognitive Sciences* 10, no. 4 (2011): 481–98. http://dx.doi.org/10.1007/s11097-011-9210-6.

Buchanan, Brett. *Onto-Ethologies: The Animal Environments of Uexküll, Heidegger, Merleau-Ponty, and Deleuze*. Albany: SUNY Press, 2008.

Busch, Thomas W. "Husserl and Merleau-Ponty on Rationality, Universality, and the Ethical Subject." In *Merleau-Ponty's Later Works and Their Practical Implications*, ed. Duane H. Davis, 87–100. New York: Humanity Books, 2001.

Butterworth, George. "Pointing Is the Royal Road to Language." In *Pointing: Where Language, Culture, and Cognition Meet*, ed. Sotaro Kita, 9–33. Mahwah: Lawrence Erlbaum Associates, 2003.

Carbone, Mauro. *The Thinking of the Sensible: Merleau-Ponty's A-Philosophy*. Evanston: Northwestern University Press, 2004.

Carr, Amanda, and Alison Pike. "Maternal Scaffolding Behavior: Links with Parenting Style and Maternal Education." *Developmental Psychology* 48, no. 2 (2012): 543–51. http://dx.doi.org/10.1037/a0025888.

Casey, Edward S. "Attending and Glancing." In *The World at a Glance*. Bloomington: Indiana University Press, 2007.

– *Getting Back into Place*. Bloomington: Indiana University Press, 1993.

– "Habitual Body and Memory in Merleau-Ponty." *Man and World* 17, nos. 3–4 (1984): 279–97. http://dx.doi.org/10.1007/BF01250454.

– *The World at a Glance*. Bloomington: Indiana University Press, 2007.

Cataldi, Sue. *Emotion, Depth, and Flesh: A Study of Sensitive Space: Reflections on Merleau-Ponty's Philosophy of Embodiment*. Albany: SUNY Press, 1993.

Celan, Paul. *Gesammelte Werke*. Frankfurt am Main: Suhrkamp, 1985.

Chall, Jeanne S. *Stages of Reading Development*, 2nd ed. San Diego: Harcourt Brace, 1995.

Charmaz, Kathy. "Loss of Self: A Fundamental Form of Suffering in the Chronically Ill." *Sociology of Health and Illness* 5, no. 2 (1983): 168–95. http://dx.doi.org/10.1111/1467-9566.ep10491512.

Cohn, Jeffrey F., and Edward Z. Tronick. "Specificity of Infants' Response to Mothers' Affective Behavior." *Journal of the American Academy of Child and Adolescent Psychiatry* 28, no. 2 (1989): 242–8. http://dx.doi.org/10.1097/00004583-198903000-00016.

Coole, Diana. *Merleau-Ponty and Modern Politics after Anti-Humanism*. Lanham: Rowman and Littlefield, 2007.

– "Thinking Politically with Merleau-Ponty." *Radical Philosophy* 108 (2001): 17–28.

Costello, Peter R. "The Life of the Life-World: The Flesh of the Transcendental Ego." *Gramma* 14 (2006): 27–42.

Costello, Peter, and Licia Carlson, eds. *Phenomenology and the Arts*. Lanham, MD: Lexington Books, 2016.

Crowther, Paul. "Merleau-Ponty: Perception into Art." *British Journal of Aesthetics* 22, no. 2 (1982): 138–49. http://dx.doi.org/10.1093/bjaesthetics/22.2.138.

Dastur, Françoise. "World, Flesh, Vision." In *Chiasms: Merleau-Ponty's Notion of Flesh*, ed. Fred Evans and Leonard Lawlor, trans. Ted Toadvine, 23–50. Albany: SUNY Press, 2000.

de Beauvoir, Simone. *A Very Easy Death*. New York: Penguin, 1969.

Depraz, Natalie. "Where Is the Phenomenology of Attention That Husserl Intended to Perform? A Transcendental Pragmatic-Oriented Description of Attention." *Continental Philosophy Review* 37, no. 1 (2004): 5–20. http://dx.doi.org/10.1023/B:MAWO.0000049309.87813.f7.

Descartes, René. *Meditations on First Philosophy*, 3rd ed., trans. Donald A. Cress. Indianapolis: Hackett, 1993.

– *Passions of the Soul, 3rd article*, trans. Stephen H. Voss. Indianapolis: Hackett, 1990.

– *The Philosophical Writings of Descartes*, 3 vols., trans. John Cottingham, Robert Stoothoff, and Dugald Murdoch. Cambridge: Cambridge University Press, 1985.

Derrida, Jacques. *Edmund Husserl's Origin of Geometry: An Introduction*. Lincoln: University of Nebraska Press, 1989.

– *Margins of Philosophy*, trans. Alan Bass. Chicago: University of Chicago Press, 1982.

– *Of Grammatology*, corrected ed. Baltimore: Johns Hopkins University Press, 1997.

– *The Politics of Friendship*. New York: Verso, 2005.
– *The Problem of Genesis in Husserl's Philosophy*. Chicago: University of Chicago Press, 2003.
– *The Truth in Painting*. Chicago: University of Chicago Press, 1987.
de Saint Aubert, Emmanuel. "La 'Promiscuité.' Merleau-Ponty à la Recherche d'une Psychanalyse Ontologique." *Archives de Philosophie* 69 (2006): 11–35.
De Waehlens, Alphonse. *Une Philosophie de l'Ambiguité*. Louvain: Nauwelaerts, 1951.
Dewey, John. *Art as Experience*. New York: Penguin, 1934.
– *Democracy and Education: An Introduction to the Philosophy of Education*. New York: Free Press (Simon and Schuster), 1944.
– *Experience and Education*. New York: Free Press (Simon and Schuster), 1997.
– *Human Nature and Conduct: An Introduction to Social Psychology*. New York: Modern Library, 1957.
Dillon, M.C. "Apriority in Kant and Merleau-Ponty." *Kant-Studien* 78, nos. 1–4 (1987): 403–23. http://dx.doi.org/10.1515/kant.1987.78.1-4.403.
– "Gestalt Theory and Merleau-Ponty's Concept of Intentionality." *Man and World* 4, no. 4 (1971): 436–59. http://dx.doi.org/10.1007/BF01579035.
– *Merleau-Ponty's Ontology*. Evanston: Northwestern University Press, 1998.
Didion, Joan. *The Year of Magical Thinking*. New York: Alfred A. Knopf, 2005.
Dolto-Marette, Françoise. "Hypothèse nouvelle concernant les réactions dites de jalousie à la naissance d'un puîné." *Psyché* 7 (1947): 524–30; 8 (1947): 788–98.
Duncker, Karl. "On Problem-Solving," trans. Lynne S. Lees. *Psychological Monographs* 58, no. 5 (1945): i–113. http://dx.doi.org/10.1037/h0093599.
Eglinton, Elizabeth, and Marylyn Annett. "Handedness and Dyslexia: A Meta-Analysis." *Perceptual and Motor Skills* 79, no. 3 (1994): 1611–16. http://dx.doi.org/10.2466/pms.1994.79.3f.1611.
Elkins, James. *The Object Stares Back: On the Nature of Seeing*. New York: Simon and Schuster, 1996.
Evans, Fred, and Leonard Lawlor. "The Value of Flesh: Merleau-Ponty's Philosophy and the Modernism/Postmodernism Debate." In *Chiasms: Merleau-Ponty's Notion of Flesh*, ed. Fred Evans and Leonard Lawlor, 1–20. Albany: SUNY Press, 2000.
Fer, Briony. "Celluloid Circus: Gordon Matt-Clark's Color Cibachromes." In *Gordon Matta-Clark: You Are the Measure*, ed. Elisabeth Sussman, 136–45. New Haven: Yale University Press, 2007.
Field, Tiffany. *The Amazing Infant*. Malden: Wiley-Blackwell, 2007.

Flynn, Bernard. "Merleau-Ponty and Nietzsche on the Visible and the Invisible." In *Merleau-Ponty: Difference, Materiality, Painting*, ed. Véronique Fóti, 2–15. Atlantic Highlands: Humanities Press, 1996.

Fóti, Véronique. "The Evidences of Paintings: Merleau-Ponty and Contemporary Abstraction." In *Merleau-Ponty: Difference, Materiality, Painting*, ed. Véronique Fóti, 137–68. Atlantic Highlands: Humanities Press, 1996.

– "Expression in Merleau-Ponty's Aesthetics, Philosophy of Nature, and Ontology." In *Time, Memory, Institution: Merleau-Ponty's New Ontology of Self*, ed. David Morris and Kym Maclaren. Athens: Ohio University Press, 2015.

– *Tracing Expression in Merleau-Ponty: Aesthetics, Philosophy of Biology, and Ontology*. Evanston: Northwestern University Press, 2013.

Fox Keller, Evelyn. *Making Sense of Life: Explaining Biological Development with Models, Metaphors, and Machines*. Cambridge, MA: Harvard University Press, 2002.

Freud, Sigmund. *Civilization and Its Discontents*, trans. James Strachey. New York: W.W. Norton, 1989.

– "Mourning and Melancholia." In *The Standard Edition of the Complete Psychological Works of Sigmund Freud*, vol. 14, 243–58. London: Hogarth Press, 1957.

Froman, Wayne J. "At the Limits of Phenomenology: Merleau-Ponty and Derrida." In *Merleau-Ponty: Difference, Materiality, Painting*, ed. Véronique Fóti, 16–32. Atlantic Highlands: Humanities Press, 1996.

Gallagher, Shaun. *How the Body Shapes the Mind*. Oxford: Oxford University Press, 2005. http://dx.doi.org/10.1093/0199271941.001.0001.

– "Lived Body and Environment." *Research in Phenomenology* 16, no. 1 (1986): 139–70. http://dx.doi.org/10.1163/156916486X00103.

– "The Practice of Mind." *Journal of Consciousness Studies* 8 (2001): 83–108.

Gallagher, Shaun, and Jonathan Cole. "Body Image and Body Schema in a Deafferented Subject." In *Body and Flesh*, ed. Donn Welton, 131–48. Malden: Blackwell, 1998.

Gallagher, Shaun, and Andrew N. Meltzoff. "The Earliest Sense of Self and Others: Merleau-Ponty and Recent Developmental Studies." *Philosophical Psychology* 9, no. 2 (1996): 211–33. http://dx.doi.org/10.1080/09515089608573181.

Gibson, James J. *The Ecological Approach to Visual Perception*. Boston: Houghton Mifflin, 1979.

Goldstein, Kurt. *The Organism: A Holistic Approach to Biology Derived from Pathological Data in Man*. New York: Zone Books, 1995.

– *Kurt Goldstein: Selected Papers / Ausgewählte Schriften*, ed. Aron Gurwitsch, E.M. Goldstein-Haudek, and R.W. Haudek. The Hague: Martinus Nijhoff, 1971.

Goodale, M.A., A.D. Milner, L.S. Jakobson, et al. "A Neurological Dissociation between Perceiving Objects and Grasping Them." *Nature* 349, no. 6305 (1991): 154–6. http://dx.doi.org/10.1038/349154a0.

Greeno, James G. "Gibson's Affordances." *Psychological Review* 101, no. 2 (1994): 336–42. http://dx.doi.org/10.1037/0033-295X.101.2.336.

Grene, Marjorie. "The Aesthetic Dialogue of Sartre and Merleau-Ponty." In *The Merleau-Ponty Aesthetics Reader*, ed. Galen A. Johnson, 212–33. Evanston: Northwestern University Press, 1993.

Halligan, Peter W., and John C. Marshall. "Neglect of Awareness." *Consciousness and Cognition* 7, no. 3 (1998): 356–80. http://dx.doi.org/10.1006/ccog.1998.0362.

Haslum, Mary. "Predictors of Dyslexia?" *Irish Journal of Psychology* 10, no. 4 (1989): 622–30. http://dx.doi.org/10.1080/03033910.1989.10557776.

Hass, Lawrence. *Merleau-Ponty's Philosophy*. Bloomington: Indiana University Press, 2008.

Hass, Marjorie, and Lawrence Hass. "Merleau-Ponty and the Origin of Geometry." In *Chiasms: Merleau-Ponty's Notion of Flesh*, ed. Fred Evans and Leonard Lawlor, 177–88. Albany: SUNY Press, 2000.

Hegel, G.W.F. *Phenomenology of Spirit*, trans. A.V. Miller. Oxford: Oxford University Press, 1977.

Heidegger, Martin. *Being and Time*, trans. Joan Stambaugh. Albany: SUNY Press, 1996.

– *Being and Time*, trans. John Macquarrie and Edward Robinson. Cambridge, MA: Blackwell, 1962, 2001.

– *The Fundamental Concepts of Metaphysics: World, Finitude, Solitude*, trans. William McNeill and Nicholas Walker. Bloomington: Indiana University Press, 1995.

– "The Question Concerning Technology." In *Basic Writings*, ed. David Farrell Krell, 307–41. San Francisco: HarperCollins, 1993.

Heinämaa, Sara. "Phenomenological Responses to Gestalt Psychology." In *Psychology and Philosophy: Inquiries into the Soul from Late Scholasticism to Contemporary Thought*, ed. Sara Heinämaa and Martina Reuter, 263–84. Dordrecht: Springer, 2009.

Henry, Marcia Klinger. "Structured, Sequential, Multisensory Teaching: The Orton Legacy." *Annals of Dyslexia* 48, no. 1 (1998): 1–26. http://dx.doi.org/10.1007/s11881-998-0002-9.

Hesiod. "Theogony." In *The Homeric Hymns, and Homerica*, trans. Hugh G. Evelyn-White. Cambridge, MA: Harvard University Press, 1914.

Homer. *The Odyssey*, trans. A.T. Murray. Cambridge, MA: Harvard University Press, 1919. http://dx.doi.org/10.4159/DLCL.homer-odyssey.1919.

– *The Odyssey*, trans. Robert Fagles. New York: Viking, 1996.

Hooper, Scott L. "Motor Control: The Importance of Stiffness." *Current Biology* 16, no. 8 (2006): R283–5. http://dx.doi.org/10.1016/j.cub.2006.03.045.

Hull, John. *On Sight and Insight: A Journey into the World of Blindness*. Oxford: Oneworld Publications, 1990, 1997.

Humphreys, Glyn W., and M. Jane Riddoch. "Detecting Action: Neuropsychological Evidence for Action-Defined Templates in Search." *Nature Neuroscience* 4, no. 1 (2001): 84–8. http://dx.doi.org/10.1038/82940.

– "Knowing What You Need But Not What You Want: Affordances and Action-Defined Templates in Neglect." *Behavioral Neurology* 13 (2001/2): 75–87.

Husserl, Edmund. *Analyses Concerning Passive and Active Synthesis: Lectures on Transcendental Logic*, trans. Anthony J. Steinbock. Dordrech: Kluwer, 2001. http://dx.doi.org/10.1007/978-94-010-0846-4.

– *Cartesian Meditations*, trans. Dorion Cairns. Dordrecht: Kluwer, 1960, 1999.

– *Ideas Pertaining to a Pure Phenomenology and to a Phenomenological Philosophy, First Book*, trans. F. Kersten. Boston: Kluwer Academic Publishers, 1982.

– *The Crisis of the European Sciences and Transcendental Phenomenology: An Introduction to Phenomenological Philosophy*, trans. David Carr. Evanston: Northwestern University Press, 1970.

– "The Origin of Geometry." In *The Crisis of European Sciences and Transcendental Phenomenology: An Introduction to Phenomenological Philosophy*, ed. and trans. David Carr, 353–78. Evanston: Northwestern University Press, 1970.

Jacobson, Kirsten. "Agoraphobia and Hypochondria as Disorders of Dwelling." *International Studies in Philosophy* 36, no. 2 (2004): 31–44. http://dx.doi.org/10.5840/intstudphil2004362165.

– "A Developed Nature: A Phenomenological Account of the Experience of Home." *Continental Philosophy Review* 42, no. 3 (2009): 355–73. http://dx.doi.org/10.1007/s11007-009-9113-1.

– "The Experience of Home and the Space of Citizenship." *Southern Journal of Philosophy* 48, no. 3 (2010): 219–45. http://dx.doi.org/10.1111/j.2041-6962.2010.00029.x.

– "The Gift of Memory: Sheltering the 'I.'" In *Time, Memory, Institution: Merleau-Ponty's New Ontology of Self*, ed. David Morris and Kym Maclaren, 29–42. Athens: Ohio University Press, 2015.

– "The Interpersonal Expression of Human Spatiality: A Phenomenological Interpretation of Anorexia Nervosa." *Chiasmi International* 8 (2006): 157–73. http://dx.doi.org/10.5840/chiasmi2006822.

Johnson, Mark, and George Lakoff. *Philosophy in the Flesh*. New York: Basic Books, 1999.

Jonas, Hans. *The Phenomenon of Life: Towards a Philosophical Biology*. Evanston: Northwestern University Press, 2001.

Julesz, Béla. *Foundations of Cyclopean Perception*. Chicago: University of Chicago Press, 1971.

Kant, Immanuel. *Critique of Pure Reason*, 2nd ed., trans. Norman Kemp. New York: Palgrave Macmillan, 2007. http://dx.doi.org/10.1007/978-1-137-10016-0.

Kelly, Michael R. "The Subject as Time: Merleau-Ponty's Transition from Phenomenology to Ontology." In *Time, Memory, Institution: Merleau-Ponty's New Ontology of Self*, ed. David Morris and Kym Maclaren, 199–215. Athens: Ohio University Press, 2015.

Kelly, Sean Dorrance. "Seeing Things in Merleau-Ponty." In *The Cambridge Companion to Merleau-Ponty*, ed. Taylor Carman and Mark B.N. Hansen, 74–110. Cambridge: Cambridge University Press, 2005.

Klinke, Marianne E., Björn Thorsteinsson, and Helga Jónsdóttir. "'Advancing Phenomenological Research': Applications of 'Body Schema,' 'Body Image,' and 'Affordances' in Neglect." *Qualitative Health Research* 24, no. 6 (2014): 824–36. http://dx.doi.org/10.1177/1049732314533425.

Klinke, Marianne E., Dan Zahavi, Haukur Hjaltason, et al. "'Getting the Left Right': The Experience of Hemispatial Neglect after Stroke." *Qualitative Health Research* 25, no. 12 (2015): 1623–36. http://dx.doi.org/10.1177/1049732314566328.

Kockelmans, Joseph J. "Merleau-Ponty on Space Perception and Space." In *Phenomenology and the Natural Sciences: Essays and Translations*, ed. Joseph J. Kockelmans and Theodore J. Kisiel. Evanston: Northwestern University Press, 1976.

Köhler, Wolfgang. *Dynamics in Psychology: Vital Applications of Gestalt Psychology*. New York: Liveright, 1940, 1968.

– *The Mentality of Apes*, 2nd ed., trans. Ella Winter. London: Routledge and Kegan Paul, 1951.

Kristensen, Stefan. "Merleau-Ponty, une Esthétique du Mouvement." *Archives de Philosophie* 69 (2006): 1–24.

– "Le Mouvement de la Création: Merleau-Ponty et le Corps de l'Artiste." *Alter: Revue de Phénoménologie* 16 (2008): 243–60.

Kvigne, Kari, Eva Gjengedal, and Marit Kirkevold. "Gaining Access to the Life-World of Women Suffering from Stroke: Methodological Issues in Empirical Phenomenological Studies." *Journal of Advanced Nursing* 40, no. 1 (2002): 61–8. http://dx.doi.org/10.1046/j.1365-2648.2002.02340.x.

Lampert, Jay. *Simultaneity and Delay: A Dialectical Theory of Staggered Time.* London and New York: Bloomsbury, 2012.

– *Synthesis and Backward Reference in Husserl's Logical Investigations.* Dordrecht: Kluwer, 1995.

Landes, Donald A. *Merleau-Ponty and the Paradoxes of Expression.* New York: Bloomsbury, 2013.

Lawlor, Leonard. "The End of Phenomenology: Expressionism in Deleuze and Merleau-Ponty." *Continental Philosophy Review* 31, no. 1 (1998): 15–34. http://dx.doi.org/10.1023/A:1010004210178.

– *Thinking Through French Philosophy: The Being of the Question.* Bloomington: Indiana University Press, 2003.

Leder, Drew. *The Absent Body.* Chicago: University of Chicago Press, 1990.

Lee, Pamela. *Object to Be Destroyed.* Cambridge, MA: MIT Press, 2001.

Legerstee, Maria, Karl Corter, and Kim Kienapple. "Hand, Arm, and Facial Actions of Young Infants to a Social and Nonsocial Stimulus." *Child Development* 61, no. 3 (1990): 774–84. http://dx.doi.org/10.2307/1130962.

Legrand, E., ed. and trans. *Bucoliques Grecs*, vol. 1. Paris: Belles-Lettres, 1925.

Levinas, Emmanuel. *Humanism of the Other*, trans. Nidra Poller. Champaign: University of Illinois Press, 2003.

– "Intersubjectivity: Notes on Merleau-Ponty." In *Ontology and Alterity in Merleau-Ponty*, ed. Galen Johnson and Michael B. Smith, trans. Michael B. Smith, 55–60. Evanston: Northwestern University Press, 1990.

– "Reality and Its Shadow." In *The Levinas Reader*, ed. Seán Hand. Cambridge: Blackwell, 1989.

– "Sensibility." In *Ontology and Alterity in Merleau-Ponty*, ed. Galen Johnson and Michael B. Smith, trans. Michael B. Smith, 60–6. Evanston: Northwestern University Press, 1990.

Lewontin, Richard C. *Biology as Ideology: The Doctrine of DNA.* Toronto: House of Anansi Press, 1991.

Longcamp, Marieke, Céline Boucard, Jean-Claude Gilhodes, et al. "Learning through Hand- or Typewriting Influences Visual Recognition of New Graphic Shapes: Behavioral and Functional Imaging Evidence." *Journal of Cognitive Neuroscience* 20, no. 5 (2008): 802–15. http://dx.doi.org/10.1162/jocn.2008.20504.

Lowell, Robert. *Collected Poems*, ed. Frank Bidart and David Gewanter. New York: Farrar, Strauss and Giroux, 2003.

Maclaren, Kym. "Embodied Perceptions of Others as a Condition of Selfhood? Empirical and Phenomenological Considerations." *Journal of Consciousness Studies* 15, no. 8 (2008): 63–93.

– "Emotional Disorder and the Mind-Body Problem: A Case Study of Alexithymia." *Chiasmi International* 8 (2006): 139–54. http://dx.doi.org/10.5840/chiasmi2006819.

– "Intercorporeality, Intersubjectivity, and the Problem of 'Letting Others Be.'" *Chiasmi International: Trilingual Studies Concerning Merleau-Ponty's Thought* 4 (2002): 187–208. http://dx.doi.org/10.5840/chiasmi2002431.

– "Life Is Inherently Expressive." *Chiasmi International* 7 (2006): 241–62.

– "Merleau-Ponty's Embodied Ethics: Rethinking Traditional Ethics." In *Existential Thinkers and Ethics*, ed. Christine Daigle, 143–66. Montreal and Kingston: McGill–Queen's University Press, 2006.

Madison, Gary Brent. "Ethics and Politics of the Flesh." In *Merleau-Ponty's Later Works and Their Practical Implications*, ed. Duane H. Davis, 161–88. New York: Humanity Books, 2001.

– "Flesh as Otherness." In *Ontology and Alterity in Merleau-Ponty*, ed. Galen Johnson and Michael B. Smith, 27–34. Evanston: Northwestern University Press, 1990.

– *The Phenomenology of Merleau-Ponty: A Search for the Limits of Consciousness*. Athens: Ohio University Press, 1981.

Mallin, Samuel B. *Merleau-Ponty's Philosophy*. New Haven: Yale University Press, 1979.

Mangen, Anne. "The Haptics of Writing." In *Current Trends in European Research: Learning to Write Effectively*, ed. Mark Torrance. Bingley: Emerald, 2012.

Maratto, Scott L. *The Intercorporeal Self: Merleau-Ponty on Subjectivity*. Albany: SUNY Press, 2012.

Marotta, J.J., T.J. McKeeff, and M. Behrmann. "Hemispatial Neglect: Its Effect on Visual Perception and Visually Guided Grasping." *Neuropsychologia* 41, no. 9 (2003): 1262–71. http://dx.doi.org/10.1016/S0028-3932(03)00038-1.

Martlew, Margaret. "Handwriting and Spelling: Dyslexic Children's Abilities Compared with Children of Same Chronological Age and Younger Children of the Same Spelling Level." *British Journal of Educational Psychology* 62 (1992): 275–90.

Matthews, Eric. "Temporality, Subjectivity, and History in Merleau-Ponty's Phenomenology." *Philosophical Inquiry* 21, no. 1 (1999): 87–98. http://dx.doi.org/10.5840/philinquiry19992115.

Mazis, Glen. *Emotion and Embodiment: Fragile Ontology*. New York: Peter Lang, 1993.

– "Merleau-Ponty and the 'Backward Flow' of Time: The Reversibility of Temporality and the Temporality of Reversibility." In *Merleau-Ponty, Hermeneutics, and Postmodernism*, ed. Thomas W. Busch and Shaun Gallagher. Albany: SUNY Press, 1992.

McBride, William L. "Merleau-Ponty and Sartre: The Singular Universal, Childhood, and Social Expression." In *Merleau-Ponty's Later Works and Their Practical Implications*, ed. Duane H. Davis, 63–86. New York: Humanity Books, 2001.

McIntosh, R.D., K.I. McClements, H.C. Dijkerman, et al. "Preserved Obstacle Avoidance during Reaching in Patients with Left Visual Neglect." *Neuropsychologica* 42, no. 8 (2004): 1107–17. http://dx.doi.org/10.1016/j.neuropsychologia.2003.11.023.

McMahon, Laura. "'Thinking According to Others': Expression, Intimacy, and the Passage of Time in Merleau-Ponty and Woolf." In *Phenomenology and the Arts*, ed. Peter Costello and Licia Carlson, 193–218. Lanham, MD: Lexington Books, 2016.

Meltzoff, Andrew N., and M. Keith Moore. "Newborn Infants Imitate Adult Facial Gestures." *Child Development* 54, no. 3 (1983): 702–9. http://dx.doi.org/10.2307/1130058.

Michel, Carine, Laure Pisella, Peter W. Halligan, et al. "Simulating Unilateral Neglect in Normals Using Prism Adaptation: Implications for Theory." *Neuropsychologia* 41, no. 1 (2003): 25–39. http://dx.doi.org/10.1016/S0028-3932(02)00135-5.

Mongin, Olivier. "Since Lascaux." In *The Merleau-Ponty Aesthetics Reader*, ed. Galen A. Johnson, 245–55. Evanston: Northwestern University Press, 1993.

Moore, Ginger A., and Susan D. Calkins. "Infants' Vagal Regulation in the Still-Face Paradigm Is Related to Dyadic Coordination of Mother–Infant Interaction." *Developmental Psychology* 40, no. 6 (2004): 1068–80. http://dx.doi.org/10.1037/0012-1649.40.6.1068.

Morris, David. "Bergsonian Intuition, Husserlian Variation, Peirceian Abduction: Toward a Relation between Method, Sense, and Nature." *Southern Journal of Philosophy* 43, no. 2 (2005): 267–98. http://dx.doi.org/10.1111/j.2041-6962.2005.tb01954.x.

– "Ecstatic Body, Ecstatic Nature: Perception as Breaking with the World." *Chiasmi International* 8 (2006): 201–16. http://dx.doi.org/10.5840/chiasmi2006831.
– "Optical Idealism and the Languages of Depth in Descartes and Berkeley." *Southern Journal of Philosophy* 35 (1997): 363–92.
– "Reversibility and *Ereignis*: On Being as Kantian Imagination in Merleau-Ponty and Heidegger." *Philosophy Today* SPEP Supplement 52 (2008): 135–43.
– *The Sense of Space*. Albany: SUNY Press, 2004.
– "Touching Intelligence." *Journal of the Philosophy of Sport* 29, no. 2 (2002): 149–62. http://dx.doi.org/10.1080/00948705.2002.9714631.
– "What Is Living and What Is Non-Living in Merleau-Ponty's Philosophy of Movement and Expression." *Chiasmi International* 7 (2006): 225–38.

Morris, David, and Kym Maclaren, eds. *Time, Memory, Institution: Merleau-Ponty's New Ontology of Self*. Athens: Ohio University Press, 2015.

Nicolson, Roderick, and Angela Fawcett. "Dyslexia Is More than a Phonological Disability." *Dyslexia* 1 (1995): 19–36.

Noble, Kimberly, and Bruce McCandliss. "Reading Development and Impairment: Behavioral, Social, and Neurobiological Factors." *Journal of Developmental and Behavioral Pediatrics* 26, no. 5 (2005): 370–8. http://dx.doi.org/10.1097/00004703-200510000-00006.

Noë, Alva. *Action in Perception*. Cambridge, MA: MIT Press, 2004.

Olkowski, Dorothea E. "Merleau-Ponty's Freudianism: From the Body of Consciousness to the Body of Flesh." *Review of Existential Psychology and Psychiatry* 18 (1982–3): 97–116.

Owens, Gwendolyn. "Lessons Learned Well: The Education of Gordon Matta-Clark." In *Gordon Matta-Clark: You Are the Measure*, ed. Elisabeth Sussman, 162–73. New Haven: Yale University Press, 2007.

Papapetros, Spyros. "Oedipal and Edible: Roberto Matt Echaurren and Gordon Matta-Clark." In *Gordon Matta-Clark: You Are the Measure*, ed. Elisabeth Sussman, 70–82. New Haven: Yale University Press, 2007.

Papoušek, Mechthild. "Communication in Early Infancy: An Arena of Intersubjective Learning." *Infant Behavior and Development* 30, no. 2 (2007): 258–66. http://dx.doi.org/10.1016/j.infbeh.2007.02.003.

Parton, Andrew, and Masud Husain. "Spatial Neglect." *Advances in Clinical Neuroscience and Rehabilitation: ACNR* 4, no. 4 (2004): 117–18.

Piaget, Jean. *The Child's Conception of the World*. New York: Harcourt, Brace, and Company, 1929.

Plato. *The Republic*, trans. G.M.A. Grube. Indianapolis: Hackett, 1992.

Porges, Stephen W. "The Polyvagal Theory: Phylogenetic Substrates of a Social Nervous System." *International Journal of Psychophysiology* 42, no. 2 (2001): 123–46. http://dx.doi.org/10.1016/S0167-8760(01)00162-3.

Prigogine, I., and Isabelle Stengers. *The End of Certainty: Time, Chaos, and the New Laws of Nature*. New York: Free Press, 1997.

Proust, Marcel. *Remembrance of Things Past*, trans. C.K. Scott Moncrieff and Terence Kilmartin. New York: Random House, 1981.

Ralón de Walton, Graciela. "Symbolic Matrices and the Institution of Meaning." *Chiasmi International: Trilingual Studies Concerning Merleau-Ponty's Thought* 9 (2007): 113–29. http://dx.doi.org/10.5840/chiasmi2007922.

Ramachandran, V.S., and Sandra Blakeslee. *Phantoms in the Brain: Probing the Mysteries of the Human Mind*. New York: Quill, 1998.

Ramus, Franck, Elizabeth Pidgeon, and Uta Frith. "The Relationship between Motor Control and Phonology in Dyslexic Children." *Journal of Child Psychology and Psychiatry, and Allied Disciplines* 44, no. 5 (2003): 712–22. http://dx.doi.org/10.1111/1469-7610.00157.

Reddy, Vasudevi. *How Infants Know Minds*. Cambridge, MA: Harvard University Press, 2008.

Reuter, Martina. "Merleau-Ponty's Notion of Pre-Reflective Intentionality." *Synthese* 118, no. 1 (1999): 69–88. http://dx.doi.org/10.1023/A:1005144911619.

Riddoch, M., Glyn W. Humphreys, Sarah Edwards, Tracy Baker, and Katherine Wilson. "Seeing the Action: Neuropsychological Evidence for Action-Based Effects on Object Selection." *Nature Neuroscience* 6, no. 1 (2003): 82–9. http://dx.doi.org/10.1038/nn984.

Rilke, Rainer Maria. *Letters to a Young Poet*, trans. M.D. Herter Norton. New York: W.W. Norton, 1934.

Robertson, I.H., D. Nico, and B.M. Hood. "Believing What You Feel: Using Proprioceptive Feedback to Reduce Unilateral Neglect." *Neuropsychology* 11, no. 1 (1997): 53–8. http://dx.doi.org/10.1037/0894-4105.11.1.53.

Rojcewicz, Richard. "Depth Perception in Merleau-Ponty: A Motivated Phenomenon." *Journal of Phenomenological Psychology* 15, no. 1 (1984): 33–44. http://dx.doi.org/10.1163/156916284X00035.

Rose, Robert. "The Writing–Reading Connection." Unpublished paper.

Rossmanith, Nicole, Alan Costall, Andreas F. Reichelt, et al. "Jointly Structuring Triadic Spaces of Meaning and Action: Book Sharing from 3 Months On." *Frontiers in Psychology* 5 (2014). http://dx.doi.org/10.3389/fpsyg.2014.01390.

Rossmanith, Nicole, and Vasudevi Reddy. "Structure and Openness in the Development of Self in Infancy." *Journal of Consciousness Studies* 23 (2016): 237–57.

Rostand, François. "Grammaire et Affectivité." *Revue Française de Psychanalyse* 14 (1950): 299–310.

Russon, John. "Aristotle's Animative Epistemology." *Idealistic Studies* 25, no. 3 (1995): 241–53. http://dx.doi.org/10.5840/idstudies199525313.

– "Between Two Intimacies: The Formative Contexts of Individual Experience." *Emotion, Space, and Society* 13 (2014): 65–70. http://dx.doi.org/10.1016/j.emospa.2013.12.015.

– *Bearing Witness to Epiphany: Persons, Things, and the Nature of Erotic Life*. Albany: SUNY Press, 2009.

– "'Embodiment and Responsibility': Merleau-Ponty and the Ontology of Nature." *Man and World* 27, no. 3 (1994): 291–308. http://dx.doi.org/10.1007/BF01278468.

– "Haunted by History: Merleau-Ponty, Hegel, and the Phenomenology of Pain." *Journal of Contemporary Thought* 37 (2013): 81–94.

– *Human Experience: Philosophy, Neurosis, and the Elements of Everyday Life*. Albany: SUNY Press, 2003.

– "The Impossibilities of the I: Self, Memory, and Language in Merleau-Ponty and Derrida." In *Time, Memory, Institution: Merleau-Ponty's New Ontology of Self*, ed. David Morris and Kym Maclaren, 91–105. Athens: Ohio University Press, 2015.

– "Merleau-Ponty and the New Science of the Soul." *Chiasmi International* 8 (2006): 129–37. http://dx.doi.org/10.5840/chiasmi2006816.

– *Reading Hegel's Phenomenology of Spirit*. Bloomington: Indiana University Press, 2004.

– "The Spatiality of Self-Consciousness: Originary Passivity in Kant, Merleau-Ponty and Derrida." *Chiasmi International* 9 (2007): 219–32.

– "The Virtues of Agency: A Phenomenology of Confidence, Courage, and Creativity." In *Phenomenology and Virtue Ethics*, ed. Kevin Hermberg and Paul Gyllenhammer, 165–79. New York: Continuum, 2013.

Sachs, Joe. "Introduction." In *Aristotle's On the Soul and Memory and Recollection*, trans. Joe Sachs. Santa Fe: Green Lion Press, 2001.

Sartre, Jean-Paul. *Being and Nothingness*, trans. Hazel E. Barnes. New York: Washington Square Press, 1956.

Schiller, Paul H. "Innate Constituents of Complex Responses in Primates." *Psychological Review* 59, no. 3 (1952): 177–91. http://dx.doi.org/10.1037/h0062854.

Shanahan, Timothy. "Nature of the Reading–Writing Relation: An Exploratory Multivariate Analysis." *Journal of Educational Psychology* 76, no. 3 (1984): 466–77. http://dx.doi.org/10.1037/0022-0663.76.3.466.

Sheffield, Betty. "Handwriting: A Neglected Cornerstone of Literacy." *Annals of Dyslexia* 46, no. 1 (1996): 21–35. http://dx.doi.org/10.1007/BF02648169.

Sheets-Johnstone, Maxine. *The Primacy of Movement*. London: John Benjamins, 1999. http://dx.doi.org/10.1075/aicr.14.

Silverman, Hugh J. "Cézanne's Mirror Stage." In *The Merleau-Ponty Aesthetics Reader*, ed. Galen A. Johnson, 262–78. Evanston: Northwestern University Press, 1993.

Simms, Eva-Maria. "Egocentric Language and the Upheaval of Speech: A Merleau-Ponty Inspired Study of Language Acquisition." *Chiasmi International* 12 (2010): 287–309. http://dx.doi.org/10.5840/chiasmi20101223.

– "Milk and Flesh, A Phenomenological Reflection on Infancy and Coexistence." *Journal of Phenomenological Psychology* 32, no. 1 (2001): 22–40. http://dx.doi.org/10.1163/156916201753534723.

Simon, Joan. "Motion Pictures: Gordon Matta-Clark." In *Gordon Matta-Clark: You Are the Measure*, ed. Elisabeth Sussman, 124–35. New Haven: Yale University Press, 2007.

Singer, Linda. "Merleau-Ponty and the Concept of Style." In *The Merleau-Ponty Aesthetics Reader: Philosophy and Painting*, ed. Galen A. Johnson, 233–44. Evanston: Northwestern University Press, 1993.

Smith, Michael B. "Merleau-Ponty's Aesthetics." In *The Merleau-Ponty Aesthetics Reader*, ed. Galen A. Johnson, 192–211. Evanston: Northwestern University Press, 1993.

Sparshott, Francis. *Taking Life Seriously: A Study of the Argument of the Nicomachean Ethics*. Toronto: University of Toronto Press, 1994.

Stawarska, Beata. "Mutual Gaze and Social Cognition." *Phenomenology and the Cognitive Sciences* 5, no. 1 (2006): 17–30. http://dx.doi.org/10.1007/s11097-005-9009-4.

Steinbock, Anthony J. "Affection and Attraction: On the Phenomenology of Becoming Aware." *Continental Philosophy Review* 37, no. 1 (2004): 21–43. http://dx.doi.org/10.1023/B:MAWO.0000049298.44397.be.

Sumbre, Germán, Graziano Fiorito, Tamar Flash, and Binyamin Hochner. "Octopuses Use a Human-like Strategy to Control Precise Point-to-Point Arm Movements." *Current Biology* 16, no. 8 (2006): 767–72. http://dx.doi.org/10.1016/j.cub.2006.02.069.

Sussman, Elisabeth. "The Mind Is Vast and Ever Present." In *Gordon Matta-Clark: You Are the Measure*, ed. Elisabeth Sussman, 13–33. New Haven: Yale University Press, 2007.

Talero, Maria. "Intersubjectivity and Intermodal Perception." *Chiasmi International* 8 (2006): 175–88. http://dx.doi.org/10.5840/chiasmi2006825.

– "Merleau-Ponty and the Bodily Subject of Learning." *International Philosophical Quarterly* 46, no. 2 (2006): 191–203. http://dx.doi.org/10.5840/ipq20064622.

– "Perception, Normativity, and Selfhood in Merleau-Ponty: The Spatial

'Level' and Existential Space." *Southern Journal of Philosophy* 43, no. 3 (2005): 443–61. http://dx.doi.org/10.1111/j.2041-6962.2005.tb01962.x.

Taminaux, Jacques. "The Thinker and Painter." In *The Merleau-Ponty Aesthetics Reader*, ed. Galen A. Johnson, 278–92. Evanston: Northwestern University Press, 1993.

Tan, Li Hai, John Spinks, Guinevere Eden, et al. "Reading Depends on Writing, in Chinese." *Proceedings of the National Academy of Sciences of the United States of America* 102, no. 24 (2005): 8781–5. http://dx.doi.org/10.1073/pnas.0503523102.

Thelen, Esther, and Linda Smith. *A Dynamic Systems Approach to the Development of Cognition and Action*. Cambridge, MA: MIT Press, 1996.

Theocritus. *Idylls*, trans. Anthony Verity. Oxford: Oxford University Press, 2002.

– *A Selection: Idylls 2, 3, 4, 6, 7, 10, 11 and 13*, ed. and trans. Richard Hunter. Cambridge: Cambridge University Press, 1999.

Thompson, Evan. *Mind in Life: Biology, Phenomenology, and the Sciences of Mind*. Cambridge, MA: Bellknap Press, 2007.

Thomson, Patience, and Peter Gilchrist. *Dyslexia: A Multidisciplinary Approach*. Nashville: Nelson Thornes, 1996.

Toadvine, Ted. *Merleau-Ponty's Philosophy of Nature*. Evanston: Northwestern University Press, 2009.

Trevarthen, Colwyn. "Communication and Cooperation in Early Infancy: A Description of Primary Intersubjectivity." In *Before Speech: The Beginning of Interpersonal Communication*, ed. M. Bullowa, 321–47. New York: Cambridge University Press, 1979.

– "The Concept and Foundations of Infant Intersubjectivity." In *Intersubjective Communication and Emotion in Early Ontogeny*, ed. Stein Bråten. Cambridge: Cambridge University Press, 1998.

Vallier, Robert. "Institution: The Significance of Merleau-Ponty's 1954 Course at the Collège de France." *Chiasmi International: Trilingual Studies Concerning Merleau-Ponty's Thought* 7 (2005): 281–302. http://dx.doi.org/10.5840/chiasmi2005746.

Varela, Francisco J. "Organism: A Meshwork of Selfless Selves." In *Organism and the Origins of Self*, ed. Alfred I. Tauber. Boston Studies in the Philosophy of Science, 79–107. Dordrecht: Kluwer, 1991. http://dx.doi.org/10.1007/978-94-011-3406-4_5.

Vernon, Sofia, and Emilia Ferreiro. "Writing Development: A Neglected Variable in the Consideration of Phonological Awareness." *Harvard Educational Review* 69, no. 4 (1999): 395–416. http://dx.doi.org/10.17763/haer.69.4.p411667586738x0w.

Vermersch, Pierre. "Attention between Phenomenology and Experimental Psychology." *Continental Philosophy Review* 37, no. 1 (2004): 45–81. http://dx.doi.org/10.1023/B:MAWO.0000049300.54905.b7.

Waldenfels, Bernhard. *Bruchlinien der Erfahrung*. Frankfurt am Main: Suhrkamp, 2002.

– "The Paradox of Expression." In *Chiasms: Merleau-Ponty's Notion of Flesh*, ed. Fred Evans and Leonard Lawlor, 89–102. Albany: SUNY Press, 2000.

– "Time Lag: Motifs for a Phenomenology of the Experience of Time." *Research in Phenomenology* 30, no. 1 (2000): 107–19. http://dx.doi.org/10.1163/156916400746632.

– "Verité à Faire: Merleau-Ponty's Question Concerning Truth." *Philosophy Today* 35, no. 2 (1991): 185–94. http://dx.doi.org/10.5840/philtoday199135223.

Weiss, Gail. "Ambiguity." In *Merleau-Ponty: Key Concepts*, ed. Rosalyn Diprose and Jack Reynolds, 132–41. Stocksfield: Acumen, 2008.

Welsh, Talia. *The Child as Natural Phenomenologist*. Evanston: Northwestern University Press, 2013.

Whiteside, Kerry. *Merleau-Ponty and the Foundation of an Existential Politics*. Princeton: Princeton University Press, 1988. http://dx.doi.org/10.1515/9781400859733.

Winnicott, D.W. *The Family and Individual Development*. New York: Routledge, 1990.

Wiskus, Jessica. *The Rhythm of Thought: Art, Literature, and Music after Merleau-Ponty*. Chicago: University of Chicago Press, 2013. http://dx.doi.org/10.7208/chicago/9780226031088.001.0001.

Wolff, Peter, George Michel, Marsha Ovrut, et al. "Rate and Timing Precision of Motor Coordination in Developmental Dyslexia." *Developmental Psychology* 26, no. 3 (1990): 349–59. http://dx.doi.org/10.1037/0012-1649.26.3.349.

Wood, David, Jerome S. Bruner, and Gail Ross. "The Role of Tutoring in Problem Solving." *Journal of Child Pyschology and Psychiatry* 17, no. 2 (1976): 89–100. http://dx.doi.org/10.1111/j.1469-7610.1976.tb00381.x.

Contributors

Ömer Aygün is an Assistant Professor at Galatasaray University, Istanbul. His MA thesis was about the concept of temporality in Merleau-Ponty. He has translated *Causeries – le monde perçu* into Turkish. He specializes in ancient philosophy. His first book, *The Middle Included – Logos in Aristotle*, will be published in December 2016 by Northwestern University Press.

Don Beith is a lecturer in the Department of Philosophy at the University of Maine. Using phenomenology as an orienting method, he studies questions about the nature of bodily development, the relationship between habit and personhood, and the genesis of time and sense through movement, and is recently interested in the relationship between intercorporeal life and social responsibility. His work on Merleau-Ponty's philosophy has recently been published in *Chiasmi* (2013) and *PhaenEx* (2015), and includes a book, forthcoming from Ohio University Press, that offers an account of life as what Merleau-Ponty calls "institution" or the emergent self-grounding of organic possibilities, as well as the transformation of these organic structures into habit, self-awareness, and language.

Susan M. Bredlau is Assistant Professor of Philosophy at Emory University. Her research draws on phenomenological accounts of perception, embodiment, and the experience of other people as well as empirical work in psychology and the cognitive sciences to develop an account of perception as an interpersonal achievement. She is the author of articles on Merleau-Ponty, Husserl, and de Beavoir, including, most recently, "Husserl's 'Pairing' Relation and the Role of Others in Infant Perception" in *Journal of Consciousness Studies* and "On Perception and Trust: Merleau-Ponty and the Emotional Significance of Our Relations with Others" in *Continental Philosophy Review*. She is currently working on a book about Merleau-Ponty's conception of objectivity in *Phenomenology of Perception*.

Noah Moss Brender teaches philosophy and humanities courses at McGill University, Concordia University, and Dawson College. His research lies at the intersection of phenomenology and embodied cognitive science, with an emphasis on the phenomenon of development. Recent publications include "Symmetry-Breaking Dynamics in Development" (*Phenomenology and the Cognitive Sciences*, forthcoming), and "Sense-Making and Symmetry-Breaking: Merleau-Ponty, Cognitive Science, and Dynamic Systems Theory" (*Symposium*, 2013). He received his PhD in Philosophy from Boston College.

David Ciavatta is an Associate Professor in the Department of Philosophy at Ryerson University, Toronto. His research focuses on various aspects of Hegel's philosophy, as well as on phenomenology and existentialism. Most recently he has been exploring the phenomenological dimensions of Hegel's philosophy of art, and has been exploring the link between action and temporality in the work of Bergson, Merleau-Ponty, and Sartre. He is the author of *Spirit, the Family, and the Unconscious in Hegel's Philosophy* (SUNY Press, 2009).

Peter Costello is Professor of Philosophy at Providence College. He is an expert in Husserl and Merleau-Ponty. His first book, *Layers in Husserl's Phenomenology: On Meaning and Intersubjectivity*, was published by University of Toronto Press in 2012.

Matthew J. Goodwin is a senior lecturer of philosophy at Northern Arizona University. He teaches phenomenology – especially Husserl and Merleau-Ponty – environmental ethics, and philosophy of art. His work focuses on utilizing the works of contemporary artists to develop phenomenological accounts. He is also working on environmental and aesthetic issues inside and around the Grand Canyon. He is a regular contributor to Northern Arizona University's Philosophy in the Public Interest Program, which brings philosophical dialogue out into the community. He is co-owner of SPEX: Sedona Philosophy Experience, leading philosophical discussions outside, on trails, and on the Colorado River.

Kirsten Jacobson is Associate Professor of Philosophy at the University of Maine. She specializes in nineteenth- and twentieth-century Continental Philosophy, and her research interests include the phenomenology of spatiality, the nature of home and dwelling, and, more generally, the philosophical significance and status of the phenomenological method. Her published work has focused significantly on using Merleau-Ponty's phenomenology to conduct novel analyses of psychological and physiological illnesses and more generally to consider issues of "existential health." In 2009, she created a philosophy outreach program called Philosophy Across the Ages, which brings together undergraduate philosophy students with local high school students and retirement community members for seminar-style discussions of accessible and exciting philosophical texts. In 2015, Professor Jacobson received the University of Maine's top two awards for teaching and advising – the College of Liberal Arts and Sciences Outstanding Faculty in Teaching and Advising Award, and the Presidential Outstanding Teaching Award.

Stefan Kristensen was a postdoctoral research fellow at the Art History Department, University of Geneva, until August 2016. He holds a PhD in philosophy from the Universities of Geneva and Paris 1 on Merleau-Ponty and the question of expression. He has been a research fellow of the Alexander von Humboldt Foundation at the University of Heidelberg (2013–15). He has published extensively on the theory of subjectivity, on the problem of witnessing, and on the sources and limits of Merleau-Ponty's philosophy, among other topics in contemporary Continental Philosophy and aesthetics. He recently completed his habilitation thesis at the University of Toulouse with a work titled "The Sensitive Machine," an essay articulating the phenomenological perspective of Merleau-Ponty and the schizopanalysis of Félix Guattari (to be published by Herrman, Paris). His latest book is *Jean-Luc Godard Philosophe* (2014).

Kym Maclaren is Associate Professor of Philosophy at Ryerson University in Toronto, Canada. Her published work has focused primarily on the nature of social life, the affective, bodily, and social conditions of selfhood and individual development, and the social nature and transformative potential of emotion. She draws especially on the work of Merleau-Ponty and tends to incorporate literature from developmental psychology, studies of psychopathology, evolutionary theory, and social thought. In addition to articles in these areas, she has co-edited, with

David Morris, *Time, Memory, Institution: Merleau-Ponty's New Ontology of Self* (Ohio University Press, 2015), and edited a collection of essays titled *Intimacy and Embodiment: Phenomenological Perspectives* in the journal *Emotion, Space, and Society* (2014).

Scott Marratto is an Associate Professor of Philosophy at Michigan Technological University. His research interests include twentieth-century Continental Philosophy, especially phenomenology; political thought; and philosophical issues in science and technology. In his 2012 book *The Intercorporeal Self: Merleau-Ponty on Subjectivity* (SUNY Press), he examines the contribution of French philosopher Maurice Merleau-Ponty to contemporary discussions of subjectivity, embodiment, language, and our relations with others. He is also co-author (with Lawrence E. Schmidt) of *The End of Ethics in a Technological Society* (McGill–Queen's University Press, 2008). His current research focuses on the political implications of contemporary philosophical accounts of spatiality and embodiment. Beginning from contemporary phenomenology's insights into the fundamentally spatial character of self-consciousness, he critically evaluates neoliberal thinking about selfhood, agency, and choice and proposes new ways of thinking about the spatial and material conditions of political community and human development.

Laura McMahon is an Assistant Professor of Philosophy at Eastern Michigan University. She works predominantly in the fields of Phenomenology (especially Merleau-Ponty) and Existentialism, and Social and Political Philosophy. She is currently working on a book project on resources in Merleau-Ponty's phenomenology for political thought, and has plans for future research on the topic of character formation in the philosophies of Aristotle, Dewey, and Merleau-Ponty.

David Morris is Professor of Philosophy at Concordia University, Montreal, and Assistant General Secretary of the International Merleau-Ponty Circle. His main interests are in phenomenology (esp. Merleau-Ponty), with a focus on the philosophy of the body, mind, and nature in relation to current biology, cognitive science, and also cosmology; other interests include Hegel, Bergson, and ancient (esp. Aristotle) and modern philosophy. He has recently completed a book project, *Merleau-Ponty's Developmental Ontology*, and is embarking on a new project focusing on the interrelation of time, meaning, and nature. He has written numerous articles and chapters, especially on phenomenology and

Merleau-Ponty, in relation to issues of philosophical method, ontology, nature, science, and biology; and a book, *The Sense of Space*, published by SUNY Press.

John Russon is Professor of Philosophy at the University of Guelph. In addition to numerous scholarly articles on Merleau-Ponty and phenomenology, he has published three books of original phenomenological research: *Human Experience: Philosophy, Neurosis, and the Elements of Everyday Life* (SUNY, 2003); *Bearing Witness to Epiphany: Persons, Things, and the Nature of Erotic Life* (SUNY, 2009); and *Sites of Exposure: Art, Politics, and the Nature of Experience* (Indiana, 2017). He has also published three books on the philosophy of G.W.F. Hegel.

Maria Talero held faculty positions at Rhodes College and at the University of Colorado at Denver, but, believing that philosophy is most significant outside the classroom, she left academia to become a freelance educator; specifically, she brings a phenomenological, enactivist approach to grassroots workshops studying climate change.

Index

www.ingramcontent.com/pod-product-compliance
Lightning Source LLC
LaVergne TN
LVHW090147080826
844660LV00013B/705/J